D1625088

Joseph Smith

Begins His Work

Volume Two

Joseph Smith

Begins His Work

Volume II

✧ ✧

The Book of Commandments

✧ ✧ ✧

The Doctrine and Covenants

✧ ✧ ✧ ✧

The Lectures on Faith

✧ ✧ ✧ ✧ ✧

Fourteen Articles of Faith

✧ ✧ ✧ ✧ ✧ ✧ ✧

FOREWORD

Among all life, only Man has risen above the law of the jungle. It is more than coincidence that only Man has achieved the capacity to believe.

Among men, the Mormon is a significant believer—one who has established a great Church based upon love, understanding, temperance and tolerance.

As is true with all great works of men, understanding results not only from reading and observing their works, but from understanding the men themselves, their motivations and their objectives.

This book is an endeavor to examine not only their works, which are reproduced from ancient original texts, but also the minds and souls of the men themselves. Through pictures and other printed media, I have striven to place the reader—if only for a moment—in the shoes of the men who founded our Mormon faith. By looking through their eyes you may be able to catch a brief glimpse of their souls—and thus of their eternal faith. In so doing, you may, as have I, find the deeper and more everlasting elements of a faith which has done much to make the Mormon indeed a man of God among men.

Wilford C. Wood

Read

THE BOOK OF COMMANDMENTS

which contains the first published revelations given to the Prophet Joseph Smith. It was published in 1833 in Independence, Missouri.

Read

THE DOCTRINE AND COVENANTS

This Book is the first Doctrine and Covenants which contains the revelations given to the Prophet Joseph Smith for the Church. It also contains the Lectures on Faith which were used in the School of the Prophets held in the Kirtland Temple and was published in 1835 at Kirtland, Ohio.

This Book is prepared and published in memory of the Prophet Joseph Smith and in appreciation for his great work of the restoration of the Gospel of Jesus Christ. It is the second of the publications of how and where the Church was made in picture and story in a series entitled *Joseph Smith Begins His Work*.

THE AUTHOR.

A F F I D A V I T

STATE OF UTAH)
                  : ss
County of Davis)

    WILFORD C. WOOD, being first duly sworn upon his oath, deposes and bears testimony:

    1. That he has in his possession and does own an original edition of the Book of Commandments published by the Prophet Joseph Smith at Independence, Missouri, in 1833.

    2. That he has in his possession and does own a first edition of the Doctrine and Covenants which contains the Lectures on Faith and the revelations given to the Prophet Joseph Smith for the Church. This edition of the Doctrine and Covenants was published in Kirtland, Ohio, in 1835.

    3. That the Book of Mormon published in 1830 which is contained within Volume 1 of this series titled "Joseph Smith Begins His Work", was the first printed publication for the Church.

    4. That the Book of Commandments above referred to is an original edition published in 1833 at Independence, Missouri, and was the second printed publication for the Church.

    5. That the Doctrine and Covenants above referred to is an original edition published in 1835 at Kirtland, Ohio, and was the third printed publication for the Church.

    6. That the Book of Commandments of 1833 and the Doctrine and Covenants of 1835 have been reproduced in this Volume 2 from the original books by photo-offset method in their original unchanged condition.

                              _____
                                  Wilford C. Wood

    Subscribed and sworn to before me this 21st day of February, 1962.

                              _____
My commission expires: Notary Public
October 4, 1963

We the undersigned of the Deseret News Publishing Company certify

that the printing of these original books, A BOOK OF COMMANDMENTS—1833,

and DOCTRINE AND COVENANTS—1835, as contained herein, were produced

by photo-offset method from books in Wilford C. Wood's possession and

owned by him.

According to Wilford C. Wood, A BOOK OF COMMANDMENTS is one of

the only edition published in 1833. The DOCTRINE AND COVENANTS,

containing the Lectures on Faith, is the first edition of the book and was

published in 1835. The page size of A BOOK OF COMMANDMENTS has been

en larged from a page size of 2 7/8 x 4 3/4 inches to 6 x 9 inches, and

the page size of the DOCTRINE AND COVENANTS has been enlarged from

3 3/4 x 5 3/4 inches to 6 x 9 inches for easier reading.

_____
Plant Manager

_____
Assistant Plant Manager

_____
Director of Sales

Subscribed and sworn to before me this 21st day of February, 1962.

_____
Notary Public
Residing at Salt Lake City, Utah

Joseph Smith
Begins His Work
Volume Two

The Book of Commandments
1833

A

BOOK

OF

COMMANDMENTS,

FOR THE GOVERNMENT OF THE

Church of Christ,

ORGANIZED ACCORDING TO LAW, ON THE

6th of April, 1830.

ZION:

PUBLISHED BY W. W. PHELPS & CO.

....

1833.

CHAPTER I.

1 A Preface or instruction unto the Book of Commandments, which were given of the Lord unto his church, through him whom he appointed to this work, by the voice of his saints through the prayer of faith: This church being organized according to the will of him, who rules all things, on the sixth day of April, in the year of our Lord, one thousand eight hundred and thirty:

HEARKEN, O ye people of my church, saith the voice of Him who dwells on high, and whose eyes are upon all men; yea, verily I say, hearken ye people from afar, and ye that are upon the islands of the sea, listen together; for verily the voice of the Lord is unto all men, and there is none to escape, and there is no eye that shall not see, neither ear that shall not hear, neither heart that shall not be penetrated; and the rebellious shall be pierced with much sorrow, for their iniquties shall be spoken upon the house-tops, and their secret acts shall be revealed; and the voice of warning shall be unto all people, by the mouths of my disciples, whom I have chosen in these last days, and they shall go forth and none shall stay them, for I the Lord have commanded them.

2 Behold, this is mine authority, and the authority of my servants, and my Preface unto the Book of my Commandments, which I have given them to publish unto you, O inhabitants of the earth:— Wherefore fear and tremble, O ye people for what I the Lord have decreed, in them, shall be fulfilled.

And verily, I say unto you, that they who go forth, bearing these tidings unto the inhabitants of the earth, to them is power given, to seal both on earth and in heaven, the unbelieving and rebellious; yea, verily, to seal them up unto the day when the wrath of God shall be poured out upon the wicked, without measure, unto the day when the Lord shall come to recompence unto every man according to his work, and measure to every man according to the measure which he has measured to his fellow man.

3 Wherefore the voice of the Lord is unto the ends of the earth, that all that will hear may hear: Prepare ye, prepare ye for that which is to come, for the Lord is nigh; and the anger of the Lord is kindled, and his sword is bathed in heaven, and it shall fall upon the inhabitants of the earth; and the arm of the Lord shall be revealed; and the day cometh, that they who will not hear the voice of the Lord, neither the voice of his servants, neither give heed to the words of the prophets, and apostles, shall be cut off from among the people: For they have strayed from mine ordinances, and have broken mine everlasting covenant, they seek not the Lord to establish his righteousness, but every man walketh in his own way, and after the image of his own god, whose image is in the likeness of the world, and whose substance is that of an idol, which waxeth old and shall perish in Babylon, even Babylon the great, which shall fall:

4 Wherefore I the Lord, knowing the calamity which should come upon the inhabitants of the earth, called upon my servant Joseph, and spake unto him from heaven, and gave him commandments; and also gave commandments to others, that they

should proclaim these things unto the world, and all this that it might be fulfilled, which was written by the prophets: The weak things of the world should come forth and break down the mighty and strong ones; that man should not counsel his fellow man, neither trust in the arm of flesh, but that every man might speak in the name of God, the Lord, even the savior of the world; that faith also might increase in the earth; that mine everlasting covenant might be established; that the fulness of my gospel might be proclaimed by the weak and the simple, unto the ends of the world; and before kings and rulers.

5 Behold I am God and have spoken it: these commandments are of me, and were given unto my servants in their weakness, after the manner of their language, that they might come to understanding; and inasmuch as they erred, it might be made known: and inasmuch as they sought wisdom, they might be instructed; and inasmuch as they sinned, they might be chastened, that they might repent; and inasmuch as they were humble, they might be made strong, and blessed from on high, and receive knowledge from time to time: after they, having received the record of the Nephites; yea, even my servant Joseph might have power to translate through the mercy of God, by the power of God, the book of Mormon: And also, those to whom these commandments were given, might have power to lay the foundation of this church, and to bring it forth out of obscurity, and out of darkness, the only true and living church upon the face of the whole earth, with which I the Lord am well pleased, speaking unto the church collectively and not individually, for I the Lord can not look upon sin

with the least degree of allowance: Nevertheless, he that repenteth and doeth the commandments of the Lord, shall be forgiven, and he that repenteth not from him shall be taken even the light which he hath received, for my Spirit shall not always strive with man, saith the Lord of hosts.

6 And again, verily I say unto you, O inhabitants of the earth, for I the Lord am willing to make these things known unto all flesh, for I am no respecter to persons, and willeth that all men shall know that the day speedily cometh, the hour is not yet, but is nigh at hand, when peace shall be taken from the earth, and the devil shall have power over his own dominion; and also, the Lord shall have power over his saints, and shall reign in their midst, and shall come down in judgment upon Idumea, or the world.

7 Search these commandments, for they are true and faithful, and the prophecies and promises which are in them, shall all be fulfilled. What I the Lord have spoken, I have spoken, and I excuse not myself, and though the heavens and the earth pass away, my word shall not pass away, but shall all be fulfilled, whether by mine own voice, or by the voice of my servants, it is the same: For behold, and lo, the Lord is God, and the Spirit beareth record, and the record is true, and the truth abideth forever and ever: Amen.

CHAPTER II.

1 *A Revelation given to Joseph, in Harmony, Pennsylvania, July, 1828, after Martin had lost the Manuscript of the forepart of the book of Mormon, translated from the book of Lehi, which was abridged by the hand of Mormon, saying:*

THE works, and the designs, and the purposes of God, can not be rustrated, neither can they come to nought, for God doth not walk in crooked paths; neither doth he turn to the right hand nor to the left; neither doth he vary from that which he hath said: Therefore his paths are strait and his course is one eternal round.

2 Remember, remember, that it is not the work of God that is frustrated, but the work of men: for although a man may have many revelations, and have power to do many mighty works, yet, if he boasts in his own strength, and sets at nought the counsels of God, and follows after the dictates of his own will, and carnal desires, he must fall and incur the vengeance of a just God upon him.

3 Behold, you have been intrusted with these things, but how strict were your commandments; and remember, also, the promises which were made to you, if you did not transgress them; and behold, how oft you have transgressed the commandments and the laws of God, and have gone on in the persuasions of men: for behold, you should not have feared man more than God, although men set at nought the counsels of God, and despise his words, yet you should have been faithful and he would have extended his arm, and supported you against all the fiery darts of the adversary; and he would have been with you in every time of trouble.

4 Behold thou art Joseph, and thou wast chosen to do the work of the Lord, but because of transgression, if thou art not aware thou wilt fall, but remember God is merciful: Therefore, repent of that which thou hast done, and he will only cause thee to be afflicted for a season, and thou art still chosen, and wilt again be called to the work; and except thou do this, thou shalt be delivered up and become as other men, and have no more gift.

5 And when thou deliveredst up that which God had given thee sight and power to translate, thou deliveredst up that which was sacred, into the hands of a wicked man, who has set at nought the counsels of God, and has broken the most sacred promises, which were made before God, and has depended upon his own judgment, and boasted in his own wisdom, and this is the reason that thou hast lost thy privileges for a season, for thou hast suffered the counsel of thy director to be trampled upon from the beginning..

6 Nevertheless, my work shall go forth and accomplish my purposes, for as the knowledge of a Savior has come into the world, even so shall the knowledge of my people, the Nephites, and the Jacobites, and the Josephites, and the Zoramites, come to the knowledge of the Lamanites, and the Lemuelites and the Ishmaelites, which dwindled in unbelief, because of the iniquities of their fathers, who have been suffered to destroy their brethren, because of their iniquities, and their abominations: and for this very purpose are these plates preserved which contain these records, that the promises of the Lord might be fulfilled, which he made to his people; and that the Lamanites might come to the knowledge of their fathers, and

that they might know the promises of the Lord, and that they may believe the gospel and rely upon the merits of Jesus Christ, and be glorified through faith in his name; and that through their repentance they might be saved: Amen.

CHAPTER III.

1 *A Revelation given to Joseph, the father of Joseph, in Harmony, Pennsylvania, February, 1829, saying:*

NOW, behold, a marvelous work is about to come forth among the children of men, therefore, O ye that embark in the service of God, see that ye serve him with all your heart, might, mind and strength, that ye may stand blameless before God at the last day: Therefore, if ye have desires to serve God, ye are called to the work, for behold, the field is white already to harvest, and lo, he that thrusteth in his sickle with his might, the same layeth up in store that he perish not, but bringeth salvation to his soul, and faith, hope, charity, and love, with an eye single to the glory of God, qualifies him for the work.

2 Remember temperance, patience, humility, diligence, &c., ask and ye shall receive, knock and it shall be opened unto you: Amen.

CHAPTER IV.

1 *A Revelation given to Joseph and Martin, in Harmony, Pennsylvania, March, 1829, when Martin desired of the Lord to know whether Joseph had, in his possession, the record of the Nephites.*

BEHOLD, I say unto you, that my servant Martin has desired a witness from my hand, that my servant Joseph has got the things of which he has testified, and borne record that he has received of me.

2 And now, behold, this shall you say unto him:—I the Lord am God, and I have given these things unto my servant Joseph, and I have commanded him that he should stand as a witness of these things, nevertheless I have caused him that he should enter into a covenant with me, that he should not show them except I command him, and he has no power over them except I grant it unto him; and he has a gift to translate the book, and I have commanded him that he shall pretend to no other gift, for I will grant him no other gift.

3 And verily I say unto you, that wo shall come unto the inhabitants of the earth, if they will not hearken unto my words, for, behold, if they will not believe my words, they would not believe my servant Joseph, if it were possible that he could show them all things. O ye unbelieving, ye stiffnecked generation, mine anger is kindled against you!

4 Behold, verily I say, I have reserved the things of which I have spoken, which I have intrusted to my servant, for a wise purpose in me, and it shall be made known unto future generations: But this generation shall have my words, yea and the testi-

mony of three of my servants shall go forth with my
words unto this generation; yea, three shall know of
a surety that these things are true, for I will give
them power, that they may behold and view these
things as they are, and to none else will I grant this
power, to receive this same testimony among this
generation. And the testimony of three witnesses
will I send forth and my word, and behold, whosoever believeth in my word, them will I visit with the
manifestation of my Spirit, and they shall be born
of me, and their testimony shall also go forth.

5 And thus, if the people of this generation harden
not their hearts, I will work a reformation among
them, and I will put down all lyings, and deceiv-
ings, and priestcrafts, and envyings, and strifes, and
idolatries, and sorceries, and all manner of iniquities, and I will establish my church, like unto the
church which was taught by my disciples in the
days of old.

6 And now if this generation do harden their
hearts against my word, behold I will deliver them
up unto satan, for he reigneth and hath much power at this time, for he hath got great hold upon the
hearts of the people of this generation: and not far
from the iniquities of Sodom and Gomorrah, do
they come at this time: and behold the sword of
justice hangeth over their heads, and if they persist
in the hardness of their hearts, the time cometh that
it must fall upon them. Behold I tell you these
things even as I also told the people of the destruction of Jerusalem, and my word shall be verified at
this time as it hath hitherto been verified.

7 And now I command my servant Joseph to repent, and walk more uprightly before me, and yield
to the persuasions of men no more; and that he be

firm in keeping the commandments wherewith I
have commanded him; and if he doeth this, behold
I grant unto him eternal life, even if he should be
slain.

8 And now I speak again concerning the man that
desireth a witness: behold I say unto him, he exalteth himself and doth not humble himself sufficiently
before me, but if he will go out and bow down before me, and humble himself in mighty prayer and
faith, in the sincerity of his heart, then will I grant
unto him a view of the things which he desireth to
know: an then he shall say unto the people of this
generation, behold I have seen the things and I
know of a surety that they are true, for I have seen
them, and they have been shown unto me by the
power of God and not of man. And I command
him that he shall say no more unto them, concerning
these things, except he shall say, I have seen them,
and they have been shown unto me by the power of
God.

9 And these are the words which he shall say.—
But if he deny this, he will break the covenant which
he has before covenanted with me, and behold he
is condemned. And now except he humble himself and acknowledge unto me the things that he
has done, which are wrong, and covenant with me
that he will keep my commandments, and exercise
faith in me, behold I say unto him, he shall have
no such views, for I will grant unto him no views
of the things of which I have spoken. And if this
be the case, I command him that he shall do no
more, nor trouble me any more concerning this
matter.

10 And if this be the case, behold I say unto you,
Joseph, when thou hast translated a few more pages,

thou shalt stop for a season, even until I command thee again : then thou mayest translate again. And except thou do this, behold thou shalt have no more gift, and I will take away the things which I have intrusted with thee.

11 And now, because I foresee the lying in wait to destroy thee: Yea, I foresee that if my servant humbleth not himself, and receive a witness from my hand, that he will fall into transgression; and there are many that lie in wait to destroy thee from off the face of the earth: And for this cause, that thy days may be prolonged, I have given unto thee these commandments; yea, for this cause I have said, stop and stand still until I command thee, and I will provide means whereby thou mayest accomplish the thing which I have commanded thee; and if thou art faithful in keeping my commandments, thou shalt be lifted up at the last day :— Amen.

A7

CHAPTER V.

1 A Revelation to Oliver, given in Harmony, Pennsylvania, April, 1829, when employed a scribe for Joseph, while translating the book of Mormon.

A GREAT and marvelous work is about to come forth unto the children of men : behold I am God, and give heed unto my word, which is quick and powerful, sharper than a two-edged sword, to the dividing asunder of both joints and marrow :— Therefore give heed unto my words.

2 Behold the field is white already to harvest, therefore whoso desireth to reap, let him thrust in his sickle with his might and reap while the day lasts, that he may treasure up for his soul everlasting salvation in the kingdom of God : Yea, whosoever will thrust in his sickle and reap, the same is called of God; therefore, if you will ask of me you shall receive; if you will knock it shall be opened unto you.

3 Now as you have asked, behold I say unto you, keep my commandments, and seek to bring forth and establish the cause of Zion : seek not for riches but for wisdom, and behold the mysteries of God shall be unfolded unto you, and then shall you be made rich. Behold he that hath eternal life is rich.

4 Verily, verily I say unto you, even as you desire of me, so shall it be unto you; and, if you desire, you shall be the means of doing much good in this generation. Say nothing but repentance unto this generation; keep my commandments and assist to bring forth my work according to my commandments, and you shall be blessed.

5 Behold thou hast a gift, and blessed art thou be cause of thy gift. Remember it is sacred and cometh from above; and if thou wilt inquire, thou shalt know mysteries which are great and marvelous: therefore thou shalt exercise thy gift, that thou mayest find out mysteries, that thou mayest bring many to the knowledge of the truth; yea, convince them of the error of their ways. Make not thy gift known unto any, save it be those which are of thy faith.— Trifle not with sacred things. If thou wilt do good, yea and hold out faithful to the end, thou shalt be saved in the kingdom of God, which is the greatest of all the gifts of God; for there is no gift greater than the gift of salvation.

6 Verily, verily I say unto thee, blessed art thou for what thou hast done, for thou hast inquired of me, and behold as often as thou hast inquired, thou hast received instruction of my Spirit. If it had not been so, thou wouldst not have come to the place where thou art at this time.

7 Behold thou knowest that thou hast inquired of me, and I did enlighten thy mind; and now I tell thee these things, that thou mayest know that thou hast been enlightened by the Spirit of truth; yea, I tell thee, that thou mayest know that there is none else save God, that knowest thy thoughts and the intents of thy heart: I tell thee these things as a witness unto thee, that the words or the work which thou hast been writing is true:

8 Therefore be diligent, stand by my servant Joseph faithfully in whatsoever difficult circumstances he may be, for the word's sake. Admonish him in his faults and also receive admonition of him. Be patient; be sober; be temperate; have patience, faith, hope and charity.

9 Behold thou art Oliver, and I have spoken unto thee because of thy desires, therefore, treasure up these words in thy heart. Be faithful and diligent in keeping the commandments of God, and I will incircle thee in the arms of my love.

10 Behold I am Jesus Christ, the Son of God. I am the same that came unto my own and my own received me not. I am the light which shineth in darkness, and the darkness comprehendeth it not.

11 Verily, verily I say unto you, if you desire a further witness, cast your mind upon the night that you cried unto me in your heart, that you might know concerning the truth of these things; did I not speak peace to your mind concering the matter?— What greater witness can you have than from God? And now behold, you have received a witness, for if I have told you things which no man knoweth, have you not received a witness? And behold I grant unto you a gift if you desire of me, to translate even as my servant Joseph.

12 Verily, verily I say unto you, that there are records which contain much of my gospel, which have been kept back because of the wickedness of the people; and now I command you, that if you have good desires, a desire to lay up treasures for yourself in heaven, then shall you assist in bringing to light, with your gift, those parts of my scriptures which have been hidden because of iniquity.

13 And now behold I give unto you, and also unto my servant Joseph, the keys of this gift, which shall bring to light this ministry; and in the mouth of two or three witnesses, shall every word be established.

14 Verily, verily I say unto you, if they reject my words, and this part of my gospel and ministry, bles

sed are ye, for they can do no more unto you than unto me; and if they do unto you, even as they have done unto me, blessed are ye, for you shall dwell with me in glory: but if they reject not my words, which shall be established by the testimony which shall be given, blessed are they; and then shall ye have joy in the fruit of your labors.

15 Verily, verily I say unto you, as I said unto my disciples, where two or three are gathered together in my name, as touching one thing, behold there will I be in the midst of them: even so am I in the midst of you. Fear not to do good my sons, for whatsoever ye sow, that shall ye also reap: therefore, if ye sow good, ye shall also reap good for your reward:

16 Therefore fear not little flock, do good, let earth and hell combine against you, for if ye are built upon my Rock, they cannot prevail. Behold I do not condemn you, go your ways and sin no more: perform with soberness the work which I have commanded you: look unto me in every thought, doubt not, fear not: behold the wounds which pierced my side, and also the prints of the nails in my hands and feet: be faithful; keep my commandments, and ye shall inherit the kingdom of heaven; Amen.

CHAPTER VI.

1 *A Revelation given to Joseph and Oliver, in Harmony, Pennsylvania, April, 1829, when they desired to know whether John, the beloved disciple, tarried on earth. Translated from parchment, written and hid up by himself.*

AND the Lord said unto me, John my beloved, what desirest thou? and I said Lord, give unto me power that I may bring souls unto thee.— And the Lord said unto me: Verily, verily I say unto thee, because thou desiredst this, thou shalt tarry till I come in my glory:

2 And for this cause, the Lord said unto Peter:— If I will that he tarry till I come, what is that to thee? for he desiredst of me that he might bring souls unto me: but thou desiredst that thou might speedily come unto me in my kingdom: I say unto thee, Peter, this was a good desire, but my beloved has undertaken a greater work.

3 Verily I say unto you, ye shall both have according to your desires, for ye both joy in that which ye have desired.

CHAPTER VII.

1 *A Revelation given to Oliver, in Harmony, Pennsylvania, April, 1829.*

OLIVER, verily, verily I say unto you, that assuredly as the Lord liveth, which is your God and your Redeemer, even so sure shall you receive a knowledge of whatsoever things you shall ask in faith, with an honest heart, believing that you shall receive a knowledge concerning the engravings of old records, which are ancient, which contain those parts of my scripture of which have been spoken, by the manifestation of my Spirit; yea, behold I will tell you in your mind and in your heart by the Holy Ghost, which shall come upon you and which shall dwell in your heart.

2 Now, behold this is the Spirit of revelation :— behold this is the spirit by which Moses brought the children of Israel through the Red sea on dry ground : therefore, this is thy gift; apply unto it and blessed art thou, for it shall deliver you out of the hands of your enemies, when, if it were not so, they would slay you and bring your soul to destruction.

3 O remember, these words and keep my commandments. Remember this is your gift. Now this is not all, for you have another gift, which is the gift of working with the rod : behold it has told you things : behold there is no other power save God, that can cause this rod of nature, to work in your hands, for it is the work of God; and therefore whatsoever you shall ask me to tell you by that means, that will I grant unto you, that you shall know.

4 Remember that without faith you can do noth-

ing. Trifle not with these things. Do not ask for that which you ought not. Ask that you may know the mysteries of God, and that you may translate all those ancient records, which have been hid up, which are sacred, and according to your faith shall it be done unto you.

5 Behold it is I that have spoken it, and I am the same which spake unto you from the beginning:—Amen.

CHAPTER VIII.

1 *A Revelation given to Oliver, in Harmony, Pennsylvania, April,* 1829.

BEHOLD I say unto you, my son, that, because you did not translate according to that which you desired of me, and did commence again to write for my servant Joseph, even so I would that you should continue until you have finished this record, which I have intrusted unto you: and then behold, other records have I, that I will give unto you power that you may assist to translate.

2 Be patient my son, for it is wisdom in me, and it is not expedient that you should translate at this present time. Behold the work which you are called to do, is to write for my servant Joseph; and behold it is because that you did not continue as you commenced, when you begun to translate, that I have taken away this privilege from you. Do not murmur my son, for it is wisdom in me that I have dealt with you after this manner.

3 Behold you have not understood, you have supposed that I would give it unto you, when you took

no thought, save it was to ask me; but behold I say
unto you, that you must study it out in your mind;
then you must ask me if it be right, and if it is right,
I will cause that your bosom shall burn within you:
therefore, you shall feel that it is right; but if it be
not right, you shall have no such feelings, but you
shall have a stupor of thought, that shall cause you
to forget the thing which is wrong: therefore, you
cannot write that which is sacred, save it be given
you from me.

4 Now if you had known this, you could have
translated: nevertheless, it is not expedient that you
should translate now. Behold it was expedient
when you commenced, but you feared and the time
is past, that it is not expedient now: for, do you not
behold that I have given unto my servant Joseph
sufficient strength, whereby it is made up? and neither of you have I condemned.

5 Do this thing which I have commanded you,
and you shall prosper. Be faithful, and yield to no
temptation. Stand fast in the work wherewith I
have called you, and a hair of your head shall not
be lost, and you shall be lifted up at the last day:
Amen.

CHAPTER IX.

A Revelation given to Joseph, in Harmony, Pennsylvania, May, 1829, informing him of the alteration of the Manuscript of the fore part of the book of Mormon.

NOW, behold I say unto you, that because you delivered up so many writings, which you had power to translate, into the hands of a wicked man, you have lost them, and you also lost your gift at the same time, nevertheless it has been restored unto you again : therefore, see that you are faithful and go on unto the finishing of the remainder of the work as you have begun. Do not run faster than you have strength and means provided to translate, but be diligent unto the end, that you may come off conquerer; yea, that you may conquer satan, and those that do uphold his work.

2 Behold they have sought to destroy you; yea, even the man in whom you have trusted, and for this cause I said, that he is a wicked man, for he has sought to take away the things wherewith you have been intrusted; and he has also sought to destroy your gift, and because you have delivered the writings into his hands, behold they have taken them from you: therefore, you have delivered them up; yea, that which was sacred unto wickedness. And behold, satan has put it into their hearts to alter the words which you have caused to be written, or which you have translated, which have gone out of your hands; and behold I say unto you, that because they have altered the words, they read contrary from that which you translated and caused to be written; and on this wise the devil has sought to lay a cunning

plan, that he may destroy this work; for he has put it into their hearts to do this, that by lying they may say they have caught you in the words which you have pretended to translate.

3 Verily I say unto you, that I will not suffer that satan shall accomplish his evil design in this thing, for behold he has put it into their hearts to tempt the Lord their God; for behold they say in their hearts, We will see if God has given him power to translate, if so, he will also give him power again; and if God giveth him power again, or if he translate again, or in other words, if he bringeth forth the same words, behold we have the same with us, and we have altered them: Therefore, they will not agree, and we will say that he has lied in his words, and that he has no gift, and that he has no power: therefore, we will destroy him, and also the work, and we will do this that we may not be ashamed in the end, and that we may get glory of the world.

4 Verily, verily I say unto you, that satan has great hold upon their hearts; he stirreth them up to do iniquity against that which is good, that he may lead their souls to destruction, and thus he has laid a cunning plan to destroy the work of God; yea, he stirreth up their hearts to anger against this work; yea, he saith unto them, Deceive and lie in wait to catch, that ye may destroy: behold this is no harm, and thus he flattereth them and telleth them that it is no sin to lie, that they may catch a man in a lie, that they may destroy him, and thus he flattereth them, and leadeth them along until he draggeth their souls down to hell; and thus he causeth them to catch themselves in their own snare; and thus he goeth up and down, to and fro in the earth, seeking to destroy the souls of men.

5 Verily, verily I say unto you, wo be unto him that lieth to decieve, because he supposeth that another lieth to decieve, for such are not exempt from the justice of God.

6 Now, behold they have altered those words, because satan saith unto them, He hath decieved you, and thus he flattereth them away to do iniquity, to tempt the Lord their God.

7 Behold I say unto you, that you shall not translate again those words which have gone forth out of your hands; for behold, they shall not lie any more against those words; for behold, if you should bring forth the same words, they would say that you have lied; that you have pretended to translate, but that you have contradicted your words; and behold they would publish this, and satan would harden the hearts of the people, to stir them up to anger against you, that they might not believe my words: thus satan would overpower this generation, that the work might not come forth in this generation: but behold here is wisdom, and because I show unto you wisdom, and give you commandments concerning these things, what you shall do, show it not unto the world until you have accomplished the work.

8 Marvel not that I said unto you, here is wisdom, show it not unto the world, for I said, show it not unto the world, that you may be preserved. Behold I do not say that you shall not show it unto the righteous; but as you cannot always judge the righteous, or as you cannot always tell the wicked from the righteous: therefore, I say unto you, hold your peace until I shall see fit to make all things known unto the world concerning the matter.

9 And now, verily I say unto you, that an account of those things that you have written, which have

gone out of your hands, are engraven upon the plates of Nephi; yea, and you remember, it was said in those writings, that a more particular account was given of these things upon the plates of Nephi.

10 And now, because the account which is engraven upon the plates of Nephi, is more particular concerning the things, which in my wisdom I would bring to the knowledge of the people in this account: therefore, you shall translate the engravings which are on the plates of Nephi, down even till you come to the reign of king Benjamin, or until you come to that which you have translated, which you have retained; and behold, you shall publish it as the record of Nephi, and thus I will confound those who have altered my words. I will not suffer that they shall destroy my work; yea, I will show unto them that my wisdom is greater than the cunning of the devil.

11 Behold they have only got a part, or an abridgment of the account of Nephi. Behold there are many things engraven on the plates of Nephi, which do throw greater views upon my gospel: therefore, it is wisdom in me, that you should translate this first part of the engravings of Nephi, and send forth in this work. And behold, all the remainder of this work, does contain all those parts of my gospel which my holy prophets; yea, and also my disciples desired in their prayers, should come forth unto this people. And I said unto them, that it should be granted unto them according to their faith in their prayers; yea, and this was their faith, that my gospel which I gave unto them, that they might preach in their days, might come unto their brethren, the Lamanites, and also, all that had become Lamanites, because of their dissensions.

12 Now this is not all, their faith in their prayers were, that this gospel should be made known also, if it were possible that other nations should possess this land; and thus they did leave a blessing upon this land in their prayers, that whosoever should believe in this gospel, in this land, might have eternal life; yea, that it might be free unto all of whatsoever nation, kindred, tongue, or people, they may be.

13 And now, behold, according to their faith in their prayers, will I bring this part of my gospel to the knowledge of my people. Behold, I do not bring it to destroy that which they have received, but to build it up.

14 And for this cause have I said, if this generation harden not their hearts, I will establish my church among them. Now I do not say this to destroy my church, but I say this to build up my church: therefore, whosoever belongeth to my church need not fear, for such shall inherit the kingdom of heaven: but it is they who do not fear me, neither keep my commandments, but buildeth up churches unto themselves, to get gain; yea, and all those that do wickedly, and buildeth up the kingdom of the devil; yea, verily, verily I say unto you, that it is they that I will disturb, and cause to tremble and shake to the centre.

15 Behold, I am Jesus Christ, the Son of God: I came unto my own, and my own received me not. I am the light which shineth in darkness, and the darkness comprehendeth it not. I am he who said: other sheep have I which are not of this fold, unto my disciples, and many there were that understood me not.

16 And I will show unto this people, that I had

other sheep, and that they were a branch of the house of Jacob; and I will bring to light their marvelous works, which they did in my name; yea, and I will also bring to light my gospel, which was ministered unto them, and behold they shall not deny that which you have received, but they shall build it up, and shall bring to light the true points of my doctrine: Yea, and the only doctrine which is in me; and this I do, that I may establish my gospel, that there may not be so much contention: Yea, satan doth stir up the hearts of the people to contention, concerning the points of my doctrine; and in these things they do err, for they do wrest the scriptures, and do not understand them: therefore, I will unfold unto them this great mystery, for behold, I will gather them as a hen gathereth her chickens under her wings, if they will not harden their hearts: Yea, if they will come, they may, and partake of the waters of life freely.

17 Behold this is my doctrine: whosoever repenteth, and cometh unto me, the same is my church: whosoever declareth more or less than this, the same is not of me, but is against me: therefore, he is not of my church.

18 And now, behold whosoever is of my church, and endureth of my church to the end, him will I establish upon my Rock, and the gates of hell shall not prevail against them.

19 And now, remember the words of him who is the life and the light of the world, your Redeemer, your Lord and your God: Amen.

CHAPTER X.

1 *A Revelation given to Hyrum, in Harmony, Pennsylvania, May,* 1829.

A GREAT and marvelous work is about to come forth among the children of men : behold I am God and give heed to my word, which is quick and powerful, sharper than a two-edged sword, to the dividing asunder of both joints and marrow : therefore, give heed unto my word.

2 Behold the field is white already to harvest, therefore, whoso desireth to reap, let him thrust in his sickle with his might, and reap while the day lasts, that he may treasure up for his soul everlasting salvation in the kingdom of God; yea, whosoever will thrust in his sickle and reap, the same is called of God : therefore, if you will ask of me, you shall receive ; if you will knock, it shall be opened unto you.

3 Now as you have asked, behold I say unto you, keep my commandments, and seek to bring forth and establish the cause of Zion. Seek not for riches but for wisdom, and behold the mysteries of God shall be unfolded unto you, and then shall you be made rich ; behold he that hath eternal life is rich.

4 Verily, verily I say unto you, even as you desire of me, so shall it be done unto you ; and, if you desire you shall be the means of doing much good in this generation. Say nothing but repentance unto this generation. Keep my commandments, and assist to bring forth my work according to my commandments, and you shall be blessed.

5 Behold thou hast a gift, or thou shalt have a gift, if thou wilt desire of me in faith, with an honest

heart, believing in the power of Jesus Christ, or in my power which speaketh unto thee : for behold it is I that speaketh : behold I am the light which shineth in darkness, and by my power I give these words unto thee.

6 And now, verily, verily I say unto thee, put your trust in that Spirit which leadeth to do good : Yea, to do justly ; to walk humbly ; to judge righteously ; and this is my Spirit.

7 Verily, verily I say unto you, I will impart unto you of my Spirit, which shall enlighten your mind, which shall fill your soul with joy, and then shall you know, or by this shall you know, all things whatsoever you desire of me, which is pertaining unto things of righteousness, in faith believing in me that you shall receive.

8 Behold I command you, that you need not suppose that you are called to preach until you are called : wait a little longer, until you shall have my word, my Rock, my church, and my gospel, that you may know of a surety my doctrine ; and then behold, according to your desires, yea, even according to your faith, shall it be done unto you.

9 Keep my commandments ; hold your peace ; appeal unto my Spirit : Yea, cleave unto me with all your heart, that you may assist in bringing to light those things of which have been spoken : Yea, the translation of my work : be patient until you shall accomplish it.

10 Behold this is your work, to keep my commandments : Yea, with all your might, mind, and strength : seek not to declare my word, but first seek to obtain my word, and then shall your tongues be loosed ; then, if you desire you shall have my Spirit, and my word : Yea, the power of God unto the

convincing of men : but now hold your peace ; study my word which hath gone forth among the children of men; and also study my word which shall come forth among the children of men; or that which you are translating : Yea, until you have obtained all which I shall grant unto the children of men in this generation; and then shall all things be added thereunto.

11 Behold thou art Hyrum, my son; seek the kingdom of God and all things shall be added according to that which is just. Build upon my Rock, which is my gospel; deny not the spirit of revelation, nor the spirit of prophecy, for wo unto him that denieth these things: therefore, treasure up in your hearts until the time which is in my wisdom, that you shall go forth: Behold I speak unto all who have good desires, and have thrust in their sickles to reap.

12 Behold I am Jesus Christ, the Son of God: I am the life and the light of the world: I am the same which came unto my own, and my own received me not: but verily, verily I say unto you, that as many as receiveth me, them will I give power to become the sons of God, even to them that believe on my name: Amen.

CHAPTER XI.

A Revelation given to Joseph (K.,) in Harmony, Pennsylvania, May, 1829, informing him how he must do, to be worthy to assist in the work of the Lord.

A GREAT and marvelous work is about to come forth among the children of men : behold I am God, and give heed to my word, which is quick and powerful, sharper than a two-edged sword, to the dividing asunder of both joints and marrow : therefore, give heed unto my word.

2 Behold the field is white already to harvest, therefore whoso desireth to reap, let him thrust in his sickle with his might, and reap while the day lasts, that he may treasure up for his soul everlasting salvation in the kingdom of God : Yea, whosoever will thrust in his sickle and reap, the same is called of God : therefore, if you will ask of me you shall receive ; if you will knock it shall be opened unto you.

3 Now as you have asked, behold I say unto you, keep my commandments, and seek to bring forth and establish the cause of Zion.

4 Behold I speak unto you, and also to all those who have desires to bring forth and establish this work, and no one can assist in this work, except he shall be humble and full of love, having faith, hope and charity, being temperate in all things, whatsoever shall be intrusted to his care.

5 Behold I am the light and the life of the world, that speaketh these words : therefore, give heed with your might, and then you are called : Amen,

CHAPTER XII,

1 *A Revelation given to David, in Fayette, New York, June,* 1829.

A GREAT and marvelous work is about to come forth unto the children of men: behold I am God, and give heed to my word, which is quick and powerful, sharper than a two-edged sword, to the dividing asunder of both joints and marrow: therefore, give heed unto my word.

2 Behold the field is white already to harvest, therefore, whoso desireth to reap, let him thrust in his sickle with his might, and reap while the day lasts, that he may treasure up for his soul everlasting salvation in the kingdom of God: Yea, whosoever will thrust in his sickle and reap, the same is called of God: therefore, if you will ask of me you shall receive; if you will knock it shall be opened unto you.

3 Seek to bring forth and establish my Zion.— Keep my commandments in all things, and if you keep my commandments, and endure to the end, you shall have eternal life; which gift is the greatest of all the gifts of God.

4 And it shall come to pass, that if you shall ask the Father in my name, in faith believing, you shall receive the Holy Ghost, which giveth utterance, that you may stand as a witness of the things of which you shall both hear and see; and also, that you may declare repentance unto this generation.

5 Behold I am Jesus Christ the Son of the living God, which created the heavens and the earth; a light which cannot be hid in darkness: wherefore, I must bring forth the fulness of my gospel from the

Gentiles unto the house of Israel. And behold thou art David, and thou art called to assist: Which thing if ye do, and are faithful, ye shall be blessed both spiritually and temporally, and great shall be your reward: Amen.

CHAPTER XIII.

1 A Revelation given to John, in Fayette, New York, June, 1829.

HEARKEN my servant John, and listen to the words of Jesus Christ, your Lord and your Redeemer, for behold I speak unto you with sharpness and with power, for mine arm is over all the earth, and I will tell you that which no man knoweth save me and thee alone: for many times you have desired of me to know that which would be of the most worth unto you.

2 Behold, blessed are you for this thing, and for speaking my words which I have given you, according to my commandments:

3 And now behold I say unto you, that the thing which will be of the most worth unto you, will be to declare repentance unto this people, that you may bring souls unto me, that you may rest with them in the kingdom of my Father. Amen.

CHAPTER XIV.

1 *A Revelation given to Peter, in Fayette, New York, June,* 1829.

HEARKEN my servant Peter, and listen to the words of Jesus Christ, your Lord and your Redeemer, for behold I speak unto you with sharpness and with power, for mine arm is over all the earth, and I will tell you that which no man knoweth save me and thee alone: for many times you have desired of me to know that which would be of the most worth unto you.

2 Behold, blessed are you for this thing, and for speaking my words which I have given you, according to my commandments:

2 And now behold I say unto you, that the thing which will be of the most worth unto you, will be to declare repentance unto this people, that you may bring souls unto me, that you may rest with them in the kingdom of my Father. Amen.

———————

CHAPTER XV.

1 *A Revelation to Joseph, Oliver and David, making known the calling of twelve disciples in these last days, and also, instructions relative to building up the church of Christ, according to the fulness of the gospel: Given in Fayette, New-York, June,* 1829.

NOW behold, because of the thing which you have desired to know of me, I give unto you these words:

2 Behold I have manifested unto you, by my

Spirit in many instances, that the things which you have written are true :

3 Wherefore you know that they are true ; and if you know that they are true, behold I give unto you a commandment, that you rely upon the things which are written ; for in them are all things written, concerning my church, my gospel, and my rock.

4 Wherefore if you shall build up my church, and my gospel, and my rock, the gates of hell shall not prevail against you.

5 Behold the world is ripening in iniquity, and it must needs be, that the children of men are stirred up unto repentance, both the Gentiles, and also the house of Israel :

6 Wherefore as thou hast been baptized by the hand of my servant, according to that which I have commanded him :

7 Wherefore he hath fulfilled the thing which I commanded him.

8 And now marvel not that I have called him unto mine own purpose, which purpose is known in me :

9 Wherefore if he shall be diligent in keeping my commandments, he shall be blessed unto eternal life, and his name is Joseph.

10 And now Oliver, I speak nnto you, and also unto David, by the way of commandment :

11 For behold I command all men every where to repent, and I speak unto you, even as unto Paul mine apostle, for you are called even with that same calling with which he was called.

12 Remember the worth of souls is great in the sight of God :

13 For behold the Lord your God suffered death

in the flesh: wherefore he suffered the pain of all men, that all men might repent and come unto him.

14 And he hath risen again from the dead, that he might bring all men unto him on conditions of repentance.

15 And how great is his joy in the soul that repenteth.

16 Wherefore you are called to cry repentance unto this people.

17 And if it so be that you should labor in all your days, in crying repentance unto this people, and bring save it be one soul only unto me, how great shall be your joy with him in the kingdom of my Father?

18 And now if your joy will be great with one soul, that you have brought unto me into the kingdom of my Father, how great will be your joy, if you should bring many souls unto me?

19 Behold you have my gospel before you, and my rock, and my salvation:

20 Ask the Father in my name in faith believing that you shall receive, and you shall have the Holy Ghost which manifesteth all things, which is expedient unto the children of men.

21 And if you have not faith, hope and charity, you can do nothing.

22 Contend against no church, save it be the church of the devil.

23 Take upon you the name of Christ, and speak the truth in soberness, and as many as repent, and are baptized in my name, which is Jesus Christ, and endure to the end, the same shall be saved.

24 Behold Jesus Christ is the name which is given of the Father, and there is none other name given whereby man can be saved;

25 Wherefore all men must take upon them the name which is given of the Father, for in that name shall they be called at the last day:

26 Wherefore if they know not the name by which they are called, they cannot have place in the kingdom of my Father.

27 And now behold, there are others which are called to declare my gospel, both unto Gentile and unto Jew: Yea, even unto twelve:

28 And the twelve shall be my disciples, and they shall take upon them my name:

29 And the twelve are they which shall desire to take upon them my name, with full purpose of heart:

30 And if they desire to take upon them my name, with full purpose of heart, they are called to go into all the world to preach my gospel unto every creature:

31 And they are they which are ordained of me to baptize in my name, according to that which is written; and you have that which is written before you:

32 Wherefore you must perform it according to the words which are written.

33 And now I speak unto the twelve:

34 Behold my grace is sufficient for you: You must walk uprightly before me and sin not.

35 And behold you are they which are ordained of me to ordain priests and teachers to declare my gospel, according to the power of the Holy Ghost which is in you, and according to the callings and gifts of God unto men:

36 And I Jesus Christ, your Lord and your God, have spoken it.

37 These words are not of men, nor of man, but of me:

38 Wherefore you shall testify they are of me, and not of man; for it is my voice which speaketh them unto you:

39 For they are given by my Spirit unto you:

40 And by my power you can read them one to another; and save it were by my power, you could not have them:

41 Wherefore you can testify that you have heard my voice, and know my words.

42 And now behold I give unto you, Oliver, and also unto David, that you shall search out the twelve which shall have the desires of which I have spoken; and by their desires and their works, you shall know them:

43 And when you have found them you shall show these things unto them.

44 And you shall fall down and worship the Father in my name:

45 And you must preach unto the world, saying, you must repent and be baptized in the name of Jesus Christ:

46 For all men must repent and be baptized; and not only men, but women and children, which have arriven to the years of accountability.

47 And now, after that you have received this, you must keep my commandments in all things:

48 And by your hands I will work a marvelous work among the children of men, unto the convincing of many of their sins, that they may come unto repentance; and that they may come unto the kingdom of my Father:

49 Wherefore the blessings which I give unto you are above all things.

50 And after that you have received this, if you keep not my commandments, you cannot be saved

in the kingdom of my Father. Behold I Jesus Christ, your Lord and your God, and your Redeemer, by the power of my Spirit, have spoken it: Amen.

CHAPTER XVI.

1 *A commandment of God and not of man to you, Martin, given (Manchester, New-York, March, 1830,) by him who is eternal :*

YEA, even I, I am he, the beginning and the end: Yea, Alpha and Omega, Christ the Lord, the Redeemer of the world :

2 I having accomplished and finished the will of him whose I am, even the Father :

3 Having done this, that I might subdue all things unto myself :

4 Retaining all power, even to the destroying of satan and his works at the end of the world, and the last great day of judgment, which I shall pass upon the inhabitants thereof, judging every man according to his works, and the deeds which he hath done.

5 And surely every man must repent or suffer, for I God am endless :

6 Wherefore, I revoke not the judgments which I shall pass, but woes shall go forth, weeping, wailing and gnashing of teeth :

7 Yea, to those who are found on my left hand, nevertheless, it is not written, that there shall be no end to this torment; but it is written endless torment.

8 Again, it is written eternal damnation : wherefore it is more express than other scriptures, that it

might work upon the hearts of the children of men, altogether for my name's glory :

9 Wherefore, I will explain unto you, this mystery, for it is mete unto you, to know even as mine apostles.

10 I speak unto you that are chosen in this thing, even as one, that you may enter into my rest.

11 For behold, the mystery of Godliness how great is it? for behold I am endless, and the punishment which is given from my hand, is endless punishment, for endless is my name :

12 Wherefore—

   Eternal punishment   ) Endless punishment
   is God's punishment :(is God's punishment :

13 Wherefore, I command you by my name, and by my Almighty power, that you repent: repent, lest I smite you by the rod of my mouth, and by my wrath, and by my anger, and your sufferings be sore : .

14 How sore you know not!

15 How exquisite you know not!

16 Yea, how hard to bear you know not!

17 For behold, I God have suffered these things for all, that they might not suffer, if they would repent, but if they would not repent, they must suffer even as I:

18 Which suffering caused myself, even God, the greatest of all, to tremble because of pain, and to bleed at every pore, both body and spirit:

19 And would that I might not drink the bitter cup and shrink :

20 Nevertheless, glory be to the Father, and I partook and finished my preparations unto the children of men :

21 Wherefore, I command you again by my Al-

mighty power, that you confess your sins, lest you suffer these punishments of which I have spoken, of which in the smallest, yea, even in the least degree you have tasted at the time I withdrew my Spirit.

22 And I command you, that you preach nought but repentance; and show not these things, neither speak these things unto the world, for they can not bear meat, but milk they must receive:

23 Wherefore, they must not know these things lest they perish:

24 Wherefore, learn of me, and listen to my words; walk in the meekness of my Spirit and you shall have peace in me, Jesus Christ by the will of the Father.

25 And again: I command you, that thou shalt not covet thy neighbor's wife.

26 Nor seek thy neighbor's life.

27 And again: I command you, that thou shalt not covet thine own property, but impart it freely to the printing of the book of Mormon, which contains the truth and the word of God, which is my word to Gentile, that soon it may go to the Jew, of which the Lamanites are a remnant; that they may believe the gospel, and look not for a Messiah to come which has already come.

28 And again: I command you, that thou shalt pray vocally as well as to thyself:

29 Yea, before the world as well as in secret; in public as well as in private.

30 And thou shalt declare glad tidings; yea, publish it upon the mountains, and upon every high place, and among every people which thou shalt be permitted to see.

31 And thou shalt do it with all humility, trusting in me, reviling not against revilers.

32 And of tenets thou shalt not talk, but thou shalt declare repentance and faith on the Savior and remission of sins by baptism and by fire; yea, even the Holy Ghost.

33 Behold this is a great and the last commandment which I shall give unto you:

34 For this shall suffice for thy daily walk even unto the end of thy life.

35 And misery thou shalt receive, if thou wilt slight these counsels; Yea, even destruction of thyself and property.

36 Impart a portion of thy property; Yea, even a part of thy lands and all save the support of thy family.

37 Pay the printer's debt. .

38 Release thyself from bondage.

39 Leave thy house and home, except when thou shalt desire to see them.

40 And speak freely to all: Yea, preach, exhort, declare the truth, even with a loud voice; with a sound of rejoicing, crying hosanna! hosanna! blessed be the name of the Lord God.

41 Pray always and I will pour out my Spirit upon you, and great shall be your blessing:

42 Yea, even more than if you should obtain treasures of earth, and corruptibleness to the extent thereof.

43 Behold, canst thou read this without rejoicing, and lifting up thy heart for gladness; or canst thou run about longer as a blind guide; or canst thou be humble and meek and conduct thyself wisely before me:

44 Yea, come unto me thy Savior. Amen.

CHAPTER XVII.

1 *A Revelation to Oliver, given in Manchester, New-York, April 6, 1830.*

BEHOLD I speak unto you, Oliver, a few words. 2 Behold thou art blessed, and art under no condemnation.

3 But beware of pride, lest thou shouldst enter into temptation.

4 Make known thy calling unto the church, and also before the world; and thy heart shall be opened to preach the truth from henceforth and forever. Amen.

CHAPTER XVIII.

1 *A Revelation to Hyrum, given in Manchester, New-York, April 6, 1830.*

BEHOLD I speak unto you, Hyrum, a few words:

2 For thou also art under no condemnation, and thy heart is opened, and thy tongue loosed;

3 And thy calling is to exhortation, and to strengthen the church continually.

4 Wherefore thy duty is unto the church forever; and this because of thy family. Amen.

CHAPTER XIX.

1 *A Revelation to Samuel, given in Manchester, New-York, April 6, 1830.*

BEHOLD I speak a few words unto you, Samuel:

2 For thou also art under no condemnation, and thy calling is to exhortation, and to strengthen the church.

3 And thou art not as yet called to preach before the world. Amen.

CHAPTER XX.

1 *A Revelation to Joseph, the father of Joseph, given in Manchester, New-York, April 6, 1830.*

BEHOLD I speak a few words unto you, Joseph:

2 For thou also art under no condemnation, and thy calling also is to exhortation, and to strengthen the church.

3 And this is thy duty from henceforth and forever. Amen.

CHAPTER XXI.

1 *A Revelation to Joseph (K.,) given in Manchester, New-York, April 6, 1830.*

BEHOLD I manifest unto you by these words, that you must take up your cross, in the which you must pray vocally before the world, as well as in secret, and in your family, and among your friends, and in all places.

2 And behold it is your duty to unite with the true church, and give your language to exhortation continually, that you may receive the reward of the laborer. Amen.

CHAPTER XXII.

1 *A Revelation to Joseph, given in Manchester, New-York, April 6, 1830.*

BEHOLD there shall be a record kept among you, and in it thou shalt be called a seer, a translator, a prophet, an apostle of Jesus Christ, an elder of the church through the will of God the Father, and the grace of our Lord Jesus Christ;

2 Being inspired of the Holy Ghost to lay the foundation thereof, and to build it up unto the most holy faith;

3 Which church was organized and established, in the year of our Lord eighteen hundred and thirty, in the fourth month, and on the sixth day of the month, which is called April.

4 Wherefore, meaning the church, thou shalt give heed unto all his words, and commandments, which he shall give unto you, as he receiveth them, walking in all holiness before me:

5 For his word ye shall receive, as if from mine own mouth, in all patience and faith;

6 For by doing these things, the gates of hell shall not prevail against you:

7 Yea, and the Lord God will disperse the powers of darkness from before you; and cause the

heavens to shake for your good, and his name's glory.

8 For thus saith the Lord God, him have I inspired to move the cause of Zion in mighty power for good; and his diligence I know, and his prayers I have heard:

9 Yea, his weeping for Zion I have seen, and I will cause that he shall mourn for her no longer, for his days of rejoicing are come unto the remission of his sins, and the manifestations of my blessings upon his works.

10 For behold, I will bless all those who labor in my vineyard, with a mighty blessing, and they shall believe on his words, which are given him through me, by the Comforter:

11 Which manifesteth that Jesus was crucified by sinful men for the sins of the world;

12 Yea, for the remission of sins unto the contrite heart.

13 Wherefore, it behooveth me, that he should be ordained by you, Oliver, mine apostle;

14 This being an ordinance unto you, that you are an elder under his hand, he being the first unto you, that you might be an elder unto this church of Christ, bearing my name;

15 And the first preacher of this church, unto the church, and before the world; yea, before the Gentiles:

16 Yea, and thus saith the Lord God, lo, lo, to the Jews also. Amen.

CHAPTER XXIII.

1 *A Commandment unto the church of Christ, which was established in these last days, in the year of our Lord one thousand eight hundred and thirty: Given in Fayette, New-York, April, 1830, in consequence of some desiring to unite with the church without re-baptism, who had previously been baptized.*

BEHOLD I say unto you, that all old covenants have I caused to be done away in this thing, and this is a new and an everlasting covenant; even that which was from the beginning.

2 Wherefore although a man should be baptized an hundred times, it availeth him nothing;

3 For you cannot enter in at the straight gate by the law of Moses, neither by your dead works;

4 For it is because of your dead works, that I have caused this last covenant, and this church to be built up unto me; even as in days of old.

5 Wherefore enter ye in at the gate, as I have commanded, and seek not to counsel your God.— Amen.

CHAPTER XXIV.

1 *The Articles and Covenants of the church of Christ, given in Fayette, New-York, June, 1830;*

THE rise of the church of Christ in these last days, being one thousand eight hundred and thirty years since the coming of our Lord and Saviour Jesus Christ, in the flesh;

D9

2 It being regularly organized and established agreeable to the laws of our country, by the will and commandments of God in the fourth month and on the sixth day of the month, which is called April:

3 Which commandments were given to Joseph, who was called of God and ordained an apostle of Jesus Christ, an elder of this church;

4 And also to Oliver, who was also called of God an apostle of Jesus Christ, an elder of this church, and ordained under his hand:

5 And this according to the grace of our Lord and Savior Jesus Christ, to whom be all glory both now and forever. Amen.

6 For, after that it truly was manifested unto this first elder, that he had received a remission of his sins, he was entangled again in the vanities of the world;

7 But after truly repenting, God ministered unto him by an holy angel, whose countenance was as lightning, and whose garments were pure and white above all whiteness, and gave unto him commandments which inspired him from on high, and gave unto him power, by the means which were before prepared, that he should translate a book;

8 Which book contained a record of a fallen people, and also the fulness of the gospel of Jesus Christ to the Gentiles;

9 And also to the Jews, proving unto them, that the holy scriptures are true;

10 And also, that God doth inspire men and call them to his holy work, in these last days as well as in days of old, that he might be the same God forever. Amen.

11 Which book was given by inspiration, and is called the book of Mormon, and is confirmed to

others by the ministering of angels, and declared unto the world by them:

12 Wherefore having so great witnesses, by them shall the world be judged, even as many as shall hereafter receive this work, either to faith and righteousness, or to the hardness of heart in unbelief, to their own condemnation, for the Lord God hath spoken it, for we, the elders of the church, have heard and bear witness to the words of the glorious Majesty on high; to whom be glory forever and ever. Amen.

13 Wherefore, by these things we know that there is a God in heaven, who is infinite and eternal, from everlasting to everlasting, the same unchangeable God, the maker of heaven and earth and all things that in them is, and that he created man male and female, and after his own image, and in his own likeness created he them;

14 And that he gave unto the children of men commandments, that they should love and serve him the only being whom they should worship, but by the transgression of these holy laws, man became sensual and devilish, and became fallen man.

15 Wherefore, the Almighty God gave his only begotton Son, as it is written in those scriptures, which have been given of him, that he suffered temptations, but gave no heed unto them;

16 That he was crucified, died, and rose again the third day, and that he ascended into heaven to sit down on the right hand of the Father, to reign with Almighty power according to the will of the Father.

17 Therefore, as many as would believe and were baptized in his holy name, and endured in faith to the end, should be saved;

18 Yea, even as many as were before he came in the flesh, from the beginning, who believed in the words of the holy prophets, who were inspired by the gift of the Holy Ghost, which truly testified of him in all things, as well as those who should come after, who should believe in the gifts and callings of God, by the Holy Ghost, which beareth record of the Father and of the Son, which Father and Son and Holy Ghost, is one God, infinite and eternal, without end. Amen.

19 And we know, that all men must repent and believe on the name of Jesus Christ, and worship the Father in his name, and endure in faith on his name to the end, or they cannot be saved in the kingdom of God.

20 And we know, that justification through the grace of our Lord and Savior Jesus Christ, is just and true;

21 And we know, also, that sanctification through the grace of our Lord and Savior Jesus Christ, is just and true, to all those who love and serve God with all their mights, minds, and strength; but there is a possibility that men may fall from grace and depart from the living God.

22 Therefore, let the church take heed and pray always, lest they fall into temptation;

23 Yea, and even he that is sanctified also.

24 And we know, that these things are true and agreeable to the revelation of John, neither adding to, nor diminishing from the prophecy of his book;

25 Neither to the holy scriptures;

26 Neither to the revelations of God which shall come hereafter, by the gift and power of the Holy Ghost;

27 Neither by the voice of God:

28 Neither by the ministering of angels, and the Lord God hath spoken it; and honor, power, and glory, be rendered to his holy name both now and ever. Amen.

29 And again, by way of commandment to the church, concerning the manner of baptism;

30 Behold whosoever humbleth himself before God and desireth to be baptized, and comes forth with a broken heart and a contrite spirit, and witnesseth unto the church, that they have truly repented of all their sins and are willing to take upon them the name of Christ, having a determination to serve him unto the end, and truly manifest by their works that they have received the Spirit of Christ unto the remission of their sins, then shall they be received unto baptism into the church of Christ.

31 The duty of the elders, priests, teachers, deacons and members of the church of Christ.

32 An apostle is an elder, and it is his calling to baptize and to ordain other elders, priests, teachers and deacons, and to administer the flesh and blood of Christ according to the scriptures;

33 And to teach, expound, exhort, baptize, and watch over the church;

34 And to confirm the church by the laying on of the hands, and the giving of the Holy Ghost, and to take the lead of all meetings.

35 The elders are to conduct the meetings as they are led by the Holy Ghost.

36 The priest's duty is to preach, teach, expound, exhort and baptize, and administer the sacrament, and visit the house of each member, and exhort them to pray vocally and in secret, and also to attend to all family duties;

37 And ordain other priests, teachers and deacons,

and take the lead of meetings; but none of these offices is he to do when there is an elder present, but in all cases is to assist the elder.

38 The teacher's duty is to watch over the church always, and be with them, and strengthen them, and see that there is no iniquity in the church, neither hardness with each other, neither lying nor backbiting, nor evil speaking;

39 And see that the church meet together often, and also see that all the members do their duty;

40 And he is to take the lead of meetings in the abscence of the elder or priest, and is to be assisted always, and in all his duties in the church by the deacons;

41 But neither the teachers nor deacons have authority to baptize nor administer the sacrament, but are to warn*, expound, exhort and teach, and invite all to come unto Christ.

42 Every elder, priest, teacher or deacon, is to be ordained according to the gifts and callings of God unto him, by the power of the Holy Ghost which is in the one who ordains him.

43 The several elders composing this church of Christ, are to meet in conference once in three months, or from time to time as they shall direct or appoint, to do church business whatsoever is necessary.

44 And each priest or teacher, who is ordained by a priest, is to take a certificate from him at the time, which when presented to an elder, he is to give him a license, which shall authorize him to perform the duty of his calling.

45 The duty of the members after they are received by baptism.

46 The elders or priests are to have a sufficient

time to expound all things concerning this church of Christ to their understanding, previous to their partaking of the sacrament, and being confirmed by the laying on of the hands of the elders;

47 So that all things may be done in order.

48 And the members shall manifest before the church, and also before the elders, by a godly walk and conversation, that they are worthy of it, that there may be works and faith agreeable to the holy scriptures, walking in holiness before the Lord.

49 Every member of this church of Christ having children, is to bring them unto the elders before the church, who are to lay their hands upon them in the name of the Lord, and bless them in the name of Christ.

50 There can not any one be received into this church of Christ, who has not arrived to the years of accountability before God, and is not capable of repentance.

51 And baptism is to be administered in the following manner unto all those who repent:

52 Whosoever being called of God and having authority given them of Jesus Christ, shall go down into the water with them, and shall say, calling them by name:

53 Having authority given me of Jesus Christ, I baptize you in the name of the Father, and of the Son, and of the Holy Ghost. Amen.

54 Then shall he immerse them in the water, and come forth again out of the water.

55 And it is expedient that the church meet together oft to partake of bread and wine, in remembrance of the Lord Jesus;

56 And the elder or priest shall administer it, and after this manner shall he do, he shall kneel with

the church, and call upon the Father in mighty prayer, saying:

57 O God the Eternal Father, we ask thee in the name of thy Son Jesus Christ, to bless and sanctify this bread to the souls of all those who partake of it, that they may eat in remembrance of the body of thy Son, and witness unto thee O God the Eternal Father, that they are willing to take upon them the name of thy Son, and always remember him, and keep his commandments which he hath given them, that they may always have his Spirit to be with them. Amen.

58 The manner of administering the wine:

59 Behold they shall take the cup and say, O God, the Eternal Father, we ask thee in the name of thy Son Jesus Christ, to bless and sanctify this wine to the souls of all those who drink of it, that they may do it in remembrance of the blood of thy Son, which was shed for them, that they may witness unto thee, O God the Eternal Father, that they do always remember him, that they may have his Spirit to be with them. Amen.

60 Any member of this church of Christ, transgressing or being overtaken in a fault, shall be dealt with according as the scriptures direct.

61 It shall be the duty of the several churches, composing this church of Christ, to send one or more of their teachers to attend the several conferences, held by the elders of this church, with a list of the names of the several members, uniting themselves to the church since the last conference, or send by the hand of some priest, so that there can be kept a regular list of all the names of the members of the whole church, in a book kept by one of the elders;

62 Whomsoever the other elders shall appoint from time to time:

63 And also, if any have been expelled from the church, so that their names may be blotted out of the general church record of names.

64 Any member removing from the church where he resides, if going to a church where he is not known, may take a letter certifying that he is a regular member and in good standing;

65 Which certificate may be signed by any elder or priest, if the member receiving the letter is personally acquainted with the elder or priest, or it may be signed by the teachers or deacons of the church.

CHAPTER XXV.

1 *A Revelation to Joseph, and also to Oliver, given in Harmony, Pennsylvania, July, 1830.* BEHOLD thou wast called and chosen to write the book of Mormon, and to my ministry;

2 And I have lifted thee up out of thine afflictions, and have counseled thee, that thou hast been delivered from all thine enemies, and thou hast been delivered from the powers of satan, and from darkness!

3 Nevertheless, thou art not excusable in thy transgressions; nevertheless go thy way and sin no more.

4 Magnify thine office;

5 And after thou hast sowed thy fields and secured them go speedily unto the church, which is in Colesville, Fayette and Manchester, and they shall

support thee; and I will bless them both spiritually and temporally;

6 But if they receive thee not, I will send upon them a cursing instead o a blessing.

7 And thou shalt continue in calling upon God in my name, and writing the things which shall be given thee by the Comforter;

8 And expounding all scriptures unto the church, and it shall be given thee in the very moment, what thou shalt speak and write;

9 And they shall hear it, or I will send unto them a cursing instead of a blessing:

10 For thou shalt devote all thy service in Zion.

11 And in this thou shalt have strength.

12 Be patient in afflictions, for thou shalt have many:

13 But endure them, for lo, I am with you, even unto the end of thy days.

14 And in temporal labors thou shalt not have strength, for this is not thy calling.

15 Attend to thy calling and thou shalt have wherewith to magnify thine office, and to expound all scriptures.

16 And continue in the laying on of the hands, and confirming the churches.

17 And thy brother Oliver shall continue in bearing my name before the world; and also to the church.

18 And he shall not suppose that he can say enough in my cause;

19 And lo I am with him to the end.

20 In me he shall have glory, and not of himself, whether in weakness or in strength, whether in bonds or free:

21 And at all times and in all places, he shall

open his mouth and declare my gospel as with the voice of a trump, both day and night.

22 And I will give unto him strength such as is not known among men.

23 Require not miracles, except I shall command you; except casting out devils; healing the sick; and against poisonous serpents; and against deadly poisons:

24 And these things ye shall not do, except it be required of you, by them who desire it, that the scriptures might be fulfilled, for ye shall do according to that which is written.

25 And in whatsoever place ye shall enter, and they receive you not, in my name, ye shall leave a cursing instead of a blessing, by casting off the dust of your feet against them as a testimony, and cleansing your feet by the wayside.

26 And it shall come to pass, that whosoever shall lay their hands upon you by violence, ye shall command to be smitten in my name, and behold I will smite them according to your words, in mine own due time.

27 And whosoever shall go to law with thee shall be cursed by the law.

28 And thou shalt take no purse, nor scrip, neither staves, neither two coats, for the church shall give unto thee in the very hour what thou needest for food, and for raiment, and for shoes, and for money, and for scrip:

29 For thou art called to prune my vineyard with a mighty pruning, yea, even for the last time.

30 Yea, and also, all those whom thou hast ordained.

31 And they shall do even according to this pattern. Amen.

CHAPTER XXVI.

1 *A Revelation to Emma, given in Harmony, Pennsylvania, July,* 1830.

EMMA, my daughter in Zion, a revelation I give unto you, concerning my will:

2 Behold thy sins are forgiven thee, and thou art an elect lady, whom I have called.

3 Murmur not because of the things which thou hast not seen, for they are withheld from thee, and from the world, which is wisdom in me in a time to come.

4 And the office of thy calling shall be for a comfort unto my servant Joseph, thy husband, in his afflictions with consoling words, in the spirit of meekness.

5 And thou shalt go with him at the time of his going, and be unto him for a scribe, that I may send Oliver whithersoever I will.

6 And thou shalt be ordained under his hand to expound scriptures, and to exhort the church, according as it shall be given thee by my Spirit:

7 For he shall lay his hands upon thee, and thou shalt receive the Holy Ghost, and thy time shall be given to writing, and to learning much.

8 And thou needest not fear, for thy husband shall support thee from the church:

9 For unto them is his calling, that all things might be revealed unto them, whatsoever I will according to their faith.

10 And verily I say unto thee, that thou shalt lay aside the things of this world, and seek for the things of a better.

11 And it shall be given thee, also, to make a selection of sacred hymns, as it shall be given thee;

which is pleasing unto me, to be had in my church?

12 For my soul delighteth in the song of the heart:
Yea, the song of the righteous is a prayer unto me.

13 And it shall be answered with a blessing upon
their heads.

14 Wherefore lift up thy heart and rejoice, and
cleave unto the covenants which thou hast made.

15 Continue in the spirit of meekness, and beware
of pride.

16 Let thy soul delight in thy husband, and the
glory which shall come upon him.

17 Keep my commandments continually, and a
crown of righteousness thou shalt receive.

18 And except thou do this, where I am you cannot come.

19 And verily, verily I say unto you, that this is
my voice unto all. Amen.

CHAPTER XXVII.

1 *A Revelation to Joseph, Oliver and John, given
in Harmony, Pennsylvania, July, 1830.*

BEHOLD, I say unto you, that you shall let
your time be devoted to the studying of the
scriptures, and to preaching, and to cofirming the
church at Colesville;

2 And to performing your labors on the land, such
as is required, until after you shall go to the west
to hold the next conference; and then it shall be
made known what you shall do.

3 And all things shall be done by common consent in the church, by much prayer and faith;

4 For all things you shall receive by faith. Amen.

CHAPTER XXVIII.

1 *A Commandment to the church of Christ, given in Harmony, Pennsylvania, September 4, 1830.*

LISTEN to the voice of Jesus Christ, your Lord, your God and your Redeemer, whose word is quick and powerful.

2 For behold I say unto you, that it mattereth not what ye shall eat, or what ye shall drink, when ye partake of the sacrament, if it so be that ye do it with an eye single to my glory;

3 Remembering unto the Father my body which was laid down for you, and my blood which was shed for the remission of your sins:

4 Wherefore a commandment I give unto you, that you shall not purchase wine, neither strong drink of your enemies:

5 Wherefore you shall partake of none, except it is made new among you, yea, in this my Father's kingdom which shall be built up on the earth.

6 Behold this is wisdom in me, wherefore marvel not, for the hour cometh that I will drink of the fruit of the vine with you, on the earth, and with all those whom my Father hath given me out of the world:

7 Wherefore lift up your hearts and rejoice, and gird up your loins and be faithful until I come: even so. Amen.

CHAPTER XXIX.

1 A Revelation to the church of Christ, given in the presence of six elders, in Fayette, New-York, September, 1830.

LISTEN to the voice of Jesus Christ, your Redeemer, the Great I AM, whose arm of mercy hath atoned for your sins;

2 Who will gather his people even as a hen gathereth her chickens under her wings, even as many as will hearken to my voice, and humble themselves before me, and call upon me in mighty prayer.

3 Behold, verily, verily I say unto you, that at this time your sins are forgiven you; therefore ye receive these things:

4 But remember to sin no more, lest perils shall come upon you.

5 Verily I say unto you, that ye are chosen out of the world to declare my gospel with the sound of rejoicing, as with the voice of a trump:

6 Lift up your hearts and be glad for I am in your midst, and am your advocate with the Father; and it is his good will to give you the kingdom;

7 And as it is written, Whatsoever ye shall ask in faith, being united in prayer according to my command, ye shall receive;

8 And ye are called to bring to pass the gathering of mine elect, for mine elect hear my voice and harden not their hearts:

9 Wherefore the decree hath gone forth from the Father, that they shall be gathered in unto one place, upon the face of this land, to prepare their hearts, and be prepared in all things, against the day when tribulation and desolation are sent forth upon the wicked:

10 For the hour is nigh, and the day soon at hand, when the earth is ripe:

11 And all the proud, and they that do wickedly, shall be as stubble, and I will burn them up, saith the Lord of Hosts, that wickedness shall not be upon the earth:

12 For the hour is nigh, and that which was spoken by mine apostles must be fulfilled; for as they spoke so shall it come to pass;

13 For I will reveal myself from heaven with power and great glory, with all the hosts thereof, and dwell in righteousness with men on earth a thousand years, and the wicked shall not stand.

14 And again, verily, verily I say unto you, and it hath gone forth in a firm decree, by the will of the Father, that mine apostles, the twelve which were with me in my ministry at Jerusalem, shall stand at my right hand at the day of my coming in a pillar of fire, being clothed with robes of righteousness, with crowns upon their heads, in glory even as I am, to judge the whole house of Israel, even as many as have loved me and kept my commandments, and none else;

15 For a trump shall sound both long and loud, even as upon mount Sinai, and all the earth shall quake, and they shall come forth:

16 Yea, even the dead which died in me, to receive a crown of righteousness, and to be clothed upon, even as I am, to be with me, that we may be one.

17 But behold, I say unto you, that before this great day shall come, the sun shall be darkened, and the moon shall be turned into blood, and the stars shall fall from heaven;

18 And there shall be greater signs in heaven

above, and in the earth beneath; and there shall be weeping and wailing among the hosts of men;

19 And there shall be a great hailstorm sent forth to destroy the crops of the earth:

20 And it shall come to pass, because of the wickedness of the world, that I will take vengeance upon the wicked, for they will not repent:

21 For the cup of mine indignation is full; for behold, my blood shall not cleanse them if they hear me not.

22 Wherefore I the Lord God will send forth flies upon the face of the earth, which shall take hold of the inhabitants thereof, and shall eat their flesh, and shall cause maggots to come in upon them, and their tongues shall be stayed that they shall not utter again t me, and their flesh shall fall from off their bones, and their eyes from their sockets:

23 And it shall come to pass, that the beasts of the forests, and the fowls of the air, shall devour them up:

24 And that great and abominable church, which is the whore of all the earth, shall be cast down by devouring fire, according as it was spoken by the mouth of Ezekiel the prophet, which spoke of these things, which have not come to pass, but surely must, as I live, for abominations shall not reign.

25 And again, verily, verily I say unto you, that when the thousand years are ended, and men again begin to deny their God, then will I spare the earth but for a little season;

26 And the end shall come, and the heaven and the earth shall be consumed, and pass away, and there shall be a new heaven and a new earth;

27 For all old things shall pass away, and all things shall become new, even the heaven and the

earth, and all the fulness thereof, both men and beasts;

28 The fowls of the air, and the fishes of the sea, and not one hair, neither mote, shall be lost, for it is the workmanship of mine hand.

29 But behold, verily I say unto you, before the earth shall pass away, Michael mine archangel, shall sound his trump, and then shall all the dead awake, for their graves shall be opened, and they shall come forth; yea, even all;

30 And the righteous shall be gathered on my right hand unto eternal life;

31 And the wicked on my left hand will I be ashamed to own before the Father:

32 Wherefore I will say unto them, depart from me ye cursed into everlasting fire, prepared for the devil and his angels.

33 And now behold I say unto you, never at any time, have I declared from mine own mouth, that they should return, for where I am they cannot come, for they have no power;

34 But remember, that all my judgments are not given unto men;

35 And as the words have gone forth out of my mouth, even so shall they be fulfilled, that the first shall be last, and that the last shall be first in all things, whatsoever I have created by the word of my power, which is the power of my Spirit;

36 For by the power of my Spirit, created I them:

37 Yea, all things both spiritual and temporal:

38 Firstly spiritual, secondly temporal, which is the beginning of my work:

39 And again, firstly temporal, and secondly spiritual, which is the last of my work:

40 Speaking unto you, that you may naturally

understand, but unto myself my works have no end, neither beginning; but it is given unto you, that ye may understand, because ye have asked it of me and are agreed.

41 Wherefore, verily I say unto you, that all things unto me are spiritual, and not at any time have I given unto you a law which was temporal, neither any man, nor the children of men:

42 Neither Adam your father, whom I created; behold I gave unto him that he should be an agent unto himself;

43 And I gave unto him commandment, but no temporal commandment gave I unto him; for my commandments are spiritual;

44 They are not natural, nor temporal, neither carnal nor sensual.

45 And it came to pass, that Adam being tempted of the devil, for behold the devil was before Adam, for he rebelled against me saying, Give me thine honor, which is my power: and also a third part of the hosts of heaven turned he away from me because of their agency:

46 And they were thrust down, and thus came the devil and his angels; and behold, there is a place prepared for them from the beginning, which place is hell:

47 And it must needs be that the devil should tempt the children of men, or they could not be agents unto themselves, for if they never should have bitter, they could not know the sweet.

48 Wherefore, it came to pass, that the devil tempted Adam and he partook the forbidden fruit, and transgressed the commandment, wherein he became subject to the will of the devil, because he yielded unto temptation.

49 Wherefore, I the Lord God caused that he should be cast out from the garden of Eden, from my presence, because of his transgression;

50 Wherein he became spiritually dead; which is the first death, even that same death, which is the last death, which is spiritual, which shall be pronounced upon the wicked when I shall say, Depart ye cursed.

51 But behold I say unto you, that I the Lord God gave unto Adam and unto his seed, that they should not die as to the temporal death, until I the Lord God should send forth angels to declare unto them repentance and redemption, through faith on the name of mine only begotten Son:

52 And thus did I the Lord God appoint unto man the days of his probation; that by his natural death he might be raised in immortality unto eternal life, even as many as would believe, and they that believe not, unto eternal damnation, for they cannot be redeemed from their spiritual fall, because they repent not, for they will love darkness rather than light, and their deeds are evil, and they receive their wages of whom they list to obey.

53 But behold I say unto you, that little children are redeemed from the foundation of the world, through mine only Begotten:

54 Wherefore they cannot sin, for power is not given unto satan to tempt little children, until they begin to become accountable before me;

55 For it is given unto them even as I will, according to mine own pleasure, that great things may be required at the hand of their fathers.

56 And again I say unto you, that whoso having knowledge, have I not commanded to repent? and he that hath no understanding, it remaineth in me

to do according as it is written. And now, I declare no more unto you at this time. Amen.

CHAPTER XXX.

1 *A Revelation to Oliver, given in Fayette, New York, September, 1830.*

BEHOLD I say unto you, Oliver, that it shall be given unto thee, that thou shalt be heard by the church, in all things whatsoever thou shalt teach them by the Comforter, concerning the revelations and commandments which I have given.

2 But behold, verily, verily I say unto you, no one shall be appointed to receive commandments and revelations in this church, excepting my servant Joseph, for he receiveth them even as Moses:

3 And thou shalt be obedient unto the things which I shall give unto him, even as Aaron, to declare faithfully the commandments and the revelations, with power and authority unto the church.

4 And if thou art led at any time by the Comforter to speak or teach, or at all times by the way of commandment unto the church, thou mayest do it.

5 But thou shalt not write by way of commandment, but by wisdom:

6 And thou shalt not command him who is at thy head, and at the head of the church, for I have given him the keys of the mysteries and the revelations which are sealed, until I shall appoint unto them another in his stead.

7 And now, behold I say unto you, that you shall go unto the Lamanites and preach my gospel unto them, and cause my church to be established among

them. And thou shalt have revelations but write them not by way of commandment.

8 And now behold I say unto you, that it is not revealed, and no man knoweth where the city shall be built, but it shall be given hereafter.

9 Behold I say unto you, that it shall be on the borders by the Lamanites.

10 Thou shalt not leave this place until after the conference, and my servant Joseph shall be appointed to rule the conference by the voice of it, and what he saith to thee, that thou shalt tell.

11 And again, thou shalt take thy brother Hiram between him and thee alone, and tell him that those things which he hath written from that stone are not of me, and that satan deceiveth him:

12 For behold these things have not been appointed unto him:

13 Neither shall any thing be appointed unto any of this church contrary to the church covenants, for all things must be done in order and by common consent in the church, by the prayer of faith.

14 And thou shalt settle all these things according to the covenants of the church before thou shalt take thy journey among the Lamanites.

15 And it shall be given thee from the time that thou shalt go, until the time that thou shalt return, what thou shalt do.

16 And thou must open thy mouth at all times declaring my gospel with the sound of rejoicing.—Amen.

CHAPTER XXXI.

A Revelation to David, given in Fayette, New-York, September, 1830.

BEHOLD I say unto you, David, that you have feared man and have not relied upon me for strength, as you ought:

2 But your mind has been on the things of the earth more than on the things of me, your Maker, and the ministry whereunto you have been called; and you have not given heed unto my Spirit, and to those who were set over you, but have been persuaded by those whom I have not commanded:

3 Wherefore you are left to inquire for yourself, at my hand, and ponder upon the things which you have received.

4 And your home shall be at your father's house, until I give unto you further commandments.

5 And you shall attend to the ministry in the church, and before the world, and in the regions round about. Amen.

CHAPTER XXXII,

A Revelation to Peter, given in Fayette, New-York, September, 1830.

BEHOLD I say unto you, Peter, that you shall take your journey with your brother Oliver, for the time has come, that it is expedient in me, that you shall open your mouth to declare my gospel:

2 Therefore, fear not but give heed unto the words and advice of your brother, which he shall give you.

3

3 And be you afflicted in all his afflictions, ever lifting up your heart unto me in prayer, and faith, for his and your deliverance:

4 For I have given unto him to build up my church among your brethren, the Lamanites.

5 And none have I appointed to be over him in the church, except it is his brother Joseph.

6 Wherefore give heed unto these things and be diligent in keeping my commandments, and you shall be blessed unto eternal life. Amen.

CHAPTER XXXIII.

A Revelation to John, given in Fayette, New-York, September, 1830.

BEHOLD I say unto you my servant, John, that thou shalt commence from this time forth to proclaim my gospel, as with the voice of a trump.

2 And your labor shall be at your brother Philip's, and in that region round about:

3 Yea, wherever you can be heard, until I command you to go from hence.

4 And your whole labor shall be in my Zion, with all your soul, from henceforth; yea, you shall ever open your mouth in my cause not fearing what man can do for I am with you. Amen.

CHAPTER XXXIV.

A Revelation to Thomas, given in Fayette, New-York, September, 1830.

THOMAS, my son, blessed are you because of your faith in my work.

2 Behold you have had many afflictions because of your family: nevertheless I will bless you, and your family:

3 Yea, your little ones, and the day cometh that they will believe and know the truth and be one with you in my church.

4 Lift up your heart and rejoice for the hour of your mission is come; and your tongue shall be loosed: and you shall declare glad tidings of great joy unto this generation.

5 You shall declare the things which have been revealed to my servant Joseph.

6 You shall begin to preach from this time forth; yea, to reap in the field which is white already to be burned:

7 Therefore thrust in your sickle with all your soul; and your sins are forgiven you; and you shall be laden with sheaves upon your back, for the laborer is worthy of his hire.

8 Wherefore your family shall live.

9 Behold, verily I say unto you, go from them only for a little time, and declare my word, and I will prepare a place for them; yea, I will open the hearts of the people and they will receive you.

10 And I will establish a church by your hand; and you shall strengthen them and prepare them against the time when they shall be gathered.

11 Be patient in afflictions, and in sufferings, revile not against those that revile.

12 Govern your house in meekness, and be steadfast.

13 Behold I say unto you, that you shall be a physician unto the church, but not unto the world, for they will not receive you.

14 Go your way whithersoever I will, and it shall be given you by the Comforter what you shall do, and whither you shall go.

15 Pray always, lest you enter into temptation, and loose your reward.

16 Be faithful unto the end, and lo, I am with you.

17 These words are not of man nor of men, but of me, even Jesus Christ, your Redeemer, by the will of the Father. Amen.

CHAPTER XXXV.

A Revelation to Ezra, and Northrop, given in Fayette, New-York, October, 1830.

BEHOLD I say unto you, my servants Ezra, and Northrop, open ye your ears and hearken to the voice of the Lord your God, whose word is quick and powerful, sharper than a two-edged sword, to the dividing asunder of the joints and marrow, soul and spirit; and is a discerner of the thoughts and intents of the heart.

2 For verily, verily I say unto you, that ye are called to lift up your voices as with the sound of a trump, to declare my gospel unto a crooked and a perverse generation:

3 For behold the field is white already to harvest; and it is the eleventh hour, and for the last time

that I shall call laborers into my vineyard.   And
my vineyard has become corrupted every whit;
and there is none which doeth good save it be a
few; and they err in many instances, because of
priestcrafts, all having corrupt minds.

4 And verily, verily I say unto you, that this
church have I established and called forth out of
the wilderness:

5 And even so will I gather mine elect from the
four quarters of the earth, even as many as will believe in me, and hearken unto my voice:

6 Yea, verily, verily I say unto you, that the field
is white already to harvest:

7 Wherefore thrust in your sickles, and reap with
all your might, mind, and strength.

8 Open your mouths and they shall be filled; and
you shall become even as Nephi of old, who journeyed from Jerusalem in the wilderness:

9 Yea, open your mouths and spare not, and you
shall be laden with sheaves upon your backs, for lo
I am with you:

10 Yea, open your mouths and they shall be filled, saying Repent, repent and prepare ye the way
of the Lord, and make his paths strait: for the kingdom of heaven is at hand:

11 Yea, repent and be baptized every one of you,
for a remission of your sins; yea, be baptized even
by water, and then cometh the baptism of fire and
of the Holy Ghost.

12 Behold, verily, verily I say unto you, this is
my gospel, and remember that they shall have faith
in me, or they can in no wise be saved:

13 And upon this Rock I will build my church;
yea, upon this Rock ye are built, and the gates of
hell shall not prevail against you; and ye shall re-

member the church articles and covenants to keep them:

14 And whoso having faith you shall confirm in my church, by the laying on of the hands, and I will bestow the gift of the Holy Ghost upon them.

15 And the book of Mormon, and the holy scriptures, are given of me for your instruction; and the power of my Spirit quickeneth all things:

16 Wherefore be faithful, praying always, having your lamps trimmed and burning, and oil with you, that you may be ready at the coming of the Bridegroom; for behold, verily, verily I say unto you, that I come quickly; even so: Amen.

CHAPTER XXXVI.

A Revelation to Orson (P.) given in Fayette, New-York, November, 1830.

MY son Orson, hearken and hear and behold what I the Lord God shall say unto you, even Jesus Christ your Redeemer, the light and the life of the world:

2 A light which shineth in darkness and the darkness comprehendeth it not:

3 Who so loved the world that he gave his own life, that as many as would believe might become the sons of God:

4 Wherefore you are my son, and blessed are you because you have believed, and more blessed are you because you are called of me to preach my gospel; to lift up your voice as with the sound of a trump, both long and loud, and cry repentance unto a crooked and perverse generation; preparing

the way of the Lord for his second coming: for behold, verily, verily I say unto you, the time is soon
at hand, that I shall come in a cloud with power
and great glory, and it shall be a great day at the
time of my coming, for all nations shall tremble.

5 But before that great day shall come, the sun
shall be darkened, and the moon be turned into
blood, and the stars shall refuse their shining, and
some shall fall, and great destructions await the
wicked:

6 Wherefore lift up your voice and spare not, for
the Lord God hath spoken.

7 Therefore prophesy and it shall be given by the
power of the Holy Ghost; and if you are faithful
behold I am with you until I come:

8 And verily, verily I say unto you, I come quickly.

9 I am your Lord and your Redeemer; even so?
Amen.

CHAPTER XXXVII.

*A Revelation to Joseph, and Sidney, given in
Fayette, New-York, December, 1830.*

LISTEN to the voice of the Lord your God,
even Alpha and Omega, the beginning and
the end, whose course is one eternal round, the same
today as yesterday and forever.

2 I am Jesus Christ, the Son of God, who was
crucified for the sins of the world, even as many as
will believe on my name, that they may become
the sons of God, even one in me as I am in the Father, as the Father is one in me, that we may be one.

3 Behold, verily, verily I say unto my servant Sidney, I have looked upon thee and thy works.

4 I have heard thy prayers and prepared thee for a greater work.

5 Thou art blessed for thou shalt do great things.

6 Behold thou wast sent forth, even as John, to prepare the way before me, and before Elijah which should come, and thou knew it not.

7 Thou didst baptize by water unto repentance, but they received not the Holy Ghost; but now I give unto thee a commandment, that thou shalt baptize by water, and they shall receive the Holy Ghost by the laying on of hands, even as the apostles of old.

8 And it shall come to pass, that there shall be a great work in the land even among the Gentiles, for their folly and their abominations shall be made manifest, in the eyes of all people:

9 For I am God and mine arm is not shortened and I will show miracles, signs and wonders, unto all those who believe on my name.

10 And whoso shall ask it in my name, in faith, they shall cast out devils; they shall heal the sick; they shall cause the blind to receive their sight, and the deaf to hear, and the dumb to speak, and the lame to walk:

11 And the time speedily cometh, that great things are to be shown forth unto the children of men:

12 But without faith shall not any thing be shown forth except desolations upon Babylon, the same which has made all nations drink of the wine of the wrath of her fornication.

13 And there are none that doeth good except those who are ready to receive the fullness of my gospel, which I have sent forth to this generation.

14 Wherefore, I have called upon the weak things of the world, those who are unlearned and despised, to thresh the nations by the power of my Spirit:

15 And their arm shall be mine arm, and I will be their shield and their buckler, and I will gird up their loins, and they shall fight manfully for me:

16 And their enemies shall be under their feet; and I will let fall the sword in their behalf; and by the fire of mine indignation will I preserve them.

17 And the poor and the meek shall have the gospel preached unto them, and they shall be looking forth for the time of my coming, for it is nigh at hand:

18 And they shall learn the parable of the fig-tree: for even now already summer is nigh, and I have sent forth the fulness of my gospel by the hand of my servant Joseph:

19 And in weakness have I blessed him, and I have given unto him the keys of the mystery of those things which have been sealed, even things which were from the foundation of the world, and the things which shall come from this time until the time of my coming, if he abide in me, and if not, another will I plant in his stead.

20 Wherefore watch over him that his faith fail not, and it shall be given by the Comforter, the Holy Ghost, that knoweth all things:

21 And a commandment I give unto thee, that thou shalt write for him:

22 And the scriptures shall be given even as they are in mine own bosom, to the salvation of mine own elect:

23 For they will hear my voice, and shall see me, and shall not be asleep, and shall abide the day of my coming, for they shall be purified even as I am

pure. And now I say unto you, tarry with him and he shall journey with you; forsake him not and surely these things shall be fulfilled.

24 And inasmuch as ye do not write, behold it shall be given unto him to prophesy.

25 And thou shalt preach my gospel, and call on the holy prophets to prove his words, as they shall be given him.

26 Keep all the commandments and covenants by which ye are bound, and I will cause the heavens to shake for your good:

27 And satan shall tremble; and Zion shall rejoice upon the hills, and flourish; and Israel shall be saved in mine own due time.

28 And by the keys which I have given, shall they be led and no more be confounded at all.

29 Lift up your hearts and be glad: your redemption draweth nigh.

30 Fear not little flock, the kingdom is yours until I come.

31 Behold I come quickly; even so: Amen.

CHAPTER XXXVIII.

A Revelation to Edward, given in Fayette, New-York, December, 1830.

THUS saith the Lord God, the mighty One of Israel, behold I say unto you, my servant Edward, that you are blessed, and your sins are forgiven you, and you are called to preach my gospel as with the voice of a trump; and I will lay my hand upon you by the hand of my servant Sidney, and you shall receive my Spirit, the Holy Ghost, even the Comforter, which shall teach you the peaceable things of the kingdom:

2 And you shall declare it with a loud voice saying, Hosanna, blessed be the name of the most high God.

3 And now this calling and commandment give I unto all men, that as many as shall come before my servant Sidney and Joseph, embracing this calling and commandment, shall be ordained and sent forth to preach the everlasting gospel among the nations, crying repentance, saying, Save yourselves from this untoward generation, and come forth out of the fire, hating even the garment spotted with the flesh.

4 And this commandment shall be given unto the elders of my church, that every man which will embrace it with singleness of heart, may be ordained and sent forth, even as I have spoken.

5 I am Jesus Christ, the Son of God:

6 Wherefore gird up your loins and I will suddenly come to my temple; even so: Amen.

CHAPTER XXXIX.

A Revelation to Joseph and Sidney, given in Canandaigua, New-York, December, 1830.

BEHOLD I say unto you, that it is not expedient in me that ye should translate any more until ye shall go to the Ohio; and this because of the enemy and for your sakes.

2 And again, I say unto you, that ye shall not go until ye have preached my gospel in those parts, and have strengthened up the church whithersoev-

ef it is found, and more especially in Colesville;

3 For behold they pray unto me in much faith.

4 And again a commandment I give unto the church, that it is expedient in me that they should assemble together at the Ohio, against the time that my servant Oliver shall return unto them.

5 Behold here is wisdom, and let every man choose for himself until I come; even so: Amen.

CHAPTER XL.

A Revelation to the churches in New-York, commanding them to remove to Ohio, given in Fayette, New-York, January, 1831.

THUS saith the Lord your God, even Jesus Christ, the Great I AM, Alpha and Omega, the beginning and the end, the same which looked upon the wide expanse of eternity, and all the seraphic hosts of heaven, before the world was made, the same which knoweth all things, for all things are present before mine eyes:

2 I am the same which spake and the world was made, and all things came by me:

3 I am the same which hath taken the Zion of Enoch into mine own bosom:

4 And verily I say, even as many as have believed on my name, for I am Christ, and in mine own name, by the virtue of the blood which I have spilt, have I plead before the Father for them:

5 But behold the residue of the wicked have I kept in chains of darkness until the judgment of the great day, which shall come at the end of the earth, and even so will I cause the wicked to be kept, that

will not hear my voice but harden their hearts, and wo, wo, wo is their doom.

6 But behold, verily, verily I say unto you, that mine eyes are upon you; I am in your midst and ye cannot see me, but the day soon cometh that ye shall see me and know that I am:

7 For the vail of darkness shall soon be rent, and he that is not purified shall not abide the day:

8 Wherefore gird up your loins and be prepared.

9 Behold the kingdom is yours and the enemy shall not overcome.

10 Verily I say unto you, ye are clean but not all; and there is none else with whom I am well pleased, for all flesh is corruptible before me, and the powers of darkness prevail upon the earth, among the children of men, in the presence of all the hosts of heaven, which causeth silence to reign, and all eternity is pained, and the angels are waiting the great command, to reap down the earth, to gather the tares that they may be burned:

11 And behold the enemy is combined.

12 And now I show unto you a mystery, a thing which is had in secret chambers, to bring to pass even your destruction, in process of time, and ye knew it not, but now I tell it unto you, and ye are blessed, not because of your iniquity, neither your hearts of unbelief, for verily some of you are guilty before me; but I will be merciful unto your weakness.

13 Therefore, be ye strong from henceforth; fear not for the kingdom is yours:

14 And for your salvation I give unto you a commandment, for I have heard your prayers, and the poor have complained before me, and the rich have I made, and all flesh is mine, and I am no respect-

er to persons. And I have made the earth rich, and behold it is my footstool: wherefore, again I will stand upon it:

15 And I hold forth and deign to give unto you greater riches, even a land of promise; a land flowing with milk and honey, upon which there shall be no curse when the Lord cometh, and I will give it unto you for the land of your inheritance, if you seek it with all your hearts:

16 And this shall be my covenant with you, ye shall have it for the land of your inheritance, and for the inheritance of your children forever, while the earth shall stand, and ye shall possess it again in eternity, no more to pass away:

17 But verily I say unto you, that in time ye shall have no king nor ruler, for I will be your King and watch over you.

18 Wherefore, hear my voice and follow me, and you shall be a free people, and ye shall have no laws but my laws, when I come, for I am your Lawgiver, and what can stay my hand.

19 But verily I say unto you, teach one another according to the office wherewith I have appointed you, and let every man esteem his brother as himself, and practice virtue and holiness before me.

20 And again I say unto you, let every man esteem his brother as himself:

21 For what man among you, having twelve sons, and is no respecter to them, and they serve him obediently, and he saith unto the one, be thou clothed in robes and sit thou here; and to the other, be thou clothed in rags and sit thou there, and looketh upon his sons and saith I am just.

22 Behold, this I have given unto you a parable, and it is even as I am, I say unto you, be one;

and if ye are not one, ye are not mine. And again I say unto you, that the enemy in the secret chambers, seeketh your lives:

23 Ye hear of wars in far countries, and you say in your hearts there will soon be great wars in far countries, but ye know not the hearts of them in your own land:

24 I tell you these things because of your prayers:

25 Wherefore, treasure up wisdom in your bosoms, lest the wickedness of men reveal these things unto you, by their wickedness, in a manner which shall speak in your ears, with a voice louder than that which shall shake the earth:

26 But if ye are prepared, ye shall not fear.

27 And that ye might escape the power of the enemy, and be gathered unto me a righteous people, without spot and blameless:

28 Wherefore, for this cause I gave unto you the commandment, that ye should go to the Ohio: and there I will give unto you my law, and there you shall be endowed with power from on high, and from thence, whomsoever I will shall go forth among all nations, and it shall be told them what they shall do, for I have a great work laid up, in store:

29 For Israel shall be saved, and I will lead them whithersoever I will, and no power shall stay my hand.

30 And now I give unto the church in these parts, a commandment, that certain men among them shall be appointed, and they shall be appointed by the voice of the church; and they shall look to the poor and the needy, and administer to their relief, that they shall not suffer; and send them forth to the place which I have commanded them; and this shall be their work, to govern the affairs of the

property of this church. And they that have farms, that can not be sold, let them be left or rented as seemeth them good.

31 See that all things are preserved, and when men are endowed with power from on high, and are sent forth, all these things shall be gathered unto the bosom of the church.

32 And if ye seek the riches which it is the will of the Father to give unto you, ye shall be the richest of all people, for ye shall have the riches of eternity:

33 And it must needs be that the riches of the earth is mine to give:

34 But beware of pride, lest ye become as the Nephites of old.

35 And again: I say unto you, I give unto you a commandment, that every man both elder, priest, teacher and also member, go to with his might, with the labor of his hands, to prepare and accomplish the things which I have commanded.

36 And let your preaching be the warning voice, every man to his neighbor, in mildness and in meekness.

37 And go ye out from among the wicked. Save yourselves.

38 Be ye clean that bear the vessels of the Lord; even so: Amen.

CHAPTER XLI.

A Revelation to James (C.,) given in Fayette, New-York, January, 1831.

HEARKEN and listen to the voice of him who is from all eternity to all eternity, the Great I AM, even Jesus Christ, the light and the life of the world; a light which shineth in darkness and the darkness comprehendeth it not:

2 The same which came in the meridian of time unto my own, and my own received me not; but to as many as received me, gave I power to become my sons, and even so will I give unto as many as will receive me, power to become my sons.

3 And verily, verily I say unto you, he that receiveth my gospel, receiveth me; and he that receiveth not my gospel, receiveth not me.

4 And this is my gospel: Repentance and baptism by water, and then cometh the baptism of fire and the Holy Ghost, even the Comforter, which showeth all things, and teacheth the peaceable things of the kingdom.

5 And now behold I say unto you, my servant James, I have looked upon thy works and I know thee:

6 And verily I say unto thee, thine heart is now right before me at this time, and behold I have bestowed great blessings upon thy head:

7 Nevertheless thou hast seen great sorrow, for thou hast rejected me many times because of pride, and the cares of the world:

8 But behold the days of thy deliverance are come.

9 Arise and be baptized, and wash away your sins, calling on my name and you shall receive my Spirit, and a blessing so great as you never have

known. And if thou do this, I have prepared thee for a greater work.

10 Thou shalt preach the fulness of my gospel which I have sent forth in these last days; the covenant which I have sent forth to recover my people, which are of the house of Israel.

11 And it shall come to pass that power shall rest upon thee; thou shalt have great faith and I will be with thee and go before thy face.

12 Thou art called to labor in my vineyard, and to build up my church, and to bring forth Zion, that it may rejoice upon the hills and flourish.

13 Behold, verily, verily I say unto thee, thou art not called to go into the eastern countries, but thou art called to go to the Ohio.

14 And inasmuch as my people shall assemble themselves to the Ohio, I have kept in store a blessing such as is not known among the children of men, and it shall be poured forth upon their heads.

15 And from thence men shall go forth into all nations.

16 Behold, verily, verily I say unto you, that the people in Ohio call upon me in much faith, thinking I will stay my hand in judgment upon the nations, but I can not deny my word:

17 Wherefore lay to with your might and call faithful laborers into my vineyard, that it may be pruned for the last time.

18 And inasmuch as they do repent and receive the fulness of my gospel, and become sanctified, I will stay mine hand in judgment:

19 Wherefore go forth, crying with a loud voice, saying, The kingdom of heaven is at hand; crying Hosanna! blessed be the name of the most high God.

20 Go forth baptizing with water, preparing the way before my face, for the time of my coming; for the time is at hand:

21 The day nor the hour no man knoweth, but it surely shall come, and he that receiveth these things receiveth me; and they shall be gathered unto me in time and in eternity.

22 And again, it shall come to pass, that on as many as ye shall baptize with water, ye shall lay your hands, and they shall receive the gift of the Holy Ghost, and shall be looking forth for the signs of my coming, and shall know me.

23 Behold I come quickly; even so: Amen.

CHAPTER XLII.

A Revelation to Joseph, and Sidney, given in Fayette, New-York, January, 1831, explaining why James (C.,) obeyed not the revelation which was given unto him.

BEHOLD, verily I say unto you, that his heart was right before me, for he covenanted with me, that he would obey my word.

2 And he received the word with gladness, but straitway satan tempted him; and the fear of persecution, and the cares of the world, caused him to reject the word:

3 Wherefore he broke my covenant, and it remaineth in me to do with him as seemeth me good. Amen.

CHAPTER XLIII.

A Revelation to the church in Kirtland, Ohio, and also the calling of Edward to the office of bishop, given February, 1831.

HEARKEN and hear, O ye my people, saith your Lord and your God, ye whom I delight to bless with the greatest of blessings, ye that hear me:

2 And ye that hear me not will I curse, that have professed my name, with the heaviest of all cursings.

3 Hearken, O ye elders of my church whom I have called;

4 Behold I give unto you a commandment, that ye shall assemble yourselves together to agree upon my word, and by the prayer of your faith ye shall receive my law, that ye may know how to govern my church, and have all things right before me.

5 And I will be your Ruler when I come: and behold, I come quickly: and ye shall see that my law is kept.

6 He that receiveth my law and doeth it the same is my disciple;

7 And he that saith he receiveth it and doeth it not, the same is not my disciple, and shall be cast out from among you:

8 For it is not meet that the things which belong to the children of the kingdom, should be given to them that are not worthy, or to dogs, or the pearls to be cast before swine.

9 And again, it is meet that my servant Joseph should have a house built, in which to live and translate.

10 And again, it is meet that my servant Sidney should live as seemeth him good.

11 And again, I have called my servant Edward, and give a commandment, that he should be appointed by the voice of the church, and ordained a bishop unto the church, to leave his merchandise and to spend all his time in the labors of the church; to see to all things as it shall be appointed unto him, in my laws in the day that I shall give them.

12 And this because his heart is pure before me, for he is like unto Nathaniel of old, in whom there is no guile.

13 These words are given unto you, and they are pure before me:

14 Wherefore beware how you hold them, for they are to be answered upon your souls in the day of judgment; even so: Amen.

CHAPTER XLIV.

A Revelation given to twelve elders assembled in Kirtland, Ohio; and also the law for the government of the church, given in the presence of the same, February, 1831.

HEARKEN, O ye elders of my church who have assembled yourselves together, in my name, even Jesus Christ, the Son of the living God, the Savior of the world;

2 Inasmuch as they believe on my name and keep my commandments;

3 Again I say unto you, hearken and hear and obey the law which I shall give unto you:

4 For verily I say, as ye have assembled yourselves together according to the commandment wherewith I commanded you, and are agreed as touch-

ing this one thing, and have asked the Father in my name, even so ye shall receive.

5 Behold, verily I say unto you, I give unto you this first commandment, that ye shall go forth in my name, every one of you, excepting my servants Joseph and Sidney.

6 And I give unto them a commandment that they shall go forth for a little season, and it shall be given by the power of my Spirit when they shall return:

7 And ye shall go forth in the power of my Spirit, preaching my gospel, two by two, in my name, lifting up your voices as with the voice of a trump, declaring my word like unto angels of God:

8 And ye shall go forth baptizing with water, saying, Repent ye, repent ye, for the kingdom of heaven is at hand.

9 And from this place ye shall go forth into the regions westward, and inasmuch as ye shall find them that will receive you, ye shall build up my church in every region, until the time shall come when it shall be revealed unto you, from on high, when the city of the New Jerusalem shall be prepared that ye may be gathered in one, that ye may be my people and I will be your God.

10 And again, I say unto you, that my servant Edward shall stand in the office wherewith I have appointed him.

11 And it shall come to pass that if he transgress another shall be appointed in his stead; even so: Amen.

12 Again I say unto you, that it shall not be given to any one to go forth to preach my gospel, or to build up my church, except he be ordained by some one who has authority, and it is known to the church

that he has authority, and has been regularly ordained by the hands of the church.

13 And again, the elders, priests, and teachers of
this church, shall teach the scriptures which are in
the bible, and the book of Mormon, in the which is
the fulness of the gospel; and they shall observe the
covenants and church articles to do them; and
these shall be their teachings.

14 And they shall be directed by the Spirit, which
shall be given them by the prayer of faith; and if
they receive not the Spirit, they shall not teach.

15 And all this they shall observe to do, as I have
commanded concerning their teaching, until the fulness of my scriptures are given.

16 And as they shall lift up their voices by the
Comforter, they shall speak and prophesy as seemeth me good; for behold the Comforter knoweth all
things, and beareth record of the Father, and of the
Son.

17 And now behold I speak unto the church:

18 Thou shalt not kill; and he that killeth, shall
not have forgiveness, neither in this world, nor in
the world to come.

19 And again, thou shalt not kill; he that killeth
shall die.

20 Thou shalt not steal; and he that stealeth and
will not repent, shall be cast out.

21 Thou shalt not lie; he that lieth and will not
repent, shall be cast out.

22 Thou shalt love thy wife with all thy heart,
and shall cleave unto her and none else; and he
that looketh upon a woman to lust after her, shall
deny the faith, and shall not have the Spirit, and if
he repent not, he shall be cast out.

23 Thou shalt not commit adultery; and he that

committeth adultery and repenteth not, shall be cast out; and he that committeth adultery and repenteth with all his heart, and forsaketh and doeth it no more, thou shalt forgive him; but if he doeth it again, he shall not be forgiven, but shall be cast out.

24 Thou shalt not speak evil of thy neighbor, or do him any harm.

25 Thou knowest my laws, they are given in my scriptures, he that sinneth and repenteth not, shall be cast out.

26 If thou lovest me, thou shalt serve me and keep all my commandments; and behold, thou shalt consecrate all thy properties, that which thou hast unto me, with a covenant and a deed which can not be broken; and they shall be laid before the bishop of my church, and two of the elders, such as he shall appoint and set apart for that purpose.

27 And it shall come to pass, that the bishop of my church, after that he has received the properties of my church, that it can not be taken from the church, he shall appoint every man a steward over his own property, or that which he has received, inasmuch as is sufficient for himself and family:

28 And the residue shall be kept to administer to him who has not, that every man may receive according as he stands in need:

29 And the residue shall be kept in my storehouse, to administer to the poor and needy, as shall be appointed by the elders of the church and the bishop; and for the purpose of purchasing lands, and the building up of the New Jerusalem, which is hereafter to be revealed; that my covenant people may be gathered in one, in the day that I shall come to my temple:

30 And this I do for the salvation of my people.

31 And it shall come to pass, that he that sinneth and repenteth not shall be cast out, and shall not receive again that which he has consecrated unto me:

32 For it shall come to pass, that which I spake by the mouths of my prophets shall be fulfilled; for I will consecrate the riches of the Gentiles, unto my people which are of the house of Israel.

33 And again, thou shalt not be proud in thy heart; let all thy garments be plain, and their beauty the beauty of the work of thine own hands, and let all things be done in cleanliness before me.

34 Thou shalt not be idle; for he that is idle shall not eat the bread, nor wear the garments of the laborer.

35 And whosoever among you that are sick, and have not faith to be healed, but believeth, shall be nourished in all tenderness with herbs and mild food, and that not of the world; and the elders of the church, two or more shall be called, and shall pray for, and lay their hands upon them in my name, and if they die, they shall die unto me; and if they live they shall live unto me.

36 Thou shalt live together in love, insomuch that thou shalt weep for the loss of them that die, and more especially for those that have not hope of a glorious resurrection.

37 And it shall come to pass, that those that die in me shall not taste of death, for it shall be sweet unto them; and they that die not in me, wo unto them; for their death is bitter.

38 And again, it shall come to pass, that he that has faith in me to be healed, and is not appointed unto death, shall be healed.

39 He who has faith to see, shall see; he who has faith to hear, shall hear; the lame who have faith to leap, shall leap; and they who have not faith to do these things, but believe in me, have power to become my sons, and inasmuch as they break not my laws, thou shalt bear their infirmities.

40 Thou shalt stand in the place of thy stewardship:

41 Thou shalt not take thy brother's garment; thou shalt pay for that which thou shalt receive of thy brother.

42 And if thou obtainest more than that which would be for thy support, thou shalt give it into my storehouse, that all things may be done according to that which I have spoken.

43 Thou shalt ask and my scriptures shall be given as I have appointed; and for thy safety it is expedient that thou shouldst hold thy peace concerning them, until ye have received them:

44 Then I give unto you a commandment that ye shall teach them unto all men; and they also shall be taught unto all nations, kindreds, tongues and people.

45 Thou shalt take the things which thou hast received, which thou knowest to have been my law, to be my law, to govern my church; and he that doeth according to these things shall be saved, and he that doeth them not shall be damned, if he continue.

46 If thou shalt ask, thou shalt receive revelation upon revelation, knowledge upon knowledge, that thou mayest know the mysteries, and the peaceable things of the kingdom; that which bringeth joy, that which bringeth life eternal.

47 Thou shalt ask and it shall be revealed unto

you in my own due time where the New Jerusalem shall be built.

48 And behold, it shall come to pass, that my servants shall be sent both to the east, and to the west, to the north, and to the south; and even now let him that goeth to the east, teach them that shall be converted to flee to the west; and this in consequence of that which is to come on the earth, and of secret combinations.

49 Behold, thou shalt observe all these things, and great shall be thy reward.

50 Thou shalt observe to keep the mysteries of the kingdom unto thyself, for it is not gi.en to the world to know the mysteries.

51 The laws which ye have received, and shall hereafter receive, shall be sufficient for you both here, and in the New Jerusalem.

52 Therefore, he that lacketh knowledge, let him ask of me and I will give him liberally and upbraid him not.

53 Lift up your hearts and rejoice, for unto you the kingdom has been given; even so: Amen.

54 The priests and teachers, shall have their stewardship given them even as the members; and the elders are to assist the bishop in all things, and he is to see that their families are supported out of the property which is consecrated to the Lord, either a stewardship, or otherwise, as may be thought best by the elders and bishop.

55 Thou shalt contract no debts with the world, except thou art commanded.

56 And again, the elders and bishop, shall counsel together, and they shall do by the direction of the Spirit as it must needs be necessary.

57 There shall be as many appointed as must

needs be necessary to assist the bishop in obtaining places for the brethren from New York, that they may be together as much as can be, and as they are directed by the Holy Spirit; and every family shall have a place, that they may live by themselves.— And every church shall be organized in as close bodies as they can be; and this for a wise purpose :— even so. Amen.

CHAPTER XLV.

A Revelation to the elders of the church, assembled in Kirtland, Ohio, given February, 1831.

O HEARKEN, ye elders of my church, and give ear to the words which I shall speak unto you:

2 For behold, verily, verily I say unto you, that ye have received a commandment for a law unto my church, through him whom I have appointed unto you, to receive commandments and revelations from my hand.

3 And this ye shall know assuredly, that there is none other appointed unto you to receive commandments and revelations until he be taken, if he abide in me.

4 But verily, verily I say unto you, that none else shall be appointed unto this gift except it be through him, for if it be taken from him he shall not have power, except to appoint another in his stead:

5 And this shall be a law unto you, that ye receive not the teachings of any that shall come before you as revelations or commandments:

6 And this I give unto you, that you may not be

deceived; that you may know they are not of me.

7 For verily I say unto you, that he that is ordained of me shall come in at the gate and be ordained as I have told you before, to teach those revelations which you have received, and shall receive through him whom I have appointed.

8 And now behold I give unto you a commandment, that when ye are assembled together ye shall note with a pen how to act, and for my church to act upon the points of my law and commandments, which I have given:

9 And thus it shall become a law unto you, being sanctified by that which ye have received, that ye shall bind yourselves to act in all holiness before me; that inasmuch as ye do this, glory shall be added to the kingdom which ye have received.

10 Inasmuch as ye do it not, it shall be taken even that which ye have received.

11 Purge ye out the iniquity which is among you; sanctifiy yourselves before me and if ye desire the glories of the kingdom, appoint ye my servant Joseph and uphold him before me by the prayer of faith.

12 And again, I say unto you, that if ye desire the mysteries of the kingdom, provide for him food and raiment and whatsoever thing he needeth to accomplish the work, wherewith I have commanded him:

13 And if ye do it not, he shall remain unto them that have received him, that I may reserve unto myself a pure people before me.

14 Again I say, hearken ye elders of my church, whom I have appointed:

15 Ye are not sent forth to be taught, but to teach the children of men the things which I have put in

to your hands by the power of my Spirit: and ye are to be taught from on high.

16 Sanctify yourselves and ye shall be endowed with power, that ye may give even as I have spoken.

17 Hearken ye, for behold the great day of the Lord is nigh at hand.

18 For the day cometh that the Lord shall utter his voice out of heaven; the heavens shall shake and the earth shall tremble, and the trump of God shall sound both long and loud, and shall say to the sleeping nations:

19 Ye saints arise and live:

20 Ye sinners stay and sleep until I shall call again:

21 Wherefore gird up your loins, lest ye be found among the wicked.

22 Lift up your voices and spare not.

23 Call upon the nations to repent, both old and young, both bond and free; saying, Prepare yourselves for the great day of the Lord:

24 For if I, who am a man, do lift up my voice and call upon you to repent, and ye hate me, what will ye say when the day cometh when the thunders shall utter their voices from the ends of the earth, speaking in the ears of all that live, saying, Repent, and prepare for the great day of the Lord;

25 Yea, and again, when the lightnings shall streak forth from the east unto the west, and shall utter forth their voices unto all that live, and make the ears of all tingle, that hear, saying these words:

26 Repent ye, for the great day of the Lord is come.

27 And again, the Lord shall utter his voice out of heaven, saying:

28 Hearken, O ye nations of the earth, and hear the words of that God who made you.

29 O ye nations of the earth, how often would I have gathered you, together as a hen gathereth her chickens under her wings, but ye would not?

30 How oft have I called upon you by the mouth of my servants; and by the ministering of angels; and by mine own voice; and by the voice of thunderings; and by the voice of lightnings; and by the voice of tempests; and by the voice of earthquakes; and great hail-storms; and by the voice of famines, and pestilences of every kind; and by the great sound of a trump; and by the voice of judgment; and by the voice of mercy all the day long; and by the voice of glory, and honor, and the riches of eternal life; and would have saved you with an everlasting salvation, but ye would not?

31 Behold the day has come, when the cup of the wrath of mine indignation, is full.

32 Behold, verily I say unto you, that these are the words of the Lord your God:

33 Wherefore, labor ye, labor ye, in my vineyard for the last time:

34 For the last time call ye upon the inhabitants of the earth, for in mine own due time will I come upon the earth in judgment:

35 And my people shall be redeemed and shall reign with me on earth:

36 For the great Millennial, which I have spoken by the mouth of my servants, shall come;

37 For satan shall be bound; and when he is loosed again, he shall only reign for a little season, and then cometh the end of the earth:

38 And he that liveth in righteousness, shall be changed in the twinkling of an eye;

39 And the earth shall pass away so as by fire;

40 And the wicked shall go away into unquench-able fire; and their end no man knoweth, on earth, nor ever shall know, until they come before me in judgment.

41 Hearken ye to these words; behold I am Jesus Christ, the Savior of the world.

42 Treasure these things up in your hearts, and let the solemnities of eternity rest upon your minds.

43 Be sober.

44 Keep all my commandments; even so: Amen.

CHAPTER XLVI.

A Revelation to Joseph, and Sidney, given in Kirtland, Ohio, February, 1831.

BEHOLD thus saith the Lord unto you my servants, it is expedient in me that the elders of my church should be called together, from the east and from the west, and from the north and from the south, by letter or some other way.

2 And it shall come to pass, that, inasmuch as they are faithful, and exercise faith in me, I will pour out my Spirit upon them in the day that they assemble themselves together.

3 And it shall come to pass that they shall go forth into the regions round about, and preach repentance unto the people;

4 And many shall be converted, insomuch that ye shall obtain power to organize yourselves, according to the laws of man;

5 That your enemies may not have power over you, that you may be preserved in all things;

29208

6 That you may be enabled to keep my laws, that every band may be broken wherewith the enemy seeketh to destroy my people.

7 Behold I say unto you, that ye must visit the poor and the needy and administer to their relief, that they may be kept until all things may be done according to my law which ye have received: Amen.

CHAPTER XLVII.

A Revelation to seven elders of the church, assembled in Kirtland, Ohio, given February 1831.

EVERY person who belongeth to this church of Christ, shall observe to keep all the commandments and covenants of the church;

2 And it shall come to pass, that if any persons among you shall kill, they shall be delivered up and dealt with according to the laws of the land;

3 For remember, that he hath no forgiveness;

4 And it shall be proven according to the laws of the land.

5 But if any man shall commit adultery, he shall be tried before two elders of the church or more, and every word shall be established against him by two witnesses of the church, and not of the world.

6 But if there are more than two witnesses it is better:

7 But he shall be condemned by the mouth of two witnesses, and the elders shall lay the case before the church, and the church shall lift up their hands against them, that they may be dealt with according to the law.

8 And if it can be, it is necessary that the bishop

is present also. And thus ye shall do in all cases which shall come before you.

9 And if a man shall rob, he shall be delivered up unto the law.

10 And if he shall steal, he shall be delivered up unto the law.

11 And if he lie, he shall be delivered up unto the law.

12 If he do any manner of iniquity, he shall be delivered up unto the law, even that of God.

13 And if thy brother offend thee, thou shalt take him between him and thee alone; and if he confess, thou shalt be reconciled.

14 And if he confess not, thou shalt take another with thee; and then if he confess not, thou shalt deliver him up unto the church, not to the members but to the elders.

15 And it shall be done in a meeting, and that not before the world.

16 And if thy brother offend many, he shall be chastened before many.

17 And if any one offend openly, he shall be rebuked openly, that he may be ashamed.

18 And if he confess not, he shall be delivered up unto the law.

19 If any shall offend in secret, he shall be rebuked in secret, that he may have opportunity to confess in secret to him whom he has offended, and to God, that the brethren may not speak reproachfully of him.

20 And thus shall ye conduct in all things.

21 Behold, verily I say unto you, that whatsoever persons among you having put away their companions, for the cause of fornication, or in other words, if they shall testify before you, in all lowliness of

heart, that this is the case, ye shall not cast them out from among you:

22 But if ye shall find that any persons, have left their companions, for the sake of adultery, and they themselves are the offenders, and their companions are living, they shall be cast out from among you.

23 And again I say unto you, that ye shall be watchful and careful, with all inquiry, that ye receive none such among you, if they are married.

24 And if they are not married, they shall repent of all their sins, or ye shall not receive them. Amen.

CHAPTER XLVIII.

A Revelation to the church, given in Kirtland, Ohio, March 1831.

HEARKEN, O ye people of my church to whom the kingdom has been given:

2 Hearken ye and give ear to him who laid the foundation of the earth; who made the heavens and all the hosts thereof, and by whom all things were made which live and move and have a being.

3 And again I say, hearken unto my voice, lest death shall overtake you:

4 In an hour when ye think not, the summer shall be past, and the harvest ended, and your souls not saved.

5 Listen to him who is the Advocate with the Father, who is pleading your case before him:

6 Saying Father behold the sufferings and death of him who did no sin, in whom thou wast well pleased; behold the blood of thy Son which was shed, the blood of him whom thou gavest that thy-

self might be glorified : wherefore Father spare these my brethren that believe on my name, that they may come unto me and have everlasting life.

7 Hearken O ye people of my church, and ye elders listen together, and hear my voice while it is called today, and harden not your hearts :

8 For verily I say unto you that I am Alpha and Omega, the beginning and the end, the light and the life of the world, a light that shineth in darkness and the darkness comprehendeth it not :

9 I came unto my own and my own received me not :

10 But unto as many as received me, gave I power to do many miracles, and to become the sons of God, and even unto them that believed on my name gave I power to obtain eternal life.

11 And even so I have sent mine everlasting covenant into the world, to be a light to the world, and to be a standard for my people, and for the Gentiles to seek to it ;

12 And to be a messenger before my face to prepare the way before me.

13 Wherefore come ye unto it, and with him that cometh I will reason as with men in days of old, and I will show unto you my strong reasoning ;

14 Wherefore hearken ye together and let me show it unto you, even my wisdom, the wisdom of him whom ye say is the God of Enoch, and his brethren, who were separated from the earth, and were reserved unto myself, a city reserved until a day of righteousness shall come, a day which was sought for by all holy men, and they found it not because of wickedness and abominations, and confessed that they were strangers and pilgrims on the earth ;

15 But obtained a promise that they should find it, and see it in their flesh.

16 Wherefore hearken and I will reason with you, and I will speak unto you and prophesy as unto men in days of old, and I will show it plainly as I showed it unto my disciples, as I stood before them in the flesh and spake unto them saying:

17 As ye have asked of me concerning the signs of my coming, in the day when I shall come in my glory, in the clouds of heaven, to fulfil the promises that I have made unto your fathers;

18 For as ye have looked upon the long absence of your spirits from your bodies to be a bondage, I will show unto you how the day of redemption shall come and also the restoration of the scattered Israel.

19 And now ye behold this temple which is in Jerusalem, which ye call the house of God, and your enemies say that this house shall never fall.

20 But verily I say unto you, that desolation shall come upon this generation as a thief in the night, and this people shall be destroyed and scattered among all nations.

21 And this temple which ye now see, shall be thrown down that there shall not be left one stone upon another.

22 And it shall come to pass, that this generation of Jews shall not pass away, until every desolation which I have told you concerning them, shall come to pass.

23 Ye say that ye know, that the end of the world cometh; ye say also that ye know, that the heavens and the earth shall pass away; and in this ye say truly, for so it is;

24 But these things which I have told you, shall not pass away until all shall be fulfilled.

25 And this I have told you concerning Jerusalem, and when that day shall come, shall a remnant be scattered among all nations, but they shall be gathered again; but they shall remain until the times of the Gentiles be fulfilled.

26 And in that day shall be heard of wars and rumors of wars, and the whole earth shall be in commotion, and men's hearts shall fail them, and they shall say that Christ delayeth his coming until the end of the earth.

27 And the love of men shall wax cold, and iniquity shall abound; and when the time of the Gentiles is come in, a light shall break forth among them that sit in darkness, and it shall be the fulness of my gospel; but they receive it not, for they perceive not the light, and they turn their hearts from me because of the precepts of men; and in that generation shall the times of the Gentiles be fulfilled :

28 And there shall be men standing in that generation, that shall not pass, until they shall see an overflowing scourge; for a desolating sickness shall cover the land :

29 But my disciples shall stand in holy places, and shall not be moved; but among the wicked, men shall lift up their voices and curse God and die.

30 And there shall be earthquakes, also, in divers places, and many desolations, yet men will harden their hearts against me; and they will take up the sword one against another, and they will kill one another.

31 And now, when I the Lord had spoken these words unto my disciples, they were troubled; and I said unto them, be not troubled, for when all these

things shall come to pass, ye may know that the promises which have been made unto you, shall be fulfilled:

32 And when the light shall begin to break forth, it shall be with them like unto a parable which I will show you:

33 Ye look and behold the fig-trees, and ye see them with your eyes, and ye say when they begin to shoot forth and their leaves are yet tender, ye say that summer is now nigh at hand;

34 Even so it shall be in that day, when they shall see all these things, then shall they know that the hour is nigh.

35 And it shall come to pass that he that feareth me shall be looking for the great day of the Lord to come, even for the signs of the coming of the Son of man; and they shall see signs and wonders, for they shall be shown forth in the heavens above, and in the earth beneath; and they shall behold blood and fire, and vapors of smoke;

36 And before the day of the Lord shall come, the sun shall be darkened, and the moon be turned into blood, and stars fall from heaven;

37 And the remnant shall be gathered unto this place; and then they shall look for me, and behold I will come; and they shall see me in the clouds of heaven, clothed with power and great glory, with all the holy angels;

38 And he that watches not for me shall be cut off.

39 But before the arm of the Lord shall fall, an angel shall sound his trump, and the saints that have slept, shall come forth to meet me in the cloud.

40 Wherefore if ye have slept in peace, blessed

are you, for as you now behold me and know that I
am, even so shall ye come unto me and your souls
shall live, and your redemption shall be perfected,
and the saints shall come forth from the four quarters of the earth.

41 Then shall the arm of the Lord fall upon the
nations, and then shall the Lord set his foot upon
this mount, and it shall cleave in twain, and the
earth shall tremble and reel to and fro, and the
heavens also shall shake, and the Lord shall utter
his voice and all the ends of the earth shall hear it,
and the nations of the earth shall mourn, and they
that have laughed shall see their folly, and calamity shall cover the mocker, and the scorner shall be
consumed, and they that have watched for iniquity,
shall be hewn down and cast into the fire.

42 And then shall the Jews look upon me, and
say, What are these wounds in thine hands, and
in thy feet?

43 Then shall they know that I am the Lord; for
I will say unto them, These wounds, are the wounds
with which I was wounded in the house of my
friends.

44 I am he who was lifted up.

45 I am Jesus that was crucified.

46 I am the Son of God.

47 And then shall they weep because of their iniquities; then shall they lament because they persecuted their King.

48 And then shall the heathen nations be redeemed, and they which knew no law shall have part in
the first resurrection;

49 And it shall be tolerable for them; and satan
shall be bound that he shall have no place in the
hearts of the children of men.

50 And at that day when I shall come in my glory, shall the parable be fulfilled which I spake concerning the ten virgins:

51 For they that are wise and have received the
truth, and have taken the Holy Spirit for their guide,
and have not been deceived;

52 Verily I say unto you, they shall not be hewn
down and cast into the fire, but shall abide the day,
and the earth shall be given unto them for an inheritance:

53 And they shall multiply and wax strong, and
their children shall grow up without sin unto salvation, for the Lord shall be in their midst, and his
glory shall be upon them, and he will be their King
and their Lawgiver.

54 And now, behold I say unto you, it shall not
be given unto you to know any farther than this, until the new testament be translated, and in it all
these things shall be made known;

55 Wherefore I give unto you that ye may now
translate it, that ye may be prepared for the things
to come;

56 For verily I say unto you, that great things
await you;

57 Ye hear of wars in foreign lands, but behold I
say unto you they are nigh even unto your doors,
and not many years hence ye shall hear of wars in
your own lands.

58 Wherefore I the Lord have said gather ye out
from the eastern lands, assemble ye yourselves together ye elders of my church;

59 Go ye forth into the western countries, call
upon the inhabitants to repent, and inasmuch as
they do repent, build up churches unto me; and with
one heart and with one mind, gather up your riches

that ye may purchase an inheritance which shall hereafter be appointed unto you, and it shall be called the New Jerusalem, a land of peace, a city of refuge, a place of safety for the saints of the most high God;

60 And the glory of the Lord shall be there, and the terror of the Lord also shall be there, insomuch that the wicked will not come unto it:

61 And it shall be called Zion:

62 And it shall come to pass, among the wicked, that every man that will not take his sword against his neighbor, must needs flee unto Zion for safety.

63 And there shall be gathered unto it out of every nation under heaven:

64 And it shall be the only people that shall not be at war one with another.

65 And it shall be said among the wicked, let us not go up to battle against Zion, for the inhabitants of Zion are terrible:

66 Wherefore we can not stand.

67 And it shall come to pass that the righteous shall be gathered out from among all nations, and shall come to Zion singing, with songs of everlasting joy.

68 And now I say unto you, keep these things from going abroad unto the world, until it is expedient in me, that ye may accomplish this work in the eyes of the people, and in the eyes of your enemies, that they may not know your works until ye have accomplished the thing which I have commanded you:

69 That when they shall know it, that they may consider these things, for when the Lord shall appear he shall be terrible unto them, that fear may seize upon them, and they shall stand afar off and

tremble: and all nations shall be afraid because of the terror of the Lord, and the power of his might; even so: Amen.

CHAPTER XLIX.

A Revelation to the church, given in Kirtland, Ohio, March, 1831.

HEARKEN, O ye people of my church, for verily I say unto you, that these things were spoken unto you for your profit and learning;

2 But notwithstanding those things which are written, it always has been given to the elders of my church, from the beginning, and ever shall be, to conduct all meetings as they are directed and guided by the Holy Spirit:

3 Nevertheless ye are commanded never to cast any one out from your public meetings, which are held before the world:

4 Ye are also commanded not to cast any one, who belongeth to the church, out of your sacrament meetings:

5 Nevertheless, if any have trespassed, let him not partake until he makes reconciliation.

6 And again I say unto you, ye shall not cast any one out of your sacrament meetings, who is earnestly seeking the kingdom;

7 I speak this concerning those who are not of the church.

8 And again I say unto you, concerning your confirmation meetings, that if there be any that is not of the church, that is earnestly seeking after the kingdom, ye shall not cast them out;

9 But ye are commanded in all things to ask of God who giveth liberally, and that which the Spirit testifies unto you, even so I would that ye should do in all holiness of heart, walking uprightly before me, considering the end of your salvation, doing all things with prayer and thanksgiving, that ye may not be seduced by evil spirits, or doctrines of devils, or the commandments of men, for some are of men, and others of devils.

10 Wherefore, beware lest ye are deceived! and that ye may not be deceived, seek ye earnestly the best gifts, always remembering for what they are given;

11 For verily I say unto you, they are given for the benefit of those who love me and keep all my commandments, and him that seeketh so to do, that all may be benefitted, that seeketh or that asketh of me, that asketh and not for a sign that he may consume it upon his lusts.

12 And again, verily I say unto you, I would that ye should always remember, and always retain in your minds what those gifts are, that are given unto the church, for all have not every gift given unto them: for there are many gifts, and to every man is given a gift by the Spirit of God;

13 To some it is given one, and to some is given another, that all may be profited thereby;

14 To some it is given by the Holy Ghost to know that Jesus Christ is the Son of God, and that he was crucified for the sins of the world; to others it is given to believe on their words, that they also might have eternal life, if they continue faithful.

15 And again, to some it is given by the Holy Ghost to know the differences of administration, as it will be pleasing unto the same Lord, according

as the Lord will, suiting his mercies according to the conditions of the children of men.

16 And again it is given by the Holy Ghost to some to know the diversities of operations, whether it be of God, that the manifestations of the Spirit may be given to every man to profit withal.

17 And again, verily I say unto you, to some it is given, by the Spirit of God, the word of wisdom; to another it is given, the word of knowledge, that all may be taught to be wise and to have knowledge.

18 And again, to some it is given to have faith to be healed, and to others it is given to have faith to heal.

19 And again, to some it is given the working of miracles;

20 And to others it is given to prophesy, and to others the discerning of spirits.

21 And again, it is given to some to speak with tongues, and to another it is given the interpretation of tongues:

22 And all these gifts cometh from God, for the benefit of the children of God.

23 And unto the bishop of the church, and unto such as God shall appoint and ordain to watch over the church, and to be elders unto the church, are to have it given unto them to discern all those gifts, lest there shall be any among you professing and yet be not of God.

24 And it shall come to pass that he that asketh in spirit shall receive in spirit; that unto some it may be given to have all those gifts, that there may be a head, in order that every member may be profited thereby:

25 He that asketh in the spirit, asketh according

to the will of God, wherefore it is done even as he asketh.

26 And again I say unto you, all things must be done in the name of Christ, whatsoever you do in the spirit;

27 And ye must give thanks unto God in the spirit for whatsoever blessing ye are blessed with:

28 And ye must practice virtue and holiness before me continually; even so: Amen.

CHAPTER L.

A Revelation to Joseph and John, given in Kirtland, Ohio, March 1831.

BEHOLD it is expedient in me that my servant John should write and keep a regular history, and assist you, my servant Joseph, in transcribing all things which shall be given you.

2 Again, verily I say unto you, that he can also lift up his voice in meetings, whenever it shall be expedient.

3 And again, I say unto you, that it shall be appointed unto him to keep the church record and history continually, for Oliver I have appointed to another office:

4 Wherefore it shall be given him, inasmuch as he is faithful, by the Comforter, to write these things; even so: Amen.

CHAPTER LI.

*A Revelation to the bishop, and the church in
Kirtland, given in Kirtland, Ohio, March, 1831.*

IT is necessary that ye should remain, for the
present time, in your places of abode, as it shall
be suitable to your circumstances;

2 And inasmuch as ye have lands, ye shall impart to the eastern brethren,;

3 And inasmuch as ye have not lands, let them
buy, for the present time, in those regions round
about, as seemeth them good, for it must needs be
necessary that they have places to live for the present time.

4 It must needs be necessary, that ye save all the
money that ye can, and that ye obtain all that ye
can in righteousness, that in time ye may be enabled
to purchase lands for an inheritance, even the city.

5 The place is not yet to be revealed, but after
your brethren come from the east, there are to be
certain men appointed, and to them it shall be given to know the place, or to them it shall be revealed; and they shall be appointed to purchase the
lands, and to make a commencement, to lay the
foundation of the city;

6 And then ye shall begin to be gathered with
your families, every man according to his family,
according to his circumstances, and as is appointed
to him by the bishop and elders of the church, according to the laws and commandments, which ye
have received, and which ye shall hereafter receive;
even so: Amen.

CHAPTER LII.

A Revelation to Sidney, Parley, and Lemon,
given in Kirtland, Ohio, March, 1831.

HEARKEN unto my word, my servant Sidney, and Parley, and Lemon, for behold, verily I say unto you, that I give unto you a commandment, that you shall go and preach my gospel, which ye have received, even as ye have received it, unto the Shakers.

2 Behold I say unto you, that they desire to know the truth in part, but not all, for they are not right before me, and must needs repent:

3 Wherefore I send you, my servants Sidney and Parley, to preach the gospel unto them; and my servant Lemon shall be ordained unto this work, that he may reason with them, not according to that which he has received of them, but according to that which shall be taught him by you, my servants, and by so doing I will bless him, otherwise he shall not prosper:

4 Thus saith the Lord, for I am God and have sent mine only begotten Son into the world, for the redemption of the world, and have decreed, that he that receiveth him shall be saved, and he that receiveth him not, shall be damned:

5 And they have done unto the Son of man even as they listed;

6 And he has taken his power on the right hand of his glory, and now reigneth in the heavens, and will reign till he descends on the earth to put all enemies under his feet:

7 Which time is nigh at hand: I the Lord God have spoken it:

8 But the hour and the day no man knoweth,

neither the angels in heaven, nor shall they know until he come:

9 Wherefore I will that all men shall repent, for all are under sin, except them which I have reserved unto myself, holy men that ye know not of:

10 Wherefore I say unto you, that I have sent unto you mine everlasting covenant, even that which was from the beginning, and that which I have promised I have so fulfilled, and the nations of the earth shall bow to it;

11 And, if not of themselves, they shall come down, for that which is now exalted of itself, shall be laid low of power:

12 Wherefore I give unto you a commandment, that ye go among this people and say unto them, like unto mine apostle of old, whose name was Peter:

13 Believe on the name of the Lord Jesus, who was on the earth, and is to come, the beginning and the end;

14 Repent and be baptized in the name of Jesus Christ, according to the holy commandment, for the remission of sins;

15 And whoso doeth this, shall receive the gift of the Holy Ghost, by the laying on of the hands of the elders of this church.

16 And again, I say unto you, that whoso forbiddeth to marry, is not ordained of God, for marriage is ordained of God unto man:

17 Wherefore it is lawful that he should have one wife, and they twain shall be one flesh, and all this that the earth might answer the end of its creation; and that it might be filled with the measure of man, according to his creation before the world was made.

18 And whoso forbiddeth to abstain from meats, that man should not eat the same, is not ordained of God;

19 For behold the beasts of the field, and the fowls of the air, and that which cometh of the earth, is ordained for the use of man, for food, and for raiment, and that he might have in abundance, but it is not given that one man should possess that which is above another:

20 Wherefore the world lieth in sin; and wo be unto man that sheddeth blood or that wasteth flesh and hath no need.

21 And again, verily I say unto you, that the Son of man cometh not in the form of a woman, neither of a man travelling on the earth:

22 Wherefore be not deceived, but continue in steadfastness, looking forth for the heavens to be shaken;

23 And the earth to tremble, and to reel to and fro as a drunken man; and for the valleys to be exalted; and for the mountains to be made low; and for the rough places to become smooth:

24 And all this when the angel shall sound his trumpet.

25 But before the great day of the Lord shall come, Jacob shall flourish in the wilderness; and the Lamanites shall blossom as the rose:

26 Zion shall flourish upon the hills, and rejoice upon the mountains, and shall be assembled together unto the place which I have appointed.

27 Behold I say unto you, go forth as I have commanded you;

28 Repent of all your sins; ask and ye shall receive; knock and it shall be opened unto you:

29 Behold I will go before you, and be your rere-

ward; and I will be in your midst, and you shall not be confounded:

30 Behold I am Jesus Christ, and I come quickly; even so: Amen.

CHAPTER LIII.

A Revelation to the elders of the church assembled at Kirtland, Ohio, given May, 1831.

HEARKEN, O ye elders of my church, and give ear to the voice of the living God; and attend to the words of wisdom which shall be given unto you, according as ye have asked and are agreed as touching the church, and the spirits which have gone abroad in the earth.

2 Behold verily I say unto you, that there are many spirits which are false spirits, which have gone forth in the earth, deceiving the world:

3 And also satan hath sought to deceive you, that he might overthrow you.

4 Behold I the Lord have looked upon you, and have seen abominations in the church, which profess my name;

5 But blessed are they who are faithful and endure, whether in life or in death, for they shall inherit eternal life.

6 But wo unto them that are deceivers, and hypocrites, for thus saith the Lord, I will bring them to judgment.

7 Behold verily I say unto you, there are hypocrites among you, and have deceived some, which has given the adversary power, but behold such shall be reclaimed;

8 But the hypocrites shall be detected and shall be cut off, either in life or in death, even as I will, and wo unto them who are cut off from my church, for the same are overcome of the world:

9 Wherefore, let every man beware lest he do that which is not in truth and righteousness before me.

10 And now come, saith the Lord, by the Spirit, unto the elders of his church, and let us reason together, that ye may understand:

11 Let us reason even as a man reasoneth one with another face to face:

12 Now when a man reasoneth, he is understood of man, because he reasoneth as a man; even so will I the Lord reason with you that you may understand:

13 Wherefore I the Lord asketh you this question, unto what were ye ordained?

14 To preach my gospel by the Spirit, even the Comforter which was sent forth to teach the truth; and then received ye spirits which ye could not understand, and received them to be of God, and in this are ye justified?

15 Behold ye shall answer this question yourselves, nevertheless I will be merciful unto you:

16 He that is weak among you hereafter shall be made strong.

17 Verily I say unto you, he that is ordained of me and sent forth to preach the word of truth by the Comforter, in the spirit of truth, doth he preach it by the spirit of truth, or some other way? and if by some other way, it be not of God.

18 And again, he that receiveth the word of truth, doth he receive it by the spirit of truth, or some other way? if it be some other way, it be not of God:

19 Therefore, why is it that ye can not understand and know that he that receiveth the word by the spirit of truth, receiveth it as it is preached by the spirit of truth?

20 Wherefore, he that preacheth and he that receiveth, understandeth one another, and both are edified and rejoice together; and that which doth not edify, is not of God, and is darkness:

21 That which is of God is light, and he that receiveth light and continueth in God, receiveth more light, and that light groweth brighter and brighter, until the perfect day.

22 And again, verily I say unto you, and I say it that you may know the truth, that you may chase darkness from among you, for he that is ordained of God and sent forth, the same is appointed to be the greatest, notwithstanding he is least, and the servant of all:

23 Wherefore he is possessor of all things, for all things are subject unto him, both in heaven and on the earth, the life, and the light, the spirit, and the power, sent forth by the will of the Father, through Jesus Christ, his Son;

24 But no man is possessor of all things, except he be purified and cleansed from all sin;

25 And if ye are purified and cleansed from all sin, ye shall ask whatsoever you will in the name of Jesus, and it shall be done:

26 But know this, it shall be given you what you shall ask, and as ye are appointed to the head, the spirits shall be subject unto you:

27 Wherefore it shall come to pass, that if you behold a spirit manifested that ye can not understand, and you receive not that spirit, ye shall ask of the Father in the name of Jesus, and if he give

not unto you that spirit, then you may know that it is not of God:

28 And it shall be given unto you power over that spirit, and you shall proclaim against that spirit with a loud voice, that it is not of God;

29 Not with railing accusation, that ye be not over-come; neither with boasting, nor rejoicing, lest you be seized therewith:

30 He that receiveth of God, let him account it of God, and let him rejoice that he is accounted of God worthy to receive, and by giving heed and doing these things which ye have received, and which ye shall hereafter receive:

31 And the kingdom is given unto you of the Father, and power to overcome all things, which is not ordained of him:

32 And behold, verily I say unto you, blessed are you who are now hearing these words of mine from the mouth of my servant, for your sins are forgiven you.

33 Let my servant Joseph (W.) in whom I am well pleased, and my servant Parley, go forth among the churches and strengthen them by the word of exhortation;

34 And also my servant John (C.,) or as many of my servants as are ordained unto this office, and let them labor in the vineyard;

35 And let no man hinder them of doing that which I have appointed unto them:

36 Wherefore in this thing my servant Edward is not justified, neverthe ess let him repent and he shall be forgiven.

37 Behold ye are little children, and ye can not bear all things now; ye must grow in grace and in the knowledge of the truth.

38 Fear not, little children, for you are mine, and I have overcome the world, and you are of them that my Father hath given me;

39 And none of them which my Father hath given me shall be lost:

40 And the Father and I are one; I am in the Father and the Father in me:

41 And inasmuch as ye have received me, ye are in me, and I in you: wherefore I am in your midst; and I am the good Shepherd;

42 And the day cometh that you shall hear my voice and see me, and know that I am.

43 Watch, therefore, that ye may be ready; even so: Amen.

CHAPTER LIV.

A Revelation to the elders of the church assembled in Kirtland, Ohio, given June, 1831.

BEHOLD, thus saith the Lord unto the elders whom he hath called and chosen, in these last days, by the voice of his Spirit, saying, I the Lord will make known unto you what I will that ye shall do from this time until the next conference, which shall be held in Missouri, upon the land which I will consecrate unto my people, which are a remnant of Jacob, and them who are heirs according to the covenant.

2 Wherefore, verily I say unto you, let my servants Joseph and Sidney take their journey as soon as preparations can be made to leave their homes, and journey to the land of Missouri.

3 And inasmuch as they are faithful unto me it

shall be made known unto them what they shall do:

4 And it shall also, inasmuch as they are faithful, be made known unto them the land of your inheritance.

5 And inasmuch as they are not faithful, they shall be cut off, even as I will, as seemeth me good.

6 And again, verily I say unto you, let my servant Lyman (W.,) and my servant John (C.,) take their journey speedily:

7 And also my servant John (M.) and my servant Hyrum, take their journey unto the same place by the way of Detroit.

8 And let them journey from thence preaching the word by the way, saying none other things than that which the prophets and apostles have written, and that which is taught them by the Comforter, through the prayer of faith.

9 Let them go two by two, and thus let them preach by the way in every congregation, baptizing by water, and the laying on of the hands by the water side:

10 For thus saith the Lord, I will cut my work short in righteousness:

11 For the days cometh that I will send forth judgment unto victory.

12 And let my servant Lyman beware, for satan desireth to sift him as chaff.

13 And behold, he that is faithful shall be made ruler over many things.

14 And again, I will give unto you a pattern in all things, that ye may not be deceived, for satan is abroad in the land, and he goeth forth deceiving the nations:

15 Wherefore he that prayeth whose spirit is con-

trite, the same is accepted of me, if he obey mine ordinances:

16 He that speaketh, whose spirit is contrite, whose language is meek, and edifieth, the same is of God, if he obey mine ordinances.

17 And again, he that trembleth under my power, shall be made strong, and shall bring forth fruits of praise, and wisdom, according to the revelations, and truths which I have given you.

18 And again, he that is overcome and bringeth not forth fruits, even according to this pattern, is not of me:

19 Wherefore by this pattern ye shall know the spirits in all cases, under the whole heavens.

20 And the days have come, according to men's faith it shall be done unto them.

21 Behold this commandment is given unto all, the elders whom I have chosen.

22 And again, verily I say unto you, let my servant Thomas, and my servant Ezra, take their journey also, preaching the word by the way, unto this same land.

23 And again, let my servant Isaac and my servant Ezra (B.,) take their journey, also preaching the word by the way unto the same land.

24 And again, let my servant Edward and Martin take their journey with my servants Sidney and Joseph.

25 Let my servant David and Harvey, also take their journey, and preach by the way unto this same land.

26 Let my servants Parley and Orson (P.) take their journey, and preach by the way, even unto this same land.

27 And let my servants Solomon and Simeon,

also take their journey unto this same land, and preach by the way.

28 Let my servants Edson and Jacob (S.,) also take their journey.

29 Let my servants Levi and Zebidee, also take their journey.

30 Let my servants Reynolds and Samuel, also take their journey.

31 Let my servants Wheeler and William (C.,) also take their journey.

32 And let my servants Newel (K.) and Selah, both be ordained and also take their journey:

33 Yea, verily I say, let all these take their journey unto one place, in their several courses, and one man shall not build upon another's foundation, neither journey in another's track.

34 He that is faithful, the same shall be kept and blessed with much fruit.

35 And again, I say unto you, let my servant Joseph (W.) and Solomon (H.,) take their journey into the eastern lands.

36 Let them labor with their families, declaring none other things than the prophets and apostles, that which they have seen, and heard, and most assuredly believe, that the prophecies may be fulfilled.

37 In consequence of transgression, let that which was bestowed upon Heman, be taken from him, and placed upon the head of Simonds.

38 And again, verily I say unto you, let Jared be ordained a priest, and also George be ordained a priest.

39 Let the residue of the elders watch over the churches, and declare the word in the regions among them.

40 And let them labor with their own hands, that

there be no idolatry nor wickedness practiced. And remember in all things, the poor and the needy, the sick and the afflicted, for he that doeth not these things, the same is not my disciple.

41 And again, let my servants Joseph and Sidney and Edward, take with them a recommend from the church.

42 And let there be one obtained for my servant Oliver, also:

43 And thus, even as I have said, if ye are faithful, ye shall assemble yourselves together to rejoice upon the land of Missouri, which is the land of your inheritance, which is now the land of your enemies.

44 But behold I the Lord will hasten the city in its time;

45 And will crown the faithful with joy and with rejoicing.

46 Behold I am Jesus Christ, the Son of God, and I will lift them up at the last day; even so: Amen.

CHAPTER LV.

A Revelation to Sidney (G.,) given in Kirtland, Ohio, June, 1831.

BEHOLD I say unto you, my servant Sidney, that I have heard your prayers, and you have called upon me, that it should be made known unto you, of the Lord your God, concerning your calling, and election in this church, which I the Lord have raised up in these last days.

2 Behold I the Lord, who was crucified for the sins of the world, giveth unto you a commandment; that you shall forsake the world.

3 Take upon *you* mine ordinances, even that of an elder, to preach faith and-repentance, and remission of sins, according to my word, and the reception of the Holy Spirit by the laying on of hands.

4 And also to be an agent unto this church in the place which shall be appointed by the bishop, according to commandments which shall be given hereafter.

5 And again, verily I say unto you, you shall take your journey with my servants Joseph and Sidney.

6 Behold these are the first ordinances which you shall receive:

7 And the residue shall be made known unto you in a time to come, according to your labor in my vineyard.

8 And again, I would that ye should learn that it is he only who is saved, that endureth unto the end; even so: Amen.

CHAPTER LVI.

A Revelation to Newel (K.,) and the church in Thompson, given in Kirtland, Ohio, June, 1831.

BEHOLD, thus saith the Lord, even Alpha and Omega, the beginning and the end, even he who was crucified for the sins of the world.

2 Behold, verily, verily I say unto you, my servant Newel, you shall stand fast in the office wherewith I have appointed you:

3 And if your brethren desire to escape their enemies let them repent of all their sins, and become truly humble before me and contrite:

4 And as the covenant which they made unto me, has been broken, even so it has become void and of none effect;

5 And wo to him by whom this offence cometh, for it had been better for him that he had been drowned in the depth of the sea;

6 But blessed are they who have kept the covenant, and observed the commandment, for they shall obtain mercy:

7 Wherefore, go to now and flee the land, lest your enemies come upon you:

8 And take your journey, and appoint whom you will to be your leader, and to pay moneys for you.

9 And thus you shall take your journey into the regions westward, unto the land of Missouri, unto the borders of the Lamanites.

10 And after you have done journeying, behold I say unto you, seek ye a living like unto men, until I prepare a place for you.

11 And again, be patient in tribulation until I come:

12 And behold I come quickly, and my reward is with me, and they who have sought me early, shall find rest to their souls; even so: Amen.

CHAPTER LVII.

A Revelation to William, given in Kirtland, Ohio, June, 1831.

BEHOLD thus saith the Lord unto you, my servant William; yea, even the Lord of the whole earth,

2 Thou art called and chosen and after thou hast

been baptized by water, which if you do with an eye single to my glory, you shall have a remission of your sins, and a reception of the Holy Spirit, by the laying on of hands:

3 And then thou shalt be ordained by the hand of my servant Joseph, to be an elder unto this church, to preach repentance and remission of sins by way of baptism in the name of Jesus Christ, the Son of the living God;

4 And on whomsoever you shall lay your hands, if they are contrite before me, you shall have power to give the Holy Spirit.

5 And again, you shall be ordained to assist my servant Oliver to do the work of printing, and of selecting, and writing books for schools, in this church, that little children also may receive instruction before me as is pleasing unto me.

6 And again verily I say unto you, for this cause you shall take your journey with my servants Joseph and Sidney, that you may be planted in the land of your inheritance, to do this work.

7 And again let my servant Joseph (C.) also take his journey with them.

8 The residue shall be made known hereafter; even as I will: Amen.

CHAPTER LVIII.

A Revelation to the church, and certain elders, given in Kirtland, Ohio, June, 1831.

HEARKEN O ye people which profess my name, saith the Lord your God, for behold mine anger is kindled against the rebellious, and they shall know mine arm and mine indignation in the day of visitation and of wrath upon the nations.

2 And he that will not take up his cross and follow me, and keep my commandments, the same shall not be saved.

3 Behold I the Lord commandeth, and he that will not obey shall be cut off in mine own due time:

4 And after that I have commanded and the commandment is broken, wherefore I the Lord command and revoke, as it seemeth me good; and all this to be answered upon the heads of the rebellious saith the Lord:

5 Wherefore I revoke the commandment which was given unto my servants Thomas and Ezra, and give a new commandment unto my servant Thomas, that he shall take up his journey speedily to the land of Missouri;

6 And my servant Selah shall also go with him:

7 For behold I revoke the commandment which was given unto my servants Selah and Newel, in consequence of the stiffneckedness of my people which are in Thompson; and their rebellions:

8 Wherefore let my servant Newel remain with them, and as many as will go may go, that are contrite before me   and which

                              that my ser-
                              nd of his self-
                              ndment which
                              ace upon which

                              e shall be no di-
                              all be appointed

                              the money which he

has paid, and shall leave the place, and shall be cut off out of my church, saith the Lord God of hosts:

12 And though the heaven and the earth pass away, these words shall not pass away, but shall be fulfilled.

13 And if my servant Joseph must needs pay the money, behold I the Lord will pay it unto him again in the land of Missouri, that those of whom he shall receive may be rewarded again, according to that which they do.

14 For according to that which they do, they shall receive; even in lands for their inheritance.

15 Behold thus saith the Lord unto my people, you have many things to do, and to repent of:

16 For behold your sins have come up unto me, and are not pardoned, because you seek to counsel in your own ways.

17 And your hearts are not satisfied.

18 And ye obey not the truth, but have pleasure in unrighteousness.

19 Wo unto you rich men, that will not give your substance to the poor, for your riches will canker your souls! and this shall be your lamentation in the day of visitation, and of judgment, and of indignation:

20 The harvest is past, the summer is ended, and my soul is not saved!

21 Wo unto you poor men, whose hearts are not broken, whose spirits are not contrite, and whose bellies are not satisfied, and whose hands are not stayed from laying hold upon other men's goods, whose eyes are full of greediness, who will not labor with their own hands!

22 But blessed are the poor, who are pure in heart, whose hearts are broken, and whose spirits are con-

trite, for they shall see the kingdom of God coming in power and great glory unto their deliverance:

23 For the fatness of the earth shall be theirs:

24 For behold the Lord shall .come, and his recompense shall be with him, and he shall reward every man, and the poor shall rejoice: and their generations shall inherit the earth from generation to generation, for ever and ever.

25 And now I make an end of speaking unto you; even so: Amen.

CHAPTER LIX.

A Revelation to the elders of the church, assembled on the land of Zion, given August, 1831.

HEARKEN O ye elders of my church, and give ear to my word, and learn of me what I will concerning you, and also concerning this land unto which I have sent you:

2 For verily I say unto you, blessed is he that keepeth my commandments, whether in life or in death;

3 And he that is faithful in tribulation the reward of the same is greater in the kingdom of heaven.

4 Ye can not behold with your natural eyes, for the present time, the design of your God concerning those things which shall come hereafter, and the glory which shall follow, after much tribulation.

5 For after much tribulation cometh the blessings.

6 Wherefore, the day cometh that ye shall be crowned with much glory, the hour is not yet but is nigh at hand.

7 Remember this which I tell you before, that you may lay it to heart, and receive that which shall

follow. Behold, verily I say unto you, for this cause I have sent you that you might be obedient, and that your hearts might be prepared to bear testimony of the things which are to come;

8 And also, that you might be honored of laying the foundation, and of bearing record of the land upon which the Zion of God shall stand;

9 And also, that a feast of fat things might be prepared for the poor;

10 Yea a feast of fat things, of wine on the lees well refined, that the earth may know that the mouths of the prophets shall not fail;

11 Yea, a supper of the house of the Lord, well prepared, unto which all nations shall be invited.

12 Firstly the rich, and the learned, the wise and the noble;

13 And after that cometh the day of my power:

14 Then shall the poor, the lame and the blind, and the deaf, come in unto the marriage of the Lamb, and partake of the supper of the Lord, prepared for the great day to come.

15 Behold I the Lord have spoken it.

16 And that the testimony might go forth from Zion; yea from the mouth of the city of the heritage of God:

17 Yea, for this cause I have sent you hither;

18 And have selected my servant Edward and appointed unto him his mission in this land:

19 But if he repent not of his sins, which are unbelief and blindness of heart, let him take heed lest he fall.

20 Behold his mission is given unto him and it shall not be given again.

21 And whoso standeth in this mission, is appointed to be a judge in Israel, like as it was in ancient

days, to divide the lands of the heritage of God unto his children; and to judge his people by the testimony of the just, and by the assistance of his counsellors, according to the laws of the kingdom which are given by the prophets of God:

22 For verily I say unto you, my laws shall be kept on this land.

23 Let no man think that he is ruler, but let God rule him that judgeth, according to the counsel of his own will:

24 Or in other words, him that counselleth, or sitteth upon the judgment seat.

25 Let no man break the laws of the land, for he that keepeth the laws of God, hath no need to break the laws of the land:

26 Wherefore be subject to the powers that be, until He reigns whose right it is to reign, and subdues all enemies under his feet.

27 Behold the laws which ye have received from my hand, are the laws of the church;

28 And in this light ye shall hold them forth.

29 Behold here is wisdom.

30 And now as I spake concerning my servant Edward: this land is the land of his residence, and those whom he has appointed for his counsellors.

31 And also the land of the residence of him whom I have appointed to keep my storehouse:

32 Wherefore let them bring their families to this land, as they shall counsel between themselves and me:

33 For behold it is not meet that I should command in all things, for he that is compelled in all things, the same is a slothful and not a wise servant;

34 Wherefore he receiveth no reward.

35 Verily I say, men should be anxiously engaged

in a good cause, and do many things of their own free will, and bring to pass much righteousness:

36 For the power is in them, wherein they are agents unto themselves.

37 And inasmuch as men do good, they shall in no wise loose their reward.

38 But he that doeth not any thing until he is commanded, and receiveth a commandment with doubtful heart, and keepeth it with slothfulness, the same is damned.

39 Who am I that made man, saith the Lord, that will hold him guiltless, that obey not my commandments?

40 Who am I, saith the Lord, that have promised and have not fulfilled?

41 I command and a man obeys not, I revoke and they receive not the blessing:

42 Then they say in their hearts, this is not the work of the Lord, for his promises are not fulfilled.

43 But wo unto such, for their reward lurketh beneath, and not from above.

44 And now I give unto you further directions concerning this land.

45 It is wisdom in me, that my servant Martin should be an example unto the church, in laying his moneys before the bishop of the church.

46 And also, this is a law unto every man that cometh unto this land, to receive an inheritance;

47 And he shall do with his moneys according as the law directs.

48 And it is wisdom also, that there should be lands purchased in Independence, for the place of the storehouse:

49 And also for the house of the printing.

50 And other directions, concerning my servant Martin, shall be given him of the Spirit, that he may receive his inheritance as seemeth him good. And let him repent of his sins, for he seeketh the praise of the world.

51 And also let my servant William stand in the office which I have appointed him, and receive his inheritance in the land.

52 And also, he hath need to repent, for I the Lord am not pleased with him, for he seeketh to excel, and he is not sufficiently meek before me.

53 Behold he who has repented of his sins the same is forgiven, and I the Lord remembereth them no more.

54 By this ye may know if a man repenteth of his sins.

55 Behold he will confess them and forsake them.

56 And now verily I say, concerning the residue of the elders of my church, the time has not yet come for many years, for them to receive their inheritance in this land; except they desire it through prayer, only as it shall be appointed unto them of the Lord.

57 For behold they shall push the people together from the ends of the earth:

58 Wherefore assemble yourselves together, and they who are not appointed to stay in this land, let them preach the gospel in the regions round about;

59 And after that, let them return to their homes.

60 Let them preach by the way, and bear testimony of the truth in all places, and call upon the rich, the high, and the low, and the poor, to repent;

61 And let them build up churches inasmuch as the inhabitants of the earth will repent.

62 And let there be an agent appointed by the

voice of the church, unto the church in Ohio, to receive moneys to purchase lands in Zion.

63 And I give unto my servant Sidney a commandment, that he shall write a description of the land of Zion, and a statement of the will of God, as it shall be made known by the Spirit, unto him; and an epistle and subscription, to be presented unto all the churches, to obtain moneys, to be put into the hands of the bishop, to purchase lands for an inheritance for the children of God, of himself or the agent, as seemeth him good, or as he shall direct.

· 64 For behold, verily I say unto you, the Lord willeth that the disciples, and the children of men, should open their hearts, even to purchase this whole region of country, as soon as time will permit.

65 Behold here is wisdom; let them do this lest they receive none inheritance, save it be by the shedding of blood.

66 And again, inasmuch as there is land obtained, let there be workmen sent forth, of all kinds, unto this land, to labor for the saints of God.

67 Let all these things be done in order.

68 And let the privileges of the lands be made known from time to time, by the bishop, or the agent of the church.

69 And let the work of the gathering be not in haste, nor by flight, but let it be done as it shall be counselled by the elders of the church at the conferences, according to the knowledge which they ceive from time to time.

70 And let my servant Sidney consecrate and icate this land, and the spot of the temple, v Lord.

71 And let a conference meeting be cal after that, let my servant Sidney and Josep

and also Oliver with them, to accomplish the residue of the work, which I have appointed unto them in their own land:

72 And the residue as shall be ruled by the conferences.

73 And let no man return from this land, except he bear record by the way, of that which he knows and most assuredly believes.

74 Let that which has been bestowed upon Ziba, be taken from him:

75 And let him stand as a member in the church, and labor with his own hands, with the brethren, until he is sufficiently chastened for all his sins, for he confesseth them not, and he thinketh to hide them.

76 Let the residue of the elders of this church, which are coming to this land, some of whom are exceedingly blessed even above measure, also, hold a conference upon this land.

77 And let my servant Edward direct the conference, which shall be held by them.

78 And let them also return, preaching the gospel by the way, bearing record of the things which are revealed unto them:

79 For verily the sound must go forth from this place into all the world;

80 And unto the uttermost parts of the earth, the gospel must be preached unto every creature, with signs following them that believe.

81 And behold the Son of man cometh: Amen.

CHAPTER LX.

A Revelation to the church, given in Zion, August, 1831

BEHOLD, blessed saith the Lord, are they who have come up unto this land with an eye single to my glory, according to my commandments:

2 For them that live shall inherit the earth, and them that die shall rest from all their labors, and their works shall follow them, and they shall receive a crown in the mansions of my Father, which I have prepared for them;

3 Yea, blessed are they whose feet stand upon the land of Zion, who have obeyed my gospel, for they shall receive for their reward the good things of the earth;

4 And it shall bring forth in its strength:

5 And they also shall be crowned with blessings from above;

6 Yea and with commandments not a few;

7 And with revelations in their time:

8 They that are faithful and diligent before me:

9 Wherefore I give unto them a commandment, saying thus:

10 Thou shalt love the Lord thy God with all thy heart, with all thy might, mind, and strength:

11 And in the name of Jesus Christ thou shalt serve him.

12 Thou shalt love thy neighbor as thyself.

13 Thou shalt not steal.

14 Neither commit adultery, nor kill, nor do any thing like unto it.

15 Thou shalt thank the Lord thy God in all things.

16 Thou shalt offer a sacrifice unto the Lord thy God in righteousness:

17 Even that of a broken heart and a contrite spirit.

18 And that thou mayest more fully keep thyself unspotted from the world, thou shalt go to the house of prayer and offer up thy sacraments upon my holy day:

19 For verily this is a day appointed unto you to rest from your labors, and to pay thy devotions unto the Most High;

20 Nevertheless thy vows shall be offered up in righteousness on all days, and at all times;

21 But remember that on this, the Lord's day, thou shalt offer thine oblations, and thy sacraments, unto the Most High, confessing thy sins unto thy brethren, and before the Lord.

22 And on this day thou shalt do none other thing, only let thy food be prepared with singleness of heart, that thy fasting may be perfect, or in other words, that thy joy may be full.

23 Verily this is fasting and prayer; or, in other words, rejoicing and prayer.

24 And inasmuch as ye do these things with thanksgiving, with cheerful hearts, and countenances, not with much laughter, for this is sin, but with a glad heart, and a cheerful countenance;

25 Verily I say, that inasmuch as ye do this the fulness of the earth is yours:

26 The beasts of the fields, and the fowls of the air, and that which climbeth upon the trees, and walketh upon the earth:

27 Yea, and the herb, and the good things which cometh of the earth, whether for food or for raiment, or for houses, or for barns, or for orchards, or for gardens, or for vineyards:

28 Yea, all things which cometh of the earth, in

the season thereof, is made for the benefit and the use of man, both to please the eye, and to gladden the heart:

29 Yea, for food and for raiment, for taste, and for smell, to strengthen the body, and to enliven the soul.

30 And it pleaseth God that he hath given all these things unto man:

31 For unto this end were they made, to be used with judgment, not to excess, neither by extortion:

32 And in nothing doth man offend God, or against none is his wrath kindled, save those who confess not his hand in all things, and obey not his commandments.

33 Behold this is according to the law and the prophets:

34 Wherefore trouble me no more concerning this matter, but learn that he who doeth the works of righteousness, shall receive his reward, even peace in this world, and eternal life in the world to come.

35 I the Lord have spoken it and the spirit beareth record. Amen.

CHAPTER LXI.

A Revelation to the elders of the church, given in Zion, August, 1831.

BEHOLD, thus saith the Lord unto the elders of his church, who are to return speedily to the land from whence they came.

2 Behold it pleaseth me, that you have come up hither;

3 But with some I am not well pleased, for they

will not open their mouths, but hide the talent which I have given unto them, because of the fear of man.

4 Wo unto such, for mine anger is kindled against them.

5 And it shall come to pass, if they are not more faithful unto me, it shall be taken away, even that which they have, for I the Lord ruleth in the heavens above, and among the armies of the earth;

6 And in the day when I shall make up my jewels, all men shall know what it is that bespeaketh the power of God.

7 But verily I will speak unto you concerning your journey unto the land from whence you came.

8 Let there be a craft made, or bought, as seemeth you good, it mattereth not unto me, and take your journey speedily for the place which is called St. Louis.

9 And from thence let my servants Sidney and Joseph and Oliver, take their journey for Cincinnati:

10 And in this place let them lift up their voice, and declare my word with loud voices, without wrath or doubting, lifting up holy hands upon them.

11 For I am able to make you holy, and your sins are forgiven you.

12 And let the residue take their journey from St. Louis, two by two, and preach the word, not in haste, among the congregations of the wicked, until they return to the churches from whence they came.

13 And all this for the good of the churches; for this intent have I sent them.

14 And let my servant Edward impart of the money which I have given him, a portion unto mine el-

ders, which are commanded to return : and he that is able, let him return it by the way of the agent, and he that is not, of him it is not required.

15 And now I speak of the residue which are to come unto this land.

16 Behold they have been sent to preach my gospel among the congregations of the wicked :

17 Wherefore, I give unto them a commandment, thus :

18 Thou shalt not idle away thy time :

19 Neither shalt thou bury thy talent that it may not be known.

20 And after thou hast come up unto the land of Zion, and hast proclaimed my word, thou shalt speedily return proclaiming the word among the congregations of the wicked.

21 Not in haste, neither in wrath, nor with strife :

22 And shake off the dust of thy feet against those who receive thee not, not in their presence, lest thou provoke them, but in secret, and wash thy feet as a testimony against them in the day of judgment.

23 Behold this is sufficient for you, and the will of him who hath sent you.

24 And by the mouth of my servant Joseph, it shall be made known concerning Sidney and Oliver.

25 The residue hereafter; even so : Amen.

CHAPTER LXII.

A Revelation to eleven elders, given upon the bank of the Missouri river, August, 1831.

BEHOLD, and hearken unto the voice of him who has all power, who is from everlasting to everlasting, even Alpha and Omega, the beginning and the end.

2 Behold, verily thus saith the Lord unto you O ye elders of my church, who are assembled upon this spot, whose sins are now forgiven you, for I the Lord forgiveth sins, and am merciful unto those who confess their sins with humble hearts:

3 But verily I say unto you, that it is not needful for this whole company of mine elders, to be moving swiftly upon the waters, whilst the inhabitants on either side are perishing in unbelief:

4 Nevertheless, I suffered it that ye might bear record:

5 Behold there are many dangers upon the waters and more especially hereafter, for I the Lord have decreed, in mine anger, many destructions upon the waters;

6 Yea, and especially upon these waters;

7 Nevertheless, all flesh is in mine hand, and he that is faithful among you, shall not perish by the waters.

8 Wherefore it is expedient that my servant Sidney (G.) and my servant William be in haste upon their errand and mission:

9 Nevertheless I would not suffer that ye should part until you are chastened for all your sins, that you might be one;

10 That you might not perish in wickedness;

11 But now verily I say, it behooveth me that ye

should part: wherefore let my servants Sidney and Willliam, take their former company, and let them take their journey in haste that they may fill their mission, and through faith they shall overcome;

12 And inasmuch as they are faithful, they shall be preserved, and I the Lord will be with them.

13 And let the residue take that which is needful for clothing.

14 Let my servant Sidney take that which is not needful with him, as you shall agree.

15 And now behold, for your good I gave unto you a commandment concerning these things; and I the Lord will reason with you as with men in days of old.

16 Behold I the Lord in the beginning, blessed the waters, but in the last days by the mouth of my servant John, I cursed the waters:

17 Wherefore, the days will come that no flesh shall be safe upon the waters, and it shall be said in days to come, that none is able to go up to the land of Zion, upon the waters, but he that is upright in heart.

18 And, as I the Lord in the beginning cursed the land, even so in the last days have I blessed it, in its time, for the use of my saints, that they may partake the fatness thereof.

19 And now I give unto you a commandment, and what I say unto one I say unto all, that you shall forewarn your brethren concerning these waters, that they come not in journeying upon them, lest their faith fail and they are caught in her snares:

20 I the Lord have decreed, and the destroyer rideth upon the face thereof, and I revoke not the decree:

21 I the Lord was angry with you yesterday, but today mine anger is turned away:

22 Wherefore let those concerning whom I have spoken, that should take their journey in haste:

23 Again I say unto you, let them take their journey in haste, and it mattereth not unto me, after a little, if it so be that they fill their mission, whether they go by water or by land:

24 Let this be as it is made known unto them according to their judgments, hereafter.

25 And now, concerning my servants Sidney, and Joseph, and Oliver, let them come not again upon the waters, save it be upon the canal, while journeying unto their homes, or in other words they shall not come upon the waters to journey, save upon the canal.

26 Behold I the Lord have appointed a way for the journeying of my saints, and behold this is the way:

27 That after they leave the canal, they shall journey by land, inasmuch as they are commanded to journey and go up unto the land of Zion; and they shall do like unto the children of Israel, pitching their tents by the way.

28 And behold this commandment, you shall give unto all your brethren: nevertheless unto whom it is given power to command the waters, unto him it is given by the Spirit to know all his ways:

29 Wherefore let him do as the Spirit of the living God commandeth him, whether upon the land or upon the waters, as it remaineth with me to do hereafter;

30 And unto you it is given the course for the saints, or the way for the saints of the camp of the Lord, to journey.

31 And again, verily I say unto you, my servants Sidney, and Joseph, and Oliver, shall not open their mouths in the congregations of the wicked, until they arrive at Cincinnati;

32 And in that place they shall lift up their voices unto God against that people.

33 Yea, unto him whose anger is kindled against their wickedness; a people which is well nigh ripened for destruction;

34 And from thence let them journey for the congregations of their brethren, for their labors, even now, are wanted more abundantly among them, than among the congregations of the wicked.

35 And now concerning the residue, let them journey and declare the word among the congregations of the wicked, inasmuch as it is given, and inasmuch as they do this they shall rid their garments, and they shall be spotless before me;

36 And let them journey together, or two by two, as seemeth them good, only let my servant Reynolds, and my servant Samuel, with whom I am well pleased, be not separated until they return to their homes, and this for a wise purpose in me.

37 And now verily I say unto you, and what I say unto one I say unto all, be of good cheer little children for I am in your midst, and I have not forsaken you, and inasmuch as you have humbled yourselves before me, the blessings of the kingdom are yours:

38 Gird up your loins and be watchful, and be sober, looking forth for the coming of the Son of man, for he cometh in an hour you think not.

39 Pray always that you enter not into temptation, that you may abide the day of his coming, whether in life or in death; even so: Amen.

CHAPTER LXIII.

*A Revelation to certain elders, while journeying
to the land of Zion, given on the bank of the
Missouri river, August, 1831.*

BEHOLD and hearken, O ye elders of my
church, saith the Lord your God; even Jesus
Christ, your advocate who knoweth the weakness
of man and how to succor them who are tempted:

2 And verily mine eyes are upon those who have
not as yet gone up unto the land of Zion:

3 Wherefore your mission is not yet full:

4 Nevertheless ye are blessed, for the testimony
which ye have borne, is recorded in heaven for the
angels to look upon, and they rejoice over you; and
your sins are forgiven you.

5 And now continue your journey.

6 Assemble yourselves upon the land of Zion,
and hold a meeting and rejoice together, and offer
a sacrament unto the Most High;

7 And then you may return to bear record;

8 Yea, even all together, or two by two, as seemeth
you good;

9 It mattereth not unto me, only be faithful, and
declare glad tidings unto the inhabitants of the
earth, or among the congregations of the wicked.

10 Behold I the Lord have brought you together
that the promise might be fulfilled, that the faithful
among you should be preserved and rejoice together
in the land of Missouri.

11 I the Lord promised the faithful, and cannot
lie.

12 I the Lord am willing, if any among you desireth to ride upon horses, or upon mules, or in
chariots, shall receive this blessing, if he receive it

from the hand of the Lord, with a thankful heart in all things.

13 These things remain with you to do according to judgment and the directions of the Spirit.

14 Behold the kingdom is yours.

15 And behold, and lo I am with the faithful always; even so: Amen.

CHAPTER LXIV.

A Revelation given in Kirtland, Ohio, August, 1831.

HEARKEN O ye people, and open your hearts, and give ear from afar:

2 And listen, you that call yourselves the people of the Lord, and hear the word of the Lord, and his will concerning you:

3 Yea, verily I say, hear the word of him whose anger is kindled against the wicked, and rebellious; who willeth to take even them whom he will take, and preserveth in life them whom he will preserve:

4 Who buildeth up at his own will and pleasure; and destroyeth when he please; and is able to cast the soul down to hell.

5 Behold I the Lord uttereth my voice, and it shall be obeyed.

6 Wherefore verily I say, let the wicked take heed, and let the rebellious fear, and tremble.

7 And let the unbelieving hold their lips, for the day of wrath shall come upon them as a whirlwind, and all flesh shall know that I am God.

8 And he that seeketh signs shall see signs, but not unto salvation.

9 Verily I say unto you, there are those among you, who seeketh signs; and there have been such even from the beginning.

10 But behold, faith cometh not by signs, but signs follow those that believe.

11 Yea, signs cometh by faith, not by the will of men, nor as they please, but by the will of God.

12 Yea, signs cometh by faith, unto mighty works, for without faith no man pleaseth God: and with whom God is angry, he is not well pleased:

13 Wherefore, unto such he sheweth no signs, only in wrath unto their condemnation.

14 Wherefore I the Lord am not pleased with those among you, who have sought after signs and wonders for faith, and not for the good of men unto my glory:

15 Nevertheless, I gave commandments and many have turned away from my commandments, and have not kept them.

16 There were among you adulterers and adulteresses; some of whom have turned away from you, and others remain with you, that hereafter shall be revealed.

17 Let such beware and repent speedily, lest judgments shall come upon them as a snare, and their folly shall be made manifest, and their works shall follow them in the eyes of the people.

18 And verily I say unto you, as I have said before, he that looketh on a woman to lust after her, or if any shall commit adultery in their hearts, they shall not have the spirit, but shall deny the faith and shall fear:

19 Wherefore I the Lord have said that the fearful and the unbelieving, and all liars, and whosoever loveth and maketh a lie, and the whoremonger, and

the sorcerer, should have their part in that lake which burneth with fire and brimstone, which is the second death.

20 Verily I say, that they shall not have part in the first resurrection.

21 And now behold, I the Lord saith unto you, that ye are not justified because these things are among you, nevertheless he that endureth in faith and doeth my will, the same shall overcome, and shall receive an inheritance upon the earth, when the day of transfiguration shall come;

22 When the earth shall be transfigured, even according to the pattern which was shown unto mine apostles upon the mount:

23 Of which account the fulness ye have not yet received.

24 And now, verily I say unto you, that as I said that I would make known my will unto you, behold I will make it known unto you, not by the way of commandment, for there are many who observe not to keep my commandments, but unto him that keepeth my commandments, I will give the mysteries of my kingdom, and the same shall be in him a well of living water, springing up unto everlasting life.

25 And now, behold this is the will of the Lord your God concerning his saints, that they should assemble themselves together unto the land of Zion, not in haste, lest there should be confusion, which bringeth pestilence.

26 Behold the land of Zion, I the Lord holdeth it in mine own hands:

27 Nevertheless, I the Lord rendereth unto Cæsar the things which are Cæsar's:

28 Wherefore I the Lord willeth, that you should

purchase the lands, that you may have advantage of the world, that you may have claim on the world, that they may not be stirred up unto anger: ‐

29 For satan putteth it into their hearts to anger against you, and to the shedding of blood:

30 Wherefore the land of Zion shall not be obtained but by purchase, or by blood, otherwise there is none inheritance for you.

31 And if by purchase behold you are blessed;

32 And if by blood, as you are forbidden to shed blood, lo, your enemies are upon you, and ye shall be scourged from city to city, and from synagogue to synagogue, and but few shall stand to receive an inheritance.

33 I the Lord am angry with the wicked;

34 I am holding my Spirit from the inhabitants of the earth.

35 I have sworn in my wrath and decreed wars upon the face of the earth, and the wicked shall slay the wicked, and fear shall come upon every man and the saints also shall hardly escape:

36 Nevertheless, I the Lord am with them, and will come down in heaven from the presence of God, and consume the wicked with unquenchable fire.

37 And behold this is not yet, but by and by;

38 Wherefore seeing that I the Lord have decreed all these things upon the face of the earth, I willeth that my saints should be assembled upon the land of Zion;

39 And that every man should take righteousness in his hands, and faithfulness upon his loins, and lift a warning voice unto the inhabitants of the earth;

40 And declare both by word and by flight, that desolation shall come upon the wicked.

41 Wherefore let my disciples in Kirtland, arrange their temporal concerns, which dwell upon this farm.

42 Let my servant Titus, who has the care thereof dispose of the land, that he may be prepared in the coming spring, to take his journey up unto the land of Zion, with those that dwell upon the face thereof, excepting those whom I shall reserve unto myself, that shall not go until I shall command them.

43 And let all the moneys which can be spared, it mattereth not unto me whether it be little or much, sent up unto the land of Zion, unto them whom I have appointed to receive.

44 Behold I the Lord, will give unto my servant Joseph power, that he shall be enabled to discern by the Spirit those who shall go up unto the land of Zion, and those of my disciples who shall tarry.

45 Let my servant Newel retain his store, or in other words, the store yet for a little season.

46 Nevertheless let him impart all the money which he can impart, to be sent up unto the land of Zion.

47 Behold these things are in his own hands, let him do according to wisdom.

48 Verily I say, let him be ordained as an agent unto the disciples that shall tarry, and let him be ordained unto this power;

49 And now speedily visit the churches, expounding these things unto them, with my servant Oliver.

50 Behold this is my will, obtaining moneys even as I have directed.

51 He that is faithful and endureth shall overcome the world.

52 He that sendeth up treasures unto the land of Zion, shall receive an inheritance in this world, and

his works shall follow him; and also, a reward in the world to come;

53 Yea, and blessed are the dead that die in the Lord from henceforth, when the Lord shall come and old things shall pass away, and all things become new, they shall rise from the dead and shall not die, and shall receive an inheritance before the Lord, in the holy city, and he that liveth when the Lord shall come, and have kept the faith, blessed is he;

54 Nevertheless it is appointed to·him to die at the age of man:

55 Wherefore children shall grow up until they become old, old men shall die;

56 But they shall not sleep in the dust, but they shall be changed in the twinkling of an eye:

57 Wherefore, for this cause preached the apostles unto the world, the resurrection of the dead:

58 These things are the things that ye must look for, and speaking after the manner of the Lord, they are now nigh at hand;

59 And in a time to come, even in the day of the coming of the Son of man, and until that hour, there will be foolish virgins among the wise, and at that hour cometh an entire separation of the righteous and the wicked;

60 And in that day will I send mine angels, to pluck out the wicked, and cast them into unquenchable fire.

61 And now behold, verily I say unto you, I the Lord am not pleased with my servant Sidney, he exalted himself in his heart, and received not counsel, but grieved the Spirit:

62 Wherefore his writing is not acceptable unto the Lord, and he shall make another;

63 And if the Lord receive it not, behold he standeth no longer in the office which I have appointed him.

64 And again: verily I say unto you, let those who desire in their hearts, in meekness, to warn sinners to repentance, let them be ordained unto this power;

65 For this is a day of warning, and not a day of many words.

66 For I the Lord am not to be mocked in the last days.

67 Behold I am from above, and my power lieth beneath.

68 I am over all, and in all, and through all, and searcheth all things:

69 And the days cometh that all things shall be subject unto me.

70 Behold I am Alpha and Omega, even Jesus Christ.

71 Wherefore let all men beware, how they take my name in their lips:

72 For behold, verily I say, that many there be who are under this condemnation;

73 Who useth the name of the Lord, and useth it in vain, having not authority.

74 Wherefore let the church repent of their sins, and I the Lord will own them, otherwise they shall be cut off.

75 Remember, that that which cometh from above is sacred, and must be spoken with care, and by constraint of the Spirit, and in this there is no condemnation; and ye receive the Spirit through prayer:

76 Wherefore without this, there remaineth condemnation:

77 Let my servants Joseph and Sidney, seek them

a home as they are taught through prayer, by the Spirit.

78 These things remain to overcome, through patience, that such may receive a more exceeding and eternal weight of glory;

79 Otherwise, a greater condemnation: Amen.

CHAPTER LXV.

A Revelation to the elders of the church, given in Kirtland, Ohio, September, 1831.

BEHOLD, thus saith the Lord your God unto you, O ye elders of my church, hearken ye, and hear, and receive my will concerning you:

2 For verily I say unto you, I will that ye should overcome the world:

3 Wherefore I will have compassion upon you.

4 There are those among you who have sinned;

5 But verily I say, for this once, for mine own glory, and for the salvation of souls, I have forgiven you your sins.

6 I will be merciful unto you, for I have given unto you the kingdom:

7 And the keys of the mysteries of the kingdom, shall not be taken from my servant Joseph, while he liveth, inasmuch as he obeyeth mine ordinances.

8 There are those who have sought occasion against him without cause;

9 Nevertheless he has sinned, but verily I say unto you, I the Lord forgiveth sins unto those who confess their sins before me, and ask forgiveness, who have not sinned unto death.

10 My disciples, in days of old, sought occasion

against one another, and forgave not one another in their hearts, and for this evil they were afflicted, and sorely chastened :

11 Wherefore I say unto you, that ye ought to forgive one another, for he that forgiveth not his brother his trespasses, standeth condemned before the Lord, for there remaineth in him the greater sin.

12 I the Lord will forgive whom I will forgive, but of you it is required to forgive all men ;

13 And ye ought to say in your hearts, Let God judge between me and thee, and reward thee according to thy deeds.

14 And he that repenteth not of his sins, and confesseth them not, then ye shall bring him before the church, and do with him as the Scriptures saith unto you, either by commandment, or by revelation.

15 And this ye shall do that God might be glorified, not because ye forgive not, having not compassion, but that ye may be justified in the eyes of the law, that ye may not offend him who is your Lawgiver.

16 Verily I say, for this cause ye shall do these things.

17 Behold I the Lord was angry with him who was my servant Ezra (B.) ;

18 And also, my servant Isaac ; for they kept not the law, neither the commandment : they sought evil in their hearts, and I the Lord withheld my Spirit.

19 They condemned for evil, that thing in which there was no evil :

20 Nevertheless I have forgiven my servant Isaac.

21 And also my servant Edward, behold he hath sinned, and satan seeketh to destroy his soul ;

22 But when these things are made known unto

them, they repent of the evil, and they shall be forgiven.

23 And now verily I say, that it is expedient in me that my servant Sidney (G.) after a few weeks, should return upon his business, and to his agency in the land of Zion;

24 And that which he hath seen and heard may be made known unto my disciples, that they perish not.

25 And for this cause have I spoken these things.

26 And again, I say unto you, that my servant Isaac may not be tempted above that which he is able to bear, and counsel wrongfully to your hurt, I gave commandment that this farm should be sold.

27 I willeth not that my servant Frederick, should sell his farm, for I the Lord willeth to retain a strong hold in the land of Kirtland, for the space of five years, in the which I will not overthrow the wicked, that thereby I may save some;

28 And after that day, I the Lord will not hold any guilty, that shall go, with an open heart, up to the land of Zion:

29 For I the Lord requireth the hearts of the children of men.

30 Behold now it is called today, and verily it is a day of sacrifice, and a day for the tithing of my people;

31 For he that is tithed shall not be burned; for after today cometh the burning:

32 This is speaking after the manner of the Lord;

33 For verily I say, tomorrow all the proud and they that do wickedly shall be as stubble: and I will burn them up, for I am the Lord of hosts;

34 And I will not spare any that remaineth in Babylon.

35 Wherefore, if ye believe me, ye will labor while it is called today.

36 And it is not meet that my servants, Newel and Sidney (G.) should sell their store, and their possessions here, for this is not wisdom until the residue of the church, which remaineth in this place, shall go up unto the land of Zion.

37 Behold it is said in my laws, or forbidden to get in debt to thine enemies;

38 But behold it is not said at any time, that the Lord should not take when he please, and pay as seemeth him good :

39 Wherefore as ye are agents, and ye are on the Lord's errand; and whatever ye do according to the will of the Lord, is the Lord's business, and it is the Lord's business to provide for his saints in these last days, that they may obtain an inheritance in the land of Zion :

40 And behold I the Lord declare unto you, and my words are sure and shall not fail, that they shall obtain it;

41 But all things must come to pass in its time;

42 Wherefore be not weary in well doing, for ye are laying the foundation of a great work.

43 And out of small things proceedeth that which is great.

44 Behold the Lord requireth the heart and a willing mind;

45 And the willing and obedient shall eat the good of the land of Zion in these last days;

46 And the rebellious shall be cut off out of the land of Zion, and shall be sent away and shall not inherit the land :

47 For verily I say that the rebellious are not of the blood of Ephraim.

THE TEN COMMANDMENTS

I am the Lord thy God, which have brought thee out of the land of Egypt, out of the house of bondage. Thou shalt have no other gods before me. Thou shalt not make unto thee any graven image, or any likeness of any thing that is in heaven above, or that is in the earth beneath, or that is in the water under the earth: Thou shalt not bow down thyself to them, nor serve them: for I the Lord thy God am a jealous God, visiting the iniquity of the fathers upon the children unto the third and fourth generation of them that hate me; And shewing mercy unto thousands of them that love me, and keep my commandments. Thou shalt not take the name of the Lord thy God in vain; for the Lord will not hold him guiltless that taketh his name in vain. Remember the sabbath day, to keep it holy. Six days shalt thou labour, and do all thy work: But the seventh day is the sabbath of the Lord thy God: in it thou shalt not do any work, thou, nor thy son, nor thy daughter, thy manservant, nor thy maidservant, nor thy cattle, nor thy stranger that is within thy gates: For in six days the Lord made heaven and earth, the sea, and all that in them is, and rested the seventh day: wherefore the Lord blessed the sabbath day, and hallowed it. Honour thy father and thy mother: that thy days may be long upon the land which the Lord thy God giveth thee. Thou shalt not kill. Thou shalt not commit adultery. Thou shalt not steal. Thou shalt not bear false witness against thy neighbour. Thou shalt not covet thy neighbour's house, thou shalt not covet thy neighbour's wife, nor his manservant, nor his maidservant, nor his ox, nor his ass, nor any thing that is thy neighbour's.

THE LORD'S PRAYER

Our Father which art in heaven, Hallowed be thy name. Thy kingdom come. Thy will be done in earth, as it is in heaven. Give us this day our daily bread. And forgive us our debts, as we forgive our debtors. And lead us not into temptation, but deliver us from evil: For thine is the kingdom, and the power, and the glory, for ever. A'men.

ARTICLES OF FAITH

The Articles of Faith in this volume are the most complete of the seven that have been found in the old published records. These Articles of Faith contain four of the most vital doctrines taught by the Prophet Joseph Smith. In Article 4, it refers to the most sacred ordinance so necessary after baptism and confirmation, *The Lord's Supper*. In Article 7 it refers to *Powers & Gifts* and that most important gift used so much by the Master, *Discernment of Spirits*. In Article 9, it refers to that great event, *Messiah's Second Coming*. Number 11 in this Articles of Faith refers to the *literal resurrection of the body that the dead in Christ will rise first and that the rest of the dead live not again until the thousand years are expired*. This Articles of Faith numbers 14. It is easy to believe that these most important principles were taught and believed in by the Prophet Joseph Smith in his great work of restoring the fullness of the Gospel in this last dispensation.

This volume is printed to help bring back to life the great work of the Prophet Joseph Smith in the foundation of this Church so that it can be understood today as though it happened yesterday and continue to live through the eternities of tomorrow.

Wilford C. Wood

Jesus of Nazareth — an original oil painting
© Wilford C. Wood 1958

JESUS THE CHRIST

This picture of Christ represents Christ as a carpenter; Christ driving the money changers from the temple; and Christ looking so much like his apostles who were men, that He was betrayed by Judas for identification.

This is not a picture of His greatness and glory, which could not be printed or painted.

No picture could show the glorious person of the crucified, risen Redeemer, neither could the natural eye look upon the majesty of His divine presence.

He had eyes, ears, nose, mouth and a beautiful head of hair. This picture represents the reality of Christ, the Man of Galilee, our Elder Brother.

From my understanding and knowledge, it has vision, character, with power of decision and greatness of the only begotten Son of our Heavenly Father.

It shows the authority of the Redeemer of the world and those He has chosen, appointed and ordained to represent Him on the earth.

"This do ye in remembrance of Him."

LEST WE FORGET.

Wilford C. Wood

Joseph Smith the Prophet as a young man. An oil painting made during the life of the Prophet, found by Wilford Wood in the Icarian Building on the Nauvoo Temple Block.

THE ARTICLES OF FAITH OF
THE CHURCH OF JESUS CHRIST
OF LATTER-DAY SAINTS

1. We believe in God the eternal Father, and his son Jesus Christ, and in the Holy Ghost.

2. We believe that men will be punished for their own sins, and not for Adam's transgressions.

3. We believe that through the atonement of Christ all mankind may be saved, by obedience to the laws and ordinances of the Gospel.

4. We believe that these ordinances are: 1st, Faith in the Lord Jesus Christ; 2nd, Repentance; 3rd, Baptism by immersion for the remission of sins; 4th, Laying on of hands for the gift of the Holy Spirit; 5th, The Lord's Supper.

5. We believe that men must be called of God by inspiration, and by laying on of hands by those who are duly commissioned to preach the Gospel, and administer in the ordinances thereof.

6. We believe in the same organization that existed in the primitive church, viz., apostles, prophets, pastors, teachers, evangelists, etc.

7. We believe in the powers and gifts of the everlasting Gospel, viz., the gift of faith, discerning of spirits, prophecy, revelation, visions, healing, tongues, and the interpretation of tongues, wisdom, charity, brotherly love, etc.

8. We believe in the Word of God recorded in the Bible; we also believe the Word of God recorded in the Book of Mormon, and in all other good books.

9. We believe all that God has revealed; all that he does now reveal; and we believe that he will yet reveal many more great and important things pertaining to the Kingdom of God, and Messiah's second coming.

10. We believe in the literal gathering of Israel, and in the restoration of the ten tribes; that Zion will be established upon the western continent; that Christ will reign personally upon the earth a thousand years; and that the earth will be renewed, and receive its paradisaical glory.

11. We believe in the literal resurrection of the body, and that the dead in Christ will rise first, and that the rest of the dead live not again until the thousand years are expired.

12. We claim the privilege of worshipping Almighty God according to the dictates of our conscience unmolested, and allow all men the same privilege, let them worship how or where they may.

13. We believe in being subject to kings, queens, presidents, rulers, and magistrates, in obeying, honoring, and sustaining the law.

14. We believe in being honest, true, chaste, temperate, benevolent, virtuous, and upright, and in doing good to all men; indeed, we may say that we follow the admonition of Paul, we 'believe all things,' we 'hope all things,' 'we have endured very many things,' and hope to be able to 'endure all things.' Everything virtuous, lovely, praiseworthy, and of good report, we seek after, looking forward to the 'recompense of reward.'

JOSEPH SMITH

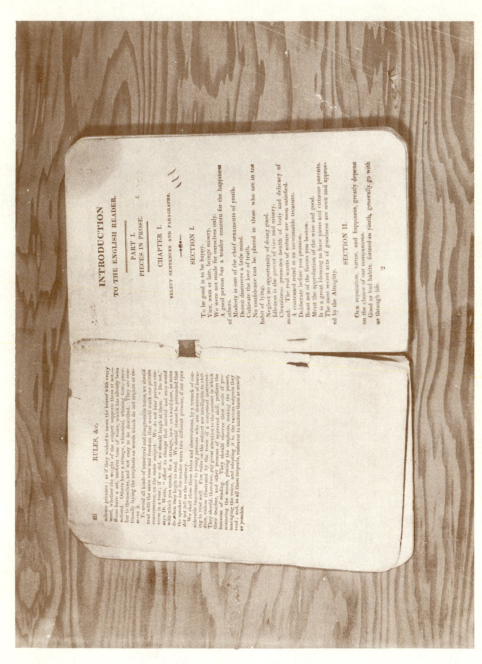

READING—Three School Books Used by the Prophet Joseph Smith

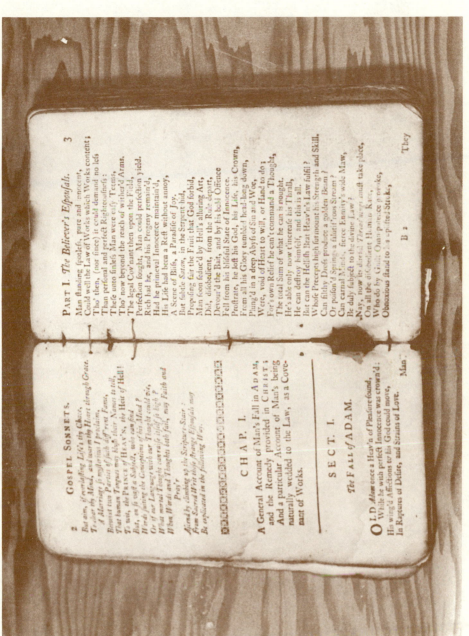

WRITING—Three School Books Used by the Prophet Joseph Smith

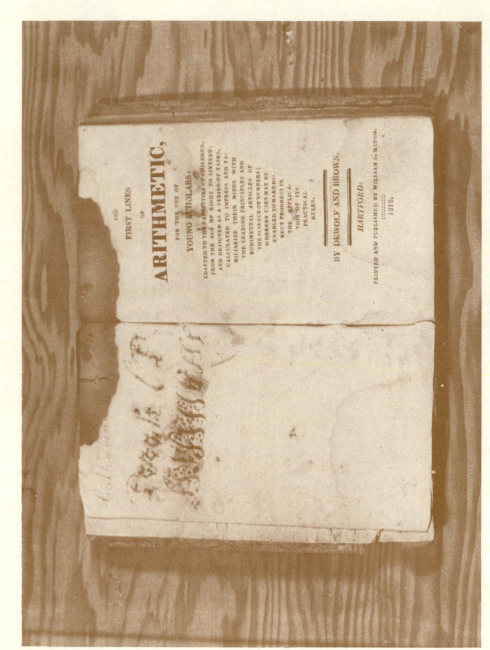

ARITHMETIC—Three School Books Used by the Prophet Joseph Smith

The Hill Cumorah

Monument at mother's home of learning, Bountiful, Utah. The monument represents Joseph Smith receiving the plates from the Angel Moroni.

Wilford Wood examines historic box used by the Prophet Joseph Smith to contain the gold plates, breast plate and urim and thummim. The Prophet Joseph Smith borrowed this box from his brother, Hyrum Smith, until a box was made for this special purpose. It has been preserved by and is now in possession of the descendants of Hyrum Smith.

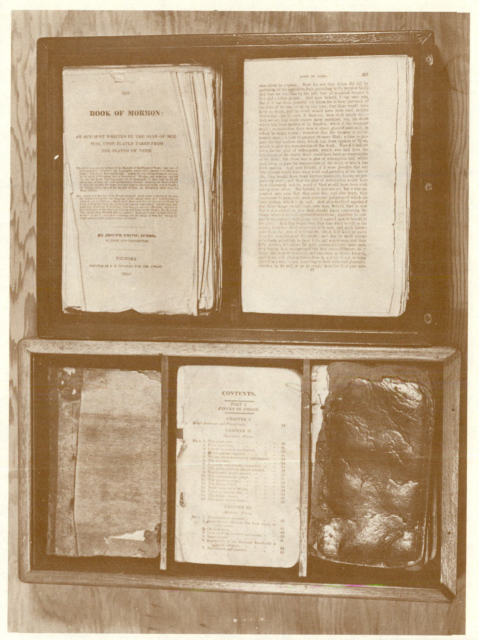

1830 Book of Mormon
Joseph Smith's Three School Books, Reading, Writing & Arithmetic

OAKLAND

Scale 200 Rods to the inch

Susquehanna Depot and Oakland Business Notices

Attorneys

Hinds L. F...Attorney at Law
Post Wm. M...Attorney at Law

Agents

Barber J. D...Genl Insurance Agent
Conklin E. C...Agent Agricultural Implements, &c

Banks

First National Bank, of Susquehanna Depot...Henry W. Brandt, Prest, J. H. Cook, Vice Prest, Myron B. Wright, Cashier
Curtis & Miller, Bankers. Particular attention paid to the collection of Notes, Checks, Bills, &c, Government and other Stocks promptly executed for the usual Commission

Baker

Prendergast M. J...Baker and Confectioner, Choice Cigars and Fruits of all kinds in their season

Clergymen

Brooks P. H...Presbyterian Clergyman
O'Reilly J. V...Pastor of St John's Church, Susquehanna Depot, St. Lawrence Church, Great Bend and St. John's Church, New Milford
Phelps O...Clergyman. Res, Dist No. 4 Oakland

Hotels

Ketchum W. D...Propr of Canewacta House
Whitney F. M...Propr of Hotchkiss House

Livery Stable

Taylor M. J. & J. B...Livery, Sale and Feed Stable

Merchants

Allen Joseph...Cigar Manufr and Dealer in Choice Brands, Tobacco, &c, Ladies and Gents Oyster and Ice Cream Saloon
Crandall G. H...Dealer in Groceries, Provisions, Glass-Ware and Crockery, Main St, near Post Office
Casey D...Dealer Extra Family Flour, Teas, Coffees, Sugars, Wines and Liquors, Main St
Drake J. G...Dealer in Doors, Sash, Blinds, Mouldings, &c, &c, all from the choicest selected lumber. A general assortment of Builder's Material Constantly on hand, 29 East Main St
Frazier Geo. T...Wholesale Dealer in Flour, Feed, Meal, Grain, &c, East Main St
Foot J. O...Dry Goods, Clothing, Gloves, Hosiery, Notions, Trunks, Valises, &c, &c, Main St
Forbes Mrs. E. R...Dry Goods, Groceries, Notions, Crockery, Glass-ware and General assortment, Broad St
Gillet U. R...Dealer in Tinn Groceries, East Main St, Cash paid for Country Produce
Gilbert & Slocum...Dealers in all kinds of Fresh Meats, Poultry, Sausage, Eggs, Hides, Calf Skins, Pelts, Tallow, &c
Guttenberg, Rosenbaum & Co...Manufrs and Dealers in Clothing, Dry Goods, Carpets, and Millinery, Main St, Susquehanna Depot. Manufactory, 108 Duane St, N. Y. City. Branch Stores, Elmira, N. Y. and Montrose Pa
McDonald & Kane...Wholesale and Retail Dealers in Flour, Groceries, Provisions, Teas, &c, Main St
McDonald Thomas...Choice Groceries and Provisions and best Brands of Flour, Main St
Mitchell W. S...Drugs, Medicines, Perfumery, Fancy Articles, &c, Physicians prescriptions carefully compounded, East Main St
Miller C. A...Jeweler and Dealer in American and Swiss Watches, Clocks, Pocket Cutlery, Violin Strings, Optical Goods, Silver and Plated Ware, &c, Main Street
McKernan Thomas...Dealers in Groceries, Provisions, Flour and Feed, Main St
Myers Maurice...Genl Grocery and Provision Store, Drinker St
Parkinsan A. C...Dry Goods, Groceries, Notions, &c, Jackson St
Smith G. T...All kinds of Furniture, Coffins, Rosewood and Gilt Picture Frames, Mouldings, &c, &c, opposite Nichol's Hall
Smith B. F...Hardware, Stoves and Tin Ware
Union Store Association...Dealers in Groceries, Provisions, Coal, Best Brands of Flour, &c, Oysters by the Keg in season, all goods warranted as represented, Main St

Manufacturers and Dealers

Lyons C. J...Manufr and Dealer in Flour, Feed, and Meal, Main St, and Propr of Susquehanna Mills, Oakland
Malpass D. Jr...Manufr of Custom Boots and Shoes, East Main St
Sperl Henry...Manufr and Dealer in Fine Arms, Cutlery, Fishing Tackle, &c, General repairing, Lock Jobbing and Key fitting done at short notice
Van Nostran & Seldon...Manufrs of all kinds of Carriages and Wagons. Strict attention given to all kinds of repairing, Painting, Finishing, Trimming, &c

Mechanics

Agnew Wm. J...Blacksmith, Erie Shop. Res, cor Jackson and Cross St
Beck Arthur T...Foreman of Running Repairs, Erie Shop. Res, Jackson St
Barton E. S...Millwright, Erie Shop
Barton G. W...Carpenter and Builder, Oakland
Creighton John...Machinist, Erie Shop. Res, Oakland
Decker U...Blacksmith, Oakland
Drake Charles R...Machinist, Erie Shop. Res, Oakland
Ernst C...Burgess 1873 Machinist, Erie Shop. Res, Vine St
Falkenburg B...Foreman Erie Railroad Co's Foundry
Greeley W. B...Clerk, Erie Railroad Co
Gregory B...Pattern Maker, Erie Shop
Gregg James B...Master Mechanic, Erie Shop
Hull W. J...Engine dispatcher, Erie Railroad Co
Haven H. A...Machinist, Erie Shop
Horton A. L...Truckman, Erie Shop. Res, Oakland
Hunt William...Foreman, Erie Railroad Co's Blacksmith Shop. Res, West Church St
Irving Nicholas...Foreman, Erie Railroad Co's Boiler Shop. Res, Washington St
Johnson J...Steam Fitter, Erie Shop
Kittle J. B...Drill-press Worker, Erie Shop and Justice of the Peace. Res, Oakland
Lovett Jas...Machinist, Erie Shop. Res, Oakland
Leal Geo. E...Foreman, Erie Railroad Co's Paint Shop. Res, Oakland
Mason D...Machinist, Erie Shop
McCutcheon James...Watchman, Erie Shop. Res, Oakland
Mannering Richard...Machinist, Erie Shop. Res, Washington St
Newham Thomas...Wagon Maker, Oakland
Ferry F. A...Contractor and Builder, Broad St

Sherman M. S...Mason, Erie Shop
Skinner Nathan...Carpenter, Oakland
Taylor E. G...Moulder, Erie Shop
Van Wagner A...Carpenter and Car Maker, Erie Shop. Res, Oakland
Wallace Robert...General Foreman, Erie Shops. Res, Washington St
Wallace Samuel...Machinist, Erie Shop. Res, Washington St
Wardwell B. F...Carpenter, Erie Shop. Res, Oakland

Physicians

Birdsall Samuel...Physician and Surgeon and Pension Examiner. Surgeon's Office, Seymore Block No. 10, East Main St
Mitchell W. S...East Main St

Miscellaneous

Bartlett William H...Burgess 1871
Boyle T...Surveyor and Civil Engineer. Res, Main St
Brunetti G. S...Real Estate Dealer and Lumberman
Bravo J. R...Engineer, Erie Railroad. Res, Main St
Brush Calvin...Farmer, Dist No. 6
Brush G. A...Lumberman, Dist No. 7
Brush F. K...Lumberman, Brushville
Brush Samuel...Lumberman, Brushville
Beebe Charles...Farmer and Dairyman, Oakland
Bourne J. T...Storekeeper, Erie Railroad Co. Res, Jackson St
Canavan Thomas...Farmer, Dist No. 7
Grimes J. K...Farmer and Lumberman, Dist No. 4
Griswold Sedate...Farmer. Res, Washington St
Hartley M. J...Refreshment Saloon, Main St
Lamb C. W...Farmer and Lumberman, Dist No. 4
Lamb W. T...Farmer, Dist No. 4
Moore C. C...Conductor on Erie Railroad. Res, Oakland
McKune B. F...Farmer, Dist No. 5
Moore J. K...Farmer, Dist No. 5, Res, Oakland
Pettit L. R...Engineer, Erie Railroad. Res, Washington St
Reilly Michael...Farmer, Dist No. 4
Sweet S. O...Photographer, cor Jackson and Grand Ward
Stevens Joseph...Farmer and Brick Manufr, Dist No. 4
Webster R. M...Dealer in Lumber and Real Estate, Susquehanna Depot
Westfall Levi...Farmer, Oakland

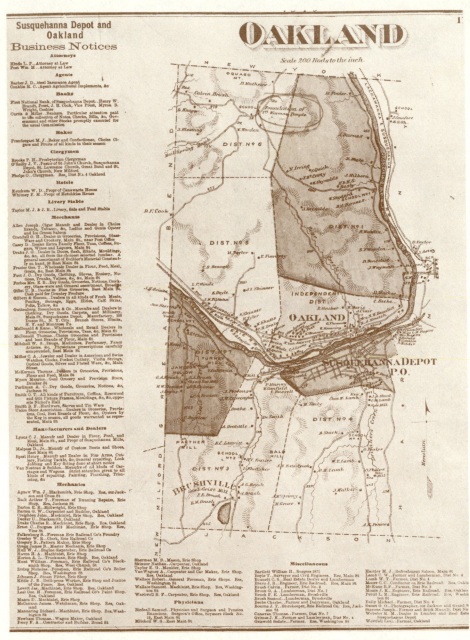

1873 Map showing foundation of first Mormon Temple where the Melchizedek Priesthood was restored, Susquehanna, Pennsylvania.

Eugene Baker of the "Evening Transcript," Susquehanna, Pennsylvania, points to the foundation of the first Mormon Temple up on the hillside of Oakland, Susquehanna, Pennsylvania.

HERE, JOSEPH SMITH, THE PROPHET AND
OLIVER COWDERY RECEIVED THE PRIESTHOOD OF
AARON ON MAY 15, 1829, SHORTLY THEREAFTER,
THEY RECEIVED THE MELCHIZEDEK PRIESTHOOD.
   FIRST BAPTISMS WERE PERFORMED HERE
IN THE SUSQUEHANNA RIVER.
   THIS PROPERTY WAS PURCHASED BY THE
CHURCH OF JESUS CHRIST OF LATTER-DAY
SAINTS OCTOBER 3, 1946.

President George Albert Smith sends Wilford Wood with sign to be placed on the Banks of the Susquehanna River where the Priesthood was restored. Property purchased by Wilford Wood in 1946.

Mrs. Wilford C. Wood standing in front of the Aaronic Priesthood
Monument at Susquehanna, Pennsylvania with her two grandchildren,
Richard and Sheila Glade.

Wilford Wood takes two of his grandchildren, Richard and Sheila Glade, to the place where the Aaronic Priesthood was restored.

The beautiful clear stream of water just down the slope of the hill from the Kirtland Temple where the baptisms were performed.

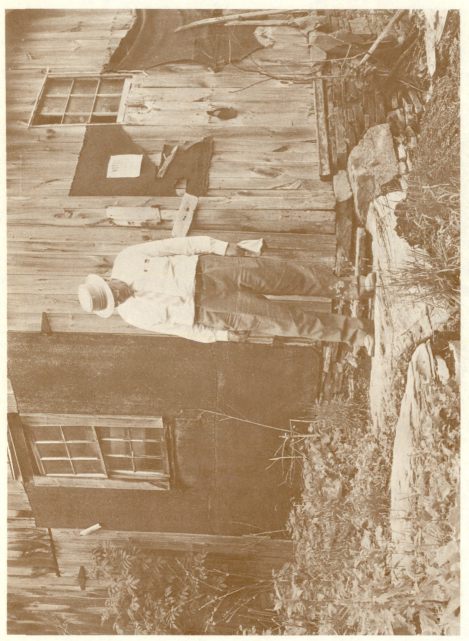

Wilford Wood examines large temple stones which were the foundation of the first Temple that the Prophet started to build in Oakland, Susquehanna, Pennsylvania. This is where the Prophet Joseph Smith received the Melchizedek Priesthood under the hands of Peter, James, and John.

Old school house near foundation of first Mormon Temple where Melchizedek Priesthood was restored by Peter, James, and John to Joseph and Oliver in Susquehanna, Pennsylvania.

Mrs. Wilford C. Wood with her granddaughter, Sheila Glade, at the beautiful Peter Whitmer home where the Church was organized.

Grandma and Grandpa take two of their grandchildren to the Peter Whitmer home and show them the room where the Church was organized telling them the story of what happened at the Peter Whitmer Home.

DIVINE

JESUS OF NAZARETH

PETER   JAMES   JOHN

1836   PROPHET JOSEPH SMITH

OLIVER COWDERY   SIDNEY RIGDON   FREDERICK G. WILLIAMS

1961   PRESIDENT DAVID O. McKAY

J. REUBEN CLARK JR.   HENRY D. MOYLE   HUGH B. BROWN

© WILFORD C. WOOD 1961

LETTERING
R. GLADE

DOCTRINE AND COVENANTS

OF

THE CHURCH OF THE

LATTER DAY SAINTS:

CAREFULLY SELECTED

FROM THE REVELATIONS OF GOD,

AND COMPILED BY

JOSEPH SMITH Junior.
OLIVER COWDERY,
SIDNEY RIGDON,
FREDERICK G. WILLIAMS,

[*Presiding Elders of said Church.*]

PROPRIETORS.

KIRTLAND, OHIO.

PRINTED BY F. G. WILLIAMS & CO

FOR THE

PROPRIETORS.

....

1835.

Joseph Smith
Begins His Work
Volume Two

The Doctrine and Covenants
1835

PREFACE.

To the members of the church of the Latter Day Saints—

DEAR BRETHREN:

We deem it to be unnecessary to entertain you with a lengthy preface to the following volume, but merely to say, that it contains in short, the leading items of the religion which we have professed to believe.

The first part of the book will be found to contain a series of Lectures as delivered before a Theological class in this place, and in consequence of their embracing the important doctrine of salvation, we have arranged them into the following work.

The second part contains items or principles for the regulation of the church, as taken from the revelations which have been given since its organization, as well as from former ones.

There may be an aversion in the minds of some against receiving any thing purporting to be articles of religious faith, in consequence of there being so many now extant; but if men believe a system, and profess that it was given by inspiration, certainly, the more intelligibly they can present it, the better. It does not make a principle untrue to *print* it, neither does it make it true not to print it.

The church viewing this subject to be of importance, appointed, through their servants and delegates the High Council, your servants to select and compile this work. Several reasons might be adduced in favor of this move of the Council, but we only add a few words. They knew that the church was evil spoken of in many places—its faith and belief misrepresented, and the

way of truth thus subverted. By some it was represented as disbelieving the bible, by others as being an
enemy to all good order and uprightness, and by others as being injurious to the peace of all governments
civil and political.

We have, therefore, endeavored to present, though
in few words, *our* belief, and when we say this, humbly trust, the faith and principles of this society as a
body.

We do not present this little volume with any other
expectation than that we are to be called to answer to
every principle advanced, in that day when the secrets of all hearts will be revealed, and the reward of
every man's labor be given him.

With sentiments of esteem
and sincere respect, we subscribe
ourselves your brethren in the bonds of
the gospel of our Lord Jesus Christ.

JOSEPH SMITH jr.
OLIVER COWDERY.
SIDNEY RIGDON.
F. G. WILLIAMS.

Kirtland, Ohio, February 17, 1835.

THEOLOGY.

LECTURE FIRST

On the doctrine of the church of the

Latter Day Saints.

Of Faith.

SECTION I.

1 FAITH being the first principle in revealed religion, and the foundation of all righteousness, necessarily claims the first place in a course of lectures which are designed to unfold to the understanding the doctrine of Jesus Christ.

2 In presenting the subject of faith, we shall observe the following order:

3 First, Faith itself—what it is:

4 Secondly, The object on which it rests; and

5 Thirdly, The effects which flow from it.

6 Agreeably to this order we have first to show what faith is.

7 The author of the epistle to the Hebrews, in the eleventh chapter of that epistle, and first verse, gives the following definition of the word faith:

8 Now faith is the substance [assurance] of things hoped for, the evidence of things not seen.

9 From this we learn, that faith is the assurance which men have of the existence of things which they have not seen; and the principle of action in all intelligent beings.

10 If men were duly to consider themselves, and turn their thoughts and reflections to the operations of

their own minds, they would readily discover that it is faith, and faith only, which is the moving cause of all action, in them; that without it, both mind and body would be in a state of inactivity, and all their exertions would cease, both physical and mental.

11 Were this class to go back and reflect upon the history of their lives, from the period of their first recollection, and ask themselves, what principle excited them to action, or what gave them energy and activity, in all their lawful avocations, callings and pursuits, what would be the answer? Would it not be that it was the assurance which we had of the existence of things which we had not seen, as yet?— Was it not the hope which you had, in consequence of your belief in the existence of unseen things, which stimulated you to action and exertion, in order to obtain them? Are you not dependant on your faith, or belief, for the acquisition of all knowledge, wisdom and intelligence? Would you exert yourselves to obtain wisdom and intelligence, unless you did believe that you could obtain them? Would you have ever sown if you had not believed that you would reap? Would you have ever planted if you had not believed that you would gather? Would you have ever asked unless you had believed that you would receive? Would you have ever sought unless you had believed that you would have found? Or would you have ever knocked unless you had believed that it would have been opened unto you? In a word, is there any thing that you would have done, either physical or mental, if you had not previously believed? Are not all your exertions, of every kind, dependant on your faith? Or may we not ask, what have you, or what do you possess, which you have not obtained by reason of your faith? Your food, your raiment, your lodgings, are they not all by reason of your faith? Reflect, and ask yourselves, if these things are not so. Turn your thoughts on

your own minds, and see if faith is not the moving cause of all action in yourselves; and if the moving cause in you, is it not in all other intelligent beings?

12 And as faith is the moving cause of all action in temporal concerns, so it is in spiritual; for the Savior has said, and that truly, that he that *believeth* and is baptized, shall be saved. Mark 16:16.

13 As we receive by faith, all temporal blessings that we do receive, so we, in like manner, receive by faith all spiritual blessings, that we do receive. But faith is not only the principle of action, but of power, also, in all intelligent beings, whether in heaven, or on earth. Thus says the author of the epistle to the Hebrews, 11:3:

14 Through faith we understand that the worlds were framed by the word of God: so that things which are seen were not made of things which do appear.

15 By this we understand that the principle of power, which existed in the bosom of God, by which the worlds were framed, was faith; and that it is by reason of this principle of power, existing in the Deity, that all created things exist—so that all things in heaven, on earth, or under the earth, exist by reason of faith, as it existed in HIM.

16 Had it not been for the principle of faith the worlds would never have been framed, neither would man have been formed of the dust—it is the principle by which Jehovah works, and through which he exercises power over all temporal, as well as eternal things. Take this principle or attribute, (for it is an attribute) from the Deity and he would cease to exist.

17 Who cannot see, that if God framed the worlds by faith, that it is by faith that he exercises power over them, and that faith is the principle of power? And that if the principle of power, it must be in all men as well as in the Deity? This is the testimony of all

the sacred writers, and the lesson which they have been endeavoring to teach to man.

18 The Savior says, Matthew 17:19,20, in explaining the reason why the disciples could not cast out the devil, that it was because of their unbelief: "For verily, I say unto you," said he, "if ye have faith as a grain of mustard-seed, ye shall say unto this mountain, Remove hence to yonder place! and it shall remove: and nothing shall be impossible unto you."

19 Moroni, while abridging and compiling the record of his fathers, has given us the following account of faith as the principle of power: He says, page 563, that it was the faith of Alma and Amulek which caused the walls of the prison to be wrent, as recorded on the 264th page; that it was the faith of Nephi and Lehi which caused a change to be wrought upon the hearts of the Lamanites, when they were immersed with the Holy Spirit, and with fire, as seen on the 421st page, and that it was by faith that the mountain Zerin was removed, when the brother of Jared spake in the name of the Lord. See also 565th page.

20 In addition to this we are told in Hebrews, 11:32, 33,34,35, that Gideon, Barak, Samson, Jephthah, David, Samuel, and the prophets, through faith subdued kingdoms, wrought righteousness, obtained promises, stopped the mouths of lions, quenched the violence of fire, escaped the edge of the sword, out of weakness were made strong, waxed valiant in fight, turned to flight the armies of the aliens; and that women received their dead raised to life again, &c. &c.

21 Also, Joshua, in the sight of all Israel, bade the sun and moon to stand still, and it was done. Josh. 10:12.

22 We here understand, that the sacred writers say, that all these things were done by faith—It was by faith that the worlds were framed—God spake, chaos heard, and worlds came into order, by reason of the faith there was in HIM. So with man also—he spake

by faith in the name of God, and the sun stood still, the moon obeyed, mountains removed, prisons fell, lions' mouths were closed, the human heart lost its enmity, fire its violence, armies their power, the sword its terror, and death its dominion; and all this by reason of the faith which was in them.

23 Had it not been for the faith which was in man, they might have spoken to the sun, the moon, the mountains, prisons, lions, the human heart, fire, armies, the sword, or to death in vain!

24 Faith, then, is the first great governing principle which has power, dominion, and authority over all things: by it they exist, by it they are upheld, by it they are changed, or by it they remain, agreeably to the will of God. Without it, there is no power, and without power there could be no creation, nor existence!

OF THEOLOGY.

Question.—What is theology?

Answer.—It is that revealed science which treats of the being and attributes of God—his relations to us—the dispensations of his providence—his will with respect to our actions—and his purposes with respect to our end. [Buck's Theological Dictionary, page 582.]

Q. What is the first principle in this revealed science?

A. Faith. [§ 1. ¶ 1.]

Q. Why is faith the first principle in this revealed science?

A. Because it is the foundation of all righteousness. Heb 11:6. Without faith it is impossible to please God. 1st. John, 3:7. Little children, let no man deceive you: he that doeth righteousness, is righteous, even as he [God] is righteous. [§ 1. ¶ 1.]

Q. What arrangement should be followed in presenting the subject of faith?

A. First, Should be shown what faith is: [§ 1. ¶ 3.] Secondly, The object upon which it rests; and [§ 1. ¶ 4.] Thirdly, The effects which flow from it. [§ 1. ¶ 5.]

Q. What is faith?

A. It is the assurance of things hoped for, the evidence of things not seen: Heb. 11:1. That is, it is the assurance we have of the existence of unseen things. And being the assurance which we have of the existence of unseen things, must be the principle of action in all intelligent beings. Heb. 11:3. Through faith we understand the worlds were framed by the word of God. [§ 1. ¶ 8,9.]

Q. How do you prove that faith is the principle of action in all intelligent beings?

A. First, By duly considering the operations of my own mind; and secondly, by the direct declaration of scripture.—Heb. 11:7. By faith Noah, being warned of things not seen as yet, moved with fear, prepared an ark to the saving of his house; by the which he condemned the world, and became heir of the righteousness which is by faith. Heb. 11:8. By faith Abraham, when he was called to go out into a place which he should after receive for an inheritance, obeyed; and he went out not knowing whither he went. Heb. 11:9. By faith he sojourned in the land of promise, as in a strange country, dwelling in tabernacles with Isaac and Jacob, the heirs with him of the same promise. Heb. 11:27. By faith Moses forsook Egypt, not fearing the wrath of the king: for he endured as seeing him who is invisible. [§ 1. ¶ 10,11.]

Q. Is not faith the principle of action in spiritual things as well as in temporal?

A. It is.

Q. How do you prove it?

A. Heb. 11:6. Without faith it is impossible to please God. Mark 16:16. 'He that believeth and is baptized, shall be saved. Rom. 4:16. Therefore, it is of faith, that it might be by grace; to the end the promise might be sure to all the seed: not to that only which is of the law, but to that also which is of the faith of Abraham, who is the father of us all.—[§ 1. ¶ 12,13.]

Q. Is faith any thing else beside the principle of action?

A. It is.

Q. What is it?

A. It is the principle of power, also. [§ 1. ¶ 13.]

Q. How do you prove it?

A. First, It is the principle of power in the Deity, as well as in man. Heb. 11:3. Through faith we understand that the worlds were framed by the word of God, so that things which are seen were not made of things which do appear.—[§ 1. ¶ 14,15,16.]

Secondly, It is the principle of power in man also. Book of Mormon, page 264. Alma and Amulek are delivered from prison. Do. page 421. Nephi and Lehi, with the Lamanites, are immersed with the Spirit. Do. page 565. The mountain Zerin, by the faith of the brother of Jared, is removed. Josh.

10:12. Then spake Joshua to the Lord in the day when the Lord delivered up the Amorites before the children of Israel, and he said in the sight of Israel, Sun, stand thou still upon Gibeon, and thou Moon, in the valley of Ajalon. Josh. 10:13. And the sun stood still, and the moon stayed, until the people had avenged themselves of their enemies. Is not this written in the book of Jasher? So the sun stood still in the midst of heaven, and hasted not to go down about a whole day. Mat. 17:19. Then came the disciples to Jesus apart, and said, Why could not we cast him out? Mat. 17:20. And Jesus said unto them, Because of your unbelief: for verily I say unto you, if ye have faith as a grain of mustard-seed, ye shall say unto this mountain, Remove hence to yonder place; and it shall remove; and nothing shall be impossible unto you.— Heb. 11:32. And what shall I say more? for the time would fail me to tell of Gideon, and of Barak, and of Samson, and of Jephthah, of David also, and Samuel, and of the prophets. Heb. 11:33. Who through faith subdued kingdoms, wrought righteousness, obtained promises, stopped the mouths of lions, Heb. 11:34. Quenched the violence of fire, escaped the edge of the sword, out of weakness were made strong, waxed valiant in fight, turned to flight the armies of the aliens. Heb. 11:35. Women received their dead raised to life again: and others were tortured, not accepting deliverance; that they might obtain a better resurrection. [§ I. ¶ 16,17,18,19,20,21, 22.]

Q. How would you define faith in its most unlimited sense? A. It is the first great governing principle, which has power, dominion and authority over all things. [§ I. ¶ 24.]

Q. How do you convey to the understanding more clearly, that faith is the first great governing principle, which has power, dominion, and authority over all things? A. By it they exist, by it they are upheld, by it they are changed, or by it they remain, agreeably to the will of God; and without it there is no power; and without power there could be no creation, nor existence! [§ I. ¶ 24.]

LECTURE SECOND.

Of Faith.

SECTION II.

1 Having shown in our previous lecture "faith itself—what it is," we shall proceed to show secondly the object on which it rests.

2 We here observe that God is the only supreme governor, and independent being, in whom all fulness and perfection dwells; who is omnipotent, omnipresent, and omnicient; without beginning of days or end of life; and that in him every good gift, and every good principle dwells; and that he is the Father of lights: In him the principle of faith dwells independently; and he is the object in whom the faith of all other rational and accountable beings centers, for life and salvation.

3 In order to present this part of the subject in a clear and conspicuous point of light, it is necessary to go back and show the evidences which mankind have had, and the foundation on which these evidences are, or were based, since the creation, to believe in the existence of a God.

4 We do not mean those evidences which are manifested by the works of creation, which we daily behold with our natural eyes: we are sensible, that after a revelation of Jesus Christ, the works of creation, throughout their vast forms and varieties, clearly exhibit his eternal power and Godhead. Romans 1:20. For the invisible things of him from the creation of the world are clearly seen, being understood by the things that are made: even his eternal power and Godhead. But we mean those evidences by which the first thoughts were suggested to the minds of men that there was a God who created all things.

5 We shall now proceed to examine the situation of

man at his first creation. Moses, the historian, has given us the following account of him in the first chapt. of the book of Genesis, beginning with the 20th verse, and closing with the 30th. We copy from the New Translation:

6 And the Lord God said unto the Only Begotten, who was with him from the beginning, Let us make man in our image, after our likeness: and it was done.

7 And the Lord God said, Let them have dominion over the fish of the sea, and over the fowl of the air, and over the cattle, and over all the earth, and over every creeping thing that creaps upon the earth.

8 So God created man in his own image, in the image of the Only Begotten created he him; male and female created he them. And God blessed them, and God said unto them, Be fruitful, and multiply, and replenish the earth, and subdue it: and have dominion over the fish of the sea, and over the fowl of the air, and over every living thing that moves upon the earth.

9 And the Lord God said unto man, Behold, I have given you every herb bearing seed, which is upon the face of all the earth, and every tree in the which is the fruit of a tree yielding seed; to you it shall be for meat.

10 Again, Genesis 2:15,16,17,19,20: And the Lord God took the man, and put him into the garden of Eden, to dress it and to keep it. And the Lord God commanded the man, saying, Of every tree of the garden you may freely eat: but of the tree of the knowledge of good and evil you shall not eat of it, neither shall you touch it; nevertheless, you may choose for yourself, for it is given unto you; but remember that I forbid it: for in the day that you eat thereof you shall surely die. -

11 And out of the ground the Lord God formed every beast of the field, and every fowl of the air, and commanded that they should be brought unto Adam, to see what he would call them.   * * * And whatever Adam called every living creature, that was the name thereof.   And Adam gave names to all cattle, and to the fowl of the air, and to every beast of the field.

12 From the foregoing we learn man's situation at his first creation; the knowledge with which he was endowed, and the high and exalted station in which he was placed—lord, or governor of all things on earth, and at the same time enjoying communion and intercourse with his Maker, without a vail to separate between.   We shall next proceed to examine the account given of his fall, and of his being driven out of the garden of Eden, and from the presence of the Lord.

13 Moses proceeds: And they [Adam and Eve] heard the voice of the Lord God as they were walking in the garden in the cool of the day, and Adam and his wife hid themselves from the presence of the Lord God among the trees of the garden.   And the Lord God called unto Adam, and said unto him, Where are you going?   And he said, I heard your voice in the garden, and I was afraid, because I beheld that I was naked, and I hid myself.

14 And the Lord God said unto Adam, Who told you that you were naked? Have you eaten of the tree whereof I told you that you should not eat? If so, you should surely die?   And the man said, The woman whom you gave me, and commanded that she should remain with me, gave me of the fruit of the tree, and I did eat.

15 And the Lord God said unto the woman, What is this which you have done?   And the woman said, The serpent beguiled me, and I did eat.

16 And again, the Lord said unto the woman, I will greatly multiply your sorrow, and your conception: in sorrow you shall bring forth children; and your desire shall be to your husband, and he shall rule over you.

17 And the Lord God said unto Adam, because you have hearkened unto the voice of your wife, and have eaten of the fruit of the tree of which I commanded you, saying, You shall not eat of it! cursed shall be the ground for your sake: in sorrow you shall eat of it all the days of your life. Thorns also, and thistles shall it bring forth to you: and you shall eat the herb of the field. By the sweat of your face shall you eat bread, until you shall return unto the ground —for you shall surely die—for out of it you were taken; for dust you were, and unto dust you shall return. This was immediately followed by the fulfillment of what we previously said: Man was driven, or sent out of Eden.

18 Two important items are shown from the former quotations: First, After man was created, he was not left without intelligence, or understanding, to wander in darkness, and spend an existence in ignorance and doubt—on the great and important point which effected his happiness,—as to the real fact by whom he was created, or unto whom he was amenable for his conduct. God conversed with him face to face: in his presence he was permitted to stand, and from his own mouth he was permitted to receive instruction—he heard his voice, walked before him, and gazed upon his glory—while intelligence burst upon his understanding, and enabled him to give names to the vast assemblage of his Maker's works.

19 Secondly, we have seen, that, though man did transgress, his transgression did not deprive him of the previous knowledge with which he was endowed, relative to the existence and glory of his Creator;

for no sooner did he hear his voice, than he sought to hide himself from his presence.

20 Having shown, then, in the first instance, that God began to converse with man, immediately after he "breathed into his nostrils the breath of life," and that he did not cease to manifest himself to him, even after his fall, we shall next proceed to show, that, though he was cast out from the garden of Eden, his knowledge of the existence of God was not lost, neither did God cease to manifest his will unto him.

21 We next proceed to present the account of the direct revelation which man received, after he was cast out of Eden, and further copy from the New Translation:

22 After Adam had been driven out of the garden, he began to till the earth, and to have dominion over all the beasts of the field, and to eat his bread by the sweat of his brow, as the Lord had commanded him: and he called upon the name of the Lord, and so did Eve his wife also. And they heard the voice of the Lord from the way toward the garden of Eden, speaking unto them; and they saw him not, for they were shut out from his presence: but he gave unto them commandments that they should worship the Lord their God, and should offer the firstlings of their flocks for an offering unto the Lord. And Adam was obedient unto the commandment.

23 And after many days an angel of the Lord appeared unto Adam, saying, why do you offer sacrifices unto the Lord? And Adam said unto him, I know not; but the Lord commanded me to offer sacrifices.

24 And the angel said unto him, This thing is a similitude of the sacrifice of the Only Begotten of the Father, who is full of grace and truth. And you shall do all that you do in the name of the Son: and you shall repent and call upon God in his name for-

ever. In that day the Holy Spirit fell upon Adam, and bore record of the Father and the Son.

25 This last quotation, or summary, shows this im-. portant fact, that though our first parents were driven out of the garden of Eden, and were even separated from the presence of God, by a vail, they still retained a knowledge of his existence, and that sufficiently to move them to call upon him. And further, that no sooner was the plan of redemption revealed to man, and he began to call upon God, than the Holy Spirit was given, bearing record of the Father and Son.

26 Moses also gives us an account, in the 4th of Genesis, of the transgression of Cain, and the righteousness of Abel, and of the revelations of God to them. He says: In process of time Cain brought of the fruit of the ground, an offering unto the Lord.— And Abel also brought of the firstlings of his flock, and of the fat thereof. And the Lord had respect unto Abel, and to his offering: but unto Cain and to his offering he had not respect. Now satan knew this, and it pleased him. And Cain was very angry, and his countenance fell. And the Lord said unto Cain, Why are you angry? why is your countenance fallen? If you do well, will you not be accepted?— And if you do not well, sin lies at the door, and satan desires to have you; and except you shall hearken unto my commandments, I will deliver you up: and it shall be unto you according to his desire.

27 And Cain went into the field and talked with his brother Abel. And while they were in the field, Cain rose up against his brother Abel, and slew him. And Cain gloried in what he had done, saying, I am free! surely the flocks of my brother will now fall into my hands.

28 But the Lord said unto Cain, Where is Abel, your brother? And he said, I know not: am I my

B

brother's keeper? And the Lord said, What have you done? the voice of your brother's blood cries unto me from the ground. And now, you shall be cursed from the earth which has opened her mouth to receive your brother's blood, from your hand. When you till the ground, she shall not henceforth yield unto you her strength. A fugitive and a vagabond also, you shall be in the earth.

29 And Cain said unto the Lord, Satan tempted me because of my brother's flocks. And I was also angry: for his offering was accepted, and mine was not: My punishment is greater than I can bear. Behold, you have driven me out this day from the face of men, and from your face shall I be hid also; and I shall be a fugitive and a vagabond in the earth; and it shall come to pass, every one that finds me will slay me, because of my oath; for these things are not hid from the Lord. And the Lord said unto him, Therefore, whoever slays Cain, vengeance shall be taken on him seven fold. And the Lord set a mark upon Cain, lest any finding him should kill him.

30 The object of the foregoing quotations is to show to this class the way by which mankind were first made acquainted with the existence of a God: that it was by a manifestation of God to man, and that God continued, after man's transgression to manifest himself to him and his posterity: and notwithstanding they were separated from his immediate presence, that they could not see his face, they continued to hear his voice.

31 Adam thus being made acquainted with God, communicated the knowledge which he had unto his posterity; and it was through this means that the thought was first suggested to their minds that there was a God. Which laid the foundation for the exercise of their faith, through which they could obtain a knowledge of his character and also of his glory.

32 Not only was there a manifestation made unto Adam of the existence of a God, but Moses informs us, as before quoted, that God condescended to talk with Cain after his great transgression, in slaying his brother, and that Cain knew that it was the Lord that was talking with him: so that when he was driven out from the presence of his brethren, he carried with him the knowledge of the existence of a God: and through this means, doubtless his posterity became acquainted with the fact that such a being existed.

33 From this we can see that the whole human family, in the early age of their existence, in all their different branches, had this knowledge disseminated among them; so that the existence of God became an object of faith, in the early age of the world. And the evidences which these men had of the existence of a God, was the testimony of their fathers in the first instance.

34 The reason why we have been thus particular on this part of our subject, is, that this class may see by what means it was that God became an object of faith among men after the fall; and what it was that stirred up the faith of multitudes to feel after him; to search after a knowledge of his character, perfections and attributes, until they became extensively acquainted with him; and not only commune with him, and behold his glory, but be partakers of his power, and stand in his presence.

35 Let this class mark particularly that the testimony which these men had of the existence of a God, was the testimony of man; for previous to the time that any of Adam's posterity had obtained a manifestation of God to themselves, Adam their common father had testified unto them of the existence of God, and of his eternal power and Godhead.

36 For instance, Abel, before he received the assu-

2*

rance from heaven that his offerings were acceptable unto God, had received the important information of his father, that such a being did exist, who had created, and who did uphold all things. Neither can there be a doubt existing on the mind of any person, that Adam was the first who did communicate the knowledge of the existence of a God, to his posterity; and that the whole faith of the world, from that time down to the present, is in a certain degree, dependent on the knowledge first communicated to them by their common progenitor; and it has been handed down to the day and generation in which we live, as we shall show from the face of the sacred records.

37 First, Adam was 130 years old when Seth was born. Gen. 5:3. And the days of Adam, after he had begotten Seth, were 800 years; making him 930 years old when he died. Gen. 5:4,5. Seth was 105 when Enos was born. 5:6. Enos was 90 when Cainan was born. 5:9. Cainan was 70 when Mahalaleel was born. 5:12. Mahalaleel was 65 when Jared was born. 5:15: Jared was 162 when Enoch was born. 5:18. Enoch was 65 when Methusaleh was born. 5:21. Methusaleh was 187 when Lamech was born. 5:25. Lamech was 182 when Noah was born. 5:28.

38 From this account it appears that Lamech, the 9th from Adam, and the father of Noah, was 56 years old when Adam died; Methuseleh, 243; Enoch, 308; Jared 470; Mahalaleel, 535; Cainan, 605; Enos, 695; and Seth, 800.

39 So that Lamech, the father of Noah; Methusaleh, Enoch, Jared, Mahalaleel, Cainan, Enos, Seth, and Adam, were all living at the same time, and beyond all controversy, were all preachers of righteousness.

40 Moses further informs us, that Seth lived, after he begat Enos, 807 years; making him 912 years old

at his death. Gen. 5:7,8. And Enos lived, after he begat Cainan, 815 years: making him 905 years old when he died. 5:10,11. And Cainan lived, after he begat Mahalaleel, 840 years: making him 910 years old at his death. 5:13,14. And Mahalaleel lived, after he begat Jared, 830 years: making him 895 years old when he died. 5:16,17. And Jared lived, after he begat Enoch, 800 years: making him 962 years old at his death. 5:19,20. And Enoch walked with God, after he begat Methuseleh 300 years: making him 365 years old when he was translated. 5:22,23. And Methuseleh lived, after he begat Lamech, 782 years: making him 969 years old when he died. 5:26,27. Lamech lived, after he begat Noah, 595 years: making him 777 years old when he died. 5:30,31.

41 Agreeably to this account, Adam died in the 930th year of the world, Enoch was translated in the 987th, Seth died in the 1042nd, Enos in the 1140th, Cainan in the 1235th, Mahalaleel in the 1290th, Jared in the 1422nd, Lamech in the 1651st, and Methusaleh in the 1656th, it being the same year in which the flood came.

42 So that Noah was 84 years old when Enos died, 176 when Cainan died, 234 when Mahalaleel died, 366 when Jared died, 595 when Lamech died, and 600 when Methusaleh died.

43 We can see from this that Enos, Cainan, Mahalaleel, Jared, Methusaleh, Lamach, and Noah all lived on the earth at the same time. And that Enos, Cainan, Mahalaleel, Jared Methusaleh, and Lamech, were all acquainted with both Adam and Noah.

44 From the foregoing it is easily to be seen, not only how the knowledge of God came into the world, but upon what principle it was preserved: that from the time it was first communicated, it was retained in the minds of righteous men, who taught, not only their own posterity, but the world; so that there was

no need of a new revelation to man, after Adam's creation, to Noah, to give them the first idea, or notion of the existence of a God: and not only of a God, but of the true and living God.

45 Having traced the chronology of the world from Adam to Noah, we will now trace it from Noah to Abraham. Noah was 502 years old when Shem was born: 98 years afterward the flood came, being the 600th year of Noah's age. And Moses informs us that Noah lived after the flood, 350 years: making him 950 years old when he died. Gen. 9:28,29.

46 Shem was 100 years old when Arphaxed was born. Gen. 11:10, Arphaxed was 35 when Salah was born 11:12. Salah was 30 when Eber was born. 11:14. Eber was 34 when Peleg was born: in whose days the earth was divided. 11:16. Peleg was 30 when Reu was born. 11:18. Reu was 32 when Serug was born. 11:20. Serug was 30 when Nahor was born. 11:22. Nahor was 29 when Terah was born. 11:24. Terah was 70 when Haran and Abraham were born. 11:26.

47 There is some difficulty in the account given by Moses, of Abraham's birth. Some have supposed, that Abraham was not born until Terah was 130 years old. This conclusion is drawn from a variety of scriptures, which are not to our purpose at present to quote. Neither is it a matter of any consequence to us, whether Abraham was born when Terah was 70 years old, or 130. But in order that there may no doubt exist upon any mind, in relation to the object lying immediately before us, in presenting the present chronology, we will date the birth of Abraham at the latest period: that is, when Terah was 130 years old. It appears from this account, that from the flood to the birth of Abraham was 352 years.

48 Moses informs us that Shem lived, after he begat Arphaxed, 500, Gen, 11:11. This added to 100

years, which was his age when Arphaxed was born, makes him 600 years old when he died. Arphaxed lived, after he begat Salah, 403 years. 11:13. This added to 35 years, which was his age when Salah was born, makes him 438 years old when he died. Salah lived, after he begat Eber, 403 years. 11:15.— This added to 30 years, which was his age when Eber was born, makes him 433 years old when he died.— Eber lived, after he begat Peleg, 430 years. 11:17. This added to 34 years, which was his age when Peleg was born, makes him 464 years old. Peleg lived, after he begat Reu, 209 years. 11:19. This added to 30 years, which was his age when Reu was born, makes him 239 years old when he died. Reu lived, after he begat Serug, 207 years. Gen. 11:21. This added to 32 years, which was his age when Serug was born, makes him 239 years old when he died. Serug lived, after he begat Nahor, 200 years. Gen. 11:23. This added to 30 years, which was his age when Nahor was born, makes him 230 years old when he died. Nahor lived, after he begat Terah, 119 years. Gen. 11:25. This added to 29 years, which was his age when Terah was born, makes him 148 years old when he died. Terah was 130 years old when Abraham was born, and is supposed to have lived 75 years after his birth: making him 205 years old when he died.

49 Agreeably to this last account, Peleg died in the 1996th year of the world. Nahor in the 1997th, and Noah in the 2006th. So that Peleg, in whose days the earth was divided, and Nahor, the grand-father of Abraham, both died before Noah: the former being 239 years old, and the latter 148. And who cannot but see, that they must have had a long and intimate acquaintance with Noah?

50 Reu died in the 2026th year of the world, Serug in 2049th, Terah in the 2083rd, Arphaxed in the

2096th, Selah in the 2126th, Shem in the 2158th, Abraham in the 2183rd, and Eber in the 2187th: which was 4 years after Abraham's death. And Eber was the fourth from Noah.

51 Nahor, Abraham's brother, was 58 years old when Noah died, Terah 128, Serug 187, Reu 219, Eber 283, Salah 313, Arphaxed 344, and Shem 448.

52 It appears from this account, that Nahor, brother of Abraham, Terah, Nahor, Scrug, Reu, Peleg, Eber, Salah, Arphaxed, Shem, and Noah, all lived on the earth at the same time. And that Abraham was 18 years old when Reu died, 41 when Serug and his brother Nahor died, 75 when Terah died, 88 when Arphaxed died, 118 when Salah died, 150 when Shem died, and that Eber lived 4 years after Abraham's death. And that Shem, Arphaxed, Salah, Eber, Reu, Serug, Terah, and Nahor, the brother of Abraham, and Abraham, lived at the same time.— And that Nahor, brother of Abraham, Terah, Serug, Reu, Eber, Salah, Arphaxed, and Shem, were all acquainted with both Noah and Abraham.

53 We have now traced the chronology of the world, agreeably to the account given in our present bible, from Adam to Abraham, and have clearly determined, beyond the power of controversy, that there was no difficulty in preserving the knowledge of God in the world, from the creation of Adam, and the manifestation made to his immediate descendants, as set forth in the former part of this lecture, so that the students, in this class need not have any dubiety resting on their minds, on this subject; for they can easily see, that it is impossible for it to be otherwise; but that the knowledge of the existence of a God, must have continued from father to son, as a matter of tradition, at least. For we cannot suppose, that a knowledge of this important fact, could have existed in the mind of any of the before mentioned individ-

uals, without their having made it known to their posterity.

54 We have now shown how it was that the first thought ever existed in the mind of any individual, that there was such a being as a God, who had created and did uphold all things: that it was by reason of the manifestation which he first made to our father Adam, when he stood in his presence, and conversed with him face to face, at the time of his creation.

55 Let us here observe, that after any portion of the human family are made acquainted with the important fact that there is a God who has created and does uphold all things, the extent of their knowledge, respecting his character and glory, will depend upon their diligence and faithfulness in seeking after him, until like Enoch the brother of Jared, and Moses, they shall obtain faith in God, and power with him to behold him face to face.

56 We have now clearly set forth how it is, and how it was, that God became an object of faith for rational beings; and also, upon what foundation the testimony was based, which excited the enquiry and diligent search of the ancient saints, to seek after and obtain a knowledge of the glory of God: and we have seen that it was human testimony, and human testimony only, that excited this enquiry, in the first instance-in their minds—it was the credence they gave to the testimony of their fathers—this testimony having aroused their minds to enquire after the knowledge of God, the enquiry frequently terminated, indeed, always terminated, when rightly persued, in the most glorious discoveries, and eternal certainty.

Question.—Is there a being who has faith in himself independently?

Answer.—There is. Q. Who is it? A. It is God.

Q. How do you prove that God has faith in himself independently?

A. Because he is omnipotent, omnipresent, and omnicient; without beginning of days or end of life, and in him all fulness dwells. Eph. 1:23. Which is his body, the fulness of him that filleth all in all. Col. 1:19. For it pleased the Father, that in him should all fulness dwell. [§ 11. ¶ 2.]

Q. Is he the object in whom the faith of all other rational and accountable beings centers, for life and salvation?

A. He is.

Q. How do you prove it?

A. Isa. 45:22. Look unto me, and be ye saved, all the ends of the earth: for I am God, and there is none else. Rom. 11: 34,35,36. For who hath known the mind of the Lord? or who hath been his counsellor? or who hath first given to him, and it shall be recompensed unto him again? For of him, and through him, and to him, are all things: to whom be glory forever. Amen. Isa. 40: from the 8th to the 18th. O Zion that bringest good tidings, [Or, O thou that tellest good tidings to Zion.] get thee up into the high mountain: O Jerusalem, that bringest good tidings, [Or, O thou that tellest good tidings to Jerusalem,] lift up thy voice with strength; lift it up, be not afraid; say unto the cities of Judah, Behold your God! Behold the Lord your God will come with strong hand, [Or, against the strong.] and his arm shall rule for him: behold, his reward is with him, and his work before him. [Or, recompense for his work.] He shall feed his flock like a shepherd: he shall gather his lambs with his arms, and carry them in his bosom, and shall gently lead those that are with young. Who hath measured the waters in the hollow of his hand, and meted out heaven with the span, and comprehended the dust of the earth in a measure, weighed the mountains in scales, and the hills in a ballance? Who hath directed the Spirit of the Lord, or being his counsellor, hath taught him? With whom took he counsel, and who instructed him, and taught him in the path of judgment, and taught him knowledge, and shewed to him the way of understanding? Behold, the nations are as a drop of a bucket, and are counted as the small dust of the ballance: behold he taketh up the isles as a very little thing. And Lebanon is not sufficient to burn, nor the beasts thereof sufficient for a burnt offering. All nations are before him as nothing; and they are counted to him less than nothing, and vanity! Jer. 51:15,16. He [the Lord] hath made the earth by his power, he hath established the world by his wisdom, and hath streached out the heaven by his understanding. When he uttereth his voice there is a multitude of waters in the heavens;

and he causeth the vapors to ascend from the ends of the earth: he maketh lightnings with rain, and bringeth forth the wind out of his treasures. 1st Cor. 8:6. But to us there is but one God, the Father, of whom are all things, and we in him; and one Lord Jesus Christ, by whom are all things, and we by him. [§ 11. ¶ 2.]

Q. How did men first come to the knowledge of the existence of a God, so as to exercise faith in him?

A. In order to answer this question, it will be necessary to go back and examine man at his creation; the circumstances in which he was placed, and the knowledge which he had of God. [§ 11. ¶ 3,4,5,6,7,8,9,10,11.]

First, When man was created he stood in the presence of God. Gen. 1:27,28. From this we learn that man, at his creation, stood in the presence of his God, and had most perfect knowledge of his existence.

Secondly, God conversed with him after his transgression. Gen. 3: from the 8th to the 22nd. [§ 11. ¶ 13,14,15,16,17.]

From this we learn, that, though man did transgress, he was not deprived of the previous knowledge which he had of the existence of God. [§ 11. ¶ 19.]

Thirdly, God conversed with man after he cast him out of the garden. [§ 11. ¶ 22,23,24,25.]

Fourthly, God also conversed with Cain after he had slain Abel. Gen. 4: from the 4th to the 6th. [§ 11. ¶ 26,27,28,29.]

Q. What is the object of the foregoing quotation?

A. It is that it may be clearly seen how it was that the first thoughts were suggested to the minds of men, of the existence of God, and how extensively this knowledge was spread among the immediate descendants of Adam. [§ 11. ¶ 30,31,32,33.]

Q. What testimony had the immediate descendants of Adam, in proof of the existence of a God?

A. The testimony of their father. And after they were made acquainted with his existence, by the testimony of their father, they were dependant upon the exercise of their own faith, for a knowledge of his character, perfections and attributes. [§ 11. ¶ 23,24,25,26.]

Q. Had any others of the human family, beside Adam, a knowledge of the existence of God, in the first instance, by any other means than human testimony?

A. They had not. For previous to the time that they could have power to obtain a manifestation for themselves, the all-important fact had been communicated to them by their common father: and so, from father to child, the knowledge was communicated as extensively, as the knowledge of his existence was known; for it was by this means, in the first instance, that men had a knowledge of his existence. [§ 11. ¶ 35,36.]

Q. How do you know that the knowledge of the existence of God was communicated in this manner, throughout the different ages of the world?

A. By the chronology obtained thro' the revelations of God.

Q. How would you divide that chronology in order to convey it to the understanding clearly?

A. Into two parts: Frst, by embracing that period of the world from Adam to Noah; and secondly, from Noah to Abraham: from which period the knowledge of the existence of God has been so general, that it is a matter of no dispute in what manner the idea of his existence has been retained in the world.

Q. How many noted righteous men lived from Adam to Noah?

A. Nine; which includes Abel, who was slain by his brother.

Q. What are their names?

A. Abel, Seth, Enos, Cainan, Mahalaleel, Jared, Enoch, Methusaleh, and Lamech.

Q. How old was Adam when Seth was born?

A. One hundred and thirty years. Gen. 5:3.

Q. How many years did Adam live after Seth was born?

A. Eight hundred. Gen. 5:4.

Q. How old was Adam when he died?

A. Nine hundred and thirty years. Gen. 5:5.

Q. How old was Seth when Enos was born?

A. One hundred and five years. Gen. 5:6.

Q. How old was Enos when Cainan was born?

A. Ninety years. Gen. 5:9.

Q. How old was Cainan when Mahalaleel was born?

A. Seventy years. Gen. 5:12.

Q. How old was Mahalaleel when Jared was born?

A. Sixty five years. Gen. 5:15.

Q. How old was Jared when Enoch was born?

A. One hundred and sixty two years. Gen. 5:18.

Q. How old was Enoch when Methusaleh was born?

A. Sixty five. Gen. 5:21.

Q. How old was Methusaleh when Lamech was born?

A. One hundred and eighty seven years. Gen. 5:25.

Q. Ho w old was Lamech when Noah was born?

A. One hundred and eighty two years. Gen. 5:28.

For this chronology see § 11. ¶ 37.

Q. How many years, according to this account, was it from Adam to Noah?

A. One thousand and fifty six years.

Q. How old was Lamech when Adam died?

A. Lamech, the ninth from Adam, (including Abel,) and father of Noah, was fifty six years old when Adam died.

Q. How old was Methusaleh?

A. Two hundred and forty three years.   Q.   How old was Enoch?
A. Three hundred nnd eight years.
Q. How old was Jared?
A.   Four hundred and seventy years.
Q. How old was Mahalaleel?
A. Five hundred and thirty five.
Q. How old was Cainan?
A. Six hundred and five years.
Q. How old was Enos?
A. Six hundred and ninety five years.
Q. How old was Seth?
A. Eight hundred.
  For this item of the account see section second, paragraph 38.
Q. How many of these noted men were cotemporary with Adam?
A. Nine.
Q. What are their names?
A. Abel, Seth, Enos, Cainan, Mahalaleel, Jared, Enoch, Methusaleh, and Lamech. [§ II. ¶ 39.]
Q. How long did Seth live after Enos was born?
A. Eight hundred and seven years. Gen. 5:7.
Q. What was Seth's age when he died?
A. Nine hundred and twelve years- Gen. 5:8.
Q. How long did Enos live after Cainan was born?
A. Eight hundred and fifteen years. Gen. 5:10.
Q. What was Enos's age when he died?
A. Nine hundred and five years. Gen. 5:11.
Q. How long did Cainan live after Mahalaleel was born?
A. Eight hundred and forty years. Gen. 5:13.
Q. What was Cainan's age when he died?
A. Nine hundred and ten years. Gen. 5:14.
Q. How long did Mahaleel live after Jared was born?
A. Eight hundred and thirty years. Gen. 5:16.
Q. What was Mahalaleel's age when he died?
A. Eight hundred and ninety five years. Gen. 5:17.
Q- How long did Jared live after Enoch was born?
A. Eight hundred years. Gen. 5:19.
Q. What was Jared's age when he died?
A. Nine hundred and sixty two years. Gen. 5:20.
Q. How long did Enoch walk with God after Methusaleh was born?
A. Three hundred years. Gen. 5:22.
Q. What was Enoch's age when he was translatedd?
A. Three hundred and sixty five years. Gen. 5:23.
Q. How long did Methusaleh live after Lamech was born?

A. Seven hundred and eighty two years.   Gen. 5:26.

Q. What was Methusaleh's age when he died?

A. Nine hundred and sixty nine years. Gen. 5:27.

Q. How long did Lamech live after Noah was born? A. Five hundred and n e y five ye rs. Gen. 5:30.

Q. What was Lamech's age when he died?

A. Seven hundred and seventy seven years. Gen. 5:31.

For the account of the last item see [§ 11. ¶ 40.]

Q. In what year of the world did Adam die?

A. In the nine hundred and thirtieth·

Q. In what year was Enoch translated?

A. In the nine hundred and eighty seventh.

Q. In what year did Seth die?

A. In the one thousand and forty second.

Q. In what year did Enos die?

A. In the eleven hundred and fortieth.

Q. In what year did Cainan die?

A. In the twelve hundred and thirty fifth.

Q. In what year did Mahalaleel die?

A. In the twelve hundred and ninetieth.

Q. In what year did Jared die?

A. In the fourteen hundred and twenty second.

Q. In what year did Lamech die?

A. In the sixteen hundred and fifty first.

Q. In what year did Methusaleh die?

A. In the sixteen hundred and fifty sixth.

For this account see § 11. ¶ 41.

Q. How old was Noah when Enos died?

A. Eighty four years.

Q. How old when Cainan died?

A. One hundred and seventy nine years.

Q. How old when Mahalaleel died?

A. Two hundred and thirty four years.

Q. How old when Jared died?

A. Three hundred and sixty six years.

Q. How old when Lamech died?

A. Five hundred and ninety five years.

Q. How old when Methusaleh died?

A. Six hundred years.

See § 11. ¶ 42, for the last item.

Q. How many of those men lived in the days of Noah?

A. Six.

Q. What are their names?

A. Seth, Enos, Cainan, Mahalaleel, Jared, Methusaleh, and Lamech. [§ 11. ¶ 43.

Q. How many of those men were cotemporary with Adam

and Noah both? A. Six. Q. What are their names?
A. Enos, Cainan, Mahalaleel, Jared, Methusaleh, and Lamech. [§ 11. ¶ 43.]

Q. According to the foregoing account, how was the knowledge of the existence of God first suggested to the minds of men?

A. By the manifestation made to our father Adam, when he was in the presence of God, both before and while he was in Eden. [§ 11. ¶ 44.]

Q. How was the knowledge of the existence of God disseminated among the inhabitants of the world?

A. By tradition from father to son. [§ 11. ¶ 44.]

Q. How old was Noah when Shem was born?
A. Five hundred and two years. Gen. 5:32. 11:10.

Q. What was the term of years from the birth of Shem to the flood?
A. Ninety eight.

Q. What was the term of years that Noah lived after the flood?
A. Three hundred and fifty. Gen. 9:28.

Q. What was Noah's age when he died?
A. Nine hundred and fifty years. Gen. 9:29. [§ 11. ¶ 45.]

Q. What was Shem's age when Arphaxed was born?
A. One hundred years. Gen. 11:10.

Q. What was Arphaxed's age when Salah was born?
A. Thirty five years. Gen. 11:12.

Q. What was Salah's age when Eber was born?
A. Thirty. Gen. 11:14.

Q. What was Eber's age when Peleg was born?
A. Thirty four years. Gen. 11:16.

Q. What was Peleg's age when Reu was born?
A. Thirty years. Gen. 11:18.

Q. What was Reu's age when Serug was born?
A. Thirty two years. Gen. 11:20.

Q. What was Serug's age when Nahor was born?
A. Thirty years. Gen. 11:22.

Q. What was Nahor's age when Terah was born?
A. Twenty nine. Gen. 11:24.

Q. What was Terah's age, when Nahor the father of Abraham was born?
A. Seventy years. Gen. 11:26.

Q. What was Terah's age when Abraham was born?
A. Some suppose one hundred and thirty years, and others seventy. Gen. 12:4. 11:26. [§ 11. ¶ 46.]

Q. What was the number of years from the flood to the birth of Abraham?

A. Supposing Abraham to have been born when Terah was one hundred and thirty years old, it was three hundred and fifty two years: but if he were born when Terah was seventy years old, it was two hundred and ninety two years. [§ ıı ¶ 47.]

Q. How long did Shem live after Arphaxed was born?
A. Five hundred years.   Gen. 11:11.
Q. What was Shem's age when he died?
A. Six hundred years.   Gen. 11:11.
Q. What number of years did Arphaxed live after Salah was born?
A. Four hundred and three years.   Gen. 21:13.
Q. What was Arphaxed's age when he died?
A. Four hundred and thirty eight years.
Q. What number of years did Salah live after Eber was born?
A. Four hundred and three years.   Gen. 11:15.
Q. What was Salah's age when he died?
A. Four hundred and thirty three years.
Q. What number of years did Eber live after Peleg was born?
A. Four hundred and thirty years.   Gen. 11:17.
Q. What was Eber's age when he died?
A. Four hundred and sixty four years.
Q. What number of years did Peleg live after Reu was born?
A. Two hundred and nine years.   Gen. 11:19.
Q. What was Peleg's age when he died?
A. Two hundred and thirty nine years.
Q. What number of years did Reu live after Serug was born?
A. Two hundred and seven years.   Gen. 11:21.
Q. What was Reu's age when he died?
A. Two hundred and thirty nine years.
Q. What number of years did Serug live after Nahor was born?
A. Two hundred years.   Gen. 11:23.
Q. What was Serug's age when he died?
A. Two hundred and thirty years.
Q. What number of years did Nahor live after Terah was born?
A. One hundred and nineteen years.   Gen. 11:25.
Q. What was Nahor's age when he died?
A. One hundred and forty eight years.
Q. What number of years did Terah live after Abraham was born?
A. Supposing Terah to have been one hundred and thirty years old when Abraham was born, he lived seventy five years; but if Abraham was born when Terah was seventy years old, he lived one hundred and thirty five.
Q. What was Terah's age when he died?

A. Two hundred and five years.   Gen. 11:32.

For this account from the birth of Arphaxed, to the death of Terah, see [§ 11.' ¶ 48.]

Q. In what year of the world did Peleg die?

A. Agreeably to the foregoing chronology, he died in the nineteen hundred and ninety sixth year of the world.

Q. In what year of the world did Nahor die?

A. In the nineteen hundred and ninety seventh.

Q. In what year of the world did Noah die?

A. In the two thousand and sixth.

Q. In what year of the world did Reu die?

A. In the two thousand and twenty sixth.

Q. In what year of the world did Serug die?

A. In the two thousand and forty ninth.

Q. In what year of the world did Terah die?

A. In the two thousand and eighty third.

Q. In what year of the world did Arphaxed die?

A. In the two thousand and ninty sixth.

Q. In what year of the world did Salah die?

A. In the twenty one hundred and twenty sixth.

Q. In what year of the world did Abraham die?

A. In the twenty one hundred and eighty third.

Q. In what year of the world did Eber die?

A. In the twenty one hundred and eighty seventh.

For this account of the year of the world in which those men died, see [§11: ¶ 49,50.]

Q. How old was Nahor, Abraham's brother, when Noah died?

A. Fifty eight years.

Q. How old was Terah?

A. One hundred and twenty eight.

Q. How old was Serug?

A. One hundred and eighty seven.

Q. How old was Reu?

A. Two hundred and nineteen.

Q. How old was Eber?

A. Two hundred and eighty three.

Q. How old was Salah?

A. Three hundred and thirteen.

Q. How old was Arphaxed?

A. Three hundred and forty eight.

Q. How old was Shem?

A. Four hundred and forty eight.

For the last account see [§ 11. ¶ 51.]

Q. How old was Abraham when Reu died?

A. Eighteen years, if he were born when Terah was one

hundred and thirty years old. Q. What was his age when Serug, and Nahor, Abraham's brother died?

A. Forty one years.

Q. What was his age when Terah died?

A. Seventy five years.

Q. What was his age when Arphaxed died?

A. Eighty eight.

Q. What was his age when Salah died?

A. One hundred and eighteen years.

Q. What was his age when Shem died?

A. One hundred and fifty years.

For this see [§ 11. ¶ 52.]

Q. How many noted characters lived from Noah to Abraham?

A. Ten.

Q. What are their names?

A. Shem, Arphaxed, Salah, Eber, Peleg, Reu, Serug, Nahor, Terah, and Nahor, Abraham's brother. [§ 11. ¶ 52.]

Q. How many of these were cotemporary with Noah?

A. The whole.

Q. How many with Abraham?

A. Eight.

Q. What are their names?

A. Nahor, Abraham's brother, Terah, Serug, Reu, Eber, Selah, Arphaxed, and Shem. [§ 11. ¶ 52.]

Q. How many were cotemporary with both Noah and Abraham?

A. Eight.

Q. What are their names?

A. Shem, Arphaxed, Salah, Eber, Reu, Serug, Terah, and
Nahor, Abraham's brother. [§ 11. ¶ 52.]

Q. Did any of these men die before Noah?

A. They did.

Q. Who were they?

A. Peleg, in whose days the earth was divided, and Nahor
Abraham's grand-father. [§ 11. ¶ 49.]

Q. Did any one of them live longer than Abraham?

A. There was one. [§ 11. ¶ 50.]

Q. Who was it?

A. Eber, the fourth from Noah. [§ 11. ¶ 50.]

Q. In whose days was the earth divided?

A. In the days of Peleg.

Q. Where have we the account given that the earth was divided in the days of Peleg?

A. Gen. 10:25.

Q. Can you repeat the sentence?

A. Unto Eber were born two sons; the name of one was Peleg; for in his days the earth was divided.

Q. What testimony have men, in the first instance, that there is a God?

A. Human testimony, and human testimony only. [§ II. ¶ 56.]

Q. What excited the ancient saints to seek diligently after a knowledge of the glory of God, his perfections and attributes?

A. The credence they gave to the testimony of their fathers. [§ II. ¶ 56.]

Q. How do men obtain a knowledge of the glory of God, his perfections and attributes?

A. By devoting themselves to his service, through prayer and supplication incessantly, strengthening their faith in him, until like Enoch, the brother of Jared, and Moses, they obtain a manifestation of God to themselves. [§ II. ¶ 55.]

Q. Is the knowledge of the existence of God a matter of mere tradition, founded upon human testimony alone, until a person receives a manifestation of God to themselves?

A. It is.

Q. How do you prove it?

A. From the whole of the first lecture of the second section.

LECTURE THIRD.

Of Faith.

SECTION III.

1 In the second lecture it was shown, how it was that the knowledge of the existence of God, came into the world, and by what means the first thoughts were suggested to the minds of men, that such a being did actually exist: and that it was by reason of the knowledge of his existence, that there was a foundation laid for the exercise of faith in him, as the only being in whom faith could center for life and salvation. For faith could not center in a being of whose existence we had no idea; because the idea of his existence in the first instance, is essential to the exercise of faith in him. Rom. 10:14: "How

3*

then shall they call on him in whom they have not believed? And how shall they believe in him of whom they have not heard? And how shall they hear without a preacher?" (or one sent to tell them?) So then faith comes by hearing the word of God. [New Translation.]

2 Let us here observe, that three things are necessary, in order that any rational and intelligent being may exercise faith in God unto life and salvation.

3 First, The idea that he actually exists.

4 Secondly, A *correct* idea of his character, perfections and attributes.

5 Thirdly, An actual knowledge that the course of life which he is pursuing, is according to his will.—For without an acquaintance with these three important facts, the faith of every rational being must be imperfect and unproductive; but with this understanding, it can become perfect and fruitful, abounding in righteousness unto the praise and glory of God the Father, and the Lord Jesus Christ.

6 Having previously been made acquainted with the way the idea of his existence came into the world, as well as the fact of his existence, we shall proceed to examine his character, perfections and attributes, in order that this class may see, not only the just grounds which they have for the exercise of faith in him, for life and salvation, but the reasons that all the world, also, as far as the idea of his existence extends, may have to exercise faith in him the Father of all living.

7 As we have been indebted to a revelation which God made of himself to his creatures in the first instance, for the idea of his existence, so in like manner we are indebted to the revelations which he has given to us, for a correct understanding of his character, perfections and attributes; because without the revelations which he has given to us, no man by searching could find out God. Job 11:7,8,9. First

Cor. 2:9,10,11: "But as it is written, eye has not seen, nor ear heard, neither have entered into the heart of man, the things which God has prepared for them that love him; but God has revealed them unto us by his Spirit: for the Spirit searches all things, yea, the deep things of God. For what man knows the things of a man, save the spirit of man which is in him? Even so, the things of God no man knows but by the Spirit of God."

8 Having said so much, we proceed to examine the character which the revelations have given of God.

9 Moses gives us the following account in Exodus, 34:6: "And the Lord passed by before him, and proclaimed, The Lord God, the Lord God, merciful and gracious, long suffering, and abundant in goodness and truth." Psalm 103:6,7,8: "The Lord executes righteousness and judgment for all that are oppressed. He made known his ways unto Moses, his acts unto the children of Israel. The Lord is merciful and gracious, slow to anger and plenteous in mercy:" Psalm 103:17,18: "But the mercy of the Lord is from everlasting to everlasting upon them that fear him, and his righteousness unto children's children, to such as keep his covenant, and to those that remember his commandments to do them." Psalm 90:2: "Before the mountains were brought forth, or ever you had formed the earth and the world, even from everlasting to everlasting, you are God." Heb. 1:10, 11,12: "And you, Lord, in the beginning have laid the foundation of the earth; and the heavens are the works of your hands: they shall perish, but you shall remain; and they shall wax old as a garment; and as a vesture shall you fold them up, and they shall be changed: but you are the same, and your years shall not fail." James 1:17: "Every good gift, and every perfect gift, is from above, and comes down from the Father of lights; with whom is no variableness,

neither shadow of turning." Malachi 3:6. "For I am the Lord, I change not; therefore ye sons of Jacob are not consumed."

10 Book of Commandments, chapt. 2nd, commencing in the third line of the first paragraph: "For God does not walk in crooked paths, neither does he turn to the right hand or the left, or vary from that which he has said, therefore his paths are strait, and his course is one eternal round:" Book of Commandments, chapt. 37:1. "Listen to the voice of the Lord your God, even Alpha and Omega, the beginning and the end, whose course is one eternal round, the same yesterday to-day and forever."

11 Numbers, 23:19. "God is not a man, that he should lie; neither the son of man that he should repent." First John, 4:8. "He that loves not, knows not God; for God is love." Acts, 10:34: "Then Peter opened his mouth and said Of a truth I perceive that God is no respecter of persons, but in every nation he that fears God and works righteousness is accepted with him."

12 From the foregoing testimonies, we learn the following things respecting the character of God.

13 First, That he was God before the world was created, and the same God that he was, after it was created.

14 Secondly, That he is merciful, and gracious, slow to anger, abundant in goodness, and that he was so from everlasting, and will be to everlasting.

15 Thirdly, That he changes not, neither is there variableness with him; but that he is the same from everlasting to everlasting, being the same yesterday to-day and forever; and that his course is one eternal round, without variation.

16 Fourthly, That he is a God of truth and cannot lie.

17 Fifthly, That he is no respecter of persons; but

in every nation he that fears God and works righteousness is accepted of him.

18 Sixthly, That he is love.

19 An acquaintance with these attributes in the divine
character, is essentially necessary, in order that the
faith of any rational being can center in him for life
and salvation. For if he did not, in the first instance,
believe him to be God, that is, the creator and upholder
of all things, he could not *center* his faith in him for
life and salvation, for fear there should be a greater
than he, who would thwart all his plans, and he, like
the gods of the heathen, would be unable to fulfil his
promises; but seeing he is God over all, from everlasting to everlasting, the creator and upholder of all
things, no such fear can exist in the minds of those
who put their trust in him, so that in this respect their
faith can be without wavering.

20 But secondly: Unless he was merciful, and gracious, slow to anger, long suffering, and full of goodness, such is the weakness of human nature, and so
great the frailties and imperfections of men, that unless they believed that these excellencies existed in the
divine character, the faith necessary to salvation
could not exist; for doubt would take the place of
faith, and those who know their weakness and lia-
bility to sin, would be in constant doubt of salvation,
if it were not for the idea which they have of the excellency of the character of God, that he is slow to anger, and long suffering, and of a forgiving disposition, and does forgive iniquity, transgression and sin.
An idea of these facts does away doubt, and makes
faith exceedingly strong.

21 But it is equally as necessary that men should
have the idea that he is a God who changes not, in order to have faith in him, as it is to have the idea that
he is gracious and long suffering. For without the
idea of unchangibleness in the character of the Deity,

doubt would take the place of faith. But with the idea that he changes not, faith lays hold upon the excellencies in his character with unshaken confidence, believing he is the same yesterday, to-day and forever, and that his course is one eternal round.

22 And again, the idea that he is a God of truth and cannot lie, is equally as necessary to the exercise of faith in him, as the idea of his unchangeableness. For without the idea that he was a God of truth and could not lie, the confidence necessary to be placed in his word in order to the exercise of faith in him, could not exist. But having the idea that he is not man that he can lie, it gives power to the minds of men to exercise faith in him.

23 But it is also necessary that men should have an idea that he is no respecter of persons; for with the idea of all the other excellencies in his character, and this one wanting, men could not exercise faith in him, because if he were a respecter of persons, they could not tell what their privileges were, nor how far they were authorized to exercise faith in him, or whether they were authorized to do it at all, but all must be confusion; but no sooner are the minds of men made acquainted with the truth on this point, that he is no respecter of persons, than they see that they have authority by faith to lay hold on eternal life the richest boon of heaven, because God is no respecter of persons, and that every man in every nation has an equal privilege.

24 And lastly, but not less important to the exercise of faith in God, is the idea that he is love; for with all the other excellencies in his character, without this one to influence them, they could not have such powerful dominion over the minds of men; but when the idea is planted in the mind that he is love, who cannot see the just ground that men of every nation, kindred

and tongue, have to exercise faith in God so as to obtain eternal life?

25 From the above description of the character of the Deity which is given him in the revelations, to men, there is a sure foundation for the exercise of faith in him among every people, nation and kindred, from age to age, and from generation to generation.

26 Let us here observe that the foregoing is the character which is given of God in his revelations to the Former Day Saints, and it is also the character which is given of him in his revelations to the Latter Day Saints, so that the saints of former days, and those of latter days, are both alike in this respect; the "Latter Day Saints" having as good grounds to exercise faith in God, as the former day saints had; because the same character is given of him to both.

———— ◆ ————

Q. What was shown in the second lecture?
A. It was shown how the knowledge of the existence of God came into the world—[§ III. ¶ 1.]
Q. What is the effect of the idea of his existence among men?
A. It lays the foundation for the exercise of faith in him.— [§ III. ¶ 1.]
Q. Is the idea of his existence, in the first instance, necessary in order for the exercise of faith in him?
A. It is. [§ III. ¶ 1.]
Q. How do you prove it?
A. By the 16 chapter to Romans and 14 verse. [§ III. ¶ 1.]
Q. How many things are necessary for us to understand, respecting the Deity and our relation to him, in order that we may exercise faith in him for life and salvation?
A. Three. [§ III. ¶ 2.]
Q. What are they?
A. First, that God does actually exist: Secondly, correct ideas of his character, his perfections and attributes; and Thirdly, that the course which we pursue is according to his mind and will. [§ III. ¶ 3,4,5.]
Q. Would the idea of any one or two of the above mentioned things, enable a person to exercise faith in God?

A. It would not, for without the idea of them all, faith would be imperfect and unproductive. [§ III. ¶ 5.]

Q. Would an idea of these three things lay a sure foundation for the exercise of faith in God, so as to obtain life and salvation?

A. It would; for by the idea of these three things, faith could become perfect, and fruitful, abounding in righteousness unto the praise and glory of God. [§ III. ¶ 5.]

Q. How are we to be made acquainted with the before mentioned things respecting the Deity, and respecting ourselves?

A. By revelation. [§ III. ¶ 6.]

Q. Could these things be found out by any other means than by revelation?

A. They could not.

Q. How do you prove it?

A. By the scriptures: Job 11:7,8:9. 1 Corinthians 2:9,10, 11. [§ III. ¶ 7.]

Q. What things do we learn in the revelations of God respecting his character?

A. We learn the six following things. First, that he was God before the world was created, and the same God that he was after it was created. Secondly, that he is merciful and gracious, slow to anger, abundant in goodness, and that he was so from everlasting, and will be so to everlasting. Thirdly, that he changes not, neither is there variableness with him, and that his course is one eternal round. Fourthly, that he is a God of truth and cannot lie. Fifthly, that he is no respecter of persons; and Sixthly, that he is love. [§ III. ¶ 12,13, 14,15,16,17,18.]

Q. Where do you find the revelations which give us this idea of the character of the Deity?

A. In the bible and book of commandments, and they are quoted in the third lecture. [§ III. ¶ 9,10,11.]

Q. What effect would it have on any rational being not to have an idea that the Lord was God, the creator and upholder of all things?

A. It would prevent him from exercising faith in him unto life and salvation.

Q. Why would it prevent him from exercising faith in God?

A. Because he would be as the heathen not knowing but there might be a being greater and more powerful than he, and thereby he be prevented from fulfilling his promises. [§ III. ¶ 19.]

Q. Does this idea prevent this doubt?

A. It does: for persons having this idea are enabled thereby to exercise faith without this doubt. [§ III. ¶ 19.]

Q. Is it not also necessary to have the idea that God is

merciful, and gracious, long suffering and full of goodness?

A. It is. [§ III. ¶ 20.]

Q. Why is it necessary?

A. Because of the weakness and imperfections of human nature, and the great frailties of man; for such is the weakness of man, and such his frailties, that he is liable to sin continually, and if God were not long suffering, and full of compassion, gracious and merciful and of a forgiving disposition, man would be cut off from before him in consequence of which, he would be in continual doubt and could not exercise faith: for where doubt is, there faith has no power, but by man's believing that God is full of compassion and forgiveness, long suffering and slow to anger, he can exercise faith in him and overcome doubt, so as to be exceedingly strong. [§ III. ¶ 20.]

Q. Is it not equally as necessary that man should have an idea that God changes not, neither is there variableness with him, in order to exercise faith in him unto life and salvation?

A. It is; because without this, he would not know how soon the mercy of God might change into cruelty, his long suffering into rashness, his love into hatred, and in consequence of which doubt, man would be incapable of exercising faith in him, but having the idea that he is unchangeable, man can have faith in him continually, believing that what he was yesterday he is to day, and will be forever. [§ III. ¶ 21.]

Q. Is it not necessary also, for men to have an idea that God is a being of truth, before they can have perfect faith in him?

A. It is; for unless men have this idea they cannot place confidence in his word, and not being able to place confidence in his word, they could not have faith in him; but believing that he is a God of truth, and that his word cannot fail, their faith can rest in him without doubt. [§ III. ¶ 22.]

Q. Could man exercise faith in God so as to obtain eternal life unless he believed that God was no respecter of persons?

A. He could not; because without this idea he could not certainly know that it was his privilege so to do, and in consequence of this doubt his faith could not be sufficiently strong to save him. [§ III. ¶ 23.]

Q. Would it be possible for a man to exercise faith in God, so as to be saved, unless he had an idea that God was love?

A. He could not; because man could not love God, unless he had an idea that God was love, and if he did not love God, he could not have faith in him. [§ III. ¶ 24.]

Q. What is the description which the sacred writers give of the character of the Deity calculated to do?

A. It is calculated to lay a foundation for the exercise of faith in him, as far as the knowledge extends among all people, tongues, languages, kindreds, and nations and that from age to age, and from generation to generation. [§ III.   ¶ 25.]

Q. Is the character which God has given of himself uniform?

A. It is, in all his revelations whether to the Former Day Saints, or to the Latter day saints, so that they all have the authority to exercise faith in him, and to expect by the exercise of their faith, to enjoy the same blessings.   [§ III. ¶ 26.]

LECTURE FOURTH.

Of Faith.

SECTION IV.

1 Having shown in the third lecture, that correct ideas of the character of God are necessary in order to the exercise of faith in him unto life and salvation, and that without correct ideas of his character, the minds of men could not have sufficient power with God to the exercise of faith necessary to the enjoyment of eternal life, and that correct ideas of his character lay a foundation as far as his character is concerned, for the exercise of faith, so as to enjoy the fulness of the blessing of the gospel of Jesus Christ, even that of eternal glory; we shall now proceed to show the connection there is between correct ideas of the attributes of God, and the exercise of faith in him unto eternal life.

2 Let us here observe, that the real design which the God of heaven had in view in making the human family acquainted with his attributes, was, that they through the ideas of the existence of his attributes, might be enabled to exercise faith in him, and through the exercise of faith in him, might obtain eternal life. For without the idea of the existence of the attributes which belong to God, the minds of men could not have power to exercise faith

on him so as to lay hold upon eternal life. The God of heaven understanding most perfectly the constitution of human nature, and the weakness of man, knew what was necessary to be revealed, and what ideas must be planted in their minds in order that they might be enabled to exercise faith in him unto eternal life.

3 Having said so much we shall proceed to examine the attributes of God, as set forth in his revelations to the human family, and to show how necessary correct ideas of his attributes are, to enable men to exercise faith in him. For without these ideas being planted in the minds of men, it would be out of the power of any person or persons to exercise faith in God so as to obtain eternal life. So that the divine communications made to man in the first instance, were designed to establish in their minds the ideas necessary to enable them to exercise faith in God, and through this means to be partakers of his glory.

4 We have, in the revelations which he has given to the human family, the following account of his attributes.

5 First, Knowledge. Acts 15:18. Known unto God are all his works from the beginning of the world. Isaiah 46:9,10. Remember the former things of old; for I am God and there is none else; I am God, and there is none like me, *declaring the end from the beginning,* and from ancient time the things that are not yet done, saying, My counsel shall stand, and I will do all my pleasure.

6 Secondly, Faith, or power. Heb. 11:3. Through faith we understand that the worlds were framed by the word of God. Gen. 1:1. In the beginning God created the heaven and the earth. Isaiah 14:24,27. The Lord of hosts has sworn, saying, Surely as I have thought so shall it come to pass; and as I have purposed, so shall it stand. For the Lord of hosts

has purposed, and who shall disannul it? and his hand is stretched out, and who shall turn it back?

7 Thirdly, Justice. Ps. 89:14. Justice and judgment are the habitation of thy throne. Isaiah 45:21. Tell ye, and bring them near; yea, let them take council together: who has declared this from the ancient time? Have not I the Lord? and there is no God else beside me; a just God and a Savior. Zeph. 3:5. The just Lord is in the midst thereof. Zech. 9:9. Rejoice greatly, O daughter of Zion; shout, O daughter of Jerusalem: behold, thy King comes unto thee: he is just, and having salvation.

8 Fourthly, Judgment. Ps. 89:14. Justice and judgment are the habitation of thy throne. Deut. 32:4. He is the Rock, his work is perfect; for all his ways are judgment: a God of truth, and without iniquity: just and right is he. Ps. 9:7. But the Lord shall endure forever: he has prepared his throne for judgment. Ps. 9:16. The Lord is known by the judgment which he executes.

9 Fifthly, Mercy. Ps. 89:15. Mercy and truth shall go before his face. Exodus 34:6. And the Lord passed by before him, and proclaimed, The Lord, the Lord God, merciful and gracious. Neh. 9:17.— But thou art a God ready to pardon, gracious and merciful.

10 And Sixthly, Truth. Ps. 89:14. Mercy and truth shall go before thy face. Exodus 34:6. Long suffering and abundant in goodness and truth. Deut. 32:4. He is the Rock, his work is perfect; for all his ways are judgment. A God of truth and without iniquity: just and right is he. Ps. 31:5. Into thy hand I commit my spirit: thou hast redeemed me, O Lord God of truth.

11 By a little reflection it will be seen, that the idea of the existence of these attributes in the Deity, is necessary to enable any rational being to exercise faith

in him. For without the idea of the existence of these attributes in the Deity, men could not exercise faith in him for life and salvation; seeing that without the knowledge of all things, God would not be able to save any portion of his creatures; for it is by reason of the knowledge which he has of all things, from the beginning to the end, that enables him to give that understanding to his creatures, by which they are made partakers of eternal life; and if it were not for the idea existing in the minds of men, that God had all knowledge, it would be impossible for them to exercise faith in him.

12 And it is not less necessary that men should have the idea of the existence of the attribute power in the Deity. For, unless God had power over all things, and was able, by his power, to control all things, and thereby deliver his creatures who put their trust in him, from the power of all beings that might seek their destruction, whether in heaven, on earth, or in hell, men could not be saved; but with the idea of the existence of this attribute, planted in the mind, men feel as though they had nothing to fear, who put their trust in God, believing that he has power to save all who come to him, to the very uttermost.

13 It is also necessary, in order to the exercise of faith in God, unto life and salvation, that men should have the idea of the existence of the attribute justice, in him. For without the idea of the existence of the attribute Justice, in the Deity, men could not have confidence sufficiently to place themselves under his guidance and direction; for they would be filled with fear and doubt, lest the Judge of all the earth would not do right; and thus fear, or doubt, existing in the mind, would preclude the possibility of the exercise of faith in him for life and salvation. But, when the idea of the existence of the attribute justice, in the Deity, is fairly planted in the mind, it leaves

no room for doubt to get into the heart, and the mind is enabled to cast itself upon the Almighty without fear and without doubt, and with most unshaken confidence, believing that the Judge of all the earth will do right.

14 It is also of equal importance that men should have the idea of the existence of the attribute judgment, in God, in order that they may exercise faith in him for life and salvation; for without the idea of the existence of this attribute in the Deity, it would be impossible for men to exercise faith in him for life and salvation, seeing that it is through the exercise of this attribute that the faithful in Christ Jesus are delivered out of the hands of those who seek their destruction; for if God were not to come out in swift judgment against the workers of iniquity and the powers of darkness, his saints could not be saved; for it is by judgment that the Lord delivers his saints out of the hands of all their enemies, and those who reject the gospel of our Lord Jesus Christ. But no sooner is the idea of the existence of this attribute, planted in the minds of men, than it gives power to the mind for the exercise of faith and confidence in God, and they are enabled, by faith, to lay hold on the promises which are set before them, and wade through all the tribulations and afflictions to which they are subjected by reason of the persecution from those who know not God, and obey not the gospel of our Lord Jesus Christ: believing, that in due time the Lord will come out in swift judgment against their enemies, and they shall be cut off from before him, and that in his own due time he will bear them off conquerers and more than conquerers in all things.

15 And again, it is equally important that men should have the idea of the existence of the attribute mercy, in the Deity, in order to exercise faith in him for life and salvation. For, without the idea of the existence

of this attribute in the Deity, the spirits of the saints
would faint in the midst of the tribulations, afflictions
and persecutions which they have to endure for righteousness' sake; but when the idea of the existence of
this attribute is once established in the mind it gives
life and energy to the spirits of the saints: believing
that the mercy of God will be poured out upon them
in the midst of their afflictions, and that he will com-
passionate them in their sufferings; and that the mercy of God will lay hold of them and secure them in
the arms of his love, so that they will receive a full
reward for all their sufferings.

16 And lastly, but not less important to the exercise of faith in God, is the idea of the existence of
the attribute truth, in him. For, without the idea of
the existence of this attribute the mind of man could
have nothing upon which it could rest with certainty:
all would be confusion and doubt; but with the idea
of the existence of this attribute in the Deity, in the
mind, all the teachings, instructions, promises and
blessings become realities, and the mind is enabled to
lay hold of them with certainty and confidence: believing that these things, and all that the Lord has
said, shall be fulfilled in their time; and that all the
cursings, denunciations and judgments, pronounced
upon the heads of the unrighteous will also be executed in the due time of the Lord: and by reason of the
truth and veracity of him, the mind beholds its deliverance and salvation as being certain.

17 Let the mind once reflect sincerely and candid-
ly upon the ideas of the existence of the before mentioned attributes in the Deity, and it will be seen,
that as far as his attributes are concerned, there is a
sure foundation laid for the exercise of faith in him
for life and salvation. For in as much as God possesses the attribute knowledge he can make all things

D

known to his saints necessary for their salvation; and as he possesses the attribute power he is able thereby to deliver them from the power of all enemies; and seeing also, that justice is an attribute of the Deity, he will deal with them upon the principles of righteousness and equity, and a just reward will be granted unto them for all their afflictions and sufferings for the truth's sake. And as judgment is an attribute of the Deity also, his saints can have the most unshaken confidence, that they will, in due time, obtain a perfect deliverance out of the hands of all their enemies, and a complete victory over all those who have sought their hurt and destruction. And as mercy is also an attribute of the Deity, his saints can have confidence that it will be exercised toward them; and through the exercise of that attribute toward them, comfort and consolation will be administered unto them abundantly, amid all their afflictions and tribulations. And lastly, realizing that truth is an attribute of the Deity, the mind is led to rejoice amid all its trials and temptations, in hope of that glory which is to be brought at the revelation of Jesus Christ, and in view of that crown which is to be placed upon the heads of the saints in the day when the Lord shall distribute rewards unto them, and in prospect of that eternal weight of glory which the Lord has promised to bestow upon them when he shall bring them into the midst of his throne to dwell in his presence eternally.

18 In view, then, of the existence of these attributes, the faith of the saints can become exceedingly strong: abounding in righteousness unto the praise and glory of God, and can exert its mighty influence in searching after wisdom and understanding, until it has obtained a knowledge of all things that pertain to life and salvation.

19 Such, then, is the foundation, which is laid,

through the revelation of the attributes of God, for the exercise of faith in him for life and salvation; and seeing that these are attributes of the Deity, they are unchangeable—being the same yesterday to day and forever—which gives to the minds of the Latter Day Saints the same power and authority to exercise faith in God, which the Former Day Saints had: so that all the saints, in this respect have been, are and will be alike, until the end of time; for God never changes, therefore his attributes and character remain forever the same. And as it is through the revelation of these that a foundation is laid for the exercise of faith in God unto life and salvation, the foundation, therefore, for the exercise of faith, was, is and ever will be the same. So that all men have had, and will have an equal privilege.

Question. What was shown in the third lecture?

Answer. It was shown that correct ideas of the character of God are necessary in order to exercise faith in him unto life and salvation; and that without correct ideas of his character, men could not have power to exercise faith in him unto life and salvation, but that correct ideas of his character, as far as his character is concerned in the exercise of faith in him, lay a sure foundation for the exercise of it. [§ iv. ¶ 1.]

Q. What object had the God of heaven in revealing his attributes to men?

A. That through an acquaintance with his attributes they might be enabled to exercise faith in him so as to obtain eternal life. [§ iv. ¶ 2.]

Q. Could men exercise faith in God without an acquaintance with his attributes, so as to be enabled to lay hold of eternal life?

A. They could not. [§ iv. ¶ 2;3.]

Q. What account is given of the attributes of God in in his revelations?

A. First, Knowledge, secondly, Faith, or power, thirdly, Justice, fourthly, Judgment, fifthly, Mercy, and sixthly truth. § iv. ¶ 4,5,6,7,8,9 and 10.]

4*

Q. Where are the revelations to be found which give this relation of the attributes of God?

A. In the Old and New Testaments, and they are quoted in the fourth lecture, fifth, sixth, seventh, eighth, ninth, and tenth paragraphs.*

Q. Is the idea of the existence of those attributes, in the Deity, necessary in order to enable any rational being to exercise faith in him unto life and salvation?

A. It is.

Q. How do you prove it?

A. By the eleventh, twelfth, thirteenth fourteenth, fifteenth and sixteenth paragraphs in this lecture.*

Q. Does the idea of the existence of these attributes in the Deity, as far as his attributes are concerned, enable a rational being to exercise faith in him unto life and salvation?

A. It does.

Q. How do you prove it?

A. By the seventeenth and eighteenth paragraphs.*

Q. Have the Latter Day Saints as much authoity given them, through the revelation of the attributes of God, to exercise faith in him as the Former Day Saints had?

A. They have.

Q. How do you prove it?

A. By the nineteenth paragraph of this lecture.*

Note. Let the student turn and commit those paragraphs to memory.

————————

LECTURE FIFTH.

Of Faith.

SECTION V.

1 In our former lectures we treated of the being, character, perfections and attributes of God. What we mean by perfections, is, the perfections which belong to all the attributes of his nature. We shall, in this lecture speak of the Godhead: we mean the Father, Son and Holy Spirit.

2 There are two personages who constitute the great, matchless, governing and supreme power over

all things—by whom all things were created and made, that are created and made, whether visible or invisible: whether in heaven, on earth, or in the earth, under the earth, or throughout the immensity of space —They are the Father and the Son: The Father being a personage of spirit, glory and power: possessing all perfection and fulness: The Son, who was in the bosom of the Father, a personage of tabernacle, made, or fashioned like unto man, or being in the form and likeness of man, or, rather, man was formed after his likeness, and in his image;—he is also the express image and likeness of the personage of the Father: possessing all the fulness of the Father, or, the same fulness with the Fathe; being begotten of him, and was ordained from before the foundation of the world to be a propitiation for the sins of all those who should believe on his name, and is called the Son because of the flesh—and descended in suffering below that which man can suffer, or, in other words, suffered greater sufferings, and was exposed to more powerful contradictions than any man can be. But notwithstanding all this, he kept the law of God, and remained without sin: Showing thereby that it is in the power of man to keep the law and remain also without sin. And also, that by him a righteous judgment might come upon all flesh, and that all who walk not in the law of God, may justly be condemned by the law, and have no excuse for their sins. And he being the only begotten of the Father, full of grace and truth, and having overcome, received a fulness of the glory of the Father—possessing the same mind with the Father, which mind is the Holy Spirit, that bears record of the Father and the Son, and these three are one, or in other words, these three constitute the great, matchless, governing and supreme power over all things: by whom all things were created and made, that were created and made: and these three constitute the Godhead, and are one: The Father and the Son possessing the same mind, the same wisdom, glory, power and fulness: Filling all in all—the Son being filled with the fulness of the Mind, glory and power, or, in other words, the Spirit, glory and power of the Father—possessing all knowledge and glory, and the same kingdom: sitting at the right hand of power, in the express image and likeness of the Father—a Mediator for man—being filled with the fulness of the Mind of the Father, or, in other words, the Spirit of the Father: which Spirit is shed forth upon all who believe on his name and keep his commandments: and all those who keep his commandments shall grow up from grace to grace, and become heirs of the heavenly kingdom, and joint heirs with Jesus Christ; possessing the same mind, being transformed into the same image or likeness, even the express image of him who fills all in all: being filled with the fulness of his glory, and become one in him, even as the Father, Son and Holy Spirit are one.

3 From the foregoing account of the Godhead, which is given in his revelations, the Saints have a sure foundation laid for the exercise of faith unto life and salvation, through the atonement and mediation of Jesus Christ, by whose blood they have a forgiveness of sins, and also, a sure reward laid up for them in heaven, even that of partaking of the fulness of the Father and the Son, through the Spirit. As the Son partakes of the fulness of the Father through the Spirit, so the saints are, by the same Spirit, to be partakers of the same fulness, to enjoy the same glory; for as the Father and the Son are one, so in like manner the saints are to be one in them, through the love of the Father, the mediation of Jesus Christ, and the gift of the Holy Spirit; they are to be heirs of God and joint heirs with Jesus Christ.

Question. Of what do the foregoing lectures treat?

Answer. Of the being, perfections and attributes of the Deity. [§5. ¶1.]

Q. What are we to understand by the perfections of the Deity?

A. The perfections which belong to his attributes.

Q. How many personages are there in the Godhead?

A. Two: the Father and the Son. [§5. ¶1.]

Q. How do you prove that there are two personages in the Godhead?

A. By the Scriptures. Gen. 1:26. Also §2. ¶6. And the Lord God said unto the Only Begotten, who was with him from the beginning, Let us make man in our image, after our likeness:—and it was done. Gen. 3: 22. And the Lord God said unto the Only Begotten, Behold, the man is become as one of us: to know good and evil. John, 17: 5. And now, O Father, glorify thou me with thine own self with the glory which I had with thee before the world was [§5. ¶2.]

Q. What is the Father?

A. He is a personage of glory and of power. [§5. ¶2.

Q. How do you prove that the Father is a personage of glory and of power?

A. Isaiah 60: 19. The Sun shall be no more thy light by day, neither for brightness shall the moon give light unto thee: but the Lord shall be unto thee an everlasting light, and thy God thy glory. 1 Chron. 29: 11. Thine, O Lord, is the greatness, and the power, and the glory. Ps. 29: 3. The voice of the Lord is upon the waters: the God of glory thunders. Ps. 79: 9. Help us, O God of our salvation, for the glory of thy name. Romans 1: 23. And changed the glory of the incorruptible God into an image made like to corruptible men.

Secondly, of power. 1 Chron. 29: 4. Thine, O Lord, is the greatness and the power, and the glory. Jer. 32: 17. Ah! Lord God, behold thou hast made the earth and the heavens by thy great power, and stretched-out arm; and there is nothing too hard for thee. Deut 4: 37. And because he loved thy fathers therefore he chose their seed after them, and bro't them out in his sight with his mighty power. 2. Samuel 22: 33. God is my strength and power. Job 26. commenceing with the 7 verse, to the end of the chapter. He stretches out the north over the empty place, and hangs the earth upon nothing. He binds up the waters in his thick clouds; and the cloud is not rent under them. He holds back the face of his throne, and spreads his cloud upon it. He has compassed the waters with bounds, until the day and night come to an end. The pillars of heaven tremble, and are astonished at his reproof. He divides the sea with his power, and by his understanding he smites through the proud. By his Spirit he has garnished the heavens; his hand has formed the crooked serpent. Lo, these are parts of his ways: but how little a portion is heard of him? But the thunder of his power who can understand?

Q. What is the Son?

A. First, he is a personage of tabernacle. [§5. ¶2.]

Q. How do you prove it?

A. John 14: 9, 10, 11, Jesus says unto him, Have I been so long time with you, and yet have you not known me, Philip? He that has seen me has seen the Father; and how do you say then, Show us the Father? Do you not believe, that I am in the Father, and the Father in me? The words that I speak unto you, I speak not of myself: but the Father that dwells in me, he does the works. Believe me that I am in the Father, and the Father in me.

Secondly, and being a personage of tabernacle, was made or fashioned like unto man, or being in the form and likeness of man. [§5. ¶2.]

Philip. 2. Let this mind be in you, which was also in Christ Jesus; who being in the form of God, thought it not robbery to be equal with God; but made himself of no reputation, and took upon him the form of a servant, and was made in the likeness of man, and, being found in fashion as a man, he humbled himself, and became obedient unto death, even the death of the cross. Heb. 2: 14, 16. Forasmuch then as the children are partakers of flesh and blood, he also himself likewise took part of the same. For verily he took not on him the nature of angels: but he took on him the seed of Abraham.

Thirdly, he is also in the likeness of the personage of the Father. [§5. ¶2.]

Heb. 1: 1,2,3. God, who at sundry times, and in divers manners, spake in time past to the fathers, by the prophets, has in these last days spoken unto us by his Son, whom he has appointed heir of all things, by whom also he made the worlds; who, being the brightness of his glory, and the express image of his person. Again, Philip. 2: 5,6. Let this mind be in you, which was also in Christ Jesus; who being in the form of God, thought it not robbery to be equal with God.

Q. Was it by the Father and the Son that all things were created and made, that were created and made?

A. It was. Col. 1: 15, 16, 17. Who is the image of the invisible God, the first born of every creature; for by him were all things created that are in heaven, and that are in earth, visible and invisible; whether they be thrones or dominions. principalities or powers; all things were created by him and for him; and he is before all things, and by him all things consist. Gen. 1: 1. In the beginning God created the heavens and the earth. Heb. 1: 2. [God] Has in these last days spoken unto us by his Son, whom he has appointed heir of all things, by whom also he made the worlds.

Q. Does he possess the fulness of the Father?

A. He does. Col. 1: 19. 2: 9. For it pleased the Father that in him should all fulness dwell. For in him dwells all the fulness of the Godhead bodily. Eph. 1: 23. Which is his [Christ's] body, the fulness of him that fills all in all.

Q. Why was he called the Son?

A. Because of the flesh. Luke 1: 33. That holy thing which shall be born of thee, shall be called the Son of God.— Math. 3: 16, 17. And Jesus, when he was baptized, went up straitway out of the water: and lo, the heavens were opened. unto him, and he [John] saw the Spirit of God descending like a dove and lighting upon him: and lo, a voice from heaven, saying, This is my beloved Son, in whom I am well pleased.

Q. Was he ordained of the Father, from before the foundation of the world, to be a propitiation for the sins of all those who should believe on his name?

A. He was. 1 Peter, 1: 18, 19, 20. For as much as you know that you were not redeemed with corruptible things, as silver and gold, from your vain conversation, received by tradition from your fathers; but with the precious blood of Christ, as of a lamb without blemish and without spot: who verily was foreordained before the foundation of the world, but was manifested in these last times for you. Rev. 13: 8. And all that dwell upon the earth shall worship him, [the beast] whose names are not written in the book of life of the Lamb slain from the foundation of the world. 1 Corin. 2: 7. But we speak the wisdom of God in a mystery, even the hidden mystery, which God ordained before the world unto our glory.

Q. Do the Father and the Son possess the same mind?

A. They do. John 5: 30. I [Christ] can of my own self do nothing: as I hear, I judge, and my judgment is just; because I seek not my own will, but the will of the Father who sent me. John 6: 38. For I [Christ] came down from heaven, not to do my own will, but the will of him that sent me. John 10: 30. I [Christ] and my Father are one.

Q. What is this mind?

A. The Holy Spirit. John 15: 26. But when the Comforter is come, whom I will send unto you from the Father, even the Spirit of truth, which proceeds from the Father, he shall testify of me. [Christ.] Gal. 4: 6. And because you are sons, God has sent forth the Spirit of his Son into your hearts.

Q. Do the Father, Son and Holy Spirit constitute the Godhead?

A. They do. [§5. ¶2.]

Let the student commit this paragraph to memory.

Q. Does the believer in Christ Jesus, through the gift of the Spirit, become one with the Father and the Son, as the Father and the Son are one?

A. They do. John 17: 20, 21. Neither pray I for these (the apostles) alone, but for them also who shall believe on me through their word; that they all may be one; as thou, Father, art in me, and I in thee, that they also may be one in us, that the world may believe that thou hast sent me.

Q. Does the foregoing account of the Godhead lay 'a sure foundation for the exercise of faith in him unto life and salvation?

A. It does.

Q. How do you prove it?

A. By the third paragraph of this lecture.

Let the student commit this also.

LECTURE SIXTH.

Of Faith.

SECTION VI.

1 Having treated, in the preceding lectures, of the ideas of the character, perfections and attributes of God, we next proceed to treat of the knowledge which personsmust have, that the course of life which they pursue is according to the will of God, in order that they may be enabled to exercise faith in him unto life and salvation.

2 This knowledge supplies an important place in revealed religion; for it was by reason of it that the ancients were enabled to endure as seeing him who is invisible. An actual knowledge to any person that

the course of life which he pursues is according to the will of God, is essentially necessary to enable him to have that confidence in God, without which no person can obtain eternal life. It was this that enabled the ancient saints to endure all their afflictions and persecutions, and to take joyfully the spoiling of their goods, knowing, (not believing merely,) that they had a more enduring substance. Heb. 10:34.

3 Having the assurance that they were pursuing a course which was agreeable to the will of God, they were enabled to take, not only the spoiling of their goods, and the wasting of their substance, joyfully, but also to suffer death in its most horrid forms; knowing, (not merely believing,) that when this earthly house of their tabernacle was dissolved, they had a building of God, a house not made with hands, eternal in the heavens. Second Cor. 5:1.

4 Such was and always will be the situation of the saints of God, that unless they have an actual knowledge that the course that they are pursuing is according to the will of God, they will grow weary in their minds and faint; for such has been and always will be the opposition in the hearts of unbelievers and those that know not God, against the pure and unadulterated religion of heaven, (the only thing which ensures eternal life,) that they will persecute, to the uttermost, all that worship God according to his revelations, receive the truth in the love of it, and submit themselves to be guided and directed by his will, and drive them to such extremities that nothing short of an actual knowledge of their being the favorites of heaven, and of their having embraced that order of things which God has established for the redemption of man, will enable them to exercise that confidence in him necessary for them to overcome the world, and obtain that crown of glory which is laid up for them that fear God.

5 For a man to lay down his all, his character and reputation, his honor and applause, his good name among men, his houses, his lands, his brothers and sisters, his wife and children, and even his own life also, counting all things but filth and dross for the excellency of the knowledge of Jesus Christ, requires more than mere belief, or supposition that he is doing the will of God, but actual knowledge: realizing, that when these sufferings are ended he will enter into eternal rest; and be a partaker of the glory of God

6 For unless a person does know that he is walking according to the will of God, it would be offering an insult to the dignity of the Creator, were he to say that he would be a partaker of his glory when he should be done with the things of this life. But when he has this knowledge, and most assuredly knows that he is doing the will of God, his confidence can be equally strong that he will be a partaker of the glory of God.

7 Let us here observe, that a religion that does not require the sacrifice of all things, never has power sufficient to produce the faith necessary unto life and salvation: for from the first existence of man, the faith necessary unto the enjoyment of life and salvation never could be obtained without the sacrifice of all earthly things: it was through this sacrifice, and this only, that God has ordained that men should enjoy eternal life; and it is through the medium of the sacrifice of all earthly things, that men do actually know that they are doing the things that are well pleasing in the sight of God. When a man has offered in sacrifice all that he has, for the truth's sake, not even withholding his life, and believing before God that he has been called to make this sacrifice, because he seeks to do his will, he does know most assuredly, that God does and will accept his sacrifice & offering, & that he has not nor will not seek his face in

vain. Under these circumstances, then, he can obtain the faith necessary for him to lay hold on eternal life.

8 It is in vain for persons to fancy to themselves that they are heirs with those, or can be heirs with them, who have offered their all in sacrifice, and by this means obtained faith in God and favor with him so as to obtain eternal life, unless they in like manner offer unto him the same sacrifice, and through that offering obtain the knowledge that they are accepted of him.

9 It was in offering sacrifices that Abel, the first martyr, obtained knowledge that he was accepted of God. And from the days of righteous Abel to the present time, the knowledge that men have that they are accepted in the sight of God, is obtained by offering sacrifice: and in the last days, before the Lord comes, he is to gather together his saints who have made a covenant with him by sacrifice. Ps. 50:3,4,5. Our God shall come, and shall not keep silence: a fire shall devour before him, and it shall be very tempestuous round about him. He shall call to the heavens from above, and to the earth, that he may judge his people. Gather my saints together unto me; those that have made a covenant unto me by sacrifice.

10 Those, then, who make the sacrifice will have the testimony that their course is pleasing in the sight of God, and those who have this testimony will have faith to lay hold on eternal life, and will be enabled, through faith, to endure unto the end, and receive the crown that is laid up for them that love the appearing of our Lord Jesus Christ. But those who do not make the sacrifice cannot enjoy this faith, because men are dependent upon this sacrifice in order to obtain this faith; therefore, they cannot lay hold upon eternal life, because the revelations of God do not guarantee unto them the authority so to do; and without this guarantee faith could not exist.

11 All the saints of whom we have account in all the revelations of God which are extant, obtained the knowledge which they had of their acceptance in his sight, through the sacrifice which they offered unto him: and through the knowledge thus obtained, their faith became sufficiently strong to lay hold upon the promise of eternal life, and to endure us seeing him who is invisible; and were enabled, through faith, to combat the powers of darkness, contend against the wiles of the adversary, overcome the world, and obtain the end of their faith, even the salvation of their souls.

12 But those who have not made this sacrifice to God, do not know that the course which they pursue is well pleasing in his sight; for whatever may be their belief or their opinion, it is a matter of doubt and uncertainty in their mind; and where doubt and uncertainty is, there faith is not, nor can it be. For doubt and faith do not exist in the same person at the same time. So that persons whose minds are under doubts and fears cannot have unshaken confidence, and where unshaken confidence is not, there faith is weak, and where faith is weak, the persons will not be able to contend against all the opposition, tribulations and afflictions which they will have to encounter in order to be heirs of God, and joint heirs with Christ Jesus; and they will grow weary in their minds, and the adversary will have power over them and destroy them.

Note. This lecture is so plain, and the facts set forth so self-evident, that it is deemed unnecessary to form a catechism upon it: the student is therefore instructed to commit the whole to memory.

LECTURE SEVENTH.

Of Faith.

SECTION VII.

1 In the preceding lectures, we treated of what faith was, and of the object on which it rested· agreeably to our plan we now proceed to speak of its effects:

2 As we have seen in our former lectures, that faith was the principle of action and of power in all intelligent beings, both in heaven and on earth, it will not be expected that we will, in a lecture of this description attempt to unfold all its effects; neither is it necessary to our purpose so to do; for it would embrace all things in heaven and on earth, and encompass all the creations of God, with all their endless varieties: for no world has yet been framed that was not framed by faith; neither has there been an intelligent being on any of God's creations who did not get there by reason of faith, as it existed in himself or in some other being; nor has there been a change or a revolution in any of the creations of God but it has been effected by faith: neither will there be a change or a revolution unless it is effected in the same way, in any of the vast creations of the Almighty; for it is by faith that the Deity works.

3 Let us here offer some explanation in relation to faith that our meaning may be clearly comprehended: We ask, then, what are we to understand by a man's working by faith? We answer: We understand that when a man works by faith he works by mental exertion instead of physical force: it is by words instead of exerting his physical powers, with which every being works when he works by faith—

God said, Let there be light, and there was light—
Joshua spake and the great lights which God had
created stood still—Elijah commanded and the heavens were stayed for the space of three years and six
months, so that it did not rain: He again commanded,
and the heavens gave forth rain,—all this was done
by faith; and the Savior says, If you have faith as
a grain of mustard seed, say to this mountain, remove, and it will remove; or say to that sycamine
tree, Be ye plucked up and planted in the midst of
the sea, and it shall obey you. Faith, then, works by
words; and with these its mightiest works have been,
and will be performed.

4 It surely will not be required of us to prove, that
this is the principle upon which all eternty has acted
and will act; for every reflecting mind must know,
that it is by reason of this power that all the hosts of
heaven perform their works of wonder, majesty and
glory: Angels move from place to place by virtue of
this power—it is by reason of it that they are enabled
to descend from heaven to earth; and were it not for
the power of faith they never could be ministering
spirits to them who should be heirs of salvation, neither could they act as heavenly messengers; for they
would be destitute of the power necessary to enable
them to do the will of God.

5 It is only necessary for us to say, that the whole
visible creation, as it now exists, is the effect of faith
—It was faith by which it was framed, and it is by
the power of faith that it continues in its organized
form, and by which the planets move round their or-
bits and sparkle forth their glory: So, then, faith is
truly the first principle in the science of THEOLOGY,
and when undrstood, leads the mind back to the beginning and carries it forward to the end; or in other
words, from eternity to eternity.

6 As faith, then, is the principle by which the heav-

only hosts perform their works, and by which they enjoy all their felicity, we might expect to find it set forth in a revelation from God as the principle upon which his creatures, here below, must act, in order, to obtain the felicities enjoyed by the saints in the eternal world, and that when God would undertake to raise up men for the enjoyment of himself, he would teach them the necessity of living by faith, and the impossibility there was of their enjoying the blessedness of eternity without it, seeing that all the blessings of eternity are the effects of faith.

7 Therefore, it is said, and appropriately too, that without faith it is impossible to please God. If it should be asked, Why is it impossible to please God without faith? the answer would be, because, without faith it is impossible for men to be saved; and as God desires the salvation of man he must of course desire that they should have faith, and he could not be pleased unless they had, or else he could be pleased with their destruction.

8 From this we learn that the many exhortations which have been given by inspired men to those who had received the word of the Lord, to have faith in him, were not mere common-place matters, but were for the best of all reasons, and that was, because, without it there was no salvation, neither in this world nor in that which is to come. When men begin to live by faith they begin to draw near to God; and when faith is perfected they are like him; and because he is saved they are saved also; for they will be in the same situation he is in, because they have come to him; and when he appears they shall be like him, for they will see him as he is.

9 As all the visible creation is an effect of faith, so is salvation, also. (We mean salvation in its most extensive latitude of interpretation, whether it is tempo-

E

ral or spiritual.) In order to have this subject clearly set before the mind, let us ask what situation must a person be in, in order to be saved? or what is the difference between a saved man and one who is not saved? We answer from what we have before seen of the heavenly worlds, they must be persons who can work by faith, and who are able, by faith to be ministering spirits to them who shall be heirs of salvation. And they must have faith to enable them to act in the presence of the Lord, otherwise they cannot be saved. And what constitutes the real difference between a saved person and one not saved, is the difference in the degree of their faith: one's faith has become perfect enough to lay hold upon eternal life, and the other's has not. But to be a little more particular, let us ask, where shall we find a prototype into whose likeness we may be assimulated, in order that we may be made partakers of life and salvation? or in other words, where shall we find a saved being? for if we can find a saved being, we may ascertain, without much difficulty, what all others must be, in order to be saved— they must be like that individual or they cannot be saved: we think, that it will not be a matter of dispute, that two beings, who are unlike each other, cannot both be saved; for whatever constitutes the salvation of one, will constitute the salvation of every creature which will be saved: and if we find one saved being in all existance, we may see what all others must be, or else not be saved. We ask, then, where is the prototype? or where is the saved being? We conclude as to the answer of this question there will be no dispute among those who believe the bible, that it is Christ: all will agree in this that he is the prototype or standard of salvation, or in other words, that he is a saved being. And if we should continue our interogation, and ask how it is that he is saved, the answer would be, because he is a just and holy being; and if he were any thing different from what he is he would not be saved; for his salvation depends on his being precisely ʃwhat he is and nothing else; for if it were possible for him to change in the least degree, so sure he would tail of salvation and lose all his dominion, power, authority and glory, which constitutes salvation; for salvation consists in the glory, authority, majesty, power and dominion which Jehovah possesses, and in nothing else; and no being can possess it but himself or one like him: Thus says John, in his first epistle, 3:2 and 3: Behold, now we are the sons of God, and it doth not appear what we shall be; but we know, that when he shall appear we shall be like him; for we shall see him as he is. And any man that has this hope in him purifies himself, even as he is pure.—Why purify himself as he is pure? because, if they do not they cannot be like him.

10 The Lord said unto Moses, Leviticus, 19:2:—Speak unto all the congregation of the children of Israel, and say unto them, Ye shall be holy: for I the Lord your God am holy. And Peter says, first epistle, 1:15 and 16: But as he who has called you is holy, so be ye holy in all manner of conversation; because it is written, Be ye holy; for I am holy. And the Savior says, Matthew, 15:48: Be ye perfect, even as your Father who is in heaven is perfect. If any should ask, why all these sayings? the answer is to be found from what is before quoted from John's epistle, that when he (the Lord) shall appear, the saints will be like him: and if they are not holy, as he is holy, and perfect as he is perfect, they cannot be like him; for no being can enjoy his glory without possessing his perfections and holiness,⸱⸱no more than they could reign in his kingdom without his power.

11 This clearly sets forth the propriety of the Sav-

5*

ior's saying, recorded in John's testimony, 4:12: Verily, verily I say unto you, he that believeth on me, the works that I do shall he do also; and greater works than these, because I go unto the Father.— This taken in connection with some of the sayings in the Savior's prayer, recorded in the 17th chapter, gives great clearness to his expressions: He says, in the 20,21, 22,23 and 24: Neither pray I for these alone; but for them also who shall believe on me through their words; that they all may be one, as thou, Father art in me, and I in thee, that they also may be one in us: that the world may believe that thou hast sent me. And the glory which thou gavest me, I have given them, that they may be one, even as we are one; I in them, and thou in me, that they may be made perfect in one; and that the world may know that thou hast sent me, and hast loved them as thou hast loved me. Father, I will that they also whom thou hast given me be with me where I am: that they may behold my glory which thou hast given me; for thou lovedest me before the foundation of the world.

12 All these sayings put together, give as clear an account of the state of the glorified saints as language could give—The works that Jesus done they were to do, and greater works than those which he done among them should they do, and that because he went to the Father. He does not say that they should do these works in time; but they should do greater works because he went to the Father. He says, in the 24th verse: Father, I will that they also whom thou hast given me, be with me where I am; that they may behold my glory. These sayings, taken in connection, make it very plain, that the greater works, which those that believed on his name, were to do, were to be done in eternity, where he was going, and where they should behold his glory. He had said, in an-

other part of his prayer, that he desired of his Father, that those who believed on him should be one in him, as he, and the Father were one in each other: Neither pray I for these (the apostles) alone, but for them also who shall believe on me through their words; that they all may be one: that is, they who believe on him through the apostles' words, as well as the apostles themselves: that they all may be one, as thou, Father, art in me and I in thee: that they also may be one in us.

13 What language can be plainer than this? The Savior surely intended to be understood by his disciples: and he so spake that they might understand him; for he declares to his Father, in language not to be easily mistaken, that he wanted his disciples, even all of them, to be as himself and the Father: for as he and the Father were one, so they might be one with them. And what is said in the 22nd verse is calculated to more firmly establish this belief, if it needs any thing to establish it. He says, And the glory which thou gavest me, I have given them, that they may be one, even as we are one. As much as to say, that unless they have the glory which the Father had given him, they could not be one with them: For he says he had given them the glory that the Father had given him, that they might be one; or in other words, to make them one.

14 This fills up the measure of information on this subject, and shows most clearly, that the Savior wished his disciples to understand, that they were to be partakers with him in all things: not even his glory excepted.

15 It is scarcely necessary here to observe what we have previously noticed: That the glory which the Father and the Son have, is because they are just and holy beings; and that if they were lacking in one attribute or perfection which they have,

the glory which they have, never could be enjoyed by them; for it requires them to be precisely what they are in order to enjoy it: and if the Savior gives this glory to any others, he must do it in the very way set forth in his prayer to his Father: by making them one with him, as he and the Father are one.— In so doing he would give them the glory which the Father has given him; and when his disciples are made one with the Father and the Son, as the Father and the Son are one, who cannot see the propriety of the Savior's saying, The works which I do, shall they do; and greater works than these shall they do, be cause I go to the Father?

16 These teachings of the Savior most clearly show unto us the nature of salvation; and what he proposed unto the human family when he proposed to save them—That he proposed to make them like unto himself; and he was like the Father, the great prototype of all saved beings: And for any portion of the human family to be assimulated into their likeness is to be saved; and to be unlike them is to be destroyed: and on this hinge turns the door of salvation.

17 Who cannot see, then, that salvation is the effect of faith? for as we have previously observed, all the heavenly beings work by this principle; and it is because they are able so to do that they are saved: for nothing but this could save them. And this is the lesson which the God of heaven, by the mouth of all his holy prophets, has been endeavoring to teach to the world. Hence we are told, that without faith it is impossible to please God; and that salvation is of faith, that it might be by grace to the end, the promise might be sure to all the seed. Romans 4:16.— And that Israel, who followed after the law of righteousness, has not attained to the law of righteousness. Wherefore? because they sought it not by faith, but as it were by the works of the law; for

they stumbled at that stumbling stone. Romans 9:32.
And Jesus said unto the man who brought his son to
him, to get the devil who tormented him, cast out, If
thou canst believe, all things are possible to him that
believeth. Mark, 9:23. These with a multitude of
other scriptures, which might be quoted, plainly set
forth the light, in which the Savior, as well as the
Former Day Saints, viewed the plan of salvation.—
That it was a system of faith—it begins with faith,
and continues by faith; and every blessing which is
obtained, in relation to it, is the effect of faith, whether it pertains to this life or that which is to come.—
To this, all the revelations of God bear witness. If
there were children of promise, they were the effects
of faith: not even the Savior of the world excepted:
Blessed is she that believed, said Elizabeth to Mary,
when she went to visit her;—for there shall be a per-
formance of the things which were told her of the
Lord; Luke, 1:45:   Nor was the birth of John the
baptist the less a matter of faith; for in order that his
father Zacharias might believe he was struck dumb.
And through the whole history of the scheme of life
and salvation, it is a matter of faith: every man received according to his faith: according as his faith
was, so were his blessings and privileges; and nothing was withheld from him when his faith was sufficient to receive it.   He could stop the mouths of lions, quench the violence of fire, escape the edge of
the sword, wax valiant in fight, and put to flight the
armies of the aliens; women could, by their faith,
receive the dead children to life again: in a word,
there was nothing impossible with them who had
faith. All things were in subjection to the Former
Day Saints, according as their faith was—By their
faith they could obtain heavenly visions, the ministering of angels, have knowledge of the spirits of just
men made perfect, of the general assembly and church

of the first born, whose names are written in heaven, of God the judge of all, of Jesus the Mediator of the new covenant, and become familiar with the third heavens, see and hear things which were not only un-utterable, but were unlawful to utter. Peter, in view of the power of faith, 2nd epistle, 1:1,2 and 3 says, to the Former Day Saints: grace and peace be multiplied unto you, through the knowledge of God, and of Je-sus our Lord, according as his divine power hath given unto us all things that pertain unto life and godliness, through the knowledge of him that has call-ed us unto glory and virtue. In the first epistle, 1:3, 4 and 5 he says, Blessed be the God and Father of our Lord Jesus Christ, who according to his abundant mercy, has begotten us again unto a lively hope by the resurrection of Jesus Christ from the dead, to an inheritance incorruptible and undefiled, and that fadeth not away, reserved in heaven for you, who are kept by the power of God through faith unto sal-vation, ready to be revealed in the last time.

16 These sayings put together, show the Apostle's views, most clearly, so as to admit of no mistake on the mind of any individual. He says that all things that pertain to life and godliness were given unto them through the knowledge of God and our Savior Jesus Christ. And if the question is asked, how were they to obtain the knowledge of God? (for there is a great difference between believing in God and knowing him: knowledge implies more than faith. And no-tice, that all things that pertain to life and godliness, were given through the knowledge of God;) the an-swer is given, through faith they were to obtain this knowledge; and having power by faith to obtain the knowledge of God, they could with it obtain all other things which pertain to life and godliness.

17 By these sayings of the Apostle we learn, that it was by obtaining a knowledge of God, that men got

the all things which pertain to life and godliness; and this knowledge was the effect of faith. So that all things which pertain to life and godliness are the effects of faith.

18 From this we may extend as far as any circumstances may require whether on earth or in heaven, and we will find it the testimony of all inspired men, or heavenly messengers, that all things that pertain to life and godliness are the effects of faith and nothing else: all learning, wisdom, and prudence fail, and every thing else as a means of salvation but faith. This is the reason that the fishermen of Gallilee could teach the world—because they sought by faith and by faith obtained. And this is the reason that Paul counted all things but filth and dross—what he formerly called his gain he called his loss; yea, and he counted all things but loss for the excellency of the knowledge of Christ Jesus the Lord. Philipians 3: 7, 8, 9 & 10. Because, to obtain the faith by which he could enjoy the knowledge of Christ Jesus the Lord, he had to suffer the loss of all things: this is the reason that the Former Day Saints knew more, and understood more of heaven, and of heavenly things than all others beside, because this information is the effect of faith—to be obtained by no other means. And this is the reason, that men, as soon as they lose their faith, run into strifes, contentions, darkness and difficulties; for the knowledge which tends to life disappears with faith, but returns when faith returns; for when faith comes, it brings its train of attendants with it—apostles, prophets, evangelists, pastors, teachers, gifts, wisdom, knowledge, miracles, healings. tongues, interpretation of tongues, &c. All these appear when faith appears on the earth, and disappear when it disappears from the earth. For these are the effects of faith and always have, and always will attend it. For where faith is, there will the knowledge

of God be also, with all things which pertain thereto
revelations, visions, and dreams, as well as every oth .
er necessary thing in order that the possessors of faith
may be perfected and obtain salvation; for God must
change, otherwise faith will prevail with him. And
he who possesses it will, through it, obtain all necessary knowledge and wisdom, until he shall know God,
and the Lord Jesus Christ, whom he has sent: whom
to know is eternal life: Amen.

PART SECOND.

COVENANTS AND COMMANDMENTS

OF THE LORD,

to his servants of the church of the

LATTER DAY SAINTS.

SECTION I.

66th given

1 Hearken, O ye people of my church, saith the voice of him who dwells on high, and whose eyes are upon all men; yea, verily I say, hearken ye people from afar, and ye that are upon the islands of the sea, listen together; for verily the voice of the Lord is unto all men, and there is none to escape, and there is no eye that shall not see, neither ear that shall not hear, neither heart that shall not be penetrated: and the rebellious shall be pierced with much sorrow, for their iniquities shall be spoken upon the house-tops, and their secret acts shall be revealed; and the voice of warning shall be unto all people, by the mouths of my disciples, whom I have chosen in these last days, and they shall go forth and none shall stay them, for I the Lord have commanded them.

2 Behold, this is mine authority, and the authority of my servants, and my preface unto the book of my commandments, which I have given them to publish unto you O inhabitants of the earth: wherefore fear and tremble, O ye people, for what I the Lord have decreed, in them, shall be fulfilled. And verily, I say unto you, that they who go forth, bearing these tidings unto the inhabitants of the earth, to them is power given to seal both on earth and in heaven, the unbelieving and rebellious; yea, verily, to seal them up unto the day when the wrath of God shall be poured out upon the wicked without measure; unto the day when the Lord shall come to recompense unto every man according to his work, and measure to every man according to the measure which he has measured to his fellow man.

3 Wherefore the voice of the Lord is unto the ends of the earth, that all that will hear may hear: prepare ye, prepare ye

for that which is to come, for the Lord is nigh; and the anger
of the Lord is kindled, and his sword is bathed in heaven, and
it shall fall upon the inhabitants of the earth; and the arm of
the Lord shall be revealed; and the day cometh, that they who
will not hear the voice of the Lord, neither the voice of his servants, neither give heed to the words of the prophets, and
apostles, shall be cut off from among the people: for they have
strayed from mine ordinances, and have broken mine everlasting covenant; they seek not the Lord to establish his righteousness, but every man walketh in his own way, and after
the image of his own god, whose image is in the likeness of the
world, and whose substance is that of an idol, which waxeth
old and shall perish in Babylon, even Babylon the great, which
shall fall:

4 Wherefore I the Lord, knowing the calamity which should
come upon the inhabitants of the earth, called upon my servant
Joseph Smith jr. and spake unto him from heaven, and gave
him commandments; and also gave commandments to others,
that they should proclaim these things unto the world; and all
this that it might be fulfilled, which was written by the prophets: the weak things of the world shall come forth and break
down the mighty and strong ones, that man should not counsel his fellow man, neither trust in the arm of flesh, but that
every man might speak in the name of God, the Lord, even
the Savior of the world; that faith also might increase in the
earth; that mine everlasting covenant might be established;
that the fulness of my gospel might be proclaimed by the weak
and the simple, unto the ends of the world, and before kings
and rulers.

5 Behold I am God and have spoken it: these commandments
are of me, and were given unto my servants in their weakness,
after the manner of their language, that they might come to
understanding; and inasmuch as they erred it might be made
known: and inasmuch as they sought wisdom, they might be
instructed; and inasmuch as they sinned they might be chastened, that they might repent; and inasmuch as they were
humble, they might be made strong, and blessed from on high,
and receive knowledge from time to time: and after having received the record of the Nephites, yea, even my servant Joseph
Smith jr. might have power to translate through the mercy of
God, by the power of God, the book of Mormon: and also,
those to whom these commandments were given, might have
power to lay the foundation of this church, and to bring it forth
out of obscurity, and out of darkness, the only true and living
church upon the face of the whole earth, with which I the
Lord am well pleased, speaking unto the church collectively

and not individually; for I the Lord cannot look upon sin with the least degree of allowance: nevertheless, he that repents and does the commandments of the Lord, shall be forgiven, and he that repents not, from him shall be taken even the light which he has received, for my Spirit shall not always strive with man, saith the Lord of hosts.

6 And again, verily I say unto you, O inhabitants of the earth, I the Lord am willing to make these things known unto all flesh, for I am no respecter of persons, and willeth that all men shall know that the day speedily cometh, the hour is not yet, but is nigh at hand, when peace shall be taken from the earth, and the devil shall have power over his own dominion; and also, the Lord shall have power over his saints, and shall reign in their midst, and shall come down in judgment upon Idumea, or the world.

7 Search these commandments, for they are true and faithful, and the prophecies and promises which are in them shall all be fulfilled.

8 What I the Lord have spoken, I have spoken, and I excuse not myself, and though the heavens and the earth pass away, my word shall not pass away, but shall all be fulfilled, whether by mine own voice, or by the voice of my servants, it is the same: for behold, and lo, the Lord is God, and the Spirit beareth record, and the record is true, and the truth abideth forever and ever: Amen.

SECTION II.

1 The rise of the church of Christ in these last days, being one thousand eight hundred and thirty years since the coming of our Lord and Savior Jesus Christ in the flesh, it being regularly organized and established agreeably to the laws of our country, by the will and commandments of God in the fourth month, and on the sixth day of the month which is called April: which commandments were given to Joseph Smith jr. who was called of God and ordained an apostle of Jesus Christ, to be the first elder of this church; and to Oliver Cowdery, who was also called of God an apostle of Jesus Christ, to be the second elder of this church, and ordained under his hand: and this according to the grace of our Lord and Savior Jesus Christ, to whom be all glory both now and forever. Amen.

2 After it was truly manifested unto this first elder that he had received a remission of his sins he was entangled again in the vanities of the world: but after repenting, and humbling himself, sincerely, through faith God ministered unto him by

an holy angel whose countenance was as lightning, and whose garments were pure and white above all other whiteness, and gave unto him commandments which inspired him, and gave him power from on high, by the means which were before prepared, to translate the book of Mormon, which contains a record of a fallen people, and the fulness of the gospel of Jesus Christ to the Gentiles, and to the Jews also, which was given by inspiration, and is confirmed to others by the ministering of angels, and is declared unto the world by them, proving to the world that the holy scriptures are true, and that God does inspire men and call them to his holy work in this age and generation, as well as in generations of old, thereby showing that he is the same God yesterday, to-day, and forever.— Amen.

3 Therefore, having so great witnesses, by them shall the world be judged, even as many as shall hereafter come to a knowledge of this work; and those who receive it in faith and work righteousness, shall receive a crown of eternal life; but those who harden their hearts in unbelief and reject it, it shall turn to their own condemnation, for the Lord God has spoken it; and we, the elders of the church, have heard and bear witness to the words of the glorious Majesty on high, to whom be glory forever and ever. Amen.

4 By these things we know that there is a God in heaven who is infinite and eternal, from everlasting to everlasting the same unchangeable God, the framer of heaven and earth and all things which are in them, and that he created man male and female: after his own image and in his own likeness created he them, and gave unto them commandments that they should love and serve him the only living and true God, and that he should be the only being whom they should worship. But by the transgression of these holy laws, man became sensual and devilish, and became fallen man.

5 Wherefore the Almighty God gave his only begotten Son, as it is written in those scriptures which have been given of him; he suffered temptations but gave no heed unto them; he was crucified, died, and rose again the third day; and ascended into heaven to sit down on the right hand of the Father, to reign with almighty power according to the will of the Father, that as many as would believe and be baptized, in his holy name, and endure in faith to the end should be saved: not only those who believed after he came in the meridian of time in the flesh, but all those from the beginning, even as many as were before he came, who believed in the words of the holy prophets, who spake as they were inspired by the gift of the Holy Ghost, who truly testified of him in all things, should

have eternal life, as well as those who should come after, who should believe in the gifts and callings of God by the Holy Ghost, which beareth record of the Father, and of the Son, which Father, Son, and Holy Ghost are one God, infinite and eternal, without end. Amen.

6 And we know that all men must repent and believe on the name of Jesus Christ and worship the Father in his name, and endure in faith on his name to the end, or they cannot be saved in the kingdom of God. And we know that justification through the grace of our Lord and Savior Jesus Christ, is just and true: and we know, also, that sanctification through the grace of our Lord and Savior Jesus Christ, is just and true, to all those who love and serve God with all their mights, minds, and strength; but there is a possibility that man may fall from grace and depart from the living God. Therefore let the church take heed and pray always, lest they fall into temptations; yea, and even let those who are sanctified, take heed also.— And we know that these things are true and according to the revelations of John, neither adding to, nor diminishing from the prophecy of his book, the holy scriptures, or the revelations of God which shall come hereafter by the gift and power of the Holy Ghost, the voice of God, or the ministering of angels: and the Lord God has spoken it; and honor, power, and glory, be rendered to his holy name, both now and ever.— Amen.

7 *And again by way of commandment to the church concerning the manner of baptism.*

All those who humble themselves before God and desire to be baptized, and come forth with broken hearts and contrite spirits, and witness before the church that they have truly repented of all their sins and are willing to take upon them the name of Jesus Christ, having a determination to serve him to the end, and truly manifest by their works that they have received of the Spirit of Christ unto the remission of their sins, shall be received by baptism into his church.

8 *The duty of the elders, priests, teachers, deacons, and members of the church of Christ.*

An apostle is an elder, and it is his calling to baptize, and to ordain other elders, priests, teachers, and deacons, and to administer bread and wine—the emblems of the flesh and blood of Christ—and to confirm those who are baptized into the church, by the laying on of hands for the baptism of fire and the Holy Ghost, according to the scriptures; and to teach, expound exhort, baptize, and watch over the church; and to confirm the church by the laying on of the hands, and the giving of the Holy Ghost—and to take the lead of all meetings.

9 The elders are to conduct the meetings as they are led by the Holy Ghost, according to the commandments and revelations of God.

10 The priest's duty is to preach, teach, expound, exhort, and baptize, and administer the sacrament, and visit the house of each member, and exhort them to pray vocally and in secret, and attend to all family duties: and he may also ordain other priests, teachers, and deacons—and he is to take the lead of meetings when there is no elder present, but when there is an elder present he is only to preach, teach, expound, exhort, and baptize, and visit the house of each member, exhorting them to pray vocally and in secret, and attend to all family duties. In all these duties the priest is to assist the elder if occasion requires.

11 The teacher's duty is to watch over the church always, and be with, and strengthen them, and see that there is no iniquity in the church, neither hardness with each other; neither lying, backbiting, nor evil speaking; and see that the church meet together often, and also see that all the members do their duty—and he is to take the lead of meetings in the absence of the elder or priest—and is to be assisted always, in all his duties in the church, by the deacons, if occasion requires: but neither teachers nor deacons have authority to baptize, administer the sacrament, or lay on hands; they are however to warn, expound, exhort, and teach, and invite all to come unto Christ.

12 Every elder, priest, teacher, or deacon, is to be ordained according to the gifts and callings of God unto him: and he is to be ordained by the power of the Holy Ghost which is in the one who ordains him.

13 The several elders composing this church of Christ are to meet in conference once in three months, or from time to time, as said conferences shall direct or appoint: and said conferences are to do whatever church business is necessary to be done at the time.

14 The elders are to receive their licences from other elders by vote of the church to which they belong, or from the conferences.

15 Each priest, teacher, or deacon, who is ordained by a priest, may take a certificate from him at the time, which certificate when presented to an elder, shall entitle him to a license, which shall authorize him to perform the duties of his calling—or he may receive it from a conference.

16 No person is to be ordained to any office in this church, where there is a regularly organized branch of the same, without the vote of that church; but the presiding elders, travel-

ling bishops, high counsellors, high priests, and elders, may have the privilege of ordaining, where there is no branch of the church, that a vote may be called.

17 Every president of the high priesthood, (or presiding elder,) bishop, high counsellor, and high priest, is to be ordained by the direction of a high counsel, or general conference.

18 *The duty of the members after they are received by baptism:*

19 The elders or priests are to have a sufficient time to expound all things concerning the church of Christ to their understanding, previous to their partaking of the sacrament, and being confirmed by the laying on of the hands of the elders; so that all things may be done in order. And the members shall manifest before the church and also before the elders, by a godly walk and conversation, that they are worthy of it, that there may be works and faith agreeable to the holy scriptures—walking in holiness before the Lord.

20 Every member of the church of Christ having children, is to bring them unto the elders before the church, who are to lay their hands upon them in the name of Jesus Christ, and bless them in his name.

21 No one can be received into the church of Christ unless he has arrived unto the years of ccountability before God, and is capable of repentance.

22 Baptism is to be administered in the following manner unto all those who repent: The person who is called of God and has authority from Jesus Christ to baptize, shall go down into the water with the person who has presented him or herself for baptism, and shall say, calling him or her by name: Having been commissioned of Jesus Christ, I baptize you in the name of the Father, and of the Son, and of the Holy Ghost, Amen. Then shall he immerse him or her in the water, and come forth again out of the water.

23 It is expedient that the church meet together often to partake of bread and wine in remembrance of the Lord Jesus: and the elder or priest shall administer it: and after this manner shall he administer it: he shall kneel with the church and call upon the Father in solemn prayer, saying, O God, the eternal Father, we ask thee in the name of thy Son Jesu Christ t bless and sanctify this bread to the souls of all those who partake of it, that they may eat in remembrance of the body of thy Son, and witness unto thee O God, the eternal Father, that they are willing to take upon them the name of thy Son, and always remember him and keep his commandments which he has given them, that they may always have his Spirit to be with them. Amen.

24 The manner of administering the wine: He shall take the cup also, and say, O God, the eternal Father, we ask thee in the name of thy Son Jesus Christ, to bless and sanctify this wine to the souls of all those who drink of it, that they may do it in remembrance of the blood of thy Son which was shed for them, that they may witness unto thee, O God, the eternal Father, that they do always remember him, that they may have his Spirit to be with them. Amen.

25 Any member of the church of Christ transgressing, or being overtaken in a fault, shall be dealt with as the scriptures direct.

26 It shall be the duty of the several churches composing the church of Christ, to send one or more of their teachers to attend the several conferences, held by the elders of the church, with a list of the names of the several members uniting themselves with the church since the last conference, or send by the hand of some priest, so that a regular list of all the names of the whole church may be kept in a book, by one of the elders, whoever the other elders shall appoint from time to time:— and also, if any have been expelled from the church; so that their names may be blotted out of the general church record of names.

27 All members removing from the church where they reside, if going to a church where they are not known, may take a letter certifying that they are regular members and in good standing; which certificate may be signed by any elder or priest, if the member receiving the letter is personally acquainted with the elder or priest, or it may be signed by the teachers, or deacons of the church.

SECTION III.

ON PRIESTHOOD.

1 There are, in the church, two priesthoods, namely: the Melchizedek, and the Aaronic, including the Levitical priesthood. Why the first is called the Melchizedek priesthood, is because Melchizedek was such a great high priest: before his day it was called *the holy priesthood, after the order of the Son of God;* but out of respect or reverence to the name of the Supreme Being, to avoid the too frequent repetition of his name, they, the church, in ancient days, called that priesthood after Melchizedek, or the Melchizedek priesthood.

2 All other authorities, or offices in the church are appendages to this priesthood; but there are two divisions, or grand heads—one is the Melchizedek priesthood, and the other is the Aaronic, or Levitical priesthood.

3 The office of an elder comes under the priesthood of Melchizedek. The Melchizedek priesthood holds the right of presidency, and has power and authority over all the offices in the church, in all ages of the world, to administer in spiritual things.

4 The presidency of the high priesthood, after the order of Melchizedek, have a right to officiate in all the offices in the church.

5 High priests, after the order of the Melchizedek priesthood, have a right to officiate in their own standing, under the direction of the presidency, in administering spiritual things, and also in the office of an elder, priest, (of the Levitical order,) teacher, deacon and member.

6 An elder has a right to officiate in his stead when the high priest is not present.

7 The high priest, and elder, are to administer in spiritual things, agreeably to the covenants and commandments of the church; and they have a right to officiate in all these offices of the church when there are no higher authorities present.

8 The second priesthood is called the priesthood of Aaron, because it was conferred upon Aaron and his seed, throughout all their generations. Why it is called the lesser priesthood, is because it is an appendage to the greater, or the Melchizedek priesthood, and has power in administering outward ordinances. The bishopric is the presidency of this priesthood and holds the keys, or authority of the same. No man has a legal right to this office, to hold the keys of this priesthood, except he be a litteral descendant of Aaron. But as a high priest, of the Melchizedek priesthood, has authority to officiate in all the lesser offices, he may officiate in the office of bishop when no literal descendant of Aaron can be found; provided he is called and set apart and ordained unto this power by the hands of the presidency of the Melchizedek priesthood.

9 The power and authority of the higher or Melchizedek priesthood, is to hold the keys of all the spiritual blessings of the church—to have the privilege of receiving the mysteries of the kingdom of heaven—to have the heavens opened unto them—to commune with the general assembly and church of the first born, and to enjoy the communion and presence of God the Father, and Jesus the Mediator of the new covenant.

10 The power and authority of the lesser, or Aaronic priesthood, is, to hold the keys of the ministring of angels, and to administer in outward ordinances—the letter of the gospel—the baptism of repentance for the remission of sins, agreeably to the covenants and commandments.

11 Of necessity there are presidents, or presiding offices growing out of, or appointed of, or from among those who are ordained to the several offices in thess two priesthoods. Of the Melchizedek priesthood, three presiding high priests, chosen by the body, appointed and ordained to that office, and upheld by the confidence, faith and prayer of the church, form a quorum of the presidency of the church. The twelve travelling counsellors are called to be the twelve apostles, or special witnesses of the name of Christ, in all the world: thus differing from other officers in the church in the duties of their calling. And they form a quorum equal in authority and power to the three presidents, previously mentioned. The seventy are also called to preach the gospel, and to be especial witnesses unto the Gentiles and in all the world. Thus differing from other officers in the church in the duties of their calling: and they form a quorum equal in authority to that of the twelve especial witnesses or apostles, just named. And every descision made by either of these quorums, must be by the unanimous voice of the same; that is, every member in each quorum must be agreed to its decisions in order to make their decisions of the same power or validity one with the other. [A majority may form a quorum when circumstances render it impossible to be otherwise.] Unless this is the case, their decisions are not entitled to the same blessings which the decisions of a quorum of three presidents were anciently, who were ordained after the order of Melchizedek, and were righteous and holy men. The decisions of these quorums, or either of them are to be made in all righteousness; in holiness and lowliness of heart; meekness and long suffering; and in faith and virtue and knowledge; temperance, patience, godliness brotherly kindness and charity, because the promise is, if these things abound in them, they shall not be unfruitful in the knowledge of the Lord. And in case that any decision, of these quorums, is made in unrighteousness, it may be brought before a general assembly of the several quorums which constitute the spiritual authorities of the church, otherwise there can be no appeal from their decision.

12 The twelve are a travelling, presiding high council, to officiate in the name of the Lord, under the direction of the presidency of the church, agreeably to the institution of heaven; to build up the church, and regulate all the affairs of the same, in all nations: first unto the Gentiles, and secondly unto the Jews.

13 The seventy are to act in the name of the Lord, under the direction of the twelve, or the travelling high council, in building up the church and regulating all the affairs of the

same, in all nations: first unto the Gentiles and then to the Jews:—the twelve being sent out, holding the keys, to open the door by the proclamation of the gospel of Jesus Christ; and first unto the Gentiles and then unto the Jews.

14 The standing high councils, at the stakes of Zion, form a quorum equal in authority, in the affairs of the church, in all their decisions, to the quorum of the presidency, or to the travelling high council.

15 The high council in Zion, forms a quorum equal in authority, in the affairs of the church, in all their decisions, to the councils of the twelve at the stakes of Zion.

16 It is the duty of the travelling high council to call upon the seventy, when they need assistance, to fill the several calls for preaching and administering the gospel, in stead of any others.

17 It is the duty of the twelve in all large branches of the church, to ordain evangelical ministers, as they shall be designated unto them by revelation.

18 The order of this priesthood was confirmed to be handed down from father to son, and rightly belongs to the literal descendants of the chosen seed, to whom the promises were made. This order was instituted in the days of Adam, and came down by lineage in the following manner:

19 From Adam to Seth, who was ordained by Adam at the age of 69 years, and was blessed by him three years previous to his (Adam's) death, and received the promise of God by his father, that his posterity should be the chosen of the Lord, and that they should be preserved unto the end of the earth, because he [Seth] was a perfect man, and his likeness was the express likeness of his father's, insomuch that he seemed to be like unto his father in all things; and could be distinguished from him only by his age.

20 Enos was ordained at the age of 134 years, and four months, by the hand of Adam.

21 God called upon Cainan in the wilderness, in the fortieth year of his age, and he met Adam in journeying to the place Shedolamak: he was eighty seven years old when he received his ordination.

22 Mahalaleel was 496 years and seven days old when he was ordained by the hand of Adam, who also blessed him.

23 Jared was 200 years old when he was ordained under the hand of Adam, who also blessed him.

24 Enoch, was 25 years old when he was ordained under the hand of Adam, and he was 65 and Adam blessed him—and he saw the Lord: and he walked with him, and was before his face continually: and he walked with God 365 years: making him 430 years old when he was translated.

25 Methuselah was 100 years old when he was ordained under the hand of Adam.

26 Lamech was 32 years old when he was ordained under
the hand of Seth.

27 Noah was 10 years old when he was ordained under the
hand of Methuselah.

28 Three years previous to the death of Adam, he called
Seth, Enos, Cainan, Mahalaleel, Jared, Enoch and Methuselah, who were all high priests, with the residue of his posterity, who were righteous, into the valley of Adam-ondi-ahman,
and there bestowed upon them his last blessing. And the
Lord appeared unto them, and they rose up and blessed Adam,
and called him Michael, the Prince, the Arch angel. And
the Lord administered comfort unto Adam, and said unto him,
I have set thee to be at the head: a multitude of nations shall
come of thee; and thou art a prince over them for ever.

29 And Adam stood up in the midst of the congregation, and
notwithstanding he was bowed down with age, being full of
the Holy Ghost, predicted whatsoever should befall his posterity unto the latest generation. These things were all written in the book of Enoch, and are to be testified of in due
time.

30 It is the duty of the twelve, also, to ordain and set in order all the other officers of the church, agreeably to the revelation which says:

31 To the church of Christ in the land of Zion, in addition
to the church laws, respecting church business: Verily, I say
unto you, says the Lord of hosts, There must needs be presiding elders, to preside over those who are of the office of an
elder; and also priests, to preside over those who are of the
office of a priest; and also teachers to preside over those who
are of the office of a teacher, in like manner; and also the
deacons: wherefore, from deacon to teacher, and from teacher
to priest, and from priest to elder, severally as they are appointed, according to the covenants and commandments of the
church; then comes the high priesthood, which is the greatest of all. Wherefore, it must needs be that one be appointed,
of the high priesthood, to preside over the priesthood; and he
shall be called president of the high priesthood of the church,
or, in other words, the presiding high priest over the high
priesthood of the church. From the same comes the administering of ordinances and blessings upon the church, by the
laying on of the hands.

32 Wherefore the office of a bishop is not equal unto it; for
the office of a bishop is in administering all temporal things:
nevertheless, a bishop must be chosen from the high priest-

hood, unless he is a literal descendant of Aaron; for unless he is a literal descendant of Aaron he cannot hold the keys of that priesthood. Nevertheless, a high priest, that is after the order of Melchizedek, may be set apart unto the ministering of temporal things, having a knowledge of them by the Spirit of truth, and also to be a judge in Israel, to do the business of the church to sit in judgment upon transgressors, upon testimony, as it shall be laid before him, according to the laws, by the assistance of his counsellors, whom he has chosen, or will chose among the elders of the church. This is the duty of a bishop who is not a literal descendant of Aaron, but has been ordained to the high priesthood after the order of Melchizedek.

33 Thus shall he be a judge, even a common judge among the inhabitants of Zion, or in a stake of Zion, or in any branch of the church where he shall be set apart unto this ministry, until the borders of Zion are enlarged, and it becomes necessary to have other bishops, or judges in Zion, or elsewhere: and inasmuch as there are other bishops appointed they shall act in the same office.

34 But a literal descendant of Aaron has a legal right to the presidency of this priesthood, to the keys of this ministry, to act in the office of bishop independently, without counsellors, except in a case where a president of the high priesthood, after the order of Melchizedek, is tried; to sit as a judge in Israel.— And the decision of either of these councils, agreeably to the commandment which says;

35 Again, verily, I say unto you: The most important business of the church, and the most difficult cases of the church, inasmuch as there is not satisfaction upon the decision of the bishop, or judges, it shall be handed over and carried up unto the council of the church, before the presidency of the high priesthood; and the presidency of the council of the high priesthood shall have power to call other high priests, even twelve, to assist as counsellors; and thus the presidency of the high priesthood, and its counsellors shall have power to decide upon testimony according to the laws of the church. And after this decision it shall be had in remembrance no more before the Lord: for this is the *highest council of the church of God, and a final decision upon controversies, in spiritual matters.

36 There is not any person belonging to the church, who is exempt from this council of the church.

37 And in as much as a president of the high priesthood shall transgress, he shall be had in remembrance before the common council of the church, who shall be assisted by twelve

counsellors of the high priesthood; and their decision upon his head shall be an end of controversy concerning him. Thus, none shall be exempted from the justice and the laws of God; that all things may be done in order and in solemnity, before him, according to truth and righteousness.

38 And again, verily I say unto you, the duty of a president over the office of a deacon, is to preside over twelve deacons, to sit in council with them, and to teach them their duty—edifying one another, as it is given according to the covenants.

39 And also the duty of the president over the office of the teachers, is to preside over twenty four of the teachers, and to sit in council with them—teaching them the duties of their office, as given in the covenants.

40 Also the duty of the president over the priesthood of Aaron, is to preside over forty eight priests, and sit in council with them, to teach them the duties of their office, as is given in the covenants. This president is to be a bishop; for this is one of the duties of this priesthood.

41 Again, the duty of the president over the office of elders is to preside over ninety six elders, and to sit in council with them, and to teach them according to the covenants. This presidency is a distinct one from that of the seventy, and is designed for those who do not travel into all the world.

42 And again, the duty of the president of the office of the high priesthood is to preside over the whole church, and to be like unto Moses. Behold, here is wisdom—yea, to be a seer, a revelator, a translator and a prophet—having all the gifts of God which he bestows upon the head of the church.

43 And it is according to the vision, showing the order of the seventy, that they should have seven presidents to preside over them, chosen out of the number of the seventy, and the seventh president of these presidents is to preside over the six; and these seven presidents are to choose other seventy besides the first seventy, to whom they belong, and are to preside over them; and also other seventy until seven times seventy, if the labor in the vineyard of necessity requires it. And these seventy are to be travelling ministers unto the Gentiles, first, and also unto the Jews, whereas other offices of the church who belong not unto the twelve neither to the seventy, are not under the responsibility to travel among all nations, but are to travel as their circumstances shall allow, notwithstanding they may hold as high and responsible offices in the church.

44 Wherefore, now let every man learn his duty, and to act in the office in which he is appointed, in all diligence. He that is slothful shall not be counted worthy to stand, and he

that learns not his duty and shows himself not approved, shall not be counted worthy to stand; even so. Amen.

SECTION IV.

A Revelation given the 22d and 23d of Sept. 1832.

ON PRIESTHOOD.

1 A revelation of Jesus Christ unto his servant Joseph Smith, jr. and six elders, as they united their hearts and lifted their voices on high; yea, the word of the Lord concerning his church, established in the last days for the restoration of his people as he has spoken by the mouth of his prophets, and for the gathering of his saints to stand upon mount Zion, which shall be the city New Jerusalem; which city shall be built, beginning at the Temple Lot, which is appointed by the finger of the Lord, in the western boundaries of the state of Missouri, and dedicated by the hand of Joseph Smith jr. and others, with whom the Lord was well pleased.

2 Verily, this is the word of the Lord, that the city New Jerusalem shall be built by the gathering of the saints, beginning at this place, even the place of the temple, which temple shall be reared in this generation; for verily, this generation shall not all pass away until an house shall be built unto the Lord and a cloud shall rest upon it, which cloud shall be even the glory of the Lord, which shall fill the house. And the sons of Moses, according to the holy priesthood, which he received under the hand of his father-in-law, Jethro, and Jethro received it under the hand of Caleb, and Caleb received it under the hand of Elihu, and Elihu under the hand of Jeremy, and Jeremy under the hand of Gad and Gad under the hand of Esaias, and Esaias received it under the hand of God; Esaias also lived in the days of Abraham and was blessed of him, which Abraham received the priesthood from Melchizedek, who received it through the lineage of his fathers, even till Noah; and from Noah till Enoch, through the lineage of their fathers; and from Enoch to Abel, who was slain by the conspiracy of his brother, who received the priesthood by the commandments of God by the hand of his father Adam, who was the first man; which priesthood continueth in the church of God in all generations, and is without beginning of days or end of years.

3 And the Lord confirmed a priesthood also upon Aaron and his seed throughout all their generations, which priesthood also continueth and abideth forever, with the priesthood which

is after the holiest order of God. And this greater priesthood administereth the gospel and holdeth the key of the mysteries of the kingdom, even the key of the knowledge of God.— Therefore, in the ordinances thereof the power of godliness is manifest; and without the ordinances thereof, and the authority of the priesthood, the power of godliness is not manifest unto men in the flesh; for without this no man can see the face of God, even the Father, and live.

4 Now this Moses plainly taught to the children of Israel in the wilderness, and sought diligently to sanctify his people that they might behold the face of God; but they hardened their hearts and could not endure his presence, therefore, the Lord, in his wrath, (for his anger was kindled against them,) swore that they should not enter into his rest, while in the wilderness, which rest is the fulness of his glory. Therefore he took Moses out of their midst and the holy priesthood also; and the lesser priesthood continued, which priesthood holdeth the key of the ministering of angels and the preparatory gospel, which gospel is the gospel of repentance and of baptism and the remission of sins and the law of carnal commandments, which the Lord, in his wrath, caused to continue with the house of Aaron among the children of Israel until John, whom God raised up, being filled with the Holy Ghost from his mother's womb: for he was baptized while he was yet in his chidhood, and was ordained by the angel of God at the time he was eight days old unto this power—to overthrow the kingdom of the Jews, an to make straight the way of the Lord before the face of his people, to prepare them for the coming of the Lord, in whose hand is given all power.

5 And again, the office of elder and bishop are necessary appendages belonging unto the high priesthood. And again, the offices of teachers and deacons are necessary appendages belonging to the lesser priesthood, which priesthood was confirmed upon Aaron and his sons.

6 Therefore, as I said concerning the Sons of Moses—for the sons of Moses and also the sons of Aaron shall offer an acceptable offering and sacrifice in the house of the Lord, which house shall be built unto the Lord in this generation upon the consecrated spot, as I have appointed—and the sons of Moses and of Aaron shall be filled with the glory of the Lord upon mount Zion in the Lord's house, whose sons are ye; and also many whom I have called and sent forth to build up my church; for whoso is faithful unto the obtaining these two priesthoods of which I have spoken, & the magnifying their calling, are sanctifyed by the Spirit unto the renewing of their bodies: they become the sons of Moses and of Aaron and the seed of Abra-

ham, and the church and kingdom and the elect of God; and also all they who receive this priesthood receiveth me, saith the Lord, for he that receiveth my servants receiveth me, and he that receiveth me receiveth my Father, and he that receiveth my Father receiveth my Father's kingdom. Therefore, all that my Father hath shall be given unto him; and this is according to the oath and covenant which belongeth to the priesthood. Therefore, all those who receive the priesthood receive this oath and covenant of my Father which he cannot break, neither can it be moved; but whoso breaketh this covenant, after he hath received it, and altogether turneth therefrom, shall not have forgiveness of sins in this world nor in the world to come. And all those who come not unto this priesthood, which ye have received, which I now confirm upon you who are present, this day, by mine own voice out of the heavens, and even I have given the heavenly hosts and mine angels charge covcerning you.

7 And I now give unto you a commandment to beware concerning yourselves, to give diligent heed to the words of eternal life; for you shall live by every word that proceedeth forth from the mouth of God. For the word of the Lord is truth, and whatsoever is truth is light, and whatsoever is light is Spirit, even the Spirit of Jesus Christ; and the Spirit giveth light to every man that cometh into the world: and the Spirit enlighteneth every man through the world, that hearkeneth to the voice of the Spirit; and every one that hearkeneth to the voice of the Spirit, cometh unto God, even the Father; and the Father teacheth him of the covenant which he has renewed and confirmed upon you, which is confirmed upon you for your sakes, and not for your sakes only, but for the sake of the whole world: and the whole world lieth in sin, and groaneth under darkness and under the bondage of sin; and by this you may know they are under the bondage of sin, because they come not unto me; for whoso cometh not unto me is under the bondage of sin; and whoso receiveth not my voice is not acquainted with my voice, and is not of me: and by this you may know the righteous from the wicked, and that the whole world groaneth under sin and darkness even now.

8 And your minds in times past have been darkened because of unbelief, and because you have treated lightly the things you have received, which vanity and unbelief hath brought the whole church under condemnation. And this condemnation resteth upon the children of Zion, even all; and they shall remain under this condemnation until they repent and remember the new covenant, even the book of Mormon and the former commandments which I have given them, not only to say, but to

do according to that which I have written, that they may bring forth fruit meet for their Father's kingdom, otherwise their remaineth a scourge and a judgment to be poured out upon the children of Zion: for shall the children of the kingdom pollute my holy land? Verily, I say unto you, Nay.

9 Verily, verily, I say you, who now have my words, which is my voice, blessed are ye inasmuch as you receive these things: for I will forgive you of your sins with this commandment, that you remain steadfast in your minds in solemnity and the spirit of prayer, in bearing testimony to all the world of those things which are communicated unto you.

10 Therefore go ye into all the world, and whatsoever place ye cannot go into ye shall send, that the testimony may go from you into all the world, unto every creature. And as I said unto mine apostles, even so I say unto you; for you are mine apostles, even God's highpriests: ye are they whom my Father hath given me: ye are my friends; therefore, as I said unto mine apostles I say unto you again, that every soul who believeth on your words, and is baptized by water for the remission of sins, shall receive the Holy Ghost; and these signs shall follow them that believe:

11 In my name they shall do many wonderful works: in my name they shall cast out devils: in my name they shall heal the sick: in my name they shall open the eys of the blind, and unstop the ears of the deaf; and the tongue of the dumb shall speak: and if any man shall administer poison unto them it shall not hurt them: and the poison of a serpent shall not have power to harm them. But a commandment I give unto them, that they shall not boast themselves of these things, neither speak them before the world; for these things are given unto you for your profit and for salvation.

12 Verily, verily, I say unto you, they who believe not on your words, and are not baptized by water, in my name, for the remission of their sins, that they may receive the Holy Ghost, shall be damned. and shall not come into my Father's kingdom, where my Father and I am. And this revelation unto you, and commandment, is in force from this very hour upon all the world, and the gospel is unto all who have not received it. But verily I say unto all those to whom the kingdom has been given, from you it must be preached unto them that they shall repent of their former evil works; for they are to be upbraided for their evil hearts of unbelief: and your brethren in Zion for their rebellion against you at the time I sent you.

13 And again, I say unto you my friends, (for from henceforth I shall call you friends,) it is expedient that I give unto you this commandment, that ye become even as my friends in

days when I was with them travelling to preach this gospel in my power; for I suffered them not to have purse or scrip, neither two coats: behold I send you out to prove the world, and the laborer is worthy of his hire. And any man that shall go and preach this gospel of the kingdom, and fail not to continue faithful in all things, shall not be weary in mind, neither darkened, neither in body, limb or joint; and an hair of his head shall not fall to the ground unnoticed. And they shall not go hungry, neither athirst.

14 Therefore, take no thought for the morrow, for what ye shall eat, or what ye shall drink, or wherewithal ye shall be clothed; for consider the lillies of the field, how they grow, they toil not, neither do they spin; and the kingdoms of the world, in all their glory, are not arrayed like one of these; for your Father who art in heaven, knoweth that you have need of all these things. Therefore, let the morrow take thought for the things of itself. Neither take ye thought beforehand what ye shall say, but treasure up in your minds continually the words of life, and it shall be given you in the very hour that portion that shall be meted unto every man.

15 Therefore let no man among you, (for this commandment is unto all the faithful who are called of God in the church, unto the ministry,) from this hour, take purse or scrip, that goeth forth to proclaim this gospel of the kingdom. Behold I send you out to reprove the world of all their unrighteous deeds, and to teach them of a judgment which is to come.— And whoso receiveth you, there I will be also: for I will go before your face: I will be on your right hand and on your left, and my Spirit shall be in your hearts, and mine angels round about you, to bear you up.

16 Whoso receiveth you, receiveth me, and the same will feed you, and clothe you, and give you money. And he who feeds you, or clothes you, or gives you money, shall in no wise lose his reward: and he that doeth not these things is not my disciple: by this you may know my disciples. He that receiveth you not, go away from him alone by yourselves, and cleanse your feet, even with water, pure water, whether in heat or in cold, and bear testimony of it unto your Father which is in heaven, and return not again unto that man. And in whatsoever village or city ye enter, do likewise. Nevertheless, search diligently and spare not; and wo unto that house, or that village, or city, that rejecteth you, or your words, or testimony concerning me. Wo, I say again, unto that house, or that village, or city, that rejecteth you, or your words, or your testimony of me; for I the Almighty, have laid my hands upon the nations to scourge them for their wickedness; and plagues

shall go forth, & they shall not be taken from the earth until I have completed my work which shall be cut short in righteousness; until all shall know me, who remain, even from the least unto the greatest, and shall be filled with the knowledge of the Lord, and shall see eye to eye, and shall lift up their voice, and with the voice together sing this new song, saying,

17 The Lord hath brought again Zion:
The Lord hath redeemed his people, Israel,
According to the election of grace,
Which was brought to pass by the faith,
And covenant of their fathers.
The Lord hath redeemed his people,
And satan is bound, and time is no longer:
The Lord hath gathered all things in one:
The Lord hath brought down Zion from above:
The Lord hath brought up Zion from beneath;
The earth hath travailed and brought forth her strength;
And truth is established in her bowels;
And the heavens have smiled upon her;
And she is clothed with the glory of her God:
For he stands in the midst of his people:
Glory, and honor, and power, and might,
Be ascribed to our God, for he is full of mercy,
Justice, grace and truth, and peace,
For ever and ever Amen.

18 And again, verily, verily I say unto you, it is expedient, that every man who goes forth to proclaim mine everlasting gospel, that inasmuch as they have families and receive moneys by gift, that they should send it unto them, or make use of it for their benefit, as the Lord shall direct them, for thus it seemeth me good. And let all those who have not families, who receive moneys, send it up unto the bishop in Zion, or unto the bishop in Ohio, that it may be consecrated for the bringing forth of the revelations and the printing thereof, and for establishing Zion.

19 And if any man shall give unto any of you a coat, or a suit, take the old and cast it unto the poor, and go your way rejoicing. And if any man among you be strong in the Spirit, let him take with him he that is weak, that he may be edified in all meekness, that he may become strong also.

20 Therefore, take with you those who are ordained unto the lesser priesthood, and send them before you to make appointments, and to prepare the way, and to fill appointments that you yourselves are not able to fill. Behold this is the way that mine apostles, in ancient days, built up my church unto me.

21 Therefore let every man stand in his own office, and labor in his own calling: and let not the head say unto the feet, it hath no need of the feet, for without the feet how shall the body be able to stand? also the body hath need of every member, that all may be edified together, that the system may be kept perfect.

24 And behold, the high priests should travel, and also the elders, and also the lesser priests; but the deacons and teachers should be appointed to watch over the church, to be standing ministers unto the church.

22 And the bishop, Newel K. Whitney, also, should travel round about and among all the churches, searching after the poor, to administer to their wants by humbling the rich and the proud: he should also, employ an agent to take charge and to do his secular business, as he shall direct; nevertheless, let the bishop go unto the city of New York, and also to the city of Albany, and also to the city of Boston, and warn the people of those cities with the sound of the gospel, with a loud voice, of the desolation and utter abolishment which awaits them if they do reject these things; for if they do reject these things the hour of their judgment is nigh: and their house shall be left unto them desolate. Let him trust in me and he shall not be confounded; and an hair of his head shall not fall to the ground unnoticed.

23 And verily, I say unto you, the rest of my servants, go ye forth as your circumstances shall permit, in your several callings, unto the great and notable cities and villages, reproving the world in righteousness of all their unrighteous and ungodly deeds, setting forth clearly and understandingly the desolation of abomination in the last days; for with you saith the Lord Almighty, I will rend their kingdoms, I will not only shake the earth, but the starry heavens shall tremble: for I the Lord have put forth my hand to exert the powers of heaven: ye cannot see it now, yet a little while and ye shall see it, and know that I am, and that I will come and reign with my people. I am Alpha and Omega, the beginning and the end: Amen.

SECTION V.

Minutes of the organization of the High Council of the church of Christ of Latter Day Saints, Kirtland, February 17, 1834.

1 This day a general council of twenty four high priests assembled at the house of Joseph Smith, jr. by revelation, and proceeded to organize the high council of the church of Christ, which was to consist of twelve high priests, and one or three

presidents, as the case might require. This high council was appointed by revelation for the purpose of settling important difficulties, which might arise in the church, which could not be settled by the church, or the bishop's council, to the satisfaction of the parties.

2 Joseph Smith, jr. Sidney Rigdon and Frederick G. Williams, were acknowledged presidents by the voice of the council; and Joseph Smith, sen. John Smith, Joseph Coe, John Johnson, Martin Harris, John S. Carter, Jared Carter, Oliver Cowdery, Samuel H. Smith, Orson Hyde, Sylvester Smith and Luke Johnson, high priests, were chosen to be a standing council for the church, by the unanimous voice of the council. The above named counsellors were then asked whether they accepted their appointments, and whether they would act in that office according to the law of heaven: to which they all answered, that they accepted their appointments, and would fill their offices according to the grace of God bestowed upon them.

3 The number composing the council, who voted in the name and for the church in appointing the above named counsellors, were forty three, as follows: nine high priests, seventeen elders, four priests and thirteen members.

4 Voted, that the high council can not have power to act without seven of the above named counsellors, or their regularly appointed successors, are present. These seven shall have power to appoint other high priests, whom they may consider worthy and capable, to act in the place of absent counsellors.

5 Voted, that whenever any vacancy shall occur by the death, removal from office for transgression, or removal from the bounds of this church government, of any one of the above named counsellors, it shall be filled by the nomination of the president or presidents, and sanctioned by the voice of a general council of high priests, convened for that purpose, to act in the name of the church.

6 The president of the church, who is also the president of the council, is appointed by revelation, and acknowledged, in his administration, by the voice of the church; and it is according to the dignity of his office, that he should preside over the high council of the church; and it is his privilege to be assisted by two other presidents, appointed after the same manner, that he himself was appointed; and in case of the absence of one or both of those who are appointed to assist him, he has power to preside over the council without an assistant; and in case that he himself is absent, the other presidents have power to preside in his stead, both or either of them.

7 Whenever a high council of the church of Christ is regu-

larly organized, according to the foregoing pattern, it shall be the duty of the twelve counsellors to cast lots by numbers, and thereby ascertain who, of the twelve, shall speak first, commencing with number 1; and so in succession to number 12.

8 Whenever this council convenes to act upon any case, the twelve counsellors shall consider whether it is a difficult one or not; if it is not, two only of the counsellors shall speak upon it, according to the form above written. But if it is thought to be difficult, four shall be appointed; and if more difficult, six: but in no case shall more than six be appointed to speak. The accused, in all cases, has a right to one half of the council, to prevent insult or injustice; and the counsellors appointed to speak before the council, are to present the case, after the evidence is examined, in its true light, before the council; and every man is to speak according to equity and justice. Those counsellors who draw even numbers, that is, 2, 4, 6, 8, 10 and 12, are the individuals who are to stand up in the behalf of the accused, and prevent insult or injustice.

9 In all cases the accuser and the accused shall have a privilege of speaking for themselves, before the council, after the evidences are heard, and the counsellors who are appointed to speak on the case, have finished their remarks. After the evidences are heard, the counsellors, accuser and accused have spoken, the president shall give a decision according to the understanding which he shall have of the case, and call upon the twelve counsellors to sanction the same by their vote. But should the remaining counsellors, who have not spoken, or any one of them, after hearing the evidences and pleadings impartially, discover an error in the decision of the president, they can manifest it, and the case shall have a re-hearing; and if, after a careful re-hearing, any additional light is shown upon the case, the decision shall be altered accordingly: but in case no additional light is given, the first decision shall stand, the majority of the council having power to determine the same.

10 In cases of difficulty respecting doctrine, or principle, (if there is not a sufficiency written to make the case clear to the minds of the council,) the president may inquire and obtain the mind of the Lord by revelation.

11 The high priests, when abroad, have power to call and organize a council after the manner of the foregoing, to settle difficulties when the parties, or either of them, shall request it: and the said council of high priests shall have power to appoint one of their own number, to preside over such council

G

for the time being. It shall be the duty of said council to transmit, immediately, a copy of their proceedings, with a full statement of the testimony accompanying their decision, to the high council of the seat of the first presidency of the church. Should the parties, or either of them, be dissatisfied with the decision of said council, they may appeal to the high council of the seat of the first presidency of the church, and have a re-hearing, which case shall there be conducted, according to the former pattern written, as though no such decision had been made.

12 This council of high priests abroad, is only to be called on the most difficult cases of church matters: and no common or ordinary case is to be sufficient to call such council. The travelling or located high priests abroad, have power to say whether it is necessary to call such a council or not.

13 There is a distinction between the high council of travelling high priests abroad, and the travelling high council composed of the twelve apostles, in their decisions: From the decision of the former there can be an appeal, but from the decision of the latter there cannot. The latter can only be called in question by the general authorities of the church in case of transgression.

14 Resolved that the president, or presidents of the seat of the first presidency of the church, shall have power to determine whether any such case, as may be appealed, is justly entitled to a re-hearing, after examining the appeal and the evidences and statements accompanying it.

15 The twelve counsellors then proceeded to cast lots, or ballot, to ascertain who should speak first, and the following was the result; namely:—

OLIVER COWDERY, No. 1   JOHN JOHNSON No. 7
JOSEPH COE   " 2   ORSON HYDE   " 8
SAMUEL H. SMITH   " 3   JARED CARTER   " 9
LUKE JOHNSON   " 4   JOSEPH SMITH sen." 10
JOHN S. CARTER   " 5   JOHN SMITH   " 11
SYLVESTER SMITH   " 6   MARTIN HARRIS   " 12

After prayer the conference adjourned.

OLIVER COWDERY, } Clerks.
ORSON HYDE,   }

SECTION VI.

Revelation explaining the parable of the wheat and the tares, December 6, 1832.

ON PRIESTHOOD.

1 Verily thus saith the Lord unto you, my servants, concerning the parable of the wheat, and of the tares: behold, verily I say, that the field was the world; and the apostles were the sowers of the seed; and after they have fallen asleep, the great persecutor of the church, the apostate, the whore, even Babylon, that maketh all nations to drink of her cup, in whose hearts the enemy, even Satan sitteth to reign: Behold he soweth the tares; wherefore the tares choke the wheat and drive the church into the wilderness.

2 But behold, in the last days, even now while the Lord is beginning to bring forth the word, and the blade is springing up and is yet tender, behold, verily I say unto you, the angels are crying unto the Lord day and night, who are ready and waiting to be sent forth to reap down the fields: but the Lord saith unto them, pluck not up the tares while the blade is yet tender: (for verily your faith is weak,) lest you destroy the wheat also: Therefore let the wheat and the tares grow together until the harvest is fully ripe, then ye shall first gather out the wheat from among the tares, and after the gathering of the wheat, behold and lo! the tares are bound in bundles, and the field remaineth to be burned.

3 Therefore thus saith the Lord unto you, with whom the priesthood hath continued through the lineage of your fathers, for ye are lawful heirs according to the flesh, and have been hid from the world with Christ in God: therefore your life and the priesthood hath remained, and must needs remain, through you and your lineage, until the restoration of all things spoken by the mouths of all the holy prophets since the world began.

4 Therefore, blessed are ye if ye continue in my goodness, a light unto the Gentiles, and through this priesthood, a savor unto my people Israel; The Lord hath said it: Amen.

7*

SECTION VI

Revelation given December 27, 183⁚

1 Verily, thus saith the Lord unto you, who have assembled yourselves together to receive his will concerning you. Be-hold, this is pleasing unto your Lord, and the angels rejoice over you; the alms of your prayers have come up into the ears of the Lord of Sabaoth, and are recorded in the book of the names of the sanctified: even them of the celestial world.— Wherefore, I now send upon you another comforter; even up-on you my friends, that it may abide in your hearts, even the Holy Spirit of promise; which other comforter is the same that I promised unto my disciples, as is recorded in the testi-mony of John.

2 This comforter is the promise which I give unto you of eternal life; even the glory of the celestial kingdom: which glory is that of the church of the first born; even of God the holiest of all, through Jesus Christ his Son: he that ascended up on high; as also he descended below all things; in that he comprehended all things, that he might be in all, and through all things; the light of truth; which truth shineth. This is the light of Christ. As also he is in the sun, and the light of the sun, and the power thereof by which it was made. As also he is in the moon, and is the light of the moon, and the pow-er thereof by which it was made. As also the light of the stars, and the power thereof by which they were made. And the earth also, and the power thereof; even the earth upon which you stand.

3 And the light which now shineth, which giveth you light, is through him who enlighteneth your eyes, which is the same light that quickeneth your understandings; which light pro-ceedeth forth from the presence of God, to fill the immensity of space. The light which is in all things; which giveth life to all things; which is the law by which all things are govern-ed: even the power of God, who sitteth upon his throne, who is in the bosom of eternity, who is in the midst of all things.

4 Now verily, I say unto you, that through the redemption which is made for you, is brought to pass the resurrection from the dead. And the spirit and the body is the soul of man.— And the resurrection from the dead is the redemption of the soul; and the redemption of the soul is through him who quickeneth all things, in whose bosom it is decreed, that the poor and the meek of the earth shall inherit it. Therefore, it must needs be sanctified from all unrighteousness, that it may be prepared for the celestial glory; for after it hath filled the measure of its creation, it shall be crowned with glory, even

with the presence of God the Father; that bodies who are of the celestial kingdom may possess it forever, and ever; for, for this intent was it made, and created; and for this intent are they sanctified.

5 And they who are not sanctified through the law which I have given unto you; even the law of Christ, must inherit another kingdom, even that of a terrestrial kingdom, or that of a telestial kingdom. For he who is not able to abide the law of a celestial kingdom, cannot abide a celestial glory: and he who cannot abide the law of a terrestrial kingdom, cannot abide a terrestrial glory: he who cannot abide the law of a telestial kingdom, cannot abide a telestial glory: therefore, he is not meet for a kingdom of glory. Therefore, he must abide a kingdom which is not a kingdom of glory.

6 And again, verily I say unto you, the earth abideth the law of a celestial kingdom, for it filleth the measure of its creation, and transgresseth not the law. Wherefore, it shall be sanctified; yea, notwithstanding it shall die, it shall be quickened again, and shall abide the power by which it is quickened. and the righteous shall inherit it: for notwithstanding they die, they also shall rise again a spiritual body: they who are of a celestial spirit, shall receive the same body which was a natural body; even ye shall receive your bodies, and your glory shall be that glory by which your bodies are quickened. Ye who are quickened by a portion of the celestial glory, shall then receive of the same, even a fulness: and they who are quickened by a portion of the terrestrial glory, shall then receive of the same, even a fulness: and also, they who are quickened by a portion of the telestial glory, shall then receive of the same, even a fulness: and they who remain, shall also be quickened; nevertheless, they shall return again to their own place, to enjoy that which they are willing to receive, because they were not willing to enjoy that which they might have received.

7 For what doth it profit a man if a gift is bestowed upon him, and he receive not the gift? Behold he rejoices not in that which is given unto him, neither rejoices in him who is the giver of the gift.

8 And again, verily I say unto you, that which is governed by law, is also preserved by law, and perfected and sanctified by the same: that which breaketh a law, and abideth not by law, but seeketh to become a law unto itself, and willeth to abide in sin, and altogether abideth in sin, cannot be sanctified by law, neither by mercy, justice, or judgment. Therefore, they must remain filthy still.

9 All kingdoms have a law given; and there are many kingdoms; for there is no space in the which there is no king-

dom; and there is no kingdom in which there is no space, either a greater or lesser kingdom. And unto every kingdom is given a law; and unto every law there are certain bounds, also, and conditions.

10 All beings who abide not in those conditions, are not justified; for intelligence cleaveth unto intelligence; wisdom receiveth wisdom; truth embraceth truth; virtue loveth virtue; light cleaveth unto light; mercy hath compassion on mercy, and claimeth her own; justice continueth its course, and claimeth its own; judgment goeth before the face of him who sitteth upon the throne, and governeth and executeth all things; he comprehendeth all things, and all things are before him, and all things are round about him; and he is above all things, and in all things, and is through all things, and is round about all things: and all things are by him, and of him; even. God, forever, and ever.

11 And again, verily I say unto you, he hath given a law unto all things by which they move in their times, and their seasons; and their courses are fixed; even the courses of the heavens, and the earth; which comprehend the earth and all the planets; and they give light to each other in their times, and in their seasons, in their minutes, in their hours, in their days, in their weeks, in their months, in their years: all these are one year with God, but not with man.

12 The earth rolls upon her wings; and the sun giveth his light by day, and the moon giveth her light by night; and the stars also giveth their light, as they roll upon their wings, in their glory, in the midst of the power of God. Unto what shall I liken these kingdoms, that ye may understand? Behold, all these are kingdoms, and any man who hath seen any or the least of these, hath seen God moving in his majesty and power. I say unto you, he hath seen him: nevertheless, he who came unto his own was not comprehended. The light shineth in darkness, and the darkness comprehendeth it not; nevertheless, the day shall come when you shall comprehend even God; being quickened in him, and by him. Then shall ye know that ye have seen me, that I am, and that I am the true light that is in you, and that you are in me, otherwise ye could not abound.

13 Behold, I will liken these kingdoms unto a man having a field, and he sent forth his servants into the field, to dig in the field; and he said unto the first, go ye and labor in the field, and in the first hour I will come unto you and ye shall behold the joy of my countenance: and he said unto the second, go ye also into the field, and in the second hour I will visit you with the joy of my countenance: and also unto the third, saying, I

will visit you; and unto the fourth, and so on unto the twelfth.

14 And the lord of the field went unto the first in the first hour, and tarried with him all that hour, and he was made glad with the light of the countenance of his lord; and then he withdrew from the first that he might visit the second also, and the third, and the fourth, and so on unto the twelfth; and thus they all received the light of the countenance of their lord: every man in his hour, and in his time, and in his season; beginning at the first, and so on unto the last, and from the last unto the first, and from the first unto the last; every man in his own order, until his hour was finished, even according as his lord had commanded him, that his lord might be glorified in him, and he in him, that they all might be glorified.

15 Therefore, unto this parable will I liken all these kingdoms, and the inhabitants thereof; every kingdom in its hour, and in its time, and in its season; even according to the decree which God hath made.

16 And again, verily I say unto you, my friends, I leave these sayings with you, to ponder in your hearts with this commandment which I give unto you, that ye shall call upon me, while I am near; draw near unto me, and I will draw near unto you; seek me dilligently and ye shall find me; ask and ye shall receive; knock and it shall be opened unto you: whatsoever ye ask the Father in my name it shall be given unto you, that is expedient for you; and if ye ask any thing that is not expedient for you, it shall turn unto your condemnation.

17 Behold, that which you hear is as the voice of one crying in the wilderness; in the wilderness, because you cannot see him: my voice, because my voice is spirit; my spirit is truth; truth abideth and hath no end; and if it be in you it shall abound.

18 And if your eye be single to my glory, your whole bodies shall be filled with light, and there shall be no darkness in you, and that body which is filled with light comprehendeth all things. Therefore, sanctify yourselves that your minds become single to God, and the days will come that you shall see him: for he will unveil his face unto you, and it shall be in his own time, and in his own way, and according to his own will.

19 Remember the great and last promise which I have made unto you: cast away your idle thoughts and your excess of laughter far from you; tarry ye, tarry ye in this place, and call a solemn assembly, even of those who are the first laborers in this last kingdom; and let those whom they have warned in their travelling, call on the Lord, and ponder the warning in their hearts which they have received, for a little season.—

Behold, and lo, I will take care of your flocks and will raise up elders and send unto them.

20 Behold, I will hasten my work in its time; and I give unto you who are the first laborers in this last kingdom, a commandment, that you assemble yourselves together, and organize yourselves, and prepare yourselves; and sanctify yourselves; yea, purify your hearts, and cleanse your hands and your feet before me, that I may make you clean; that I may testify unto your Father, and your God, and my God, that you are clean from the blood of this wicked generation: that I may fulfil this promise, this great and last promise which I have made unto you, when I will.

21 Also, I give unto you a commandment, that ye shall continue in prayer and fasting from this time forth. And I give unto you a commandment, that you shall teach one another the doctrine of the kingdom; teach ye diligently and my grace shall attend you, that you may be instructed more perfectly in theory, in principle, in doctrine, in the law of the gospel, in all things that pertain unto the kingdom of God, that is expedient for you to understand; of things both in heaven, and in the earth, and under the earth; things which have been; things which are; things which must shortly come to pass; things which are at home; things which are abroad; the wars and the perplexities of the nations; and the judgments which are on the land; and a knowledge also of countries, and of kingoms, that ye may be prepared in all things when I shall send you again, to magnify the calling whereunto I have called you, and the mission with which I have commissioned you.

22 Behold I sent you out to testify and warn the people, and it becometh every man who hath been warned, to warn his neighbor. Therefore, they are left without excuse, and their sins are upon their own heads. He that seeketh me early shall find me, and shall not be forsaken.

23 Therefore, tarry ye, and labor dilligently, that you may be perfected in your ministry, to go forth among the Gentiles for the last time, as many as the mouth of the Lord shall name, to bind up the law, and seal up the testimony, and to prepare the saints for the hour of judgment which is to come; that their souls may escape the wrath of God, the desolation of abomination, which await the wicked, both in this world, and in the world to come. Verily, I say unto you, let those who are not the first elders, continue in the vineyard, until the mouth of the Lord shall call them, for their time is not yet come; their garments are not clean from the blood of this generation.

24 Abide ye in the liberty wherewith ye are made free; entangle not yourselves in sin, but let your hands be clean, un-

til the Lord come, for not many days hence and the earth shall tremble, and reel to and fro as a drunken man, and the sun shall hide his face, and shall refuse to give light, and the moon shall be bathed in blood, and the stars shall become exceeding angry, and shall cast themselves down as a fig that falleth from off a fig-tree.

25 And after your testimony, cometh wrath and indignation upon the people; for after your testimony cometh the testimony of earthquakes, that shall cause groanings in the midst of her, and men shall fall upon the ground, and shall not be able to stand. And also cometh the testimony of the voice of thundrings, and the voice of lightnings, and the voice of tempests, and the voice of the waves of the sea, heaving themselves beyond their bounds. And all things shall be in commotion; and surely, men's hearts shall fail them; for fear shall come upon all people; and angels shall fly through the midst of heaven, crying with a loud voice, sounding the trump of God, saying, prepare ye, prepare ye, O inhabitants of the earth; for the judgment of our God is come: behold, and lo, the Bridegroom cometh, go ye out to meet him.

26 And immediately there shall appear a great sign in heaven, and all people shall see it together. And another angel shall sound his trump, saying, that great church, the mother of abominations, that made all nations drink of the wine of the wrath of her fornication, that persecuteth the saints of God, that shed their blood: her who sitteth upon many waters, and upon the islands of the sea; behold, she is the tares of the earth, she is bound in bundles, her bands are made strong, no man can loose them; therefore, she is ready to be burned. And he shall sound his trump both long and loud, and all nations shall hear it.

27 And there shall be silence in heaven for the space of half an hour, and immediately after shall the curtain of heaven be unfolded, as a scroll is unfolded after it is rolled up, and the face of the Lord shall be unveiled; and the saints that are upon the earth, who are alive, shall be quickened, and be caught up to meet him. And they who have slept in their graves, shall come forth; for their graves shall be opened, and they also shall be caught up to meet him in the midst of the pillar of heaven: they are Christ's, the first fruits: they who shall descend with him first, and they who are on the earth and in their graves, who are first caught up to meet him: and all this by the voice of the sounding of the trump of the angel of God.

28 And after this another angel shall sound, which is the second trump; and then cometh the redemption of those who

are Christ's at his coming; who have received their part in
that prison which is prepared for them, that they might receive the gospel, and be judged according to men in the flesh.

29 And again, another trump shall sound, which is the third
trump: and then cometh the spirits of men who are to be judged, and are found under condemnation: and these are the rest
of the dead, and they live not again until the thousand years
are ended, neither again, until the end of the earth.

30 And another trump shall sound, which is the fourth trump,
saying, these are found among those who are to remain until
that great and last day, even the end, who shall remain filthy
still.

31 And another trump shall sound. which is the fifth trump,
which is the fifth angel who committeth the everlasting gospel, flying through the midst of heaven, unto all nations, kindreds, tongues and people; and this shall be the sound of his
trump, saying to all people, both in heaven, and in earth, and
that are under the earth; for every ear shall hear it, and every
knee shall bow, and every tongue shall confess, while they
hear the sound of the trump, saying, fear God, and give glory to him who sitteth upon the throne, forever, and ever; for
the hour of his judgment is come.

32 And again, another angel shall sound his trump, which is
the sixth angel, saying, she is fallen, who made all nations
drink of the wine of the wrath of her fornication: she is fallen!
is fallen!

33 And again, another angel shall sound his trump, which is
the seventh angel, saying, it is finished! it is finished! the
Lamb of God hath overcome, and trodden the wine-press
alone; even the wine-press of the fierceness of the wrath of
Almighty God: and then shall the angels be crowned with
the glory of his might, and the saints shall be filled with his
glory, and receive their inheritance and be made equal with
him.

34 And then shall the first angel again sound his trump in
the ears of all living, and reveal the secret acts of men, and
the mighty works of God in the first thousandth year.

35 And then shall the second angel sound his trump, and reveal the secret acts of men, and the thoughts and intents of
their hearts, and the mighty works of God in the second thousandth year: and so on, until the seventh angel shall sound
his trump: and he shall stand forth upon the land and upon
the sea, and swear in the name of him who sitteth upon the
throne, that there shall be time no longer, and satan shall be
bound, that old serpent who is called the devil, and shall not
be loosed for the space of a thousand years. And then he shall

be loosed for a little season, that he may gather together his armies: and Michael the seventh angel, even the archangel, shall gather together his armies, even the hosts of heaven.—And the devil shall gather together his armies; even the hosts of hell, and shall come up to battle against Michael and his armies: and then cometh the battle of the great God! and the devil and his armies shall be cast away into their own place, that they shall not have power over the saints any more at all; for Michael shall fight their battles, and shall overcome him who seeketh the throne of him who sitteth upon the throne, even the Lamb. This is the glory of God, and the sanctified; and they shall not any more see death.

36 Therefore, verily I say unto you, my friends, call your solemn assembly, as I have commanded you; and as all have not faith, seek ye diligently and teach one another words of wisdom; yea, seek ye out of the best books words of wisdom: seek learning even by study, and also by faith. Organize yourselves; prepare every needful thing, and establish a house, even a house of prayer, a house of fasting, a house of faith, a house of learning, a house of glory, a house of order, a house of God; that your incomings may be in the name of the Lord; that your outgoings may be in the name of the Lord; that all your salutations may be in the name of the Lord, with uplift-ed hands unto the Most High.

37 Therefore, cease from all your light speeches; from all laughter; from all your lustful desires: from all your pride and lightmindedness, and from all your wicked doings. Appoint among yourselves a teacher, and let not all be spokesmen at once; but let one speak at a time, and let all listen unto his sayings, that when all have spoken, that all may be edified of all, and that every man may have an equal privilege.

38 See that ye love one another; cease to be covetous, learn to impart one to another as the gospel requires; cease to be idle, cease to be unclean; cease to find fault one with another; cease to sleep longer than is needful; retire to thy bed early, that ye may not be weary; arise early, that your bodies and your minds may be invigorated: and above all things, clothe yourselves with the bonds of charity, as with a mantle, which is the bond of perfectness and peace: pray always, that you may not faint until I come: behold, and lo, I will come quickly, and receive you unto myself: Amen.

39 And again, the order of the house prepared for the presidency of the school of the prophets, established for their instruction in all things that are expedient for them, even for all the officers of the church, or in other words, those who are called to the ministry in the church, beginning at the high-

priests, even down to the deacons: and this shall be the order of the house of the presidency of the school: He that is appointed to be president, or teacher, shall be found standing in his place, in the house, which shall be prepared for him. Therefore, he shall be first in the house of God, in a place that the congregation in the house may hear his words carefully and distinctly, not with loud speech. And when he cometh into the house of God, (for he should be first in the house; behold this is beautiful, that he may be an example,)

40 Let him offer himself in prayer upon his knees before God, in token, or remembrance, of the everlasting covenant, and when any shall come in after him let the teacher arise, and with uplifted hands to heaven; yea, even directly, salute his brother or brethren with these words:

41 Art thou a brother or brethren, I salute you in the name of the Lord Jesus Christ, in token, or remembrance of the everlasting covenant, in which covenant I receive you to fellowship in a determination that is fixed, immovable and unchangable, to be your friend and brother through the grace of God, in the bonds of love, to walk in all the commandments of God blameless, in thanksgiving, forever and ever. Amen.

42 And he that is found unworthy of this salutation, shall not have place among you; for ye shall not suffer that mine house shall be polluted by them.

43 And he that cometh in and is faithful before me, and is a brother, or if they be brethren, they shall salute the president or teacher with uplifted hands to heaven with this same prayer and covenant, or by saying, Amen, in token of the same.

44 Behold, verily I say unto you, this is a sample unto you for a salutation to one another in the house of God, in the school of the prophets. And ye are called to do this by prayer and thanksgiving as the Spirit shall give utterance, in all your doings in the house of the Lord, in the school of the prophets, that it may become a sanctuary, a tabernacle, of the Holy Spirit to your edification.

45 And ye shall not receive any among you, into this school save he is clean from the blood of this generation: and he shall be received by the ordinance of the washing of feet; for unto this end was the ordinance of the washing of feet instituted.

46 And again, the ordinance of washing feet is to be administered by the president, or presiding elder of the church. It is to be commenced with prayer: and after partaking of bread and wine he is to gird himself, according to the pattern given in the thirteenth chapter of John's testimony concerning me. Amen.

SECTION VIII

Revelation given April, 1829, *to Oliver Cowdery, and Joseph Smith jr.*

1 A great and marvelous work is about to come forth unto the children of men: behold I am God, and give heed unto my word, which is quick and powerful, sharper than a two-edged sword, to the dividing asunder of both joints and marrow: Therefore give heed unto my words.

2 Behold the field is white already to harvest, therefore whoso desireth to reap, let him thrust in his sickle with his might and reap while the day lasts, that he may treasure up for his soul everlasting salvation in the kingdom of God: Yea, whosoever will thrust in his sickle and reap, the same is called of God; therefore, if you will ask of me you shall receive; if you will knock it shall be opened unto you.

3 Now as you have asked, behold I say unto you, keep my commandments, and seek to bring forth and establish the cause of Zion: seek not for riches but for wisdom, and behold the mysteries of God shall be unfolded unto you, and then shall you be made rich. Behold he that hath eternal life is rich.

4 Verily, verily I say unto you, even as you desire of me, so shall it be unto you; and if you desire, you shall be the means of doing much good in this generation. Say nothing but repentance unto this generation: keep my commandments and assist to bring forth my work according to my commandments, and you shall be blessed.

5 Behold thou hast a gift, and blessed art thou because of thy gift. Remember it is sacred and cometh from above: and if thou wilt inquire, thou shalt know mysteries which are great and marvelous: therefore thou shalt exercise thy gift, that thou mayest find out mysteries, that thou mayest bring many to the knowledge of the truth; yea, convince them of the error of their ways. Make not thy gift known unto any, save it be those who are of thy faith. Trifle not with sacred things. If thou wilt do good, yea and hold out faithful to the end, thou shalt be saved in the kingdom of God, which is the greatest of all the gifts of God; for there is no gift greater than the gift of salvation.

6 Verily, verily I say unto thee, blessed art thou for what thou hast done, for thou hast inquired of me, and behold as often as thou hast inquired, thou hast received instruction of my Spirit. If it had not been so, thou wouldst not have come to the place where thou art at this time.

7 Behold thou knowest that thou hast inquired of me, and I did enlighten thy mind; and now I tell thee these things, that thou mayest know that thou hast been enlightened by the Spirit of truth; yea, I tell thee, that thou mayest know that there is none else save God, that knowest thy thoughts and the intents of thy heart: I tell thee these things as a witness unto thee, that the words or the work which thou hast been writing is true.

8 Therefore be diligent, stand by my servant Joseph faithfully in whatsoever difficult circumstances he may be, for the word's sake. Admonish him in his faults and also receive admonition of him. Be patient; be sober; be temperate: have patience, faith, hope and charity.

9 Behold thou art Oliver, and I have spoken unto thee because of thy desires; therefore, treasure up these words in thy heart. Be faithful and diligent in keeping the commandments of God, and I will encircle thee in the arms of my love.

10 Behold I am Jesus Christ, the Son of God. I am the same that came unto my own and my own received me not.— I am the light which shineth in darkness, and the darkness comprehendeth it not.

11 Verily, verily I say unto you, if you desire a further witness, cast your mind upon the night that you cried unto me in your heart, that you might know concerning the truth of these things; did I not speak peace to your mind concerning the matter? What greater witness can you have than from God? And now behold, you have received a witness, for if I have told you things which no man knoweth, have you not received a witness? And behold I grant unto you a gift, if you desire of me, to translate even as my servant Joseph.

12 Verily, verily I say unto you, that there are records which contain much of my gospel, which have been kept back because of the wickedness of the people; and now I command you, that if you have good desires, a desire to lay up treasures for yourself in heaven, then shall you assist in bringing to light, with your gift, those parts of my scriptures which have been hidden because of iniquity.

13 And now, behold I give unto you, and also unto my servant Joseph the keys of this gift, which shall bring to light this ministry; and in the mouth of two or three witnesses, shall every word be established.

14 Verily, verily I say unto you, if they reject my words, and this part of my gospel and ministry, blessed are ye, for they can do no more unto you than unto me; and if they do unto you, even as they have done unto me, blessed are ye, for you shall dwell with me in glory: but if they reject not my

words, which shall be established by the testimony which shall be given, blessed are they; and then shall ye have joy in the fruit of your labors.

15 Verily, verily I say unto you, as I said unto my disciples, where two or three are gathered together in my name, as touching one thing, behold there will I be in the midst of them: even so am I in the midst of you. Fear not to do good my sons, for whatsoever ye sow, that shall ye also reap: therefore, if ye sow good, ye shall also reap good for your reward:

16 Therefore fear not little flock, do good, let earth and hell combine against you, for if ye are built upon my Rock, they cannot prevail. Behold I do not condemn you, go your ways and sin no more: perform with soberness the work which I have commanded you; look unto me in every thought, doubt not, fear not: behold the wounds which pierced my side, and also the prints of the nails in my hands and feet: be faithful; keep my commandments, and ye shall inherit the kingdom of heaven: Amen.

SECTION IX.

Revelation given to Joseph Smith, jr. and Oliver Cowdery, July, 1830.

1 Behold thou wast called and chosen to write the book of Mormon, and to my ministry; and I have lifted thee up out of thy afflictions, and have counselled thee, that thou hast been delivered from all thine enemies, and thou hast been delivered from the powers of satan, and from darkness! Nevertheless, thou art not excusable in thy transgressions; nevertheless go thy way and sin no more.

2 Magnify thine office; and after thou hast sowed thy fields and secured them, go speedily unto the church which is in Colesville, Fayette and Manchester, and they shall support thee; and I will bless them both spiritually and temporally; but if they receive thee not, I will send upon them a cursing instead of a blessing.

3 And thou shalt continue in calling upon God in my name, and writing the things which shall be given thee by the Comforter, and expounding all scriptures unto the church, and it shall be given thee in the very moment, what thou shalt speak and write; and they shall hear it, or I will send unto them a cursing instead of a blessing:

4 For thou shalt devote all thy service in Zion. And in this thou shalt have strength. Be patient in afflictions, for thou shalt have many: but endure them, for lo, I am with you, even

unto the end of thy days. And in temporal labors thou shalt not have strength, for this is not thy calling. Attend to thy calling and thou shalt have wherewith to magnify thine office, and to expound all scriptures. And continue in laying on of the hands, and confirming the churches.

5 And thy brother Oliver shall continue in bearing my name before the world; and also to the church. And he shall not suppose that he can say enough in my cause; and lo I am with him to the end. In me he shall have glory, and not of himself, whether in weakness or in strength, whether in bonds or free: And at all times and in all places, he shall open his mouth and declare my gospel as with the voice of a trump, both day and night. And I will give unto him strength such as is not known among men.

6 Require not miracles, except I shall command you; except casting out devils; healing the sick; and against poisonous serpents; and against deadly poisons; and these things ye shall not do, except it be required of you, by them who desire it, that the scriptures might be fulfilled, for ye shall do according to that which is written. And in whatsoever place ye shall enter, and they receive you not, in my name, ye shall leave a cursing instead of a blessing, by casting off the dust of your feet against them as a testimony, and cleansing your feet by the wayside.

7 And it shall come to pass, that whosoever shall lay their hands upon you by violence, ye shall command to be smitten in my name, and behold I will smite them according to your words, in mine own due time. And whosoever shall go to law with thee shall be cursed by the law. And thou shalt take no purse, nor scrip, neither staves, neither two coats, for the church shall give unto thee in the very hour what thou needest for food, and for raiment, and for shoes, and for money, and for scrip: For thou art called to prune my vineyard with a mighty pruning, yea, even for the last time. Yea, and also, all those whom thou hast ordained. And they shall do even according to this pattern. Amen.

SECTION X.

Revelation given in the presence of six elders, in Fayette, New-York, September, 1830.

1 Listen to the voice of Jesus Christ, your Redeemer, the Great I AM, whose arm of mercy hath atoned for your sins; who will gather his people even as a hen gathereth her chickens under her wings, even as many as will hearken to my

voice, and humble themselves before me, and call upon me in mighty prayer. Behold, verily, verily I say unto you, that at this time your sins are forgiven you, therefore ye receive these things: but remember to sin no more, lest perils shall come upon you.

2 Verily I say unto you, that ye are chosen out of the world to declare my gospel with the sound of rejoicing, as with the voice of a trump: lift up your hearts and be glad for I am in your midst, and am your advocate with the Father; and it is his good will to give you the kingdom; and as it is written, Whatsoever ye shall ask in faith, being united in prayer according to my command, ye shall receive; and ye are called to bring to pass the gathering of mine elect, for mine elect hear my voice and harden not their hearts: wherefore the decree hath gone forth from the Father, that they shall be gathered in unto one place, upon the face of this land, to prepare their hearts, and be prepared in all things, against the day when tribulation and desolation are sent forth upon the wicked: for the hour is nigh, and the day soon at hand, when the earth is ripe: and all the proud, and they that do wickedly, shall be as stubble, and I will burn them up, saith the Lord of hosts, that wickedness shall not be upon the earth: for the hour is nigh, and that which was spoken by mine apostles must be fulfilled; for as they spoke so shall it come to pass; for I will reveal myself from heaven with power and great glory, with all the hosts thereof, and dwell in righteousness with men on earth a thousand years, and the wicked shall not stand.

3 And again, verily, verily I say unto you, and it hath gone forth in a firm decree, by the will of the Father, that mine apostles, the twelve which were with me in my ministry at Jerusalem, shall stand at my right hand at the day of my coming in a pillar of fire, being clothed with robes of righteousness, with crowns upon their heads, in glory even as I am, to judge the whole house of Israel, even as many as have loved me and kept my commandments, and none else; for a trump shall sound both long and loud, even as upon mount Sinai, and all the earth shall quake, and they shall come forth: yea, even the dead which died in me, to receive a crown of righteousness, and to be clothed upon, even as I am, to be with me, that we may be one.

4 But behold, I say unto you, that before this great day shall come, the sun shall be darkened, and the moon shall be turned into blood, and the stars shall fall from heaven; and there shall be greater signs in heaven above, and in the earth beneath; and there shall be weeping and wailing among the hosts of

men; and there shall be a great hailstorm sent forth to destroy the crops of the earth: and it shall come to pass, because of the wickedness of the world, that I will take vengeance upon the wicked, for they will not repent: for the cup of mine indignation is full; for behold, my blood shall not cleanse them if they hear me not.

5 Wherefore I the Lord God will send forth flies upon the face of the earth, which shall take hold of the inhabitants thereof, and shall eat their flesh, and shall cause maggots to come in upon them, and their tongues shall be stayed that they shall not utter against me, and their flesh shall fall from off their bones, and their eyes from their sockets: and it shall come to pass, that the beasts of the forests, and the fowls of the air, shall devour them up: and that great and abominable church, which is the whore of all the earth, shall be cast down by devouring fire, according as it is spoken by the mouth of Ezekiel the prophet, which spoke of these things, which have not come to pass, but surely must, as I live, for abomination shall not reign.

6 And again, verily, verily I say unto you, that when the thousand years are ended, and men again begin to deny their God, then will I spare the earth but for a little season; and the end shalt come, and the heaven and the earth shall be consumed, and pass away, and there shall be a new heaven and a new earth; for all old things shall pass away, and all things shall become new, even the heaven and the earth, and all the fulness thereof, both men and beasts: the fowls of the air, and the fishes of the sea, and not one hair, neither mote, shall be lost. for it is the workmanship of mine hand.

7 But behold, verily I say unto you, before the earth shall pass away, Michael mine archangel, shall sound his trump, and then shall all the dead awake, for their graves shall be opened, and they shall come forth; yea, even all; and the righteous shall be gathered on my right hand unto eternal life; and the wicked on my left hand will I be ashamed to own before the Father: wherefore I will say unto them, depart from me ye cursed into everlasting fire, prepared for the devil and his angels.

8 And now behold I say unto you, never at any time, have I declared from mine own mouth, that they should return, for where I am they cannot come, for they have no power; but remember, that all my judgments are not given unto men: and as the words have gone forth out of my mouth, even so shall they be fulfilled, that the first shall be last, and that the last shall be first in all things, whatsoever I have created by the word of my power, which is the power of my Spirit; for

By the power of my Spirit, created I them: yea, all things both spiritual and temporal: firstly spiritual, secondly temporal, which is the beginning of my work: and again, firstly temporal, and secondly spiritual, which is the last of my work: speaking unto you, that you may naturally understand, but unto myself my works have no end, neither beginning; but it is given unto you, that ye may understand, because ye have asked it of me and are agreed.

9 Wherefore, verily I say unto you, that all things unto me are spiritual, and not at any time have I given unto you a law which was temporal, neither any man, nor the children of men: neither Adam your father, whom I created: behold I gave unto him that he should be an agent unto himself; and I gave unto him commandment, but no temporal commandment gave I unto him; for my commandments are spiritual; they are not natural, nor temporal, neither carnal nor sensual.

10 And it came to pass, that Adam being tempted of the devil, for behold the devil was before Adam, for he rebelled against me saying, Give me thine honor, which is my power: and also a third part of the hosts of heaven turned he away from me because of their agency: and they were thrust down, and thus came the devil and his angels; and behold, there is a place prepared for them from the beginning, which place is hell: and it must needs be that the devil should tempt the children of men, or they could not be agents unto themselves, for if they never should have bitter, they could not know the sweet.

11 Wherefore, it came to pass, that the devil tempted Adam and he partook the forbidden fruit, and transgressed the commandment, wherein he became subject to the will of the devil, because he yielded unto temptation. Wherefore, I the Lord God caused that he should be cast out from the garden of Eden, from my presence, because of his transgression: wherein he became spiritually dead: which is the first death, even that same death, which is the last death, which is spiritual, which shall be pronounced upon the wicked when I shall say, Depart ye cursed.

12 But behold I say unto you, that I the Lord God gave unto Adam and unto his seed, that they should not die as to the temporal death, until I the Lord God should send forth angels to declare unto them repentance and redemption, through faith on the name of mine only begotten Son: and thus did I the Lord God appoint unto man the days of his probation; that by his natural death, he might be raised in immortality unto eternal life, even as many as would believe, and they

8*

that believe not, unto eternal damnation, for they cannot be redeemed from their spiritual fall, because they repent not, for they will love darkness rather than light, and their deeds are evil, and they receive their wages of whom they list to obey.

13 But behold I say unto you, that little children are redeemed from the foundation of the world, through mine Only begotten: Wherefore they cannot sin, for power is not given unto satan to tempt little children, until they begin to become accountable before me; for it is given unto them even as I will, according to mine own pleasure, that great things may be required at the hand of their fathers.

14 And again I say unto you, that whoso having knowledge, have I not commanded to repent? and he that hath no understanding, it remaineth in me to do according as it is written. And now, I declare no more unto you at this time. Amen.

SECTION XI.

Revelation to Joseph Smith jr. and Sidney Rigdon, December, 1830.

1 Listen to the voice of the Lord your God, even Alpha and Omega, the beginning and the end, whose course is one eternal round, the same to-day as yesterday and forever. I am Jesus Christ, the Son of God, who was crucified for the sins of the world, even as many as will believe on my name, that they may become the sons of God, even one in me as I am in the Father, as the Father is one in me, that we may be one.

2 Behold, verily, verily I say unto my servant Sidney, I have looked upon thee and thy works. I have heard thy prayers and prepared thee for a greater work. Thou art blessed, for thou shalt do great things. Behold thou wast sent forth even as John, to prepare the way before me, and before Elijah which should come, and thou knew it not. Thou didst baptize by water unto repentance, but they received not the Holy Ghost; but now I give unto thee a commandment, that thou shalt baptize by water, and they shall receive the Holy Ghost by the laying on of the hands, even as the apostles of old.

3 And it shall come to pass, that there shall be a great work in the land even among the Gentiles, for their folly and their abominations shall be made manifest, in the eyes of all people: for I am God and mine arm is not shortened and I will show miracles, signs and wonders, unto all those who believe on my name. And whoso shall ask it in my name, in faith, they shall cast out devils; they shall heal the sick; they shall cause

the blind to receive their sight, and the deaf to hear, and the dumb to speak, and the lame to walk: and the time speedily cometh that great things are to be shown forth unto the children of men: but without faith shall not any thing be shown forth except desolations upon Babylon, the same which has made all nations drink of the wine of the wrath of her fornication. And there are none that doeth good except those who are ready to receive the fulness of my gospel, which I have sent forth to this generation:

4 Wherefore, I have called upon the weak things of the world, those who are unlearned and despised, to thresh the nations by the power of my Spirit: and their arm shall be my arm, and I will be their shield and their buckler, and I will gird up their loins, and they shall fight manfully for me: and their enemies shall be under their feet; and I will let fall the sword in their behalf; and by the fire of mine indignation will I preserve them. And the poor and the meek shall have the gospel preached unto them, and they shall be looking forth for the time of my coming, for it is nigh at hand: and they shall learn the parable of the fig-tree: for even now already summer is nigh, and I have sent forth the fulness of my gospel by the hand of my servant Joseph: and in weakness have I blessed him, and I have given unto him the keys of the mystery of those things which have been sealed, even things which were from the foundation of the world, and the things which shall come from this time until the time of my coming, if he abide in me, and if not, another will I plant in his stead.

5 Wherefore watch over him that his faith fail not, and it shall be given by the Comforter, the Holy Ghost, that knoweth all things: and a commandment I give unto thee, that thou shalt write for him: and the scriptures shall be given even as they are in mine own bosom, to the salvation of mine own elect: for they will hear my voice, and shall see me, and shall not be asleep, and shall abide the day of my coming, for they shall be purified even as I am pure. And now I say unto you, tarry with him and he shall journey with you; forsake him not and surely these things shall be fulfilled. And inasmuch as ye do not write, behold it shall be given unto him to prophesy: And thou shalt preach my gospel, and call on the holy prophets to prove his words, as they shall be given him.

6 Keep all the commandments and covenants by which ye are bound, and I will cause the heavens to shake for your good: and satan shall tremble; and Zion shall rejoice upon the hills, and flourish; and Israel shall be saved in mine own due time. And by the keys which I have given, shall they be led and no more be confounded at all. Lift up your hearts and be glad:

your redemption draweth nigh. Fear not little flock, the kingdom is yours until I come. Behold I come quickly; even so: Amen.

SECTION. XII.

Revelation given January, 1831.

1 Thus saith the Lord your God, even Jesus Christ, the Great I AM, Alpha and Omega, the beginning and the end, the same which looked upon the wide expanse of eternity, and all the seraphic hosts of heaven, before the world was made: the same which knoweth all things, for all things are present before mine eyes: I am the same which spake and the world was made, and all things came by me: I am the same which have taken the Zion of Enoch into mine own bosom: and verily I say, even as many as have believed on my name, for I am Christ, and in mine own name, by the virtue of the blood which I have spilt, have I plead before the Father for them: But behold the residue of the wicked have I kept in chains of darkness until the judgment of the great day, which shall come at the end of the earth; and even so will I cause the wicked to be kept, that will not hear my voice but harden their hearts, and wo, wo, wo is their doom.

2 But behold, verily, verily I say unto you, that mine eyes are upon you; I am in your midst and ye cannot see me, but the day soon cometh that ye shall see me and know that I am: for the vail of darkness shall soon be rent, and he that is not purified shall not abide the day: wherefore gird up your loins and be prepared. Behold the kingdom is yours and the enemy shall not overcome.

3 Verily I say unto you, ye are clean but not all; and there is none else with whom I am well pleased, for all flesh is corruptible before me, and the powers of darkness prevail upon the earth, among the children of men, in the presence of all the hosts of heaven, which causeth silence to reign, and all eternity is pained, and the angels are waiting the great command to reap down the earth, to gather the tares that they may be burned: and behold the enemy is combined.

4 And now I show unto you a mystery, a thing which is had in secret chambers, to bring to pass even your destruction, in process of time, and ye knew it not, but now I tell it unto you, and ye are blessed, not because of your iniquity, neither your hearts of unbelief, for verily some of you are guilty before me; but I will be merciful unto your weakness. Therefore, be ye strong from henceforth; fear not for the kingdom is

yours: and for your salvation I give unto you a commandment, for I have heard your prayers, and the poor have complained before me, and the rich have I made, and all flesh is mine, and I am no respecter of persons. And I have made the earth rich, and behold it is my footstool: wherefore, again I will stand upon it: and I hold forth and deign to give unto you greater riches, even a land of promise; a land flowing with milk and honey, upon which there shall be no curse when the Lord cometh: and I will give it unto you for the land of your inheritance, if you seek it with all your hearts: and this shall be my covenant with you, ye shall have it for the land of your inheritance, and for the inheritance of your children forever, while the earth shall stand, and ye shall possess it again in eternity, no more to pass away.

5 But verily I say unto you, that in time ye shall have no king nor ruler, for I will be your king and watch over you--- Wherefore, hear my voice and follow me, and you shall be a free people, and ye shall have no laws but my laws, when I come, for I am your Lawgiver, and what can stay my hand? But verily I say unto you, teach one another according to the office wherewith I have appointed you, and let every man esteem his brother as himself, and practice virtue and holiness before me. And again I say unto you, let every man esteem his brother as himself: for what man among you having twelve sons, and is no respecter to them, and they serve him obediently, and he saith unto the one, be thou clothed in robes and sit thou here; and to the other, be thou clothed in rags and sit thou there, and looketh upon his sons and saith I am just.

6 Behold, this I have given unto you a parable, and it is even as I am: I say unto you, be one; and if ye are not one, ye are not mine. And again I say unto you, that the enemy in the secret chambers seeketh your lives: Ye hear of wars in far countries, and you say that there will soon be great wars in far countries, but ye know not the hearts of them in your own land: I tell you these things because of your prayers: wherefore, treasure up wisdom in your bosoms, lest the wickedness of men reveal these things unto you, by their wickedness, in a manner which shall speak in your ears, with a voice louder than that which shall shake the earth: but if ye are prepared, ye shall not fear.

7 And that ye might escape the power of the enemy, and be gathered unto me a righteous people, without spot and blameless: wherefore, for this cause I gave unto you the commandment, that ye should go to the Ohio: and there I will give unto you my law; and there you shall be endowed with power from on high, and from thence, whomsoever I will shall go

forth among all nations, and it shall be told them what they shall do: for I have a great work laid up in store: for Israel shall be saved, and I will lead them whithersoever I will, and no power shall stay my hand.

8 And now I give unto the church in these parts, a commandment, that certain men among them shall be appointed, and they shall be appointed by the voice of the church: and they shall look to the poor and the needy, and administer to their relief, that they shall not suffer; and send them forth to the place which I have commanded them; and this shall be their work, to govern the affairs of the property of this church. And they that have farms that cannot be sold, let them be left, or rented as seemeth them good. See that all things are preserved, and when men are endowed with power from on high, and sent forth, all these things shall be gathered unto the bosom of the church.

9 And if ye seek the riches which it is the will of the Father to give unto you, ye shall be the richest of all people; for ye shall have the riches of eternity: and it must needs be that the riches of the earth is mine to give: but beware of pride, lest ye become as the Nephites of old. And again I say unto you, I give unto you a commandment, that every man, both elder, priest, teacher and also member, go to with his might, with the labor of his hands, to prepare and accomplish the things which I have commanded. And let your preaching be the warning voice, every man to his neighbor, in mildness and in meekness. And go ye out from among the wicked. Save yourselves. Be ye clean that bear the vessels of the Lord; even so: Amen.

SECTION XIII.

Revelation given February, 1831.

1 Hearken, O ye elders of my church who have assembled yourselves together, in my name, even Jesus Christ, the Son of the living God, the Savior of the world; inasmuch as they believe on my name and keep my commandments; again I say unto you, hearken and hear and obey the law which I shall give unto you: for verily I say, as ye have assembled yourselves together according to the commandment wherewith I commanded you, and are agreed as touching this one thing, and have asked the Father in my name, even so ye shall receive.

2 Behold, verily I say unto you, I give unto you this first commandment, that ye shall go forth in my name, every one

of you, excepting my servants Joseph Smith, jr. and Sidney Rigdon. And I give unto them a commandment that they shall go forth for a little season, and it shall be given by the power of my Spirit when they shall return: and ye shall go forth in the power of my Spirit, preaching my gospel, two by two, in my name, lifting up your voices as with the voice of a trump, declaring my word like unto angels of God: and ye shall go forth baptizing with water, saying, Repent ye, repent ye, for the kingdom of heaven is at hand.

3 And from this place ye shall go forth into the regions westward, and inasmuch as ye shall find them that will receive you, ye shall build up my church in every region, until the time shall come when it shall be revealed unto you, from on high, when the city of the New Jerusalem shall be prepared that ye may be gathered in one, that ye may be my people and I will be your God. And again, I say unto you, that my servant Edward Partridge shall stand in the office wherewith I have appointed him. And it shall come to pass that if he transgress another shall be appointed in his stead; even so: Amen.

4 Again I say unto you, that it shall not be given to any one to go forth to preach my gospel, or to build up my church, except he be ordained by some one who has authority, and it is known to the church that he has authority, and has been regularly ordained by the heads of the church.

5 And again, the elders, priests and teachers of this church, shall teach the principles of my gospel which are in the bible and the book of Mormon, in the which is the fulness of the gospel; and they shall observe the covenants and church articles to do them, and these shall be their teachings, as they shall be directed by the Spirit: and the Spirit shall be given unto you by the prayer of faith, and if ye receive not the Spirit, ye shall not teach. And all this ye shall observe to do as I have commanded, concerning your teaching, until the fulness of my scriptures are given. And as ye shall lift up your voices by the Comforter, ye shall speak and prophesy as seemeth me good; for behold, the Comforter knoweth all things, and beareth record of the Father and of the Son.

6 And now, behold I speak unto the church: Thou shalt not kill; and he that kills shall not have forgiveness, in this world, nor in the world to come.

7 And again, I say, thou shalt not kill; but he that killeth shall die. Thou shalt not steal; and he that stealeth and will not repent, shall be cast out. Thou shalt not lie; he that lieth and will not repent, shall be cast out. Thou shalt love thy wife with all thy heart, and shall cleave unto her and none

else; and he that looketh upon a woman to lust after her, shall deny the faith, and shall not have the Spirit, and if he repents not he shall be cast out. Thou shalt not commit adultery; and he that committeth adultery and repenteth not, thall be cast out; but he that has committed adultery and repents with all his heart, and forsaketh it, and doeth it no more, thou shalt forgive; but if he doeth it again, he shall not be forgiven, but shall be cast out. Thou shalt not speak evil of thy neighbor, nor do him any harm. Thou knowest my laws concerning these things are given in my scriptures: he that sinneth and repenteth not, shall be cast out.

8 If thou lovest me thou shalt serve me and keep all my commandments. And behold, thou wilt remember the poor, and consecrate of thy properties for their support, that which thou hast to impart unto them, with a covenant and a deed which cannot be broken—and inasmuch as ye impart of your substance unto the poor, ye will do it unto me—and they shall be laid before the bishop of my church and his counsellors, two of the elders, or high priests, such as he shall or has appointed and set apart for that purpose.

9 And it shall come to pass, that after they are laid before the bishop of my church, and after that he has received these testimonies concerning the consecration of the properties of my church, that they cannot be taken from the church, agreeable to my commandments, every man shall be made accountable unto me, a steward over his own property, or that which he has received by consecration, inasmuch as is sufficient for himself and family.

10 And again, if there shall be properties in the hands of the church, or any individuals of it, more than is necessary for their support, after this first consecration, which is a residue, to be consecrated unto the bishop, it shall be kept to administer to those who have not, from time to time, that every man who has need may be amply supplied, and receive according to his wants. Therefore, the residue shall be kept in my store house, to administer to the poor and the needy, as shall be appointed by the high council of the church, and the bishop and his council, and for the purpose of purchasing lands for the public benefit of the church, and building houses of worship, and building up of the New Jerusalem which is hereafter to be revealed, that my covenant people may be gathered in one in that day when I shall come to my temple. And this I do for the salvation of my people.

11 And it shall come to pass, that he that sinneth and repenteth not, shall be cast out of the church, and shall not receive again that which he has consecrated unto the poor and

the needy of my church, or in other words, unto me, for inas-much as ye do it unto the least of these ye do it unto me—for it shall come to pass, that which I spake by the mouths of my prophets, shall be fulfilled; for I will consecrate of the riches of those who embrace my gospel among the Gentiles, unto the poor of my people who are of the house of Israel.

12 And again, thou shalt not be proud in thy heart, let all thy garments be plain, and their beauty the beauty of the work of thine own hands, and let all things be done in cleanliness before me. Thou shalt not be idle; for he that is idle shall not eat the bread, nor wear the garments of the laborer. And whosoever among you are sick, and have not faith to be heal-ed, but believe, shall be nourished with all tenderness with herbs and mild food, and that not by the hand of an enemy. And the elders of the church, two or more, shall be called, and shall pray for and lay their hands upon them in my name, and if they die they shall die unto me, and if they live they shall live unto me. Thou shalt live together in love, insomuch that thou shalt weep for the loss of them that die, and more especially for those that have not hope of a glorious resurrec-tion. And it shall come to pass, that those that die in me, shall not taste of death, for it shall be sweet unto them, and they that die not in me, wo unto them, for their death is bitter!

13 And again, it shall come to pass, that he that has faith in me to be healed, and is not appointed unto death, shall be healed: he who has faith to see shall see: he who has faith to hear shall hear: the lame who have faith to leap shall leap; and they who have not faith to do these things, but believe in me, have power to become my sons: and inasmuch as they break not my laws, thou shalt bear their infirmities.

14 Thou shalt stand in the place of thy stewardship: thou shalt not take thy brother's garment; thou shalt pay for that which thou shalt receive of thy brother; and if thou obtainest more than that which would be for thy support, thou shalt give it into my store house, that all things may be done accor-ding to that which I have said.

15 Thou shalt ask, and my scriptures shall be given as I have appointed, and they shall be preserved in safety; and it is ex-pedient that thou shouldst hold thy peace concerning them, and not teach them until ye have received them in full. And I give unto you a commandment, that then ye shall teach them unto all men; for they shall be taught unto all nations, kind-reds, tongues and people.

16 Thou shalt take the things which thou hast received, which have been given unto thee in my scriptures for a law, to be my law, to govern my church; and he that doeth accor-

ding to these things, shall be saved, and he that doeth them not shall be damned, if he continues.

17 If thou shalt ask, thou shalt receive revelation upon revelation; knowledge upon knowledge, that thou mayest know the mysteries, and peaceable things; that which bringeth joy, that which bringeth life eternal. Thou shalt ask, and it shall be revealed unto you in mine own due time, where the New Jerusalem shall be built.

18 And behold, it shall come to pass, that my servants shall be sent forth to the east, and to the west, to the north, and to the south; and even now, let him that goeth to the east, teach them that shall be converted to flee to the west; and this in consequence of that which is coming on the earth, and of secret combinations. Behold thou shalt observe all these things, and great shall be thy reward; for unto you it is given to know the mysteries of the kingdom, but unto the world it is not given to know them. Ye shall observe the laws which ye have received, and be faithful. And ye shall hereafter receive church covenants, such as shall be sufficient to establish you, both here, and in the New Jerusalem. Therefore, he that lacketh wisdom, let him ask of me, and I will give him liberally, and upbraid him not. Lift up your hearts and rejoice, for unto you the kingdom, or in other words, the keys of the church, have been given; even so Amen.

19 The priests and teachers shall have their stewardships, even as the members, and the elders, or high priests who are appointed to assist the bishop as counsellors, in all things are to have their families supported out of the property which is consecrated to the bishop, for the good of the poor, and for other purposes, as before mentioned; or they are to receive a just remuneration for all their services; either a stewardship, or otherwise, as may be thought best, or decided by the counsellors and bishop. And the bishop also, shall receive his support, or a just remuneration for all his services, in the church.

20 Behold, verily I say unto you, that whatever persons among you having put away their companions for the cause of fornication, or in other words, if they shall testify before you in all lowliness of heart that this is the case, ye shall not cast them out from among you; but if ye shall find that any persons have left their companions for the sake of adultery, and they themselves are the offenders, and their companions are living, they shall be cast out from among you. And again I say unto you, that ye shall be watchful and careful, with all inquiry, that ye receive none such among you if they are married, and if they are not married, they shall repent of all their sins, or ye shall not receive them.

21 And again, every person who belongeth to this church of Christ shall observe to keep all the commandments and covenants of the church; And it shall come to pass, that if any persons among you shall kill, they shall be delivered up and dealt with according to the laws of the land; For remember, that he hath no forgiveness: and it shall be proven according to the laws of the land.

22 And if any man or woman shall commit adultery, he or she shall be tried before two elders of the church or more, and every word shall be established against him or her by two witnesses of the church, and not of the enemy. But if there are more than two witnesses it is better: but he or she shall be condemned by the mouth of two witnesses, and the elders shall lay the case before the church, and the church shall lift up their hands against him or her, that they may be dealt with according to the law of God. And if it can be, it is necessary that the bishop is present also. And thus ye shall do in all cases which shall come before you. And if a man or woman shall rob, he or she shall be delivered up unto the law of the land. And if he or she shall steal, he or she shall be delivered up unto the law of the land. And if he or she shall lie, he or she shall be delivered up unto the law of the land. If he or she do any manner of iniquity, he or she shall be delivered up unto the law, even that of God.

23 And if thy brother or sister offend thee, thou shalt take him or her between him or her and thee alone; and if he or she confess, thou shalt be reconciled. And if he or she confess not, thou shalt deliver him or her up unto the church, not to the members but to the elders. And it shall be done in a meeting, and that not before the world. And if thy brother or sister offend many, he or she shall be chastened before many. And if any one offend openly, he or she shall be rebuked openly, that he or she may be ashamed. And if he or she confess not, he or she shall be delivered up unto the law of God. If any shall offend in secret, he or she shall be rebuked in secret, that he or she may have opportunity to confess in secret to him or her whom he or she has offended, and to God, that the church may not speak reproachfully of him or her. And thus shall ye conduct in all things.

SECTION XIV.

A Revelation given February, 1831.

1 O hearken, ye elders of my church, and give ear to the words which I shall speak unto you: for behold, verily, verily

I say unto you, that ye have received a commandment for a law unto my church, through him whom I have appointed unto you, to receive commandments and revelations from my hand. And this ye shall know assuredly, that there is none other appointed unto you to receive commandments and revelations until he be taken, if he abide in me.

2 But verily, verily I say unto you, that none else shall be appointed unto this gift except it be through him, for if it be taken from him he shall not have power, except to appoint another in his stead: and this shall be a law unto you, that ye receive not the teachings of any that shall come before you as revelations or commandments: and this I give unto you, that you may not be deceived; that you may know they are not of me. For verily I say unto you, that he that is ordained of me shall come in at the gate and be ordained as I have told you before, to teach those revelations which you have received, and shall receive through him whom I have appointed.

3 And now behold I give unto you a commandment, that when ye are assembled together, ye shall instruct and edify each other, that ye may know how to act and direct my church how to act upon the points of my law and commandments, which I have given: and thus ye shall become instructed in the law of my church, and be sanctified by that which ye have received, and ye shall bind yourselves to act in all holiness before me, that inasmuch as ye do this, glory shall be added to the kingdom which ye have received. Inasmuch as ye do it not, it shall be taken even that which ye have received. Purge ye out the iniquity which is among you: sanctify yourselves before me and if ye desire the glories of the kingdom, appoint ye my servant Joseph Smith, jr. and uphold him before me by the prayer of faith. And again, I say unto you, that if ye desire the mysteries of the kingdom, provide for him food and raiment and whatsoever thing he needeth to accomplish the work, wherewith I have commanded him: and if ye do it not, he shall remain unto them that have received him, that I may reserve unto myself a pure people before me.

4 Again I say, hearken ye elders of my church, whom I have appointed: ye are not sent forth to be taught, but to teach the children of men the things which I have put into your hands by the power of my Spirit: and ye are to be taught from on high. Sanctify yourselves and ye shall be endowed with power, that ye may give even as I have spoken.

5 Hearken ye, for behold the great day of the Lord is nigh at hand. For the day cometh that the Lord shall utter his voice out of heaven; the heavens shall shake and the earth

shall tremble, and the trump of God shall sound both long and loud, and shall say to the sleeping nations: Ye saints arise and live: Ye sinners stay and sleep until I shall call again: wherefore gird up your loins, least ye be found among the wicked. Lift up your voices and spare not. Call upon the nations to repent, both old and young, both bond and free: saying, Prepare yourselves for the great day of the Lord: for if I, who am a man, do lift up my voice and call upon you to repent, and ye hate me, what will ye say when the day cometh when the thunders shall utter their voices from the ends of the earth, speaking to the ears of all that live, saying: Repent, and prepare for the great day of the Lord? yea, and again, when the lightnings shall streak forth from the east unto the west, and shall utter forth their voices unto all that live, and make the ears of all tingle, that hear, saying these words: Repent ye, for the great day of the Lord is come?

6 And again, the Lord shall utter his voice out of heaven, saying: Hearken, O ye nations of the earth, and hear the words of that God who made you. O ye nations of the earth, how often would I have gathered you together as a hen gathereth her chickens under her wings, but ye would not? How oft have I called upon you by the mouth of my servants; and by the ministering of angels; and by mine own voice; and by the voice of thunderings; and by the voice of lightnings; and by the voice of tempests; and by the voice of earthquakes; and great hailstorms; and by the voice of famines, and pestilences of every kind; and by the great sound of a trump; and by the voice of judgment: and by the voice of mercy all the day long; and by the voice of glory, and honor, and the riches of eternal life; and would have saved you with an everlasting salvation, but ye would not? Behold the day has come, when the cup of the wrath of mine indignation is full.

7 Behold, verily I say unto you, that these are the words of the Lord your God: wherefore, labor ye, labor ye, in my vineyard for the last time: for the last time call upon the inhabitants of the earth, for in mine own due time will I come upon the earth in judgment: and my people shall be redeemed and shall reign with me on earth: for the great Millennial, which I have spoken by the mouth of my servants, shall come; for satan shall be bound; and when he is loosed again, he shall only reign for a little season, and then cometh the end of the earth: and he that liveth in righteousness, shall be changed in the twinkling of an eye; and the earth shall pass away so as by fire; and the wicked shall go away into unquenchable fire; and their end no man knoweth, on earth, nor ever shall know, until they come before me in judgment.

8 Hearken ye to these words; behold I am Jesus Christ.
the Savior of the world. Treasure these things up in your
hearts, and let the solemnities of eternity rest upon your
minds. Be sober. Keep all my commandments; even so:
Amen.

SECTION XV.

Revelation given March 7, 1831.

1 Hearken, O ye people of my church to whom the kingdom
has been given: hearken ye and give ear to him who laid the
foundation of the earth; who made the heavens and all the
host thereof, and by whom all things were made which live
and move and have a being. And again I say, hearken unto
my voice, lest death shall overtake you: in an hour when ye
think not the summer shall be past, and the harvest ended,
and your souls not saved. Listen to him who is the Advocate with the Father, who is pleading your cause before him;
saying, Father behold the sufferings and death of him who did
no sin, in whom thou wast well pleas d: behold the blood of
thy Son which was shed, the blood of him whom thou gavest
that thyself might be glorified: wherefore, Father spare these
my brethren that believe on my name, that they may come unto me and have everlasting life.
2 Hearken O ye people of my church, and ye elders listen together, and hear my voice while it is called to-day and harden
not your hearts; for verily I say unto you that I am Alpha
and Omega, the beginning and the end, the light and the life
of the world; a light that shineth in darkness and the darkness
comprehendeth it not: I came unto my own and my own received me not: but unto as many as received me gave I power
to do many miracles, and to become the sons of God, and even
unto them that believed on my name, gave I power to obtain
eternal life. And even so I have sent mine everlasting covenant into the world; to be a light to the world, and to be a standard for my people and for the Gentiles to seek to it: and to
be a messenger before my face to prepare the way before me.
Wherefore come ye unto it, and with him that cometh I will
reason as with men in days of old, and I will show unto you
my strong reasoning; wherefore hearken ye together and let
me show it unto you, even my wisdom, the wisdom of him
whom ye say is the God of Enoch, and his brethren, who
were separated from the earth, and were received unto myself—a city reserved until a day of righteousness shall come—
a day which was sought for by all holy men, and they found

it not because of wickedness and abominations: and confessed that they were strangers and pilgrims on the earth; but obtained a promise that they should find it, and see it in their flesh. Wherefore hearken and I will reason with you, and I will speak unto you and prophesy as unto men in days of old and I will show it plainly as I showed it unto my disciples, as I stood before them in the flesh, and spake unto them saying: As ye have asked of me concerning the signs of my coming, in the day when I shall come in my glory in the clouds of heaven, to fulfil the promises that I have made unto your fathers: for as ye have looked upon the long absence of your spirits from your bodies to be a bondage, I will show unto you how the day of redemption shall come, and also the restoration of the scattered Israel.

3 And now ye behold this temple which is in Jerusalem, which ye call the house of God, and your enemies say that this house shall never fall. But verily I say unto you, that desolation shall come upon this generation as a thief in the night, and this people shall be destroyed and scattered among all nations. And this temple which ye now see, shall be thrown down that there shall not be left one stone upon another. And it shall come to pass, that this generation of Jews shall not pass away, until every desolation which I have told you concerning them, shall come to pass. Ye say that ye know that the end of the world cometh; ye say also that ye know that the heavens and the earth shall pass away; and in this ye say truly, for so it is; but these things which I have told you, shall not pass away until all shall be fulfilled. And this I have told you concerning Jerusalem, and when that day shall come, shall a remnant be scattered among all nations, but they shall be gathered again; but they shall remain until the times of the Gentiles be fulfilled.

4 And in that day shall be heard of wars and rumors of wars, and the whole earth shall be in commotion, and men's hearts shall fail them, and they shall say that Christ delayeth his coming until the end of the earth. And the love of men shall wax cold, and iniquity shall abound; and when the time of the Gentiles is come in, a light shall break forth among them that sit in darkness, and it shall be the fulness of my gospel; but they receive it not, for they perceive not the light, and they turn their hearts from me because of the precepts of men; and in that generation shall the times of the Gentiles be fulfilled: and there shall be men standing in that generation, that shall not pass, until they shall see an overflowing scourge; for a desolating sickness shall cover the land: but my disciples shall

stand in holy places, and shall not be moved; but among the wicked, men shall lift up their voices and curse God and die. And there shall be earthquakes, also, in divers places, and many desolations, yet men will harden their hearts against me; and they will take up the sword one against another, and they will kill one another.

5 And now, when I the Lord had spoken these words unto my disciples, they were troubled; and I said unto them, be not troubled, for when all these things shall come to pass, ye may know that the promises which have been made unto you, shall be fulfilled: and when the light shall begin to break forth, it shall be with them like unto a parable which I will show you: ye look and behold the fig-trees, and ye see them with your eyes, and ye say when they begin to shoot forth and their leaves are yet tender, that summer is now nigh at hand: even so it shall be in that day, when they shall see all these things, then shall they know that the hour is nigh.

6 And it shall come to pass that he that feareth me shall be looking forth for the great day of the Lord to come, even for the signs of the coming of the Son of man; and they shall see signs and wonders, for they shall be shown forth in the heavens above, and in the earth beneath; and they shall behold blood and fire, and vapors of smoke; and before the day of the Lord shall come, the sun shall be darkened, and the moon be turned into blood, and stars fall from heaven; and the remnant shall be gathered unto this place; and then they shall look for me, and behold I will come: and they shall see me in the clouds of heaven, clothed with power and great glory, with all the holy angels; and he that watches not for me shall be cut off.

7 But before the arm of the Lord shall fall, an angel shall sound his trump, and the saints that have slept, shall come forth to meet me in the cloud. Wherefore if ye have slept in peace, blessed are you, for as you now behold me and know that I am, even so shall ye come unto me and your souls shall live, and your redemption shall be perfected, and the saints shall come forth from the four quarters of the earth.

8 Then shall the arm of the Lord fall upon the nations, and then shall the Lord set his foot upon this mount, and it shall cleave in twain, and the earth shall tremble and reel to and fro, and the heavens also shall shake, and the Lord shall utter his voice and all the ends of the earth shall hear it, and the nations of the earth shall mourn, and they that have laughed shall see their folly, and calamity shall cover the mocker, and the scorner shall be consumed, and they that have watched for iniquity, shall be hewn down and cast into the fire.

9 And then shall the Jews look upon me and say, What are

these wounds in thine hands, and in thy feet? Then shall
they know that I am the Lord; for I will say unto them, These
wounds are the wounds with which I was wounded in the
house of my friends. I am he who was lifted up. I am Jesus
that was crucified. I am the Son of God. And then shall
they weep because of their iniquities; then shall they lament
because they persecuted their King.

10 And then shall the heathen nations be redeemed, and they
that knew no law shall have part in the first resurrection;
and it shall be tolerable for them: and satan shall be bound
that he shall have no place in the hearts of the children of
men. And at that day when I shall come in my glory, shall
the parable be fulfilled which I spake concerning the ten virgins: for they that are wise and have received the truth, and
have taken the Holy Spirit for their guide, and have not been
deceived, verily I say unto you, they shall not be hewn down
and cast into the fire, but shall abide the day, and the earth
shall be given unto them for an inheritance: and they shall
multiply and wax strong, and their children shall grow up
without sin unto salvation, for the Lord shall be in their midst,
and his glory shall be upon them, and he will be their King
and their Lawgiver.

11 And now, behold I say unto you, it shall not be given unto you to know any farther concerning this chapter, until the
new testament be translated, and in it all these things shall be
made known: wherefore I give unto you that ye may now translate it, that ye may be prepared for the things to come; for
verily I say unto you, that great things await you; ye hear of
wars in foreign lands, but behold I say unto you, they are nigh
even at your doors and not many years hence ye shall hear of
wars in your own lands.

12 Wherefore I the Lord have said gather ye out from the
eastern lands, assemble ye yourselves together ye elders of my
church; go ye forth into the western countries, call upon the
inhabitants to repent, and inasmuch as they do repent, build
up churches unto me; and with one heart and with one mind,
gather up your riches that ye may purchase an inheritance
which shall hereafter be appointed unto you, and it shall be
called the New Jerusalem, a land of peace, a city of refuge, a
place of safety for the saints of the most high God; and the
glory of the Lord shall be there, and the terror of the Lord also shall be there, insomuch that the wicked will not come unto it: and it shall be called Zion:

13 And it shall come to pass, among the wicked, that every
man that will not take his sword against his neighbor, must

needs flee unto Zion for safety. And there shall be gathered unto it out of every nation under heaven: and it shall be the only people that shall not be at war one with another. And it shall be said among the wicked, Let us not go up to battle against Zion, for the inhabitants of Zion are terrible. Wherefore we cannot stand.

14 And it shall come to pass that the righteous shall be gathered out from among all nations, and shall come to Zion singing, with songs of everlasting joy.

15 And now I say unto you, keep these things from going abroad unto the world, until it is expedient in me, that ye may accomplish this work in the eyes of the people, and in the eyes of your enemies, that they may not know your works until ye have accomplished the thing which I have commanded you: that when they shall know it, that they may consider these things, for when the Lord shall appear he shall be terrible unto them, that fear may seize upon them, and they shall stand afar off and tremble: and all nations shall be afraid because of the terror of the Lord, and the power of his might; even so: Amen.

SECTION XVI.

Revelation given March, 1831.

1 Hearken, O ye people of my church, for verily I say unto you, that these things were spoken unto you for your profit and learning; but notwithstanding those things which are written, it always has been given to the elders of my church, from the beginning, and ever shall be, to conduct all meetings as they are directed and guided by the Holy Spirit: nevertheless ye are commanded never to cast any one out from your public meetings, which are held before the world: ye are also commanded not to cast any one, who belongeth to the church, out of your sacrament meetings: nevertheless, if any have trespassed, let him not partake until he makes reconciliation.

2 And again I say unto you, ye shall not cast any one out of your sacrament meetings, who is earnestly seeking the kingdom: I speak this concerning those who are not of the church.

3 And again I say unto you, concerning your confirmation meetings, that if there be any that is not of the church, that is earnestly seeking after the kingdom, ye shall not cast them out; but ye are commanded in all things to ask of God who giveth liberally, and that which the Sprit testifies unto you, even so I would that ye should do in all holiness of heart, walking uprightly before me, considering the end of your sal-

vation, doing all things with prayer and thanksgiving, that ye may not be seduced by evil spirits, or doctrines of devils, or the commandments of men, for some are of men, and others of devils.

4 Wherefore, beware lest ye are deceived! and that ye may not be deceived, seek ye earnestly the best gifts, always remembering for what they are given; for verily I say unto you, they are given for the benefit of those who love me and keep all my commandments, and him that seeketh so to do, that all may be benefited, that seeketh or that asketh of me, that asketh and not for a sign that he may consume it upon his lusts.

5 And again, verily I say unto you, I would that ye should always remember, and always retain in your minds what those gifts are, that are given unto the church, for all have not every gift given unto them: for there are many gifts, and to every man is given a gift by the Spirit of God: to some it is given one, and to some is given another, that all may be profited thereby; to some it is given by the Holy Ghost to know that Jesus Christ is the Son of God, and that he was crucified for the sins of the world; to others it is given to believe on their words, that they also might have eternal life, if they continue faithful.

6 And again, to some it is given by the Holy Ghost to know the differences of administration, as it will be pleasing unto the same Lord, according as the Lord will, suiting his mercies according to the conditions of the children of men. And again it is given by the Holy Ghost to some to know the diversities of operations, whether it be of God, that the manifestations of the Spirit may be given to every man to profit withal.

7 And again, verily I say unto you, to some it is given, by the Spirit of God, the word of wisdom; to another it is given the word of knowledge, that all may be taught to be wise and to have knowledge. And again, to some it is given to have faith to be healed, and to others it is given to have faith to heal. And again, to some it is given the working of miracles; and to others it is given to prophesy, and to others the discerning of spirits. And again, it is given to some to speak with tongues, and to another it is given the interpretation of tongues: and all these gifts cometh from God, for the benefit of the children of God. And unto the bishop of the church, and unto such as God shall appoint and ordain to watch over the church, and to be elders unto the church, are to have it given unto them to discern all those gifts, lest there shall be any among you professing and yet be not of God.

8 And it shall come to pass that he that asketh in spirit shall receive in spirit; that unto some it may be given to have all

those gifts, that there may be a head, in order that every member may be profited thereby: he that asketh in the spirit, asketh according to the will of God, wherefore it is done even as he asketh.

9 And again I say unto you, all things must be done in the name of Christ, whatsoever you do in the spirit; and ye must give thanks unto God in the spirit for whatsoever blessing ye are blessed with: and ye must practice virtue and holiness before me continually; even so: Amen.

SECTION XVII.

A Revelation given May, 1831.

1 Hearken, O ye elders of my church, and give ear to the voice of the living God; and attend to the words of wisdom which shall be given unto you, according as ye have asked and are agreed as touching the church, and the spirits which have gone abroad in the earth. Behold verily I say unto you, that there are many spirits which are false spirits, which have gone forth in the earth, deceiving the world: and also satan hath sought to deceive you, that he might overthrow you.

2 Behold I the Lord have looked upon you, and have seen abominations in the church, that profess my name; but blessed are they who are faithful and endure, whether in life or in death, for they shall inherit eternal life. But wo unto them that are deceivers, and hypocrites, for thus saith the Lord, I will bring them to judgment.

3 Behold verily I say unto you, there are hypocrites among you, and have deceived some, which has given the adversary power, but behold such shall be reclaimed; but the hypocrites shall be detected and shall be cut off, either in life or in death, even as I will, and wo unto them who are cut off from my church, for the same are overcome of the world: wherefore, let every man beware lest he do that which is not in truth and righteousness before me.

4 And now come, saith the Lord, by the Spirit, unto the elders of his church, and let us reason together, that ye may understand: let us reason even as a man reasoneth one with another face to face: now when a man reasoneth, he is understood of man, because he reasoneth as a man; even so will I the Lord reason with you that you may understand: wherefore I the Lord asketh you this question, unto what were ye ordained? To preach my gospel by the Spirit, even the Comforter which was sent forth to teach the truth; and then received ye spirits which ye could not understand, and received them to

be of God, and in this are ye justified? Behold ye shall answer this question yourselves, nevertheless I will be merciful unto you: he that is weak among you hereafter shall be made strong.

5 Verily I say unto you, he that is ordained of me and sent forth to preach the word of truth by the Comforter, in the spirit of truth, doth he preach it by the spirit of truth, or some other way? and if it be by some other way, it be not of God. And again, he that receiveth the word of truth, doth he receive it by the spirit of truth, or some other way? if it be some other way, it be not of God: therefore, why is it that ye cannot understand and know that he that receiveth the word by the spirit of truth, receiveth it as it is preached by the spirit of truth?

6 Wherefore, he that preacheth and he that receiveth, understandeth one another, and both are edified and rejoice together; and that which doth not edify, is not of God, and is darkness: that which is of God is light, and he that receiveth light and continueth in God, receiveth more light, and that light groweth brighter and brighter, until the perfect day. And again, verily I say unto you, and I say it that you may know the truth, that you may chase darkness from among you, for he that is ordained of God and sent forth, the same is appointed to be the greatest, notwithstanding he is least, and the servant of all: wherefore he is possessor of all things, for all things are subject unto him, both in heaven and on the earth, the life, and the light, the spirit, and the power, sent forth by the will of the Father, through Jesus Christ, his Son; but no man is possessor of all things, except he be purified and cleansed from all sin; and if ye are purified and cleansed from all sin, ye shall ask whatsoever you will in the name of Jesus, and it shall be done: but know this, it shall be given you what you shall ask, and as ye are appointed to the head, the spirits shall be subject unto you:

7 Wherefore it shall come to pass, that if you behold a spirit manifested that you cannot understand, and you receive not that spirit, ye shall ask of the Father in the name of Jesus, and if he give not unto you that spirit, that you may know that it is not of God: and it shall be given unto you power over that spirit, and you shall proclaim against that spirit with a loud voice, that it is not of God; not with railing accusation, that ye be not overcome; neither with boasting, nor rejoicing, lest you be seized therewith: he that receiveth of God, let him account it of God, and let him rejoice that he is accounted of God worthy to receive, and by giving heed and doing these things which ye have received, and which ye shall hereafter receive: and the kingdom is given you of the Father, and pow-

er to overcome all things, which is not ordained of him: and behold, verily I say unto you, blessed are you who are now hearing these words of mine from the mouth of my servant, for your sins are forgiven you.

8 Let my servant Joseph Wakefield, in whom I am well pleased, and my servant Parley P. Pratt, go forth among the churches and strengthen them by the word of exhortation; and also my servant John Corrill, or as many of my servants as are ordained unto this office, and let them labor in the vineyard; and let no man hinder them of doing that which I have appointed unto them: wherefore in this thing my servant Edward Partridge, is not justified, nevertheless let him repent and he shall be forgiven. Behold ye are little children, and ye cannot bear all things now; ye must grow in grace and in the knowledge of the truth. Fear not, little children, for you are mine, and I have overcome the world, and you are of them that my Father hath given me; and none of them that my Father hath given me shall be lost: and the Father and I are one: I am in the Father and the Father in me: and inasmuch as ye have received me, ye are in me, and I in you: wherefore I am in your midst; and I am the good Shepherd, (and the stone of Israel: He that buildeth upon this rock shall never fall.) And the day cometh that you shall hear my voice and see me, and know that I am. Watch, therefore, that ye may be ready; even so: Amen.

SECTION XVIII.

Revelation given in Zion, August, 1831.

1 Hearken O ye elders of my church, and give ear to my word, and learn of me what I will concerning you, and also concerning this land unto which I have sent you: for verily I say unto you, blessed is he that keepeth my commandments, whether in life or in death; and he that is faithful in tribulation the reward of the same is greater in the kingdom of heaven.

2 Ye cannot behold with your natural eyes, for the present time, the design of your God concerning those things which shall come hereafter, and the glory which shall follow, after much tribulation. For after much tribulation cometh the blessings. Wherefore, the day cometh that ye shall be crowned with much glory, the hour is not yet but is nigh at hand.

3 Remember this which I tell you before, that you may lay it to heart, and receive that which shall follow. Behold, verily I say unto you, for this cause I have sent you that you might be obedient, and that your hearts might be prepared to

bear testimony of the things which are to come; and also that you might be honored of laying the foundation, and of bearing record of the land upon which the Zion of God shall stand; and also, that a feast of fat things might be prepared for the poor; yea a feast of fat things, of wine on the lees well refined, that the earth may know that the mouths of the prophets shall not fail; yea, a supper of the house of the Lord, well prepared unto which all nations shall be invited. Firstly the rich, and the learned, the wise and the noble; and after that cometh the day of my power: then shall the poor, the lame and the blind, and the deaf, come in unto the marriage of the Lamb, and partake of the supper of the Lord, prepared for the great day to come. Behold I the Lord have spoken it.

4 And that the testimony might go forth from Zion; yea from the mouth of the city of the heritage of God: yea, for this cause I have sent you hither; and have selected my servant Edward Partridge and have appointed unto him his mission in this land: but if he repent not of his sins, which are unbelief and blindness of heart, let him take heed lest he fall. Behold his mission is given unto him and it shall not be given again. And whoso standeth in this mission, is appointed to be a judge in Israel, like as it was in ancient days, to divide the lands of the heritage of God unto his children; and to judge his people by the testimony of the just, and by the assistance of his counsellors, according to the laws of the kingdom which are given by the prophets of God; for verily I say unto you, my laws shall be kept on this land.

5 Let no man think that he is ruler, but let God rule him that judgeth, according to the counsel of his own will: or in other words, him that counselleth, or sitteth upon the judgment seat. Let no man break the laws of the land, for he that keepeth the laws of God, hath no need to break the laws of the land: wherefore be subject to the powers that be, until He reigns whose right it is to reign, and subdues all enemies under his feet. Behold the laws which ye have received from my hand, are the laws of the church; and in this light ye shall hold them forth. Behold here is wisdom.

6 And now as I spake concerning my servant Edward Partridge: this land is the land of his residence, and those whom he has appointed for his counsellors. And also the land of the residence of him whom I have appointed to keep my storehouse: wherefore let them bring their families to this land, as they shall counsel between themselves and me: for behold it is not meet that I should command in all things, for he that is compelled in all things, the same is a slothful and not a wise servant: wherefore he receiveth no reward. Verily I say, men

should be anxiously engaged in a good cause, and do many things of their own free will, and bring to pass much righteousness: for the power is in them, wherein they are agents unto themselves. And inasmuch as men do good they shall in no wise lose their reward. But he that doeth not any thing until he is commanded, and receiveth a commandment with doubtful heart, and keepeth it with slothfulness, the same is damned. Who am I that made man, saith the Lord, that will hold him guiltless that obeys not my commandments? Who am I, saith the Lord, that have promised and have not fulfilled? I command and a man obeys not, I revoke and they receive not the blessing: then they say in their hearts, this is not the work of the Lord, for his promises are not fulfilled.—But wo unto such, for their reward lurketh beneath, and not from above.

7 And now I give unto you further directions concerning this land. It is wisdom in me, that my servant Martin Harris should be an example unto the church, in laying his moneys before the bishop of the church. And also, this is a law unto every man that cometh unto this land, to receive an inheritance; and he shall do with his moneys according as the law directs. And it is wisdom also, that there should be lands purchased in Independence, for the place of the storehouse: and also for the house of the printing.

8 And other directions, concerning my servant Martin Harris, shall be given him of the Spirit, that he may receive his inheritance as seemeth him good. And let him repent of his sins, for he seeketh the praise of the world.

9 And also let my servant William W. Phelps stand in the office which I have appointed him, and receive his inheritance in the land. And also, he hath need to repent, for I the Lord am not well pleased with him, for he seeketh to excell and he is not sufficiently meek before me. Behold he who has repented of his sins the same is forgiven, and I the Lord remembereth them no more. By this ye may know if a man repenteth of his sins. Behold he will confess them and forsake them. And now verily I say, concerning the residue of the elders of my church, the time has not yet come for many years, for them to receive their inheritance in this land; except they desire it through the prayer of faith, only as it shall be appointed unto them of the Lord. For behold they shall push the people together from the ends of the earth: wherefore assemble yourselves together, and they who are not appointed to stay in this land, let them preach the gospel in the regions round about; and after that, let them return to their homes. Let them preach by the way, and bear testimony of

the truth in all places, and call upon the rich, the high, and the low, and the poor, to repent; and let them build up churches inasmuch as the inhabitants of the earth will repent.

10 And let there be an agent appointed by the voice of the church, unto the church in Ohio, to receive moneys to purchase lands in Zion.

11 And I give unto my servant Sidney Rigdon, a commandment, that he shall write a description of the land of Zion, and a statement of the will of God, as it shall be made known by the Spirit, unto him; and an epistle and subscription, to be presented unto all the churches, to obtain moneys, to be put into the hands of the bishop, to purchase lands for an inheritance for the children of God, of himself or the agent, as seemeth him good, or as he shall direct. For behold, verily I say unto you, the Lord willeth that the disciples, and the children of men, should open their hearts even to purchase this whole region of country, as soon as time will permit. Behold here is wisdom; let them do this lest they receive none inheritance, save it be by the shedding of blood.

12 And again, inasmuch as there is land obtained, let there be workmen sent forth, of all kinds, unto this land, to labor for the saints of God. Let all these things be done in order. And let the privileges of the lands be made known from time to time, by the bishop, or the agent of the church. And let the work of the gathering be not in haste, nor by flight, but let it be done as it shall be counselled by the elders of the church at the conferences, according to the knowledge which they receive from time to time.

13 And let my servant Sidney Rigdon consecrate and dedicate this land, and the spot of the temple, unto the Lord. And let a conference meeting be called, and after that, let my servant Sidney Rigdon and Joseph Smith, jr. return, and also Oliver Cowdery with them, to accomplish the residue of the work, which I have appointed unto them in their own land: and the residue as shall be ruled by the conferences.

14 And let no man return from this land, except he bear record by the way, of that which he knows and most assuredly believes. Let that which has been bestowed upon Ziba Peterson, be taken from him: and let him stand as a member in the church, and labor with his own hands, with the brethren, until he is sufficiently chastened for all his sins, for he confesseth them not, and he thinketh to hide them.

15 Let the residue of the elders of this church, who are coming to this land, some of whom are exceedingly blessed even above measure, also, hold a conference upon this land. And let my servant Edward Partridge direct the conference, which

shall be held by them. And let them also return, preaching the gospel by the way, bearing record of the things which are revealed unto them: for verily the sound must go forth from this place into all the world; and unto the uttermost parts of the earth, the gospel must be preached unto every creature, with signs following them that believe. And behold the Son of man cometh: Amen.

SECTION XIX.

Revelation given in Zion, August, 1831.

1 Behold, blessed, saith the Lord, are they who have come up unto this land with an eye single to my glory, according to my commandments: for them that live shall inherit the earth, and them that die shall rest from all their labors, and their works shall follow them, and they shall receive a crown in the mansions of my Father, which I have prepared for them; yea, blessed are they whose feet stand upon the land of Zion, who have obeyed my gospel, for they shall receive for their reward the good things of the earth; and it shall bring forth in its strength: and they shall also be crowned with blessings from above; yea and with commandments not a few; and with revelations in their time: they that are faithful and diligent before me:

2 Wherefore I give unto them a commandment, saying thus: Thou shalt love the Lord thy God, with all thy heart, with all thy might, mind, and strength: and in the name of Jesus Christ thou shalt serve him. Thou shalt love thy neighbor as thyself. Thou shalt not steal. Neither commit adultery, nor kill, nor do any thing like unto it. Thou shalt thank the Lord thy God in all things. Thou shalt offer a sacrifice unto the Lord thy God in righteousness: even that of a broken heart and a contrite spirit. And that thou mayest more fully keep thyself unspotted from the world, thou shalt go to the house of prayer and offer up thy sacraments upon my holy day; for verily this is a day appointed unto you to rest from your labors, and to pay thy devotions unto the Most High; nevertheless thy vows shall be offered up in righteousness on all days, and at all times; but remember that on this, the Lord's day, thou shalt offer thine oblations, and thy sacraments, unto the Most High, confessing thy sins unto thy brethren, and before the Lord.

3 And on this day thou shalt do none other thing, only let thy food be prepared with singleness of heart, that thy fasting may be perfect, or in other words, that thy joy may be full.—

Verily this is fasting and prayer; or, in other words, rejoicing and prayer.

4 And inasmuch as ye do these things, with thanksgiving, with cheerful hearts, and countenances; not with much laughter, for this is sin, but with a glad heart and a cheerful countenance; verily I say, that inasmuch as ye do this the fulness of the earth is yours: the beasts of the fields, and the fowls of the air, and that which climbeth upon the trees, and walketh upon the earth: yea, and the herb, and the good things which cometh of the earth, whether for food or for raiment, or for houses or for barns, or for orchards, or for gardens, or for vineyards: yea, all things which cometh of the earth, in the season thereof, is made for the benefit and the use of man, both to please the eye, and to gladden the heart: yea, for food and for raiment, for taste, and for smell, to strengthen the body, and to enliven the soul.

5 And it pleaseth God that he hath given all these things unto man: for unto this end were they made, to be used with judgment, not to excess, neither by extortion: and in nothing doth man offend God, or against none is his wrath kindled, save those who confess not his hand in all things, and obey not his commandments. Behold this is according to the law and the prophets: wherefore trouble me no more concerning this matter, but learn that he who doeth the works of righteousness, shall receive his reward, even peace in this world, and eternal life in the world to come. I the Lord have spoken it and the Spirit beareth record. Amen.

SECTION XX.

Revelation given in Kirtland, August, 1831.

1 Hearken, O ye people, and open your hearts, and give ear from afar: and listen, you that call yourselves the people of the Lord, and hear the word of the Lord, and his will concerning you: yea, verily, I say, hear the word of him whose anger is kindled against the wicked, and rebellious; who willeth to take even them whom he will take, and preserveth in life them whom he will preserve: who buildeth up at his own will and pleasure; and destroyeth when he please; and is able to cast the soul down to hell.

2 Behold I the Lord utter my voice, and it shall be obeyed. Wherefore verily I say, let the wicked take heed, and let the rebellious fear, and tremble. And let the unbelieving hold their lips, for the day of wrath shall come upon them as a whirlwind, and all flesh shall know that I am God. And he that seeketh signs shall see signs, but not unto salvation.

3 Verily I say unto you, there are those among you who seek signs: and there have been such even from the beginning. But behold, faith cometh not by signs, but signs follow those that believe. Yea, signs cometh by faith, not by the will of men, nor as they please, but by the will of God. Yea, signs cometh by faith, unto mighty works, for without faith, no man pleaseth God: and with whom God is angry, he is not well pleased: wherefore, unto such he showeth no signs, only in wrath unto their condemnation.

4 Wherefore I the Lord am not pleased with those among you, who have sought after signs and wonders for faith, and not for the good of men unto my glory: nevertheless, I gave commandments and many have turned away from my commandments, and have not kept them. There were among you adulterers and adulteresses; some of whom have turned away from you, and others remain with you: that hereafter shall be revealed. Let such beware and repent speedily, lest judgments shall come upon them as a snare, and their folly shall be made manifest, and their works shall follow them in the eyes of the people.

5 And verily I say unto you, as I have said before, he that looketh on a woman to lust after her, or if any shall commit adultery in their hearts, they shall not have the Spirit, but shall deny the faith and shall fear: wherefore I the Lord have said that the fearful, and the unbelieving, and all liars, and whosoever loveth and maketh a lie, and the whoremonger, and the sorcerer, shall have their part in that lake which burneth with fire and brimstone, which is the second death. Verily I say, that they shall not have part in the first resurrection.

6 And now behold, I the Lord saith unto you, that ye are not justified because these things are among you, nevertheless he that endureth in faith and doeth my will, the same shall overcome, and shall receive an inheritance upon the earth, when the day of transfiguration shall come; when the earth shall be transfigured, even according to the pattern which was shown unto mine apostles upon the mount: of which account the fulness ye have not yet received.

7 And now, verily I say unto you, that as I said that I would make known my will unto you, behold I will make it known unto you, not by the way of commandment, for there are many who observe not to keep my commandments, but unto him that keepeth my commandments, I will give the mysteries of my kingdom, and the same shall be in him a well of living water, springing up unto everlasting life.

8 And now, behold this is the will of the Lord your God concerning his saints, that they should assemble themselves to-

gether unto the land of Zion, not in haste, lest there should be confusion, which bringeth pestilence. Behold the land of Zion, I the Lord holdeth it in mine own hands: nevertheless, I the Lord renderth unto Cæsar the things which are Cæsar's: wherefore I the Lord willeth, that you should purchase the lands, that you may have advantage of the world, that you may have claim on the world, that they may not be stirred up unto anger: for satan putteth it into their hearts to anger against you, and to the shedding of blood: wherefore the land of Zion shall not be obtained but by purchase, or by blood, otherwise there is none inheritance for you. And if by purchase behold you are blessed; and if by blood, as you are forbidden to shed blood, lo, your enemies are upon you, and ye shall be scourged from city to city, and from synagogue to synagogue, and but few shall stand to receive an inheritance.

9 I the Lord am angry with the wicked; I am holding my Spirit from the inhabitants of the earth. I have sworn in my wrath and decreed wars upon the face of the earth, and the wicked shall slay the wicked, and fear shall come upon every man and the saints also shall hardly escape: nevertheless, I the Lord am with them, and will come down in heaven from the presence of my Father, and consume the wicked with unquenchable fire. And behold this is not yet, but by and by: wherefore seeing that I the Lord have decreed all these things upon the face of the earth, I willeth that my saints should be assembled upon the land of Zion; and that every man should take righteousness in his hands, and faithfulness upon his loins, and lift a warning voice unto the inhabitants of the earth; and declare both by word and by flight, that desolation shall come upon the wicked. Wherefore let my disciples in Kirtland, arrange their temporal concerns, which dwell upon this farm.

10 Let my servant Titus Billings, who has the care thereof dispose of the land, that he may be prepared in the coming spring, to take his journey up unto the land of Zion, with those that dwell upon the face thereof, excepting those whom I shall reserve unto myself, that shall not go until I shall command them. And let all the moneys which can be spared, it mattereth not unto me whether it be little or much, sent up unto the land of Zion, unto them whom I have appointed to receive.

11 Behold I the Lord will give unto my servants Joseph Smith, Jr. power, that he shall be enabled to discern by the Spirit those who shall go up unto the land of Zion, and those of my disciples who shall tarry.

12 Let my servant Newel K. Whitney retain his store, or in other words, the store yet for a little season. Nevertheless let him impart all the money which he can impart, to be sent up un-

to the land of Zion. Behold these things are in his own hands, let him do according to wisdom. Verily I say, let him be ordained as an agent unto the disciples that shall tarry, and let him be ordained unto this power; and now speedily visit the churches, expounding these things unto them, with my servant Oliver Cowdery. Behold this is my will, obtaining moneys even as I have directed.

13 He that is faithful and endureth shall overcome the world. He that sendeth up treasures unto the land of Zion, shall receive an inheritance in this world, and his works shall follow him; and also, a reward in the world to come; yea, and blessed are the dead that die in the Lord from henceforth, when the Lord shall come and old things shall pass away, and all things become new, they shall rise from the dead and shall not die after, and shall receive an inheritance before the Lord, in the holy city, and he that liveth when the Lord shall come, and have kept the faith, blessed is he; nevertheless it is appointed to him to die at the age of man: wherefore children shall grow up until they become old, old men shall die; but they shall not sleep in the dust, but they shall be changed in the twinkling of an eye: wherefore, for this cause preached the apostles unto the world, the resurrection of the dead: these things are the things that ye must look for, and speaking after the manner of the Lord, they are now nigh at hand; and in a time to come, even in the day of the coming of the Son of man, and until that hour, there will be foolish virgins among the wise, and at that hour cometh an entire separation of the righteous and the wicked; and in that day will I send mine angels, to pluck out the wicked, and cast them into unquenchable fire.

14 And now behold, verily I say unto you, I the Lord am not pleased with my servant Sidney Rigdon, he exalted himself in his heart, and received not counsel, but grieved the Spirit: wherefore his writing is not acceptable unto the Lord, and he shall make another; and if the Lord receive it not, behold he standeth no longer in the office which I have appointed him.

15 And again, verily I say unto you, those who desire in their hearts, in meekness, to warn sinners to repentance, let them be ordained unto this power: for this is a day of warning, and not a day of many words. For I the Lord am not to be mocked in the last days. Behold I am from above, and my power lieth beneath. I am over all, and in all, and through all, and searcheth all things: and the day cometh that all things shall be subject unto me. Behold I am Alpha and Omega, even Jesus Christ. Wherefore let all men be-

ware, how they take my name in their lips: for behold verily I
say, that many there be who are under this condemnation;
who useth the name of the Lord, and useth it in vain, having
not authority. Wherefore let the church repent of their sins,
and I the Lord will own them, otherwise they shall be cut off.

16 Remember, that that which cometh from above is sacred,
and must be spoken with care, and by constraint of the Spirit,
and in this there is no condemnation; and ye receive the Spirit through prayer: wherefore without this, there remaineth
condemnation: Let my servant Joseph Smith, jr. and Sidney
Rigdon, seek them a home as they are taught through prayer,
by the Spirit. These things remain to overcome, through patience, that such may receive a more exceeding and eternal
weight of glory; otherwise, a greater condemnation: Amen.

SECTION XXI.

A Revelation given in Kirtland, September, 1831.

1 Behold, thus saith the Lord your God unto you, O ye elders
of my church, hearken ye, and hear, and receive my will concerning you: for verily I say unto you, I will that ye should
overcome the world: wherefore I will have compassion upon
you. There are those among you who have sinned; but verily
I say, for this once, for mine own glory, and for the salvation
of souls, I have forgiven you your sins.

2 I will be merciful unto you, for I have given unto you the
kingdom: and the keys of the mysteries of the kingdom, shall
not be taken from my servant Joseph Smith, jr. through the
means I have appointed, while he liveth, inasmuch as he
obeyeth mine ordinances. There are those who have sought
occasion against him without cause; nevertheless he has sinned, but verily I say unto you, I the Lord forgiveth sins unto
those who confess their sins before me, and ask forgiveness,
who have not sinned unto death. My disciples, in days of
old, sought occasion against one another, and forgave not one
another in their hearts, and for this evil they were afflicted,
and sorely chastened: wherefore I say unto you, that ye ought
to forgive one another, for he that forgiveth not his brother
his trespasses, standeth condemned before the Lord, for there
remaineth in him the greater sin. I the Lord will forgive
whom I will forgive, but of you it is required to forgive all
men; and ye ought to say in your hearts, let God judge between me and thee, and reward thee according to thy deeds.
And he that repenteth not of his sins, and confesseth them

J

not, then ye shall bring him before the church, and do with him as the Scriptures saith unto you, either by commandment, or by revelation. And this ye shall do that God might be glorified, not because ye forgive not, having not compassion, but that ye may be justified in the eyes of the law, that ye may not offend him who is your Lawgiver.

3 Verily I say, for this cause ye shall do these things. Behold I the Lord was angry with him who was my servant Ezra Booth; and also, my servant Isaac Morley; for they kept not the law, neither the commandment; they sought evil in their hearts, and I the Lord withheld my Spirit. They condemned for evil, that thing in which there was no evil; nevertheless I have forgiven my servant Isaac Morley. And also my servant Edward Partridge, behold he hath sinned, and satan seeketh to destroy his soul; but when these things are made known unto them, they repent of the evil, and they shall be forgiven.

4 And now verily I say, that it is expedient in me that my servant Sidney Gilbert, after a few weeks, should return upon his business, and to his agency in the land of Zion; and that which he hath seen and heard may be made known unto my disciples, that they perish not. And for this cause have I spoken these things. And again, I say unto you, that my servant Isaac Morley may not be tempted above that which he is able to bear, and counsel wrongfully to your hurt, I gave commandment that this farm should be sold. I willeth not that my servant Frederick G. Williams should sell his farm, for I the Lord willeth to retain a strong hold in the land of Kirtland, for the space of five years, in the which I will not overthrow the wicked, that thereby I may save some; and after that day, I the Lord will not hold any guilty, that shall go, with an open heart, up to the land of Zion: for I the Lord requireth the hearts of the children of men.

5 Behold now it is called to-day, (until the coming of the Son of man) and verily it is a day of sacrifice, and a day for the tithing of my people; for he that is tithed shall not be burned (at his coming;) for after to-day cometh the burning: this is speaking after the manner of the Lord; for verily I say, to-morrow all the proud and they that do wickedly shall be as stubble: and I will burn them up, for I am the Lord of hosts; and I will not spare any that remaineth in Babylon. Wherefore, if ye believe me, ye will labor while it is called to-day.— And it is not meet that my servants, Newel K. Whitney and Sidney Gilbert should sell their store, and their possessions here, for this is not wisdom until the residue of the church, which remaineth in this place, shall go up unto the land of Zion.

6 Behold it is said in my laws, or forbidden to get in debt to thine enemies; but behold it is not said at any time, that the Lord should not take when he please, and pay as seemeth him good: wherefore as ye are agents, and ye are on the Lord's errand; and whatever ye do according to the will of the Lord, is the Lord's business, and he hath set you to provide for his saints in these last days, that they may obtain an inheritance in the land of Zion; and behold I the Lord declare unto you, and my words are sure and shall not fail, that they shall obtain it; but all things must come to pass in their time; wherefore be not weary in well doing, for ye are laying the foundation of a great work. And out of small things proceedeth that which is great.

7 Behold the Lord requireth the heart and a willing mind; and the willing and obedient shall eat the good of the land of Zion in these last days; and the rebellious shall be cut off out of the land of Zion, and shall be sent away and shall not inherit the land: for verily I say that the rebellious are not of the blood of Ephraim, wherefore they shall be plucked out. Behold I the Lord have made my church in these last days, like unto a judge sitting on an hill, or in an high place, to judge the nations: for it shall come to pass, that the inhabitants of Zion shall judge all things pertaining to Zion: and liars, and hypocrites shall be proved by them, and they who are not apostles and prophets shall be known.

8 And even the bishop, who is a judge, and his counsellors, if they are not faithful in their stewardships, shall be condemned, and others shall be planted in their stead: for behold I say unto you that Zion shall flourish, and the glory of the Lord shall be upon her, and she shall be an ensign unto the people: and there shall come unto her out of every nation under heaven. And the day shall come, when the nations of the earth shall tremble because of her, and shall fear because of her terrible ones: the Lord hath spoken it: Amen.

SECTION XXII.

A Revelation, given November, 1831, to Orson Hyde, Luke Johnson, Lyman Johnson and William E. McLellin. The mind and will of the Lord, as made known by the voice of the Spirit to a conference concerning certain elders; and also certain items, as made known, in addition to the covenants and commandments.

1 My servant, Orson Hyde, was called, by his ordinance, to proclaim the everlasting gospel, by the Spirit of the living God,

from people to people, and from land to land, in the congregations of the wicked, in their synagogues, reasoning with and
expounding all scriptures unto them: and behold and lo, this
is an ensample unto all those who were ordained unto this
priesthood, whose mission is appointed unto them to go forth:
and this is the ensample unto them, that they shall speak as
they are moved upon by the Holy Ghost; and whatsoever they
shall speak when moved upon by the Holy Ghost, shall be
scripture; shall be the will of the Lord; shall be the mind of
the Lord; shall be the word of the Lord; shall be the voice of
the Lord, and the power of God unto salvation; behold this
is the promise of the Lord unto you, O ye my servants: wherefore, be of good cheer, and do not fear, for I the Lord am with
you, and will stand by you; and ye shall bear record of me
even Jesus Christ, that I am the Son of the living God; that
I was; that I am; and that I am to come.   This is the word of
the Lord unto you my servant, Orson Hyde; and also unto
my servant, Luke Johnson, and unto my servant, Lyman
Johnson, and unto my servant, William E. McLellin; and unto all the faithful elders of my church: Go ye into all the
world; preach the gospel to every creature; acting in the authority which I have given you; baptizing in the name of the
Father, and of the Son, and of the Holy Ghost, and he that
believeth, and is baptized, shall be saved, and he that believeth
not shall be damned; and he that believeth shall be blessed
with signs following, even as it is written: and unto you it
shall be given to know the signs of the times, and the signs of
the coming of the Son of man; and of as many as the Father
shall bear record, to you it shall be given power to seal them
up unto eternal life: Amen.

2 And now concerning the items in addition to the covenants
and commandments, they are these: There remaineth hereafter
in the due time of the Lord, other bishops to be set apart unto the church to minister even according to the first: wherefore they shall be high priests who are worthy, and they shall
be appointed by the first presidency of the Melchizedek priesthood, except they be literal descendants of Aaron; and if they
be literal descendants of Aaron, they have a legal right to the
bishopric, if they are the first born among the sons of Aaron:
for the first born holds the right of presidency over this priesthood, and the keys or authority of the same.   No man has a
legal right to this office, to hold the keys of this priesthood,
except he be a literal descendant and the first born of Aaron:
but as a high priest of the Melchizedek priesthood, has authority to officiate in all the lesser offices, he may officiate in the
office of bishop when no literal descendant of Aaron can be

found; provided he is called and set apart, and ordained unto this power under the hands of the first presidency of the Melchizedek priesthood. And a literal descendant of Aaron, also, must be designated by this presidency, and found worthy, and anointed, and ordained under the hands of this presidency, otherwise they are not legally authorized to officiate in their priesthood: but by virtue of the decree concerning their right of the priesthood descending from father to son, they may claim their annointing, if at any time they can prove their lineage, or do ascertain it by revelation from the Lord under the hands of the above named presidency.

3 And again, no bishop or high priest, who shall be set apart for this ministry, shall be tried or condemned for any crime save it be before the first presidency of the church; and inasmuch as he is found guilty before this presidency, by testimony that cannot be impeached, he shall be condemned, and if he repents he shall be forgiven, according to the covenants and commandments of the church.

4 And again, inasmuch as parents have children in Zion, or in any of her stakes which are organized, that teach them not to understand the doctrine of repentance; faith in Christ the Son of the living God; and of baptism and the gift of the Holy Ghost by the laying on of the hands, when eight years old, the sin be upon the head of the parents, for this shall be a law unto the inhabitants of Zion, or in any of her stakes which are organized: and their children shall be baptized for the remission of their sins when eight years old, and receive the laying on of the hands: and they shall also teach their children to pray, and to walk uprightly before the Lord. And the inhabitants of Zion shall also observe the Sabbath day to keep it holy. And the inhabitants of Zion, also, shall remember their labors, inasmuch as they are appointed to labor, in all faithfulness, for the idler shall be had in remembrance before the Lord. Now I the Lord am not well pleased with the inhabitants of Zion, for there are idlers among them; and their children are also growing up in wickedness: They also seek not earnestly the riches of eternity, but their eyes are full of greediness. These things ought not to be, and must be done away from among them: wherefore let my servant Oliver Cowdery, carry these sayings unto the land of Zion. And a commandment I give unto them, that he that observeth not his prayers before the Lord in the season thereof, let him be had in remembrance before the judge of my people. These sayings are true and faithful: wherefore transgress them not, neither take therefrom. Behold I am Alpha and Omega, and I come quickly: Amen.

SECTION XXIII.

Revelation given May, 1831.

1 Hearken unto me, saith the Lord your God, and I will speak unto my servant Edward Partridge, and give unto him directions: for it must needs be that he receive directions how to organize this people: for it must needs be that they are organized according to my laws, if otherwise they will be cut off: wherefore let my servant Edward Partridge, and those whom he has chosen, in whom I am well pleased, appoint unto this people their portion, every man equal according to their families, according to their circumstances, and their wants and needs; and let my servant Edward Partridge, when he shall appoint a man his portion, give unto him a writing that shall secure unto him his portion, that he shall hold it, even this right and this inheritance in the church, until he transgresses and is not accounted worthy by the voice of the church, according to the laws and covenants of the church, to belong to the church: and if he shall transgress, and is not accounted worthy to belong in the church, he shall not have power to claim that portion which he has consecrated unto the bishop for the poor and the needy of my church: therefore, he shall not retain the gift, but shall only have claim on that portion that is deeded unto him. And thus, all things shall be made sure according to the laws of the land.

2 And let that which belongs to this people, be appointed unto this people; and the money which is left unto this people, let there be an agent appointed unto this people, to take the money to provide food and raiment, according to the wants of this people. And let every man deal honestly, and be alike among this people, and receive alike, that ye may be one, even as I have commanded you.

3 And let that which belongeth to this people not be taken and given unto that of another church; wherefore if another church would receive money of this church, let them pay unto this church again according as they shall agree; and this shall be done through the bishop or the agent, which shall be appointed by the voice of the church.

4 And again, let the bishop appoint a storehouse unto this church, and let all things, both in money and in meat, which is more than is needful for the want of this people, be kept in the hands of the bishop. And let him also reserve unto himself, for his own wants, and for the wants of his family, as he shall be employed in doing this business. And thus I grant unto this people a privilege of organizing themselves according

to my laws; and I consecrate unto them this land for a little season, until I the Lord shall provide for them otherwise, and command them to go hence; and the hour and the day is not given unto them: wherefore let them act upon this land as for years; and this shall turn unto them for their good.

5 Behold, this shall be an example unto my servant Edward Partridge, in other places, in all churches. And whoso is found a faithful, a just and a wise steward, shall enter into the joy of his Lord, and shall inherit eternal life. Verily I say unto you, I am Jesus Christ, who cometh quickly, in an hour you think not: even so. Amen.

SECTION XXIV.

Revelation on prayer; given October, 1831.

1 Hearken, and lo, a voice as of one sent down from on high, who is mighty and powerful, whose going forth is unto the ends of the earth; yea, whose voice is unto men, Prepare ye the way of the Lord make his paths straight. The keys of the kingdom of God are committed unto man on the earth, and from thence shall the gospel roll forth unto the ends of the earth, as the stone which is cut out of the mountain without hands shall roll forth, until it has filled the whole earth; yea, a voice crying, Prepare ye the way of the Lord, prepare ye the supper of the Lamb, make ready for the bridegroom; pray unto the Lord; call upon his holy name; make known his wonderful works among the people, call upon the Lord, that his kingdom may go forth upon the earth; that the inhabitants thereof may receive it, and be prepared for the days to come, in the which the Son of man shall come down in heaven, clothed in the brightness of his glory, to meet the kingdom of God which is set up on the earth: wherefore, may the kingdom of God go forth, that the kingdom of heaven may come, that thou O God may be glorified in heaven, so on earth, that thy enemies may be subdued; for thine is the honor, power and glory, forever and ever: Amen.

SECTION XXV.

Revelation given November, 1831.

1 Behold, and hearken, O ye elders of my church, who have assembled yourselves together, whose prayers I have heard, and whose hearts I know, and whose desires have come up before me. Behold and lo, mine eyes are upon you; and the

heavens and the earth are in mine hands, and the riches of eternity are mine to give. Ye endeavored to believe that ye should receive the blessing which was offered unto you, but behold, verily I say unto you, there were fears in your hearts; and verily this is the reason that ye did not receive.

2 And now I the Lord give unto you a testimony of the truth of these commandments which are lying before you: your eyes have been upon my servant Joseph Smith, jr.; and his language you have known; and his imperfections you have known; and you have sought in your hearts knowledge, that you might express beyond his language: this you also know: now seek ye out of the book of commandments, even the least that is among them, and appoint him that is the most wise among you; or if there be any among you, that shall make one like unto it, then ye are justified in saying that ye do not know that they are true: but if ye cannot make one like unto it, ye are under condemnation if ye do not bear record that they are true: for ye know that there is no unrighteousness in them; and that which is righteous cometh down from above, from the Father of lights..

3 And again, verily I say unto you, that it is your privilege, and a promise I give unto you that have been ordained unto this ministry, that inasmuch as you strip yourselves from jealousies and fears, and humble yourselves before me, for ye are not sufficiently humble, the vail shall be rent and you shall see me and know that I am; not with the carnal, neither natural mind, but with the spiritual; for no man has seen God at any time in the flesh, except quickened by the Spirit of God: neither can any natural man abide the presence of God; neither after the carnal mind; ye are not able to abide the presence of God now, neither the ministering of angels: wherefore continue in patience until ye are perfected.

4 Let not your minds turn back; and when ye are worthy, in mine own due time, ye shall see and know that which was conferred upon you by the hands of my servant Joseph Smith, jr. Amen.

SECTION XXVI.

Revelation given November, 1831.

1 Behold and hearken, O ye inhabitants of Zion, and all ye people of my church, who are far off, and hear the word of the Lord which I give unto my servant Joseph Smith, jr. ; and also unto my servant Martin Harris; and also unto my servant Oliver Cowdery; and also unto my servant John Whit-

mer; and also unto my servant Sidney Rigdon; and also unto my servant Wm. W. Phelps: by the way of commandment unto them, for I give unto them a commandment: wherefore hearken and hear, for thus saith the Lord unto them, I the Lord have appointed them, and ordained them to be stewards over the revelations, and commandments which I have given unto them, and which I shall hereafter give unto them; and an account of this stewardship will I require of them in the day of judgment: wherefore I have appointed unto them, and this is their business in the church of God, to manage them and the concerns thereof, yea, the benefits thereof:

2 Wherefore a commandment I give unto them, that they shall not give these things unto the church, neither unto the world, nevertheless, inasmuch as they receive more than is needful for their necessities, and their wants, it shall be given into my storehouse, and the benefits shall be consecrated unto the inhabitants of Zion, and unto their generations, inasmuch as they become heirs according to the laws of the kingdom.

3 Behold this is what the Lord requires of every man in his stewardship; even as I the Lord have appointed, or shall hereafter appoint unto any man. And behold none are exempt from this law who belong to the church of the living God; yea, neither the bishop, neither the agent, who keepeth the Lord's storehouse; neither he who is appointed in a stewardship over temporal things: He who is appointed to administer spiritual things, the same is worthy of his hire, even as those who are appointed to a stewardship, to administer in temporal things; yea, even more abundantly, which abundance is multiplied unto them through the manifestations of the Spirit: nevertheless, in your temporal things you shall be equal, and this not grudgingly, otherwise the abundance of the manifestations of the Spirit, shall be withheld.

4 Now this commandment I give unto my servants for their benefit while they remain, for a manifestation of my blessings upon their heads, and for a reward of their diligence; and for their security for food and for raiment, for an inheritance; for houses and for lands, in whatsoever circumstances I the Lord shall place them, and whithersoever I the Lord shall send them: for they have been faithful over many things, and have done well inasmuch as they have not sinned. Behold I the Lord am merciful and will bless them, and they shall enter into the joy of these things: even so. Amen:

SECTION XXVII.

Revelation given in Zion, July, 1831.

1 Hearken, O ye elders of my church, saith the Lord your God, who have assembled yourselves together, according to my commandments, in this land which is the land of Missouri, which is the land which I have appointed and consecrated for the gathering of the saints: wherefore this is the land of promise, and the place for the city of Zion. And thus saith the Lord your God, if you will receive wisdom here is wisdom.— Behold the place which is now called Independence, is the center place, and the spot for the temple is lying westward upon a lot which is not far from the court house: wherefore it is wisdom that the land should be purchased by the saints; and also every tract lying westward, even unto the line running directly between Jew and Gentile. And also every tract bordering by the prairies, inasmuch as my disciples are enabled to buy lands. Behold this is wisdom, that they may obtain it for an everlasting inheritance.

2 And let my servant Sidney Gilbert, stand in the office which I have appointed him, to receive moneys, to be an agent unto the church, to buy land in all the regions round about, inasmuch as can be in righteousness, and as wisdom shall direct.

3 And let my servant Edward Partridge, stand in the office which I have appointed him, to divide the saints their inheritance, even as I have commanded: and also those whom he has appointed to assist him.

4 And again, verily I say unto you, let my servant Sidney Gilbert plant himself in this place, and establish a store, that he may sell goods without fraud, that he may obtain money to buy lands for the good of the saints; and that he may obtain whatsoever things the disciples may need to plant them in their inheritance. And also let my servant Sidney Gilbert obtain a licence, (behold here is wisdom, and whoso readeth let him understand,) that he may send goods also unto the people, even by whom he will as clerks, employed in his service, and thus provide for my saints, that my gospel may be preached unto those who sit in darkness and in the region and shadow of death.

5 And again, verily I say unto you, let my servant William W. Phelps be planted in this place, and be established as a printer unto the church: and lo, if the world receiveth his writings, (behold here is wisdom,) let him obtain whatsoever he can obtain in righteousness, for the good of the saints. And

let my servant Oliver Cowdery assist him, even as I have commanded, in whatsoever place I shall appoint unto him, to copy, and to correct, and select, that all things may be right before me, as it shall be proved by the Spirit through him.—And thus let those of whom I have spoken, be planted in the land of Zion, as speedily as can be, with their families, to do those things even as I have spoken.

6 And now concerning the gathering, let the bishop and the agent make preparations for those families which have been commanded to come to this land, as soon as possible, and plant them in their inheritance. And unto the residue of both elders and members, further directions shall be given hereafter: even so. Amen.

SECTION XXVIII.

Revelation given November, 1831.

1 Hearken unto me, saith the Lord your God, for my servant Oliver Cowdery's sake, it is not wisdom in me that he should be entrusted with the commandments and the moneys which he shall carry unto the land of Zion, except one go with him who will be true and faithful: wherefore I the Lord willeth that my servant John Whitmer, should go with my servant Oliver Cowdery. And also that he shall continue in writing and making a history of all the important things which he shall observe and know, concerning my church, and also that he receive counsel and assistance from my servant Oliver Cowdery, and others.

2 And also, my servants who are abroad in the earth, should send forth the accounts of their stewardships to the land of Zion; for the land of Zion shall be a seat and a place to receive and do all these things; nevertheless, let my servant John Whitmer travel many times from place to place, and from church to church, that he may the more easily obtain knowledge: preaching and expounding, writing, copying, selecting and obtaining all things which shall be for the good of the church, and for the rising generations, that shall grow up on the land of Zion, to possess it from generation to generation, forever and ever. Amen.

SECTION XXIX.

A Revelation to Joseph Smith, jr. and Sidney Rigdon, January, 1832. The word of the Lord unto them concerning the elders of the church of the living God, established in the last days, making known the will of the Lord unto the elders, what they shall do until conference.

1 For verily thus saith the Lord, it is expedient in me, that they should continue preaching the gospel, and in exhortation to the churches, in the regions round about, until conference: and then behold it shall be made known unto them, by the voice of the conference, their several missions.

2 Now verily I say unto you, my servants Joseph Smith, jr. and Sidney Rigdon, saith the Lord, it is expedient to translate again, and inasmuch as it is practicable, to preach in the regions round about until conference, and after that it is expedient to continue the work of translation, until it be finished. And let this be a pattern unto the elders until further knowledge, even as it is written. Now I give no more unto you at this time. Gird up your loins and be sober: even so. Amen.

ON PRIESTHOOD AND CALLING.

SECTION XXX.

Revelation to Joseph Smith, jr. given July, 1828, concerning certain manuscripts on the first part of the book of Mormon, which had been taken from the possession of Martin Harris.

1 The works, and the designs, and the purposes of God, cannot be frustrated, neither can they come to nought, for God doth not walk in crooked paths; neither doth he turn to the right hand nor to the left; neither doth he vary from that which he hath said: therefore his paths are strait and his course is one eternal round.

2 Remember, remember, that it is not the work of God that is frustrated, but the work of men: for although a man may have many revelations, and have power to do many mighty works, yet, if he boasts in his own strength, and sets at nought the counsels of God, and follows after the dictates of his own will, and carnal desires, he must fall and incur the vengeance of a just God upon him.

3 Behold, you have been intrusted with these things, but how strict were your commandments; and remember, also, the promises which were made to you, if you did not transgress

them; and behold, how oft you have transgressed the commandments and the laws of God, and have gone on in the persuasions of men: for behold, you should not have feared man more
than God, although men set at nought the counsels of God,
and despise his words, yet you should have been faithful and
he would have extended his arm, and supported you against
all the fiery darts of the adversary; and he would have been
with you in every time of trouble.

4 Behold thou art Joseph, and thou wast chosen to do the
work of the Lord, but because of transgression, if thou art not
aware thou wilt fall, but remember God is merciful: therefore,
repent of that which thou hast done, which is contrary to the
commandment which I gave you, and thou art still chosen,
and art again called to the work; except thou do this, thou
shalt be delivered up and become as other men, and have no
more gift.

5 And when thou deliveredst up that which God had given
thee sight and power to translate, thou deliveredst up that
which was sacred, into the hands of a wicked man, who has
set at nought the counsels of God, and has broken the most
sacred promises, which were made before God, and has depended upon his own judgment, and boasted in his own wisdom,
and this is the reason that thou hast lost thy privileges for a
season, for thou hast suffered the counsel of thy director to be
trampled upon from the beginning.

6 Nevertheless my work shall go forth, for, inasmuch as the
knowledge of a Savior has come unto the world, through the
testimony of the Jews, even so shall the knowledge of a Savior come unto my people; and to the Nephites, and the Jacobites, and the Josephites, and the Zoramites, through the testimony of their fathers; and this testimony shall come to the
knowledge of the Lamanites, and the Lemuelites, and the
Ishmaelites, who dwindled in unbelief because of the iniquity
of their fathers, whom the Lord has suffered to destroy their
brethren the Nephites, because of their iniquities and their
abominations: and for this very purpose are these plates preserved which contain these records, that the promises of the
Lord might be fulfilled, which he made to his people; and that
the Lamanites might come to the knowledge of their fathers,
and that they might know the promises of the Lord, and that
they may believe the gospel and rely upon the merits of Jesus
Christ, and be glorified through faith in his name; and that
through their repentance they might be saved: Amen.

SECTION XXXI.

Revelation to Joseph Smith, Sen., given February, 1829.

1 Now, behold, a marvellous work is about to come forth among the children of men, therefore, O ye that embark in the service of God, see that ye serve him with all your heart, might, mind and strength, that ye may stand blameless before God at the last day: therefore, if ye have desires to serve God, ye are called to the work, for behold the field is white already to harvest, and lo, he that thrusteth in his sickle with his might, the same layeth up in store that he perish not, but bringeth salvation to his soul, and faith, hope, charity, and love, with an eye single to the glory of God, qualifies him for the work.

2 Remember faith, virtue, knowledge, temperance, patience, brotherly kindness, godliness, charity, humility, diligence.—Ask and ye shall receive, knock and it shall be opened unto you. Amen.

SECTION XXXII.

Revelation given March, 1829.

1 Behold I say unto you, that as my servant Martin Harris has desired a witness at my hand, that you, my servant Joseph Smith, jr. have got the plates of which you have testified and borne record that you have received of me: and now behold, this shall you say unto him, He who spake unto you said unto you, I the Lord am God, and have given these things unto you, my servant Joseph Smith, jr. and have commanded you that you shall stand as a witness of these things, and I have caused you that you should enter into a covenant with me that you should not show them except to those persons to whom I command you; and you have no power over them except I grant it unto you. And you have a gift to translate the plates; and this is the first gift that I bestowed upon you, and I have commanded that you should pretend to no other gift until my purpose is fulfilled in this; for I will grant unto you no other gift until it is finished.

2 Verily I say unto you, that wo shall come unto the inhabitants of the earth if they will not hearken unto my words: for hereafter you shall be ordained and go forth and deliver my words unto the children of men. Behold if they will not believe my words, they would not believe you, my servant Joseph, if it were possible that you could show them all these

things which I have committed unto you. O this unbelieving and stiffnecked generation, mine anger is kindled against them.

3 Behold verily, I say unto you, I have reserved those things which I have entrusted unto you, my servant Joseph, for a wise purpose in me, and it shall be made known unto future generations; but this generation shall have my word through you; and in addition to your testimony the testimony of three of my servants, whom I shall call and ordain, unto whom I will show these things: and they shall go forth with my words that are given through you, yea, they shall know of a surety that these things are true: for from heaven will I declare it unto them: I will give them power that they may behold and view these things as they are; and to none else will I grant this power, to receive this same testimony, among this generation, in this, the beginning of the rising up, and the coming forth of my church out of the wilderness—clear as the moon and fair as the sun, and terrible as an army with banners. And the testimony of three witnesses will I send forth of my word; and behold whosoever believeth on my words them will I visit with the manifestation of my Spirit and they shall be born of me, even of water and of the Spirit. And you must wait yet a little while; for ye are not yet ordained—and their testimony shall also go forth unto the condemnation of this generation if they harden their hearts against them: for a desolating scourge shall go forth among the inhabitants of the earth, and shall continue to be poured out, from time to time, if they repent not, until the earth is empty, and the inhabitants thereof are consumed away, and utterly destroyed by the brightness of my coming. Behold, I tell you these things even as I also told the people of the destruction of Jerusalem, and my word shall be verified at this time as it hath hitherto been verified.

4 And now I command you, my servant Joseph, to repent and walk more uprightly before me, and yield to the persuasions of men no more; and that you be firm in keeping the commandments wherewith I have commanded you, and if you do this, behold I grant unto you eternal life, even if you should be slain.

5 And now again I speak unto you, my servant Joseph, concerning the man that desires the witness: Behold I say unto him he exalts himself and does not humble himself sufficiently before me: but if he will bow down before me, and humble himself in mighty prayer and faith, in the sincerity of his heart, then will I grant unto him a view of the things which he desires to see. And then he shall say unto the people of this generation, behold I have seen the things which the Lord has shown unto Joseph Smith, jr. and I know of a surety that

they are true, for I have seen them: for they have been shown unto me by the power of God and not of man. And I the Lord command him, my servant Martin Harris, that he shall say no more unto them concerning these things, except he shall say I have seen them, and they have been shown unto me by the power of God: and these are the words which he shall say. But if he deny this he will break the covenant which he has before covenanted with me, and behold he is condemned. And now except he humble himself and acknowledge unto me the things that he has done which are wrong, and covenant with me that he will keep my commandments, and exercise faith in me, behold, I say unto him, he shall have no such views; for I will grant unto him no views of the things of which I have spoken. And if this be the case I command you, my servant Joseph, that you shall say unto him, that he shall do no more, nor trouble me any more concerning this matter.

6 And if this be the case, behold I say unto thee Joseph, when thou hast translated a few more pages thou shalt stop for a season, even until I command thee again: then thou mayest translate again. And except thou do this, behold thou shalt have no more gift, and I will take away the things which I have intrusted with thee. And now because I foresee the lying in wait to destroy thee: yea, I foresee that if my servant Martin Harris humbleth not himself, and receive a witness from my hand, that he will fall into transgression; and there are many that lie in wait to destroy thee from off the face of the earth: and for this cause, that thy days may be prolonged, I have given unto thee these commandments; yea, for this cause I have said, stop and stand still until I command thee, and I will provide means whereby thou mayest accomplish the thing which I have commanded thee; and if thou art faithful in keeping my commandments, thou shalt be lifted up at the last day. Amen.

SECTION XXXIII.

A Revelation given to Joseph Smith, jr. and Oliver Cowdery, in Harmony, Pennsylvania, April, 1829, when they desired to know whether John, the beloved disciple, tarried on earth.— Translated from parchment, written and hid up by himself.

1 And the Lord said unto me, John, my beloved, what desirest thou? For if ye shall ask, what you will, it shall be granted unto you. And I said unto him, Lord, give unto me power over death, that I may live and bring souls unto thee.

And the Lord said unto me, Verily, verily, I say unto thee, because thou desiredst this thou shalt tarry until I come in my glory, and shall prophesy before nations, kindreds, tongues and people.

2 And for this cause the Lord said unto Peter, If I will that he tarry till I come, what is that to thee? For he desiredst of me that he might bring souls unto me; but thou desiredst that thou might speedily come unto me in my kingdom. I say unto thee, Peter, this was a good desire, but my beloved has desired that he might do more, or a greater work, yet among men than what he has before done; yea, he has undertaken a greater work; therefore, I will make him as flaming fire and a ministering angel: he shall minister for those who shall be heirs of salvation who dwell on the earth; and I will make thee to minister for him and for thy brother James: and unto you three I will give this power and the keys of this ministry until I come.

3 Verily I say unto you, ye shall both have according to your desires, for ye both joy in that which ye have desired.

SECTION XXXIV.

Revelation given April, 1829.

1 Oliver Cowdery, verily, verily I say unto you, that assuredly as the Lord liveth, who is your God and your Redeemer, even so sure shall you receive a knowledge of whatsoever things you shall ask in faith, with an honest heart, believing that you shall receive a knowledge concerning the engravings of old records, which are ancient, which contain those parts of my scripture of which have been spoken, by the manifestation of my Spirit; yea, behold I will tell you in your mind and in your heart by the Holy Ghost, which shall come upon you and which shall dwell in your heart

2 Now, behold this is the Spirit of Revelation: behold this is the Spirit by which Moses brought the children of Israel through the Red sea on dry ground: therefore this is thy gift; apply unto it and blessed art thou, for it shall deliver you out of the hands of your enemies, when, if it were not so, they would slay you and bring your soul to destruction.

3 O remember these words, and keep my commandments.— Remember this is your gift. Now this is not all thy gift; for you have another gift, which is the gift of Aaron: behold it has told you many things: behold there is no other power save the power of God that can cause this gift of Aaron to be with

K

you; therefore, doubt not, for it is the gift of God, and you shall hold it in your hands, and do marvelous works; and no power shall be able to take it away out of your hands; for it is the work of God. And therefore, whatsoever you shall ask me to tell you by that means, that will I grant unto you and you shall have knowledge concerning it: remember, that without faith you can do nothing. Therefore, ask in faith. Trifle not with these things: do not ask for that which you ought not: ask that you may know the mysteries of God, and that you may translate and receive knowledge from all those ancient records which have been hid up, that are sacred, and according to your faith shall it be done unto you. Behold, it is I that have spoken it: and I am the same who spake unto you from the beginning. Amen.

SECTION XXXV.

Revelation given to Oliver Cowdery, April, 1829.

1 Behold I say unto you, my son, that because you did not translate according to that which you desired of me, and did commence again to write for my servant Joseph Smith, jr. even so I would that you should continue until you have finished this record, which I have intrusted unto him: and then behold, other records have I, that I will give unto you power that you may assist to translate.

2 Be patient my son, for it is wisdom in me, and it is not expedient that you should translate at this present time. Behold the work which you are called to do, is to write for my servant Joseph; and behold it is because that you did not continue as you commenced, when you began to translate, that I have taken away this privilege from you. Do not murmur my son, for it is wisdom in me that I have dealt with you after this manner.

3 Behold you have not understood, you have supposed that I would give it unto you, when you took no thought, save it was to ask me; but behold I say unto you, that you must study it out in your mind; then you must ask me if it be right, and if it is right, I will cause that your bosom shall burn within you: therefore, you shall feel that it is right; but if it be not right, you shall have no such feelings, but you shall have a stupor of thought, that shall cause you to forget the thing which is wrong: therefore, you cannot write that which is sacred, save it be given you from me.

4 Now if you had known this, you could have translated; nevertheless, it is not expedient that you should translate now.

Behold it was expedient when you commenced, but you feared and the time is past, and it is not expedient now: for, do you not behold that I have given unto my servant Joseph sufficient strength, whereby it is made up? and neither of you have I condemned.

5 Do this thing which I have commanded you, and you shall prosper. Be faithful, and yield to no temptation. Stand fast in the work wherewith I have called you, and a hair of your head shall not be lost, and you shall be lifted up at the last day. Amen.

SECTION XXXVI.

Revelation given to Joseph Smith, jr. May, 1829, informing him of the alteration of the Manuscript of the fore part of the book of Mormon.

1 Now, behold I say unto you, that because you delivered up those writings which you had power given unto you to translate, by the means of the Urim and Thummim, into the hands of a wicked man, you have lost them; and you also lost your gift at the same time, and your mind became darkened; nevertheless, it is now restored unto you again, therefore see that you are faithful and continue on unto the finishing of the remainder of the work of translation as you have begun: do not run faster, or labor more than you have strength and means provided to enable you to translate; but be diligent unto the end: pray always, that you may come off conqueror; yea, that you may conquer satan and that you may escape the hands of the servants of satan, that do uphold his work. Behold, they have sought to destroy you; yea, even the man in whom you have trusted, has sought to destroy you. And for this cause I said, that he is a wicked man, for he has sought to take away the things wherewith you have been intrusted; and he has also sought to destroy your gift, and because you have delivered the writings into his hands, behold wicked men have taken them from you: therefore, you have delivered them up; yea, that which was sacred unto wickedness. And behold satan has put it into their hearts to alter the words which you have caused to be written, or which you have translated, which have gone out of your hands; and behold I say unto you, that because they have altered the words, they read contrary from that which you translated and caused to be written; and on this wise the devil has sought to lay a cunning plan, that he may destroy this work; for he has put it into their

hearts to do this, that by lying they may say they have caught you in the words which you have pretended to translate.

2 Verily I say unto you, that I will not suffer that satan shall accomplish his evil design in this thing, for behold he has put it into their hearts to get thee to tempt the Lord thy God, in asking to translate it over again; and then behold they say and think in their hearts, we will see if God has given him power to translate, if so, he will also give him power again; and if God giveth him power again, or if he translate again, or in other words, if he bringeth forth the same words, behold we have the same with us, and we have altered them: therefore, they will not agree, and we will say that he has lied in his words, and that he has no gift, and that he has no power: therefore, we will destroy him, and also the work, and we will do this that we may not be ashamed in the end, and that we may get glory of the world.

3 Verily, verily I say unto you, that satan has great hold upon their hearts; he stirreth them up to iniquity against that which is good, and their hearts are corrupt, and full of wickedness and abominations, and they love darkness rather than light, because their deeds are evil: therefore they will not ask of me. Satan stirreth them up, that he may lead their souls to destruction. And thus he has laid a cunning plan, thinking to destroy the work of God, but I will require this at their hands, and it shall turn to their shame and condemnation in the day of judgment; yea, he stirreth up their hearts to anger against this work; yea, he saith unto them, Deceive and lie in wait to catch, that ye may destroy: behold this is no harm, and thus he flattereth them and telleth them that it is no sin to lie, that they may catch a man in a lie, that they may destroy him, and thus he flattereth them, and leadeth them along until he draggeth their souls down to hell; and thus he causeth them to catch themselves in their own snare; and thus he goeth up and down, to and fro in the earth, seeking to destroy the souls of men.

4 Verily, verily I say unto you, wo be unto him that lieth to deceive, because he supposes that another lieth to deceive, for such are not exempt from the justice of God.

5 Now, behold they have altered those words, because satan saith unto them, He hath deceived you: and thus he flattereth them away to do iniquity, to get thee to tempt the Lord thy God.

6 Behold I say unto you, that you shall not translate again those words which have gone forth out of your hands; for behold they shall not accomplish their evil designs in lying against those words. For, behold, if you should bring forth

the same words they will say that you have lied; that you have pretended to translate, but that you have contradicted yourself: and behold they will publish this, and satan will harden the hearts of the people to stir them up to anger against you, that they will not believe my words. Thus satan thinketh to overpower your testimony in this generation, that the work may not come forth in this generation: but behold here is wisdom, and because I show unto you wisdom, and give you commandments concerning these things, what you shall do, show it not unto the world until you have accomplished the work of translation.

7 Marvel not that I said unto you, here is wisdom, show it not unto the world, for I said, show it not unto the world, that you may be preserved. Behold I do not say that you shall not show it unto the righteous; but as you cannot always judge the righteous, or as you cannot always tell the wicked from the righteous: therefore, I say unto you, hold your peace until I shall see fit to make all things known unto the world concerning the matter.

8 And now, verily I say unto you, that an account of those things that you have written, which have gone out of your hands, are engraven upon the plates of Nephi: yea, and you remember, it was said in those writings, that a more particular account was given of these things upon the plates of Nephi.

9 And now, because the account which is engraven upon the plates of Nephi, is more particular concerning the things, which in my wisdom I would bring to the knowledge of the people in this account: therefore, you shall translate the engravings which are on the plates of Nephi, down even till you come to the reign of king Benjamin, or until you come to that which you have translated, which you have retained; and behold, you shall publish it as the record of Nephi, and thus I will confound those who have altered my words. I will not suffer that they shall destroy my work; yea, I will show unto them that my wisdom is greater than the cunning of the devil.

10 Behold they have only got a part, or an abridgment of the account of Nephi. Behold there are many things engraven on the plates of Nephi, which do throw greater views upon my gospel: therefore, it is wisdom in me, that you should translate this first part of the engravings of Nephi, and send forth in this work. And behold, all the remainder of this work, does contain all those parts of my gospel which my holy prophets, yea, and also my disciples desired in their prayers, should come forth unto this people. And I said unto them, that it should be granted unto them according to their faith in their prayers; yea, and this was their faith, that my gospel

which I gave unto them, that they might preach in their days, might come unto their brethren, the Lamanites, and also, all that had become Lamanites, because of their dissensions.

11 Now this is not all, their faith in their prayers were, that this gospel should be made known also, if it were possible that other nations should possess this land; and thus they did leave a blessing upon this land in their prayers, that whosoever should believe in this gospel, in this land, might have eternal life; yea, that it might be free unto all of whatsoever nation, kindred, tongue, or people, they may be.

12 And now, behold, according to their faith in their prayers, will I bring this part of my gospel to the knowledge of my people. Behold, I do not bring it to destroy that which they have received, but to build it up.

13 And for this cause have I said, if this generation harden not their hearts, I will establish my church among them. Now I do not say this to destroy my church, but I say this to build up my church: therefore, whosoever belongeth to my church need not fear, for such shall inherit the kingdom of heaven: but it is they who do not fear me, neither keep my commandments, but buildeth up churches unto themselves, to get gain; yea, and all those that do wickedly, and buildeth up the kingdom of the devil; yea, verily, verily I say unto you, that it is they that I will disturb, and cause to tremble and shake to the centre.

14 Behold, I am Jesus Christ, the Son of God: I came unto my own, and my own received me not. I am the light which shineth in darkness, and the darkness comprehendeth it not. I am he who said other sheep have I which are not of this fold, unto my disciples, and many there were that understood me not.

15 And I will show unto this people, that I had other sheep, and that they were a branch of the house of Jacob: and I will bring to light their marvelous works, which they did in my name: yea, and I will also bring to light my gospel, which was ministered unto them, and behold they shall not deny that which you have received, but they shall build it up, and shall bring to light the true points of my doctrine: yea, and the only doctrine which is in me; and this I do, that I may establish my gospel, that there may not be so much contention: yea, satan doth stir up the hearts of the people to contention, concerning the points of my doctrine; and in these things they do err, for they do wrest the scriptures, and do not understand them: therefore, I will unfold unto them this great mystery, for behold, I will gather them as a hen gathereth her chickens under her wings, if they will not harden their hearts: yea, if

they will come, they may, and partake of the waters of life freely.

16 Behold this is my doctrine: whosoever repenteth' and cometh unto me, the same is my church: whosoever declareth more or less than this, the same is not of me, but is against me: therefore, he is not of my church.

17 And now, behold whosoever is of my church, and endureth of my church to the end, him will I establish upon my Rock, and the gates of hell shall not prevail against them.

18 And now, remember the words of him who is the life and the light of the world, your Redeemer, your Lord and your God. Amen.

SECTION XXXVII.

Revelation given to Hyrum Smith, May, 1829.

1 A great and marvelous work is about to come forth among the children of men: behold I am God and give heed to my word, which is quick and powerful, sharper than a two-edged sword, to the dividing asunder of both joints and marrow: therefore, give heed unto my word.

2 Behold the field is white already to harvest, therefore, whoso desireth to reap, let him thrust in his sickle with his might, and reap while the day lasts, that he may treasure up for his soul everlasting salvation in the kingdom of God; yea, whosoever will thrust in his sickle and reap, the same is called of God: therefore, if you will ask of me, you shall receive; if you will knock, it shall be opened unto you.

3 Now as you have asked, behold I say unto you, keep my commandments, and seek to bring forth and establish the cause of Zion. Seek not for riches but for wisdom, and behold the mysteries of God shall be unfolded unto you, and then shall you be made rich; behold he that hath eternal life is rich.

4 Verily, verily I say unto you, even as you desire of me, so shall it be done unto you; and, if you desire you shall be the means of doing much good in this generation. Say nothing but repentance unto this generation. Keep my commandments, and assist to bring forth my work according to my commandments, and you shall be blessed.

5 Behold thou hast a gift, or thou shalt have a gift if thou wilt desire of me in faith, with an honest heart, believing in the power of Jesus Christ, or in my power which speaketh unto thee: for behold it is I that speaketh: behold I am the light which shineth in darkness, and by my power I give these words unto thee.

6 And now, verily, verily I say unto thee, put your trust in that Spirit which leadeth to do good: yea, to do justly; to walk humbly; to judge righteously; and this is my Spirit.

7 Verily, verily I say unto you, I will impart unto you of my Spirit, which shall enlighten your mind, which shall fill your soul with joy, and then shall ye know, or by this shall you know, all things whatsoever you desire of me, which is pertaining unto things of righteousness, in faith believing in me that you shall receive.

8 Behold I command you, that you need not suppose that you are called to preach until you are called: wait a little longer, until you shall have my word, my rock, my church, and my gospel, that you may know of a surety my doctrine; and then behold, according to your desires, yea, even according to your faith, shall it be done unto you.

9 Keep my commandments; hold your peace; appeal unto my Spirit: yea, cleave unto me with all your heart, that you may assist in bringing to light those things of which have been spoken: yea, the translation of my work: be patient until you shall accomplish it.

10 Behold this is your work, to keep my commandments: yea, with all your might, mind, and strength: seek not to declare my word, but first seek to obtain my word, and then shall your tongue be loosed; then, if you desire, you shall have my Spirit, and my word: yea, the power of God unto the convincing of men: but now hold your peace; study my word which hath gone forth among the children of men; and also study my word which shall come forth among the children of men; or that which is now translating: yea, until you have obtained all which I shall grant unto the children of men in this generation; and then shall all things be added thereunto.

11 Behold thou art Hyrum, my son; seek the kingdom of God and all things shall be added according to that which is just. Build upon my rock, which is my gospel; deny not the Spirit of revelation, nor the Spirit of prophecy, for wo unto him that denieth these things: therefore, treasure up in your hearts until the time which is in my wisdom, that you shall go forth: behold I speak unto all who have good desires, and have thrust in their sickles to reap.

12 Behold I am Jesus Christ, the Son of God: I am the life and the light of the world: I am the same who came unto my own, and my own received me not: but verily, verily I say unto you, that as many as receiveth me, them will I give power to become the sons of God, even to them that believe on my name. Amen.

SECTION XXXVIII.

Revelation given to Joseph Knight, Sen. May, 1829.

1 A great and marvelous work is about to come forth among the children of men: behold I am God, and give heed to my word, which is quick and powerful, sharper than a two-edged sword, to the dividing asunder of both joints and marrow: therefore, give heed unto my word.

2 Behold the field is white already to harvest, therefore whoso desireth to reap, let him thrust in his sickle with his might, and reap while the day lasts, that he may treasure up for his soul everlasting salvation in the kingdom of God: yea, whosoever will thrust in his sickle and reap, the same is called of God: therefore if you will ask of me you shall receive; if you will knock it shall be opened unto you.

3 Now as you have asked, behold I say unto you, keep my commandments, and seek to bring forth and establish the cause of Zion.

4 Behold I speak unto you, and also to all those who have desires to bring forth and establish this work, and no one can assist in this work, except he shall be humble and full of love, having faith, hope and charity, being temperate in all things, whatsoever shall be intrusted to his care.

5 Behold I am the light and the life of the world, that speaketh these words: therefore, give heed with your might, and then you are called. Amen.

SECTION XXXIX.

Revelation given to David Whitmer, June, 1829.

1 A great and marvelous work is about to come forth unto the children of men: behold I am God, and give heed to my word, which is quick and powerful, sharper than a two edged sword, to the dividing asunder of both joints and marrow: therefore, give heed unto my word.

2 Behold the field is white already to harvest, therefore, whoso desireth to reap, let him thrust in his sickle with his might, and reap while the day lasts. that he may treasure up for his soul everlasting salvation in the kingdom of God: yea, whosoever will thrust in his sickle and reap, the same is called of God: therefore. if you will ask of me you shall receive; if you will knock it shall be opened unto you.

3 Seek to bring forth and establish my Zion. Keep my commandments in all things, and if you keep my commandment

and endure to the end, you shall have eternal life; which gift is the greatest of all the gifts of God.

4 And it shall come to pass, that if you shall ask the Father in my name, in faith believing, you shall receive the Holy Ghost, which giveth utterance, that you may stand as a witness of the things of which you shall both hear and see; and also, that you may declare repentance unto this generation.

5 Behold I am Jesus Christ the Son of the living God, who created the heavens and the earth; a light which cannot be hid in darkness: wherefore, I must bring forth the fulness of my gospel from the Gentiles unto the house of Israel. And behold thou art David, and thou art called to assist: which thing if ye do, and are faithful, ye shall be blessed both spiritually and temporally, and great shall be your reward. Amen.

SECTION XL.

Revelation given to John Whitmer, jr. *June*, 1829.

1 Hearken my servant John, and listen to the words of Jesus Christ, your Lord and your Redeemer, for behold I speak unto you with sharpness and with power, for mine arm is over all the earth, and I will tell you that which no man knoweth save me and thee alone: for many times you have desired of me to know that which would be of the most worth unto you.

2 Behold, blessed are you for this thing, and for speaking my words which I have given you, according to my commandments:

3 And now behold I say unto you, that the thing which will be of the most worth unto you, will be to declare repentance unto this people, that you may bring souls unto me, that you may rest with them in the kingdom of my Father. Amen.

SECTION XLI.

Revelation given to Peter Whitmer, June, 1829.

1 Hearken my servant Peter, and listen to the words of Jesus Christ, your Lord and your Redeemer, for behold I speak unto you with sharpness and with power, for mine arm is over all the earth, and I will tell you that which no man knoweth save me and thee alone: for many times you have desired of me to know that which would be of the most worth unto you.

2 Behold, blessed are you for this thing, and for speaking my words which I have given you according to my commandments:

3 And now behold I say unto you, that the thing which will be of the most worth unto you, will be to declare repentance unto this people, that you may bring souls unto me, that you may rest with them in the kingdom of my Father. Amen.

SECTION XLII.

Revelation to Oliver Cowdery, David Whitmer and Martin Harris, June, 1829, given previous to their viewing the plates containing the book of Mormon:

1 Behold I say unto you, that you must rely upon my word, which if you do, with full purpose of heart, you shall have a view of the plates, and also the breastplate, the sword of Laban, the Urim and Thummim, which were given to the brother of Jared upon the mount, when he talked with the Lord face to face, and the miraculous directors which were given to Lehi while in the wilderness, on the borders of the red sea; and it is by your faith that you shall obtain a view of them, even by that faith which was had by the prophets of old.

2 And after that you have obtained faith, and have seen them with your eyes, you shall testify of them, by the power of God; and this you shall do that my servant Joseph Smith, jr. may not be destroyed, that I may bring about my righteous purposes unto the children of men, in this work. And ye shall testify that you have seen them, even as my servant Joseph Smith, jr. has seen them, for it is by my power that he has seen them, and it is because he had faith: and he has translated the book, even that part which I have commanded him, and as your Lord and your God liveth it is true.

3 Wherefore you have received the same power, and the same faith, and the same gift like unto him; and if you do these last commandments of mine, which I have given you, the gates of hell shall not prevail against you; for my grace is sufficient for you: and you shall be lifted up at the last day.— And I, Jesus Christ, your Lord and your God, have spoken it unto you, that I might bring about my righteous purposes unto the children of men. Amen.

SECTION XLIII.

Revelation to Joseph Smith, jr. Oliver Cowdery and David Whitmer, making known the calling of twelve apostles in these last days, and also, instructions relative to building up the church of Christ, according to the fulness of the gospel: Given in Fayette, New York, June, 1829.

1 Now behold, because of the thing which you, my servant Oliver Cowdery, have desired to know of me, I give unto you these words: behold I have manifested unto you, by my Spirit in many instances, that the things which you have written are true: wherefore you know that they are true; and if you know that they are true, behold I give unto you a commandment, that you rely upon the things which are written; for in them are all things written concerning the foundation of my church, my gospel and my rock; wherefore, if you shall build up my church upon the foundation of my gospel and my rock, the gates of hell shall not prevail against you.

2 Behold the world is ripening in iniquity, and it must needs be, that the children of men are stirred up unto repentance, both the Gentiles, and also the house of Israel: wherefore as thou hast been baptized by the hand of my servant, Joseph Smith, jr. according to that which I have commanded him, he hath fulfilled the thing which I commanded him. And now marvel not that I have called him unto mine own purpose, which purpose is known in me: wherefore if he shall be diligent in keeping my commandments, he shall be blessed unto eternal life, and his name is Joseph.

3 And now Oliver Cowdery, I speak unto you, and also unto David Whitmer, by the way of commandment: for behold I command all men every where to repent, and I speak unto you, even as unto Paul mine apostle, for you are called even with that same calling with which he was called. Remember the worth of souls is great in the sight of God: for behold the Lord your Redeemer suffered death in the flesh: wherefore he suffered the pain of all men, that all men might repent and come unto him. And he hath risen again from the dead, that he might bring all men unto him on conditions of repentance. And how great is his joy in the soul that repenteth.— Wherefore you are called to cry repentance unto this people. And if it so be that you should labor all your days, in crying repentance unto this people, and bring save it be one soul unto me, how great shall be your joy with him in the kingdom of my Father?

4 And now if your joy will be great with one soul, that you

have brought unto me into the kingdom of my Father, how great will be your joy, if you should bring many souls unto me? Behold you have my gospel before you, and my rock, and my salvation: ask the Father in my name in faith believing that you shall receive, and you shall have the Holy Ghost which manifesteth all things, which is expedient unto the children of men. And if you have not faith, hope and charity, you can do nothing. Contend against no church, save it be the church of the devil. Take upon you the name of Christ, and speak the truth in soberness, and as many as repent, and are baptized in my name, which is Jesus Christ, and endure to the end, the same shall be saved. Behold Jesus Christ is the name which is given of the Father, and there is none other name given whereby man can be saved: wherefore all men must take upon them the name which is given of the Father, for in that name shall they be called at the last day: wherefore if they know not the name by which they are called, they cannot have place in the kingdom of my Father.

5 And now behold, there are others who are called to declare my gospel, both unto Gentile and unto Jew: yea, even twelve: and the twelve shall be my disciples, and they shall take upon them my name; and the twelve are they who shall desire to take upon them my name, with full purpose of heart: and if they desire to take upon them my name, with full purpose of heart, they are called to go into all the world to preach my gospel unto every creature: and they are they who are ordained of me to baptize in my name, according to that which is written; and you have that which is written before you: wherefore you must perform it according to the words which are written. And now I speak unto the twelve: Behold my grace is sufficient for you: you must walk uprightly before me and sin not. And behold you are they who are ordained of me to ordain priests and teachers to declare my gospel, according to the power of the Holy Ghost which is in you, and according to the callings and gifts of God unto men: and I Jesus Christ, your Lord and your God, have spoken it. These words are not of men, nor of man, but of me: wherefore you shall testify they are of me, and not of man; for it is my voice which speaketh them unto you: for they are given by my Spirit unto you: and by my power you can read them one to another; and save it were by my power, you could not have them: wherefore you can testify that you have heard my voice, and know my words.

6 And now behold I give unto you, Oliver Cowdery, and also unto David Whitmer, that you shall search out the twelve who shall have the desires of which I have spoken; and by

their desires and their works, you shall know them: and when you have found them you shall show these things unto them. And you shall fall down and worship the Father in my name: and you must preach unto the world, saying, you must repent and be baptized in the name of Jesus Christ: for all men must repent and be baptized; and not only men, but women and children, who have arriven to the years of accountability.

7 And now, after that you have received this, you must keep my commandments in all things: and by your hands I will work a marvelous work among the children of men, unto the convincing of many of their sins, that they may come unto repentance; and that they may come unto the kingdom of my Father: wherefore the blessings which I give unto you, are above all things. And after that you have received this, if you keep not my commandments, you cannot be saved in the kingdom of my Father. Behold I Jesus Christ, your Lord and your God, and your Redeemer, by the power of my Spirit, have spoken it. Amen.

SECTION XLIV.

A commandment of God and not of man to Martin Harris, given (Manchester, New York, March. 1830,) by him who is eternal:

1 I am Alpha and Omega, Christ the Lord; yea, even I am He, the beginning and the end, the Redeemer of the world: I having accomplished and finished the will of him whose I am, even the Father concerning me: having done this, that I might subdue all things unto myself: retaining all power, even to the destroying of satan and his works at the end of the world, and the last great day of judgment, which I shall pass upon the inhahitants thereof, judging every man according to his works, and the deeds which he hath done. And surely every man must repent or suffer, for I God am endless: wherefore, I revoke not the judgments which I shall pass, but woes shall go forth, weeping, wailing and gnashing of teeth: yea, to those who are found on my left hand; nevertheless it is not written, that there shall be no end to this torment; but it is written endless torment.

2 Again, it is written eternal damnation: wherefore it is more express than other scriptures, that it might work upon tl e hearts of the children of men, altogether for my name's glory: wherefore, I will explain unto you, this mystery, for it is meet unto you, to know even as mine apostles. I speak unto you that are chosen in this thing, even as one, that you may enter into my rest. For behold, the mystery of Godliness, how

great is it? for behold I am endless, and the punishment which is given from my hand, is endless punishment, for endless is my name; wherefore—

Eternal punishment	Endless punishment
is God's punishment:	is God's punishment:

wherefore, I command you to repent, and keep the commandments which you have received by the hand of my servant Joseph Smith, jr. in my name: and it is by my almighty power that you have received them: therefore I command you to repent, repent, lest I smite you by the rod of my mouth, and by my wrath, and by my anger, and your sufferings be sore: how sore you know not! how exquisite you know not! yea, how hard to bear you know not! For behold, I God have suffered these things for all, that they might not suffer, if they would repent, but if they would not repent, they must suffer even as I: which suffering caused myself, even God, the greatest of all to tremble because of pain, and to bleed at every pore, and to suffer both body and spirit: and would that I might not drink the bitter cup and shrink: nevertheless, glory be to the Father, and I partook and finished my preparations unto the children of men: wherefore, I command you again to repent lest I humble you by my almighty power, and that you confess your sins lest you suffer these punishments of which I have spoken, of which in the smallest, yea, even in the least degree you have tasted at the time I withdrew my Spirit. And I command you, that you preach nought but repentance; and show not these things unto the world until it is wisdom in me; for they cannot bear meat now, but milk they must receive: wherefore, they must not know these things lest they perish: learn of me, and listen to my words; walk in the meekness of my Spirit and you shall have peace in me: I am Jesus Christ; I came by the will of the Father, and I do his wil'.

3 And again: I command thee, that thou shalt not covet thy neighbor's wife. Nor seek thy neighbor's life. And again: I command thee, that thou shalt not covet thine own property, but impart it freely to the printing of the book of Mormon, which contains the truth and the word of God, which is my word to the Gentile, that soon it may go to the Jew, of whom the Lamanites are a remnant: that they may believe the gospel, and look not for a Messiah to come who has already come.

4 And again: I command thee, that thou shalt pray vocally as well as in thy heart: yea, before the world as well as in secret; in public as well as in private: And thou shalt declare glad tidings: yea, publish it upon the mountains, and upon every high place, and among every people that thou shalt

be permitted to see. And thou shalt do it with all humility, trusting in me, reviling not against revilers. And of tenets thou shalt not talk, but thou shalt declare repentance and faith on the Savior, and remission of sins by baptism and by fire; yea, even the Holy Ghost.

5 Behold, this is a great, and the last commandment which I shall give unto you concerning this matter: for this shall suffice for thy daily walk even unto the end of thy life. And misery thou shalt receive, if thou wilt slight these counsels; yea, even destruction of thyself and property. Impart a portion of thy property; yea, even part of thy lands and all save the support of thy family. Pay the debt thou hast contracted with the printer. Release thyself from bondage. Leave thy house and home, except when thou shalt desire to see thy family. And speak freely to all: yea, preach, exhort, declare the truth, even with a loud voice; with a sound of rejoicing, crying hosanna! hosanna! blessed be the name of the Lord God.

6 Pray always and I will pour out my Spirit upon you, and great shall be your blessing: yea, even more than if you should obtain treasures of earth, and corruptibleness to the extent thereof. Behold, canst thou read this without rejoicing and lifting up thy heart for gladness; or canst thou run about longer as a blind guide; or canst thou be humble and meek and conduct thyself wisely before me: yea, come unto me thy Savior. Amen.

SECTION XLV.

Revelation to Oliver Cowdery, Hyrum Smith, Samuel H. Smith, Joseph Smith Sen. and Joseph Knight, Sen. given April, 1830.

1 Behold I speak unto you, Oliver, a few words. Behold thou art blessed, and art under no condemnation. But be ware of pride, lest thou shouldst enter into temptation. Make known thy calling unto the church, and also before the world; and thy heart shall be opened to preach the truth from henceforth and forever. Amen.

2 Behold I speak unto you, Hyrum, a few words: for thou also art under no condemnation, and thy heart is opened, and thy tongue loosed; and thy calling is to exhortation, and to strengthen the church continually. Wherefore thy duty is unto the church forever; and this because of thy family. Amen.

3 Behold I speak a few words unto you, Samuel: for thou also art under no condemnation, and thy calling is to exhortation, and to strengthen the church. And thou art not as yet called to preach before the world. Amen.

4 Behold I speak a few words unto you, Joseph: for thou also art under no condemnation, and thy calling also is to exhortation, and to strengthen the church. And this is thy duty from henceforth and forever. Amen.

5 Behold I manifest unto you, Joseph Knight, by these
words, that you must take up your cross, in the which you
must pray vocally before the world, as well as in secret, and
in your family, and among your friends, and in all places.—
And behold it is your duty to unite with the true church, and
give your language to exhortation continually, that you may
receive the reward of the laborer. Amen.

SECTION XLVI.

Revelation to Joseph Smith, jr. given April 6, 1830.

1 Behold there shall be a record kept among you, and in
it thou shalt be called a seer, a translator, a prophet, an apostle of Jesus Christ, an elder of the church through the will of
God the Father, and the grace of your Lord Jesus Christ; being
inspired of the Holy Ghost to lay the foundation thereof, and to
build it up unto the most holy faith; which church was organized and established, in the year of your Lord eighteen hundred and thirty, in the fourth month, and on the sixth day of
the month, which is called April.

2 Wherefore, meaning the church, thou shalt give heed unto
all his words, and commandments, which he shall give unto
you, as he receiveth them, walking in all holiness before me;
for his word ye shall receive, as if from mine own mouth, in
all patience and faith; for by doing these things, the gates of
hell shall not prevail against you: yea, and the Lord God will
disperse the powers of darkness from before you; and cause
the heavens to shake for your good, and his name's glory.—
For thus saith the Lord God, him have I inspired to move the
cause of Zion in mighty power for good; and his diligence I
know, and his prayers I have heard: yea, his weeping for Zion I have seen, and I will cause that he shall mourn for her no
longer, for his days of rejoicing are come unto the remission of
his sins, and the manifestations of my blessings upon his works.

3 For behold, I will bless all those who labor in my vineyard,
with a mighty blessing, and they shall believe on his words,
which are given him through me, by the Comforter, which
manifesteth that Jesus was crucified by sinful men for the sins
of the world; yea, for the remission of sins unto the contrite
heart. Wherefore, it behooveth me, that he should be ordain-

L

ed by you, Oliver Cowdery, mine apostle; this being an ordinance unto you, that you are an elder under his hand, he
being the first unto you, that you might be an elder unto this
church of Christ, bearing my name; and the first preacher of
this church, unto the church, and before the world; yea, before the Gentiles: yea, and thus saith the Lord God, lo, lo, to
the Jews, also. Amen.

SECTION XLVII.

*Revelation to the church of Christ, which was established in these
last days, in the year of our Lord one thousand eight hundred
and thirty: Given April, 1830, in consequence of some desiring to unite with the church without re-baptism, who had previously been baptized.*

1 Behold I say unto you, that all old covenants have I caused
to be done away in this thing, and this is a new and an everlasting covenant; even that which was from the beginning.—
Wherefore, although a man should be baptized an hundred
times, it availeth him nothing; for you cannot enter in at the
straight gate by the law of Moses, neither by your dead works;
for it is because of your dead works, that I have caused this
last covenant, and this church to be built up unto me; even as
in days of old. Wherefore enter ye in at the gate, as I have
commanded, and seek not to counsel your God. Amen.

SECTION XLVIII.

Revelation given July, 1830.

1 Hearken unto the voice of the Lord your God, while I
speak unto you, Emma Smith, my daughter, for verily I say
unto you, all those who receive my gospel are sons and daughters in my kingdom. A revelation I give unto you concerning
my will, and if thou art faithful and walk in the paths of virtue before me, I will preserve thy life, and thou shalt receive
an inheritance in Zion. Behold thy sins are forgiven thee,
and thou art an elect lady, whom I have called. Murmur not
because of the things which thou hast not seen, for they are
withheld from thee, and from the world, which is wisdom in
me in a time to come.

2 And the office of thy calling shall be for a comfort unto my
servant Joseph Smith, jr. thy husband, in his afflictions with
consoling words, in the spirit of meekness. And thou shalt go
with him at the time of his going, and be unto him for a scribe,

while there is no one to be a scribe for him, that I may send my servant Oliver Cowdery, whithersoever I will. And thou shalt be ordained under his hand to expound scriptures, and to exhort the church, according as it shall be given thee by my Spirit: for he shall lay his hands upon thee, and thou shalt receive the Holy Ghost, and thy time shall be given to writing, and to learning much. And thou needst not fear, for thy husband shall support thee in the church: for unto them is his calling, that all things might be revealed unto them, whatsoever I will, according to their faith.

3 And verily I say unto thee, that thou shalt lay aside the things of this world, and seek for the things of a better. And it shall be given thee, also, to make a selection of sacred Hymns, as it shall be given thee, which is pleasing unto me, to be had in my church: for my soul delighteth in the song of the heart: yea, the song of the righteous is a prayer unto me. And it shall be answered with a blessing upon their heads.— Wherefore lift up thy heart and rejoice, and cleave unto the covenants which thou hast made.

4 Continue in the spirit of meekness, and beware of pride. Let thy soul delight in thy husband, and the glory which shall come upon him. Keep my commandments continually, and a crown of righteousness thou shalt receive. And except thou do this, where I am you cannot come. And verily, verily I say unto you, that this is my voice unto all. Amen.

SECTION XLIX.

Revelation to Joseph Smith, jr. Oliver Cowdery and John Whitmer, given July, 1830.

1 Behold, I say unto you, that you shall let your time be devoted to the studying of the scriptures, and to preaching, and to confirming the church at Colesville; and to performing your labors on the land, such as is required, until after you shall go to the west, to hold the next conference; and then it shall be made known what you shall do. And all things shall be done by common consent in the church, by much prayer and faith; for all things you shall receive by faith. Amen.

SECTION L.

Revelation given September, 1830.

1 Listen to the voice of Jesus Christ, your Lord, your God and your Redeemer, whose word is quick and powerful. For

12*

behold I say unto you, that it mattereth not what ye shall eat,
or what ye shall drink, when ye partake of the sacrament, if it
so be that ye do it with an eye single to my glory; remembering unto the Father my body which was laid down for you,
and my blood which was shed for the remission of your sins:
wherefore a commandment I give unto you, that you shall not
purchase wine, neither strong drink of your enemies: wherefore you shall partake of none, except it is made new among
you, yea, in this my Father's kingdom which shall be built up
on the earth.

2 Behold this is wisdom in me: wherefore marvel not for the
hour cometh that I will drink of the fruit of the vine with you
on the earth, and with Moroni, whom I have sent unto you to
reveal the book of Mormon, containing the fulness of my everlasting gospel; to whom I have committed the keys of the record of the stick of Ephraim; and also with Elias, to whom I
have committed the keys of bringing to pass the restoration
of all things, or the restorer of all things spoken by the mouth
of all the holy prophets since the world began, concerning the
last days: and also John the son of Zacharias, which Zacharias he (Elias) visited and gave promise that he should have a
son, and his name should be John, and he should be filled with
the spirit of Elias; which John I have sent unto you, my servants, Joseph Smith, jr. and Oliver Cowdery, to ordain you
unto this first priesthood which you have received, that you
might be called and ordained even as Aaron: and also Elijah,
unto whom I have committed the keys of the power of turning the hearts of the fathers to the children and the hearts of
the children to the fathers, that the whole earth may not be
smitten with a curse: and also, with Joseph, and Jacob, and
Isaac, and Abraham your fathers; by whom the promises remain; and also with Michael, or Adam, the father of all, the
prince of all, the ancient of days:

3 And also with Peter, and James, and John, whom I have
sent unto you, by whom I have ordained you and confirmed
you to be apostles and especial witnesses of my name, and bear
the keys of your ministry: and of the same things which I revealed unto them: unto whom I have committed the keys of
my kingdom, and a dispensation of the gospel for the last
times; and for the fulness of times, in the which I will gather
together in one all things both which are in heaven and which
are on earth: and also with all those whom my Father hath
given me out of the world: wherefore lift up your hearts and
rejoice, and gird up your loins, and take upon you my whole
armor, that ye may be able to withstand the evil day, having
done all ye may be able to stand. Stand, therefore, having

your loins girt about with truth; having on the breastplate of righteousness; and your feet shod with the preparation of the gospel of peace which I have sent mine angels to commit unto you, taking the shield of faith wherewith ye shall be able to quench all the fiery darts of the wicked; and take the helmet of salvation, and the sword of my Spirit, which I will pour out upon you, and my word which I reveal unto you, and be agreed as touching all things whatsoever ye ask of me, and be faithful until I come, and ye shall be caught up that where I am ye shall be also. Amen.

SECTION LI.

Revelation given to Oliver Cowdery, September, 1830.

1 Behold I say unto thee, Oliver, that it shall be given unto thee, that thou shalt be heard by the church, in all things whatsoever thou shalt teach them by the Comforter, concerning the revelations and commandments which I have given.

2 But behold, verily, verily I say unto thee, no one shall be appointed to receive commandments and revelations in this church, excepting my servant Joseph Smith, jr. for he receiveth them even as Moses; and thou shalt be obedient unto the things which I shall give unto him, even as Aaron, to declare faithfully the commandments and the revelations, with power and authority unto the church. And if thou art led at any time by the Comforter to speak or teach, or at all times by the way of commandment unto the church, thou mayest do it. But thou shalt not write by way of commandment, but by wisdom: And thou shalt not command him who is at thy head, and at the head of the church; for I have given him the keys of the mysteries and the revelations which are sealed, until I shall appoint unto them another in his stead.

3 And now, behold I say unto you, that you shall go unto the Lamanites and preach my gospel unto them; and inasmuch as they receive thy teachings, thou shalt cause my church to be established among them, and thou shalt have revelations but write them not by way of commandment. And now behold I say unto you, that it is not revealed, and no man knoweth where the city shall be built, but it shall be given hereafter. Behold I say unto you, that it shall be on the borders by the Lamanites.

4 Thou shalt not leave this place until after the conference and my servant Joseph shall be appointed to preside over the conference by the voice of it, and what he saith to thee thou shalt tell. And again, thou shalt take thy brother Hiram

Page between him and thee alone, and tell him that those things which he hath written from that stone are not of me, and that satan deceiveth him. for behold these things have not been appointed unto him: neither shall any thing be appointed unto any of this church contrary to the church covenants, for all things must be done in order and by common consent in the church, by the prayer of faith.

5 And thou shalt assist to settle all these things according to the covenants of the church before thou shalt take thy journey among the Lamanites. And it shall be given thee from the time that thou shalt go, until the time that thou shalt return, what thou shalt do. And thou must open thy mouth at all times declaring my gospel with the sound of rejoicing.—Amen.

SECTION LII.

Revelation to David Whitmer, Peter Whitmer, jr. and John Whitmer, given September, 1830.

1 Behold I say unto you, David, that you have feared man and have not relied on me for strength, as you ought: but your mind has been on the things of the earth more than on the things of me, your Maker, and the ministry whereunto you have been called; and you have not given heed unto my Spirit, and to those who were set over you, but have been persuaded by those whom I have not commanded: wherefore you are left to inquire for yourself, at my hand, and ponder upon the things which you have received. And your home shall be at your father's house, until I give unto you further commandments. And you shall attend to the ministry in the church, and before the world, and in the regions round about. Amen.

2 Behold I say unto you, Peter, that you shall take your journey with your brother Oliver, for the time has come, that it is expedient in me, that you shall open your mouth to declare my gospel: therefore, fear not but give heed unto the words and advice of your brother, which he shall give you.— And be you afflicted in all his afflictions, ever lifting up your heart unto me in prayer, and faith, for his and your deliverance: for I have given unto him power to build up my church among the Lamanites: and none have I appointed to be his counsellor, over him, in the church, concerning church matters, except it is his brother Joseph Smith, jr. Wherefore give heed unto these things and be diligent in keeping my commandments, and you shall be blessed unto eternal life. Amen.

3 Behold I say unto you, my servant John, that thou shalt

commence from this time forth to proclaim my gospel, as
with the voice of a trump. And your labor shall be at your
brother Philip Burroughs', and in that region round about:
yea, wherever you can be heard, until I command you to go
from hence. And your whole labor shall be in Zion, with all
your soul, from henceforth; yea, you shall ever open your
mouth in my cause not fearing what man can do, for I am
with you. Amen.

SECTION LIII.

Revelation to Thomas B. Marsh, given September, 1830.

1 Thomas, my son, blessed are you because of your faith in
my work. Behold you have had many afflictions because of
your family: nevertheless I will bless you, and your family:
yea, your little ones, and the day cometh that they will believe
and know the truth and be one with you in my church.

2 Lift up your heart and rejoice for the hour of your mission
is come; and your tongue shall be loosed; and you shall declare
glad tidings of great joy unto this generation. You shall declare the things which have been revealed to my servant Joseph Smith, jr. You shall begin to preach from this time forth;
yea, to reap in the field which is white already to be burned:
therefore thrust in your sickle with all your soul; and your
sins are forgiven you; and you shall be laden with sheaves upon your back, for the laborer is worthy of his hire. Wherefore
your family shall live.

3 Behold, verily I say unto you, go from them only for a little time, and declare my word, and I will prepare a place for
them; yea, I will open the hearts of the people and they will
receive you. And I will establish a church by your hand;
and you shall strengthen them and prepare them against the
time when they shall be gathered. Be patient in afflictions,
revile not against those that revile. Govern your house in
meekness, and be steadfast.

4 Behold I say unto you, that you shall be a physician unto
the church, but not unto the world, for they will not receive
you. Go your way whithersoever I will, and it shall be giv-
en you by the Comforter what you shall do, and whither you
shall go. Pray always, lest you enter into temptation, and
lose your reward. Be faithful unto the end and, lo, I am with
you. These words are not of man nor of men, but of me,
even Jesus Christ, your Redeemer, by the will of the Father.
Amen.

SECTION LIV.

Revelation to Parley P. Pratt and Ziba Peterson, given October, 1830.

1 And now concerning my servant Parley P. Pratt, behold I say unto him, that as I live I will that he shall declare my gospel and learn of me, and be meek and lowly of heart; and that which I have appointed unto him, is, that he shall go with my servants Oliver Cowdery and Peter Whitmer, jr. into the wilderness, among the Lamanites; and Ziba Peterson, also, shall go with them, and I myself will go with them and be in their midst: and I am their Advocate with the Father, and nothing shall prevail. And they shall give heed to that which is written and pretend to no other revelation, and they shall pray always that I may unfold them to their understanding; and they shall give heed unto these words and trifle not, and I will bless them. Amen.

SECTION LV.

Revelation to Ezra Thayre and Northrop Sweet, given October, 1830.

1 Behold I say unto you, my servants Ezra and Northrop, open ye your ears and hearken to the voice of the Lord your God, whose word is quick and powerful, sharper than a two edged sword, to the dividing asunder of the joints and marrow, soul and spirit: and is a discerner of the thoughts and intents of the heart. For verily, verily I say unto you, that ye are called to lift up your voices as with the sound of a trump, to declare my gospel unto a crooked and a perverse generation: for behold the field is white already to harvest; and it is the eleventh hour, and for the last time that I shall call laborers into my vineyard. And my vineyard has become corrupted every whit: and there is none which doeth good save it be a few; and they err in many instances, because of priestcrafts, all having corrupt minds.

2 And verily, verily I say unto you, that this church have I established and called forth out of the wilderness: and even so will I gather mine elect from the four quarters of the earth, even as many as will believe in me, and hearken unto my voice: yea, verily, verily I say unto you, that the field is white already to harvest: wherefore thrust in your sickles, and reap with all your might, mind and strength. Open your mouths and they shall be filled; and you shall become even as Nephi

of old, who journeyed from Jerusalem in the wilderness: yea, open your mouths and spare not, and you shall be laden with sheaves upon your backs, for lo I am with you: yea, open your mouths and they shall be filled, saying, Repent, repent and prepare ye the way of the Lord, and make his paths straight: for the kingdom of heaven is at hand: yea, repent and be baptized every one of you; for a remission of your sins; yea, be baptized even by water, and then cometh the baptism of fire and of the Holy Ghost.

3 Behold, verily, verily I say unto you, this is my gospel, and remember that they shall have faith in me, or they can in no wise be saved: and upon this Rock I will build my church; yea, upon this rock ye are built, and if ye continue, the gates of hell shall not prevail against you; and ye shall remember the church articles and covenants to keep them: and whoso having faith you shall confirm in my church, by the laying on of the hands, and I will bestow the gift of the Holy Ghost upon them. And the book of Mormon, and the holy scriptures, are given of me for your instruction; and the power of my Spirit quickeneth all things: wherefore be faithful, praying always, having your lamps trimmed and burning, and oil with you, that you may be ready at the coming of the Bridegroom; for behold, verily, verily I say unto you, that I come quickly; even so: Amen.

SECTION LVI.

Revelation to Orson Pratt, given November, 1830.

1 My son Orson, hearken and hear and behold what I the Lord God shall say unto you, even Jesus Christ your Redeemer, the light and the life of the world: a light which shineth in darkness and the darkness comprehendeth it not: who so loved the world that he gave his own life, that as many as would believe might become the sons of God: wherefore you are my son, and blessed are you because you have believed, and more blessed are you because you are called of me to preach my gospel; to lift up your voice as with the sound of a trump, both long and loud, and cry repentance unto a crooked and perverse generation; preparing the way of the Lord for his second coming; for behold, verily, verily I say unto you, the time is soon at hand, that I shall come in a cloud with power and great glory, and it shall be a great day at the time of my coming, for all nations shall tremble.

2 But before that great day shall come, the sun shall be darkened, and the moon be turned into blood, and the stars

shall refuse their shining, and some shall fall, and great destructions await the wicked: wherefore lift up your voice and spare not, for the Lord God hath spoken. Therefore prophesy and it shall be given by the power of the Holy Ghost; and if you are faithful behold I am with you until I come: and verily, verily I say unto you, I come quickly. I am your Lord and your Redeemer; even so. Amen.

SECTION LVII.

Revelation to Edward Partrige, given December, 1830.

1 Thus saith the Lord God, the mighty One of Israel, behold I say unto you, my servant Edward, that you are blessed, and your sins are forgiven you, and you are called to preach my gospel as with the voice of a trump; and I will lay my hand upon you by the hand of my servant Sidney Rigdon, and you shall receive my Spirit, the Holy Ghost, even the Comforter, which shall teach you the peaceable things of the kingdom: and you shall declare it with a loud voice, saying, Hosanna, blessed be the name of the most high God.

2 And now this calling and commandment give I unto you concerning all men, that as many as shall come before my servants Sidney Rigdon and Joseph Smith, jr. embracing this calling and commandment, shall be ordained and sent forth to preach the everlasting gospel among the nations, crying repentance, saying, Save yourselves from this untoward generation, and come forth out of the fire, hating even the garments spotted with the flesh.

3 And this commandment shall be given unto the elders of my church, that every man which will embrace it with singleness of heart, may be ordained and sent forth, even as I have spoken. I am Jesus Christ, the Son of God: wherefore gird up your loins and I will suddenly come to my temple; even so. Amen.

SECTION LVIII.

Revelation to Joseph Smith, jr. and Sidney Rigdon, given December, 1830.

1 Behold I say unto you, that it is not expedient in me that ye should translate any more until ye shall go to the Ohio; and this because of the enemy and for your sakes. And again, I say unto you, that ye shall not go until ye have preached my gospel in those parts, and have strengthened up the church

whithersoever it is found, and more especially in Colesville: for behold they pray unto me in much faith.

2 And again a commandment I give unto the church, that it is expedient in me that they should assemble together at the Ohio, against the time that my servant Oliver Cowdery shall return unto them. Behold here is wisdom, and let every man choose for himself until I come; even so. Amen.

SECTION LIX.

Revelation to James Covill, given January, 1831.

1 Hearken and listen to the voice of him who is from all eternity to all eternity, the Great I AM, even Jesus Christ, the light and the life of the world; a light which shineth in darkness and the darkness comprehendeth it not: the same which came in the meridian of time unto my own, and my own received me not; but to as many as received me, gave I power to become my sons, and even so will I give unto as many as will receive me, power to become my sons.

2 And verily, verily I say unto you, he that receiveth my gospel, receiveth me; and he that receiveth not my gospel. receiveth not me. And this is my gospel: repentance and baptism by water, and then cometh the baptism of fire and the Holy Ghost, even the Comforter, which showeth all things, and teacheth the peaceable things of the kingdom.

3 And now behold I say unto you, my servant James, I have looked upon thy works and I know thee: and verily I say unto thee, thine heart is now right before me at this time, and behold I have bestowed great blessings upon thy head:—nevertheless thou hast seen great sorrow for thou hast rejected me many times because of pride, and the cares of the world: but behold the days of thy deliverance are come, if thou wilt hearken to my voice, which saith unto thee, Arise and be baptized, and wash away your sins, calling on my name and you shall receive my Spirit, and a blessing so great as you never have known. And if thou do this, I have prepared thee for a greater work. Thou shalt preach the fulness of my gospel which I have sent forth in these last days; the covenant which I have sent forth to recover my people, which are of the house of Israel.

4 And it shall come to pass that power shall rest upon thee; thou shalt have great faith and I will be with thee and go before thy face. Thou art called to labor in my vineyard, and to build up my church, and to bring forth Zion, that it may rejoice upon the hills and flourish. Behold, verily, verily I

say unto thee, thou art not called to go into the eastern countries, but thou art called to go to the Ohio. And inasmuch as my people shall assemble themselves to the Ohio, I have kept in store a blessing such as is not known among the children of men, and it shall be poured forth upon their heads.— And from thence men shall go forth into all nations.

5 Behold, verily, verily I say unto you, that the people in Ohio call upon me in much faith, thinking I will stay my hand in judgment upon the nations, but I cannot deny my word: wherefore lay to with your might and call faithful laborers into my vineyard, that it may be pruned for the last time. And inasmuch as they do repent and receive the fulness of my gospel, and become sanctified, I will stay mine hand in judgment: wherefore go forth, crying with a loud voice, saying, The kingdom of heaven is at hand; crying Hosanna! blessed be the name of the most high God. Go forth baptizing with water, preparing the way before my face, for the time of my coming; for the time is at hand: the day nor the hour no man knoweth, but it surely shall come, and he that receiveth these things receiveth me; and they shall be gathered unto me in time and in eternity.

6 And again, it shall come to pass, that on as many as ye shall baptize with water, ye shall lay your hands, and they shall receive the gift of the Holy Ghost, and shall be looking forth for the signs of my coming, and shall know me. Behold I come quickly; even so. Amen.

SECTION LX.

Revelation to Joseph Smith, jr. and Sidney Rigdon, given January, 1831, explaining why James Covill, obeyed not the revelation which was given unto him.

1 Behold, verily I say unto you, that the heart of my servant James Covill was right before me, for he covenanted with me, that he would obey my word. And he received the word with gladness, but straightway satan tempted him; and the fear of persecution, and the cares of the world, caused him to reject the word; wherefore he broke my covenant, and it remaineth in me to do with him as seemeth me good. Amen.

SECTION LXI.

Revelation given February, 1831.

1 Hearken and hear, O ye my people, saith the Lord and your God, ye whom I delight to bless with the greatest bles-

sings; ye that hear me: and ye that hear me not will I curse, that have professed my name, with the heaviest of all cursings. Hearken, O ye elders of my church whom I have called: behold I give unto you a commandment, that ye shall assemble yourselves together to agree upon my word, and by the prayer of your faith ye shall receive my law, that ye may know how to govern my church, and have all things right before me.

2 And I will be your Ruler when I come: and behold, I come quickly: and ye shall see that my law is kept. He that receiveth my law and doeth it the same is my disciple; and he that saith he receiveth it and doeth it not, the same is not my disciple, and shall be cast out from among you: for it is not meet that the things which belong to the children of the kingdom, should be given to them that are not worthy, or to dogs, or the pearls to be cast before swine.

3 And again, it is meet that my servant Joseph Smith, jr. should have a house built, in which to live and translate. And again it is meet that my servant Sidney Rigdon should live as seemeth him good, inasmuch as he keepeth my commandments. And again, I have called my servant Edward Partridge, and give a commandment, that he should be appointed by the voice of the church, and ordained a bishop unto the church, to leave his merchandise and to spend all his time in the labors of the church; to see to all things as it shall be appointed unto him, in my laws in the day that I shall give them. And this because his heart is pure before me, for he is like unto Nathaniel of old, in whom there is no guile. These words are given unto you, and they are pure before me: wherefore beware how you hold them, for they are to be answered upon your souls in the day of judgment; even so. Amen.

SECTION LXII.

Revelation to Joseph Smith, jr. and Sidney Rigdon, given February, 1831.

1 Behold thus saith the Lord unto you my servants, it is expedient in me that the elders of my church should be called together, from the east and from the west, and from the north and from the south, by letter or some other way.

2 And it shall come to pass, that inasmuch as they are faithful, and exercise faith in me, I will pour out my Spirit upon them in the day that they assemble themselves together. And it shall come to pass that they shall go forth into the regions round about, and preach repentance unto the people; and many shall be converted, insomuch that ye shall obtain power to

organize yourselves, according to the laws of man; that your enemies may not have power over you, that you may be preserved in all things; that you may be enabled to keep my laws, that every band may be broken wherewith the enemy seeketh to destroy my people.

3 Behold I say unto you, that ye must visit the poor and the needy and administer to their relief, that they may be kept until all things may be done according to my law which ye have received. Amen.

SECTION LXIII.

Revelation to Joseph Smith, jr. and John Whitmer, given March, 1831.

1 Behold it is expedient in me that my servant John should write and keep a regular history, and assist you, my servant Joseph, in transcribing all things which shall be given you, until he is called to further duties. Again, verily I say unto you, that he can also lift up his voice in meetings, whenever it shall be expedient.

2 And again, I say unto you, that it shall be appointed unto him to keep the church record and history continually, for Oliver Cowdery I have appointed to another office. Wherefore it shall be given him, inasmuch as he is faithful, by the Comforter, to write these things; even so. Amen.

SECTION LXIV.

Revelation given March, 1831.

1 It is necessary that ye should remain, for the present time, in your places of abode, as it shall be suitable to your circumstances; and inasmuch as ye have lands, ye shall impart to the eastern brethren; and inasmuch as ye have not lands, let them buy for the present time in those regions round about as seemeth them good, for it must needs be necessary that they have places to live for the present time.

2 It must needs be necessary, that ye save all the money that ye can, and that ye obtain all that ye can in righteousness, that in time ye may be enabled to purchase lands for an inheritance, even the city. The place is not yet to be revealed, but after your brethren come from the east, there are to be certain men appointed, and to them it shall be given to know the place, or to them it shall be revealed; and they shall be appointed to purchase the lands, and to make a commencement, to lay the foundation of the city; and then ye shall begin to be

gathered with your families, every man according to his family, according to his circumstances, and as is appointed to him by the presidency and the bishop of the church, according to the laws and commandments, which ye have received, and which ye shall hereafter receive; even so. Amen.

SECTION LXV.

Revelation to Sidney Rigdon, Parley P. Pratt, and Lemon Copley, given March, 1831.

1 Hearken unto my word, my servant Sidney, and Parley, and Lemon, for behold, verily I say unto you, that I give unto you a commandment, that you shall go and preach my gospel, which ye have received, even as ye have received it, unto the shakers. Behold I say unto you, that they desire to know the truth in part, but not all, for they are not right before me, and must needs repent: wherefore I send you, my servants Sidney and Parley, to preach the gospel unto them; and my servant Lemon shall be ordained unto this work, that he may reason with them, not according to that which he has received of them, but according to that which shall be taught him by you, my servants, and by so doing I will bless him, otherwise he shall not prosper: thus saith the Lord, for I am God and have sent mine only begotten Son into the world, for the redemption of the world, and have decreed that he that receiveth him shall be saved, and he that receiveth him not, shall be damned.

2 And they have done unto the Son of man even as they listed; and he has taken his power on the right hand of his glory, and now reigneth in the heavens, and will reign till he descends on the earth to put all enemies under his feet: which time is nigh at hand: I the Lord God have spoken it: but the hour and the day no man knoweth, neither the angels in heaven, nor shall they know until he comes: wherefore I will that all men shall repent, for all are under sin, except them which I have reserved unto myself, holy men that ye know not of: wherefore I say unto you, that I have sent unto you mine everlasting covenant, even that which was from the beginning, and that which I have promised I have so fulfilled, and the nations of the earth shall bow to it; and, if not of themselves, they shall come down, for that which is now exalted of itself, shall be laid low of power: wherefore I give unto you a commandment, that ye go among this people and say unto them, like unto mine apostle of old, whose name was Peter: Believe on the name of the Lord Jesus, who was on the earth, and is to come, the beginning and the end; repent and be baptized in

the name of Jesus Christ, according to the holy commandment, for the remission of sins; and whoso doeth this, shall receive the gift of the Holy Ghost, by the laying on of the hands of the elders of this church.

3 And again, I say unto you, that whoso forbiddeth to marry, is not ordained of God, for marriage is ordained of God unto man: wherefore it is lawful that he should have one wife, and they twain shall be one flesh, and all this that the earth might answer the end of its creation; and that it might be filled with the measure of man, according to his creation before the world was made. And whoso forbiddeth to abstain from meats, that man should not eat the same, is not ordained of God; for behold the beasts of the field, and the fowls of the air, and that which cometh of the earth, is ordained for the use of man, for food, and for raiment, and that he might have in abundance, but it is not given that one man should possess that which is above another: wherefore the world lieth in sin; and wo be unto man that sheddeth blood or that wasteth flesh and hath no need.

4 And again, verily I say unto you, that the Son of man cometh not in the form of a woman, neither of a man travelling on the earth: wherefore be not deceived, but continue in steadfastness, looking forth for the heavens to be shaken; and the earth to tremble, and to reel to and fro as a drunken man; and for the valleys to be exalted; and for the mountains to be made low; and for the rough places to become smooth: and all this when the angel shall sound his trumpet.

5 But before the great day of the Lord shall come, Jacob shall flourish in the wilderness; and the Lamanites shall blossom as the rose: Zion shall flourish upon the hills, and rejoice upon the mountains, and shall be assembled together unto the place which I have appointed. Behold I say unto you, go forth as I have commanded you; repent of all your sins; ask and ye shall receive; knock and it shall be opened unto you: behold I will go before you, and be your rereward; and I will be in your midst, and you shall not be confounded: behold I am Jesus Christ, and I come quickly; even so. Amen.

SECTION LXVI.

Revelation given June, 1831.

1 Behold, thus saith the Lord unto the elders whom he hath called and chosen, in these last days, by the voice of his Spirit, saying, I the Lord will make known unto you what I will that ye shall do from this time until the next conference, which

shall be held in Missouri, upon the land which I will consecrate unto my people, who are a remnant of Jacob, and those
who are heirs according to the covenant.

2 Wherefore, verily I say unto you, let my servant Joseph
Smith, jr. and Sidney Rigdon take their journey as soon as
preparations can be made to leave their homes, and journey to
the land of Missouri. And inasmuch as they are faithful unto
me, it shall be made known unto them what they shall do: and
it shall also, inasmuch as they are faithful, be made known unto them the land of your inheritance. And inasmuch as they
are not faithful, they shall be cut off, even as I will, as seemeth me good.

3 And again, verily I say unto you, let my servant Lyman
Wight, and my servant John Corrill take their journey speedily: and also my servant John Murdock, and my servant Hyrum Smith, take their journey unto the same place by the way
of Detroit. And let them journey from thence preaching the
word by the way, saying none other things than that which
the prophets and apostles have written, and that which is
taught them by the Comforter, through the prayer of faith.—
Let them go two by two, and thus let them preach by the way
in every congregation, baptizing by water, and the laying on
of the hands by the water's side: for thus saith the Lord, I will
cut my work short in righteousness: for the days cometh that
I will send forth judgment unto victory. And let my servant
Lyman Wight beware, for satan desireth to sift him as chaff.

4 And behold, he that is faithful shall be made ruler over many things. And again, I will give unto you a pattern in all
things, that ye may not be deceived, for satan is abroad in the
land, and he goeth forth deceiving the nations: wherefore he
that prayeth whose spirit is contrite, the same is accepted of
me, if he obey mine ordinances: he that speaketh, whose spirit is contrite, whose language is meek, and edifieth, the same
is of God, if he obey mine ordinances. And again, he that
trembleth under my power, shall be made strong, and shall
bring forth fruits of praise, and wisdom, according to the revelations, and truths which I have given you.

5 And again, he that is overcome and bringeth not forth
fruits, even according to this pattern, is not of me: wherefore
by this pattern ye shall know the spirits in all cases, under the
whole heavens. And the days have come, according to men's
faith it shall be done unto them. Behold this commandment
is given unto all the elders whom I have chosen. And again,
verily I say unto you, let my servant Thomas B. Marsh, and my
servant Ezra Thayre, take their journey also, preaching the

M

word by the way, unto this same land. And again, let my servant Isaac Morley, and my servant Ezra Booth, take their journey, also preaching the word by the way unto the same land.

6 And again, let my servants Edward Partridge and Martin Harris, take their journey with my servants Sidney Rigdon and Joseph Smith, jr. Let my servants David Whitmer and Harvy Whitlock also take their journey, and [preach by the way unto this same land. Let my servants Parley P. Pratt and Orson Pratt take their journey, and preach by the way, even unto this same land. And let my servants Solomon Hancock and Simeon Carter also take their journey unto this same land, and preach by the way. Let my servants Edson Fuller and Jacob Scott also take their journey. Let my servants Levi Hancock and Zebedee Coltrin also take their journey. Let my servants Reynolds Cahoon and Samuel H. Smith also take their journey. Let my servants Wheeler Baldwin and William Carter also take their journey.

7 And let my servants Newel Knight and Selah J. Griffin, both be ordained and also take their journey: yea, verily I say, let all these take their journey unto one place, in their several courses, and one man shall not build upon another's foundation, neither journey in another's track. He that is faithful, the same shall be kept and blessed with much fruit.

8 And again, I say unto you, let my servants Joseph Wakefield and Solomon Humphrey take their journey into the eastern lands. Let them labor with their families, declaring none other things than the prophets and apostles, that which they have seen, and heard, and most assuredly believe, that the prophecies may be fulfilled. In consequence of transgression, let that which was bestowed upon Heman Basset, be taken from him, and placed upon the head of Simonds Rider.

9 And again, verily I say unto you, let Jared Carter be ordained a priest, and also George James be ordained a priest.— Let the residue of the elders watch over the churches, and declare the word in the regions among them. And let them labor with their own hands, that there be no idolatry nor wickedness practiced. And remember in all things, the poor and the needy, the sick and the afflicted, for he that doeth not these things, the same is not my disciple. And again, let my servants Joseph Smith, jr. and Sidney Rigdon and Edward Partridge, take with them a recommend from the church.— And let there be one obtained for my servant Oliver Cowdery also: and thus, even as I have said, if ye are faithful, ye shall assemble yourselves together to rejoice upon the land of Missouri, which is the land of your inheritance, which is now the

land of your enemies. But behold I the Lord will hasten the city in its time, and will crown the faithful with joy and with rejoicing. Behold I am Jesus Christ the Son of God, and I will lift them up at the last day; even so. Amen.

SECTION LXVI.

Revelation to Sidney Gilbert, given June, 1831.

1 Behold I say unto you, my servant Sidney Gilbert, that I have heard your prayers, and you have called upon me, that it should be made known unto you, of the Lord your God, concerning your calling, and election in this church, which I the Lord have raised up in these last days.

2 Behold I the Lord, who was crucified for the sins of the world, giveth unto you a commandment, that you shall forsake the world. Take upon you mine ordinances, even that of an elder, to preach faith and repentance, and remission of sins, according to my word, and the reception of the Holy Spirit by the laying on of hands. And also to be an agent unto this church in the place which shall be appointed by the bishop, according to commandments which shall be given hereafter.

3 And again, verily I say unto you, you shall take your journey with my servants Joseph Smith, jr. and Sidney Rigdon. Behold these are the first ordinances which you shall receive: and the residue shall be made known in a time to come, according to your labor in my vineyard. And again, I would that ye should learn that it is he only who is saved, that endureth unto the end; even so. Amen.

SECTION LXVII.

Revelation to Newel Knight, given June, 1831.

1 Behold, thus saith the Lord, even Alpha and Omega, the beginning and the end, even he who was crucified for the sins of the world. Behold, verily, verily I say unto you, my servant Newel Knight, you shall stand fast in the office wherewith I have appointed you: and if your brethren desire to escape their enemies let them repent of all their sins; and become truly humble before me and contrite: and as the covenant which they made unto me, has been broken, even so it has become void and of none effect; and wo to him by whom this offence cometh, for it had been better for him that he had been drowned in the depth of the sea; but blessed are they who have

kept the covenant, and observed the commandment, for they shall obtain mercy.

2 Wherefore, go to now and flee the land, lest your enemies come upon you: and take your journey, and appoint whom you will to be your leader, and to pay moneys for you. And thus you shall take your journey into the regions westward, unto the land of Missouri, unto the borders of the Lamanites. And after you have done journeying, behold I say unto you, seek ye a living like unto men, until I prepare a place for you.

3 And again, be patient in tribulation until I come: and behold I come quickly, and my reward is with me, and they who have sought me early, shall find rest to their souls; even so. Amen.

SECTION LXVIII.

Revelation to William W. Phelps, given June, 1831.

1 Behold thus saith the Lord unto you, my servant William; yea, even the Lord of the whole earth, thou art called and chosen and after thou hast been baptized by water, which if you do with an eye single to my glory, you shall have a remission of your sins, and a reception of the Holy Spirit, by the laying on of hands. And then thou shalt be ordained by the hand of my servant Joseph Smith, jr. to be an elder unto this church, to preach repentance and remission of sins by way of baptism in the name of Jesus Christ, the Son of the living God; and on whomsoever you shall lay your hands, if they are contrite before me, you shall have power to give the Holy Spirit.

2 And again, you shall be ordained to assist my servant Oliver Cowdery to do the work of printing, and of selecting, and writing books for schools, in this church, that little children also may receive instruction before me as is pleasing unto me. And again verily I say unto you, for this cause you shall take your journey with my servants Joseph Smith, jr. and Sidney Rigdon, that you may be planted in the land of your inheritance, to do this work.

3 And again let my servant Joseph Coe also take his journey with them. The residue shall be made known hereafter; even as I will. Amen.

SECTION LXIX.

Revelation given June, 1831.

1 Hearken O ye people who profess my name, saith the Lord your God, for behold mine anger is kindled against the rebellious, and they shall know mine arm and mine indignation in the day of visitation and of wrath upon the nations.— And he that will not take up his cross and follow me, and keep my commandments, the same shall not be saved.

2 Behold I the Lord commandeth, and he that will not obey shall be cut off in mine own due time: and after that I have commanded and the commandment is broken, wherefore I the Lord command and revoke, as it seemeth me good; and all this to be answered upon the heads of the rebellious saith the Lord: wherefore I revoke the commandment which was given unto my servants Thomas B. Marsh and Ezra Thayre, and give a new commandment unto my servant Thomas, that he shall take up his journey speedily to the land of Missouri; and my servant Selah J. Griffin shall also go with him: for behold I revoke the commandment which was given unto my servants Selah J. Griffin and Newel Knight, in consequence of the stiffneckedness of my people which are in Thompson; and their rebellions: wherefore let my servant Newel Knight remain with them, and as many as will go may go, that are contrite before me, and be led by him to the land which I have appointed.

3 And again, verily I say unto you, that my servant Ezra Thayre must repent of his pride, and of his selfishness, and obey the former commandment which I have given him concerning the place upon which he lives; and if he will do this, as there shall be no divisions made upon the land, he shall be appointed still to go to the land of Missouri; otherwise he shall receive the money which he has paid, and shall leave the place, and shall be cut off out of my church, saith the Lord God of hosts: and though the heaven and the earth pass away, these words shall not pass away, but shall be fulfilled.

4 And if my servant Joseph Smith, jr. must needs pay the money, behold I the Lord will pay it unto him again in the land of Missouri, that those of whom he shall receive may be rewarded again, according to that which they do. For according to that which they do, they shall receive; even in lands for their inheritance. Behold thus saith the Lord unto my people, you have many things to do, and to repent of: for behold your sins have come up unto me, and are not pardoned, because you seek to counsel in your own ways. And your

hearts are not satisfied. And ye obey not the truth, but have pleasure in unrighteousness.

5 Wo unto you rich men, that will not give your substance to the poor, for your riches will canker your souls! and this shall be your lamentation in the day of visitation, and of judgment, and of indignation: The harvest is past, the summer is ended, and my soul is not saved! Wo unto you poor men, whose hearts are not broken, whose spirits are not contrite, and whose bellies are not satisfied, and whose hands are not stayed from laying hold upon other men's goods, whose eyes are full of greediness, who will not labor with their own hands!

6 But blessed are the poor, who are pure in heart, whose hearts are broken, and whose spirits are contrite, for they shall see the kingdom of God coming in power and great glory unto their deliverance: for the fatness of the earth shall be theirs: for behold the Lord shall come, and his recompense shall be with him, and he shall reward every man, and the poor shall rejoice: and their generations shall inherit the earth from generation to generation, forever and ever. And now I make an end of speaking unto you; even so. Amen.

SECTION LXX.

Revelation given August, 1831.

1 Behold, thus saith the Lord unto the elders of his church, who are to return speedily to the land from whence they came. Behold it pleaseth me, that you have come up hither; but with some I am not well pleased, for they will not open their mouths, but hide the talent which I have given unto them, because of the fear of man. Wo unto such, for mine anger is kindled against them.

2 And it shall come to pass, if they are not more faithful unto me, it shall be taken away, even that which they have, for I the Lord ruleth in the heavens above, and among the armies of the earth; and in the day when I shall make up my jewels, all men shall know what it is that bespeaketh the power of God. But verily I will speak unto you concerning your journey unto the land from whence you came. Let there be a craft made, or bought, as seemeth you good, it mattereth not unto me, and take your journey speedily for the place which is called St. Louis. And from thence let my servants Sidney Rigdon, and Joseph Smith, jr. and Oliver Cowdery, take their journey for Cincinnati: and in this place let them lift up their voice, and declare my word with loud voices, without wrath

or doubting, lifting up holy hands upon them. For I am able to make you holy, and your sins are forgiven you.

3 And let the residue take their journey from St. Louis, two by two, and preach the word, not in haste, among the congregations of the wicked, until they return to the churches from whence they came. And all this for the good of the churches; for this intent have I sent them. And let my servant Edward Partridge impart of the money which I have given him, a portion unto mine elders, who are commanded to return; and he that is able, let him return it by the way of the agent, and he that is not, of him it is not required. And now I speak of the residue who are to come unto this land. Behold they have been sent to preach my gospel among the congregations of the wicked: wherefore, I give unto them a commandment thus: Thou shalt not idle away thy time: neither shalt thou bury thy talent that it may not be known.

4 And after thou hast come up unto the land of Zion, and hast proclaimed my word, thou shalt speedily return proclaiming my word among the congregations of the wicked. Not in haste, neither in wrath nor with strife: and shake off the dust of thy feet against those who receive thee not, not in their presence, lest thou provoke them, but in secret, and wash thy feet as a testimony against them in the day of judgment.— Behold this is sufficient for you, and the will of him who hath sent you. And by the mouth of my servant Joseph Smith, jr. it shall be made known concerning Sidney Rigdon and Oliver Cowdery, the residue hereafter; even so. Amen.

SECTION LXXI.

Revelation given August, 1831.

1 Behold, and hearken unto the voice of him who has all power, who is from everlasting to everlasting, even Alpha and Omega, the beginning and the end. Behold, verily thus saith the Lord unto you O ye elders of my church, who are assembled upon this spot, whose sins are now forgiven you, for I the Lord forgiveth sins, and am merciful unto those who confess their sins with humble hearts: but verily I say unto you, that it is not needful for this whole company of mine elders, to be moving swiftly upon the waters, whilst the inhabitants on either side are perishing in unbelief: nevertheless, I suffered it that ye might bear record: behold there are many dangers upon the waters and more especially hereafter, for I the Lord have decreed, in mine anger, many destructions upon the waters; yea, and especially upon these waters; neverthe-

less, all flesh is in mine hand, and he that is faithful among you, shall not perish by the waters.

2 Wherefore it is expedient that my servant Sidney Gilbert, and my servant William W. Phelps, be in haste upon their errand and mission: nevertheless I would not suffer that ye should part until you are chastened for all your sins, that you might be one; that you might not perish in wickedness; but now verily I say, it behoveth me that ye should part: wherefore let my servants Sidney Gilbert and William W. Phelps, take their former company, and let them take their journey in haste that they may fill their mission, and through faith they shall overcome; and inasmuch as they are faithful, they shall be preserved, and I the Lord will be with them. And let the residue take that which is needful for clothing. Let my servant Sidney Gilbert take that which is not needful with him, as you shall agree. And now behold, for your good I gave unto you a commandment concerning these things; and I the Lord will reason with you as with men in days of old.

3 Behold I the Lord in the beginning, blessed the waters, but in the last days by the mouth of my servant John, I cursed the waters: wherefore, the days will come that no flesh shall be safe upon the waters, and it shall be said in days to come, that none is able to go up to the land of Zion, upon the waters, but he that is upright in heart. And, as I the Lord in the beginning cursed the land, even so in the last days have I blessed it, in its time, for the use of my saints, that they may partake the fatness thereof. And now I give unto you a commandment, and what I say unto one I say unto all, that you shall forewarn your brethren concerning these waters, that they come not in journeying upon them, lest their faith fail and they are caught in her snares: I the Lord have decreed, and the destroyer rideth upon the face thereof, and I revoke not the decree: I the Lord was angry with you yesterday, but to-day mine anger is turned away. Wherefore let those concerning whom I have spoken, that should take their journey in haste, again I say unto you, let them take their journey in haste, and it mattereth not unto me, after a little, if it so be that they fill their mission, whether they go by water or by land: let this be as it is made known unto them according to their judgments, hereafter.

4 And now, concerning my servants Sidney Rigdon, and Joseph Smith, jr. and Oliver Cowdery, let them come not again upon the waters, save it be upon the canal, while journeying unto their homes, or in other words, they shall not come upon the waters to journey, save upon the canal. Behold I the Lord have appointed a way for the journeying of

my saints, and behold this is the way: that after they leave the canal, they shall journey by land, inasmuch as they are commanded to journey and go up unto the land of Zion; and they shall do like unto the children of Israel, pitching their tents by the way.

5 And behold this commandment you shall give unto all your brethren: nevertheless unto whom it is given power to command the waters, unto him it is given by the Spirit to know all his ways: wherefore let him do as the Spirit of the living God commandeth him, whether upon the land or upon the waters, as it remaineth with me to do hereafter; and unto you it is given the course for the saints, or the way for the saints of the camp of the Lord, to journey. And again, verily I say unto you, my servants Sidney Rigdon, and Joseph Smith, jr. and Oliver Cowdery, shall not open their mouths in the congregations of the wicked, until they arrive at Cincinnati; and in that place they shall lift up their voices unto God against that people: yea, unto him whose anger is kindled against their wickedness; a people who are well nigh ripened for destruction; and from thence let them journey for the congregations of their brethren, for their labors, even now, are wanted more abundantly among them, than among the congregations of the wicked.

6 And now concerning the residue, let them journey and declare the word among the congregations of the wicked, inasmuch as it is given, and inasmuch as they do this they shall rid their garments, and they shall be spotless before me; and let them journey together, or two by two, as seemeth them good, only let my servant Reynolds Cahoon, and my servant Samuel H. Smith, with whom I am well pleased, be not separated until they return to their homes, and this for a wise purpose in me. And now verily I say unto you, and what I say unto one I say unto all, be of good cheer little children, for I am in your midst, and I have not forsaken you, and inasmuch as you have humbled yourselves before me, the blessings of the kingdom are yours. Gird up your loins and be watchful, and be sober, looking forth for the coming of the Son of man, for he cometh in an hour you think not. Pray always that you enter not into temptation, that you may abide the day of his coming, whether in life or in death; even so.—Amen.

SECTION LXXII.

Revelation given August, 1831.

1 Behold and hearken, O ye elders of my church, saith the Lord your God; even Jesus Christ, your advocate who knoweth the weakness of man and how to succor them who are tempted: and verily mine eyes are upon those who have not as yet gone up unto the land of Zion: wherefore your mission is not yet full: nevertheless ye are blessed, for the testimony which ye have borne is recorded in heaven for the angels to look upon, and they rejoice over you; and your sins are forgiven you.

2 And now continue your journey. Assemble yourselves upon the land of Zion, and hold a meeting and rejoice together, and offer a sacrament unto the Most High; and then you may return to bear record; yea, even all together, or two by two, as seemeth you good; it mattereth not unto me, only be faithful, and declare glad tidings unto the inhabitants of the earth, or among the congregations of the wicked. Behold I the Lord have brought you together that the promise might be fulfilled, that the faithful among you should be preserved and rejoice together in the land of Missouri. I the Lord promised the faithful and cannot lie.

3 I the Lord am willing, if any among you desireth to ride upon horses, or upon mules, or in chariots, he shall receive this blessing, if he receive it from the hand of the Lord, with a thankful heart in all things. These things remain with you to do according to judgment and the directions of the Spirit.— Behold the kingdom is yours. And behold, and lo I am with the faithful always; even so. Amen.

SECTION LXXIII.

An explanation of the epistle to the first Corinthians, 7th chapter, 14th verse.

1 For the unbelieving husband is sanctified by the wife, and the unbelieving wife is sanctified by the husband, else were your children unclean, but now are they holy.

2 Now in the days of the apostles the law of circumcision was had among all the Jews, who believed not the gospel of Jesus Christ. And it came to pass that there arose a great contention among the people concerning the law of circumcision, for the unbelieving husband was desirous that his children should be circumcised and become subject to the law of Moses, which law was fulfilled.

2 And it came to pass that the children being brought up in subjection to the law of Moses, and give heed to the traditions of their fathers, and believed not the gospel of Christ, wherein they become unholy: wherefore, for this cause the apostle wrote unto the church, giving unto them a commandment, not of the Lord but of himself, that a believer should not be united to an unbeliever except the law of Moses should be done away among them, that their children might remain without circumcision; and that the tradition might be done away, which saith, that little children are unholy: for it was had among the Jews: but little children are holy being sanctified through the atonement of Jesus Christ: and this is what the scriptures mean.

SECTION LXXIV.

Revelation given October, 1830.

1 Behold, thus saith the Lord, unto you my servant, William E. McLelin, blessed are you, inasmuch as you have turned away from your iniquities, and have received my truths, saith the Lord your Redeemer, the Savior of the world, even of as many as believe on my name. Verily I say unto you, blessed are you for receiving mine everlasting covenant, even the fulness of my gospel, sent forth unto the children of men, that they might have life, and be made partakers of the glories, which are to be revealed in the last days, as it was written by the prophets and apostles in days of old.

2 Verily I say unto you, my servant William, that you are clean, but not all; repent therefore of those things which are not pleasing in my sight, saith the Lord, for the Lord will show them unto you. And now verily I the Lord will show unto you what I will concerning you, or what is my will concerning you, behold, verily I say unto you, that it is my will that you should proclaim my gospel from land to land, and from city to city, yea, in those regions round about where it has not been proclaimed.

3 Tarry not many days in this place: go not up unto the land of Zion, as yet; but inasmuch as you can send, send; otherwise think not of thy property. Go unto the eastern lands; bear testimony in every place, unto every people, and in their synagogues; reasoning with the people.

4 Let my servant, Samuel H. Smith go with you, and forsake him not, and give him thine instructions: and he that is faithful shall be made strong in every place, and I the Lord will go with you.

5 Lay your hands upon the sick and they shall recover. Return not till I the Lord shall send you. Be patient in affliction. Ask and ye shall receive. Knock and it shall be opened unto you. Seek not to be cumbered. Forsake all unrighteousness. Commit not adultery, a temptation with which thou hast been troubled. Keep these sayings for they are true and faithful, and thou shalt magnify thine office, and push many people to Zion, with songs of everlasting joy upon their heads. Continue in these things, even unto the end, and you shall have a crown of eternal life at the right hand of my Father, who is full of grace and truth. Verily thus saith the Lord your God, your Redeemer, even Jesus Christ. Amen.

SECTION LXXV.

Revelation given March, 1832. *The order given of the Lord to Enoch, for the purpose of establishing the poor.*

1 The Lord spake unto Enoch, saying, Hearken unto me saith the Lord your God, who are ordained unto the high priesthood of my church, who have assembled yourselves together, and listen to the counsel of him who has ordained you from on high, who shall speak in your ears the words of wisdom, that salvation may be unto you in that thing which you have presented before me, saith the Lord God: for verily I say unto you, the time has come, and is now at hand, and behold, and lo, it must needs be that there be an organization of my people, in regulating and establishing the affairs of the storehouse for the poor of my people, both in this place and in the land of Zion, or in other words, the city of Enoch, for a permanent and everlasting establishment and order unto my church, to advance the cause which ye have espoused, to the salvation of man, and to the glory of your Father who is in heaven, that you may be equal in the bands of heavenly things, yea and earthly things also, for the obtaining of heavenly things; for if ye are not equal in earthly things, ye cannot be equal in obtaining heavenly things: for if you will that I give unto you a place in the celestial world, you must prepare yourselves by doing the things which I have commanded you and required of you.

2 And now, verily thus saith the Lord, it is expedient that all things be done unto my glory, that ye should, who are joined together in this order; or in other words, let my servant Ahasdah, and my servant Gazelam, or Enoch, and my servant Pelagoram, sit in council with the saints which are in Zion; otherwise satan seeketh to turn their hearts away from the

truth, that they become blinded, and understand not the things which are prepared for them: wherefore a commandment I give unto you, to prepare and organize yourselves by a bond or everlasting covenant that cannot be broken.

3 And he who breaketh it shall lose his office and standing in the church, and shall be delivered over to the buffetings of satan until the day of redemption. Behold this is the preparation wherewith I prepare you, and the foundation, and the ensample, which I give unto you whereby you may accomplish the commandments which are given you, that through my providence, notwithstanding the tribulation which shall descend upon you, that the church may stand independent above all other creatures beneath the celestial world, that you may come up unto the crown prepared for you, and be made rulers over many kingdoms, saith the Lord God, the Holy One of Zion, who hath established the foundations of Adam-ondi-Ahman; who hath appointed Michael, your prince, and established his feet, and set him upon high; and given unto him the keys of salvation under the counsel and direction of the Holy One, who is without beginning of days or end of life.

4 Verily, verily I say unto you, ye are little children, and ye have not as yet understood how great blessings the Father has in his own hands, and prepared for you; and ye cannot bear all things now, nevertheless be of good cheer, for I will lead you along: the kingdom is yours and the blessings thereof are yours; and the riches of eternity are yours: and he who receiveth all things, with thankfulness, shall be made glorious, and the things of this earth shall be added unto him, even an hundred fold, yea more: wherefore do the things which I have commanded you, saith your Redeemer, even the Son Ahman, who prepareth all things before he taketh you; for ye are the church of the first born, and he will take you up in the cloud, and appoint every man his portion. And he that is a faithful and wise steward shall inherit all things. Amen.

SECTION LXXVI.

Revelation given March, **1832.**

1 Verily I say unto you, that it is my will that my servant Jared Carter should go again into the eastern countries, from place to place, and from city to city, in the power of the ordination wherewith he has been ordained, proclaiming glad tidings of great joy, even the everlasting gospel, and I will send upon him the Comforter which shall teach him the truth and the way whither he shall go; and inasmuch as he is faithful I

will crown him again with sheaves: wherefore let your heart be glad my servant Jared Carter, and fear not saith your Lord, even Jesus Christ. Amen.

SECTION LXXVII.

Revelation given March, 1832.

1 Verily, thus saith the Lord, unto you my servant Stephen Burnett, go ye, go ye, into the world, and preach the gospel to every creature that cometh under the sound of your voice, and inasmuch as you desire a companion I will give unto you my servant Eden Smith: wherefore go ye and preach my gospel, whether to the north, or to the south; to the east, or to the west, it mattereth not, for ye cannot go amiss: therefore declare the things which ye have heard and verily believe, and know to be true. Behold this is the will of him who hath called you, your Redeemer, even Jesus Christ. Amen.

SECTION LXXVIII.

Revelation given August, 1832.

1 Behold thus saith the Lord unto my servant John Murdock, thou art called to go into the eastern countries from house to house, from village to village, and from city to city, to proclaim mine everlasting gospel unto the inhabitants thereof, in the midst of persecution and wickedness; and whoso receiveth you receiveth me, and you shall have power to declare my word in the demonstration of my Holy Spirit; and whoso receiveth you as a little child, receiveth my kingdom and blessed are they, for they shall obtain mercy; and whoso rejecteth you shall be rejected of my Father, and his house: and you shall cleanse your feet in the secret places by the way for a testimony against them.

2 And behold, and lo, I come quickly to judgment, to convince all of their ungodly deeds which they have committed against me, as it is written of me in the volume of the book.— And now verily I say unto you, that it is not expedient that you should go until your children are provided for, and kindly sent up unto the bishop in Zion, and after a few years, if thou desirest of me thou mayest go up also unto the goodly land, to possess thine inheritance; otherwise thou shalt continue proclaiming my gospel until thou be taken. Amen.

SECTION LXXIX.

Revelation given March, 1832.

1 Verily, verily I say unto you my servant Frederick G. Williams, listen to the voice of him who speaketh, to the word of the Lord your God, and hearken to the calling wherewith you are called, even to be a high priest in my church, and a counsellor unto my servant Joseph Smith, jr. unto whom I have given the keys of the kingdom, which belongeth always unto the presidency of the high priesthood: therefore, verily I acknowledge him and will bless him, and also thee, inasmuch as thou art faithful in council, in the office which I have appointed unto you, in prayer always vocally, and in thy heart, in public and in private; also in thy ministry in proclaiming the gospel in the land of the living, and among thy brethren: and in doing these things thou wilt do the greatest good unto thy fellow-beings, and will promote the glory of him who is your Lord: wherefore, be faithful, stand in the office which I have appointed unto you, succor the weak, lift up the hands which hang down, and strengthen the feeble knees: and if thou art faithful unto the end thou shalt have a crown of immortality and eternal life in the mansions which I have prepared in the house of my Father. Behold, and lo, these are the words of Alpha and Omega, even Jesus Christ. Amen.

SECTION LXXX.

A word of wisdom for the benefit of the council of high priests, assembled in Kirtland, and church; and also, the saints in Zion: to be sent greeting: not by commandment, or constraint: but by revelation and the word of wisdom: showing forth the order and will of God in the temporal salvation of all saints in the last days. Given for a principle with promise, adapted to the capacity of the weak, and the weakest of all saints, who are or can be called saints.

1 Behold, verily thus saith the Lord unto you, in consequence of evils and designs which do, and will exist in the hearts of conspiring men in the last days, I have warned you, and forewarn you, by giving unto you this word of wisdom by revelation, that inasmuch as any man drinketh wine or strong drink among you, behold it is not good, neither meet in the sight of your Father, only in assembling yourselves together, to offer up your sacraments before him. And behold, this should be wine, yea, pure wine of the grape of the vine, o

your own make. And again, strong drinks are not for the belly, but for the washing of your bodies. And again, tobacco is not for the body, neither for the belly; and is not good for man; but is an herb for bruises, and all sick cattle, to be used with judgment and skill. And again, hot drinks are not for the body, or belly.

2 And again, verily I say unto you, all wholesome herbs God hath ordained for the constitution, nature, and use of man.— Every herb in the season thereof, and every fruit in the season thereof. All these to be used with prudence and thanksgiving. Yea, flesh also of beasts and of the fowls of the air, I the Lord hath ordained for the use of man with thanksgiving. Nevertheless, they are to be used sparingly; and it is pleasing unto me, that they should not be used only in times of winter or of cold, or famine. All grain is ordained for the use of man, and of beasts, to be the staff of life, not only for man, but for the beasts of the field, and the fowls of heaven, and all wild animals that run or creep on the earth: and these hath God made for the use of man only in times of famine, and excess of hunger.

3 All grain is good for the food of man, as also the fruit of the vine, that which yieldeth fruit, whether in the ground or above the ground. Nevertheless wheat for man, and corn for the ox, and oats for the horse, and rye for the fowls, and for swine, and for all beasts of the field, and barley for all useful animals, and for mild drinks; as also other grain. And all saints who remember to keep and do these sayings, walking in obedience to the commandments, shall receive health in their navel, and marrow to their bones and shall find wisdom, and great treasures of knowledge, even hidden treasures; and shall run and not be weary, and shall walk and not faint: and I the Lord give unto them a promise, that the destroying angel shall pass by them, as the children of Israel, and not slay them. Amen.

SECTION LXXXI.

Revelation given August, 1833.

1 Verily I say unto you my friends, I speak unto you with my voice, even the voice of my Spirit, that I may show unto you my will concerning your brethren in the land of Zion, many of whom are truly humble, and are seeking diligently to learn wisdom and to find truth: verily, verily I say unto you, blessed are all such for they shall obtain, for I the Lord showeth mercy unto all the meek, and upon all whomsoever I will,

that I may be justified, when I shall bring them into judgment.

2 Behold I say unto you, concerning the school in Zion, I the Lord am well pleased that there should be a school in Zion: and also with my servant Parley P. Pratt, for he abideth in me: and inasmuch as he continueth to abide in me, he shall continue to preside over the school, in the land of Zion, until I shall give unto him other commandments; and I will bless him with a multiplicity of blessings, in expounding all scriptures and mysteries to the edification of the school, and of the church in Zion: and to the residue of the school, I the Lord am willing to show mercy, nevertheless there are those that must needs be chastened, and their works shall be made known: The axe is laid at the root of the trees, and every tree that bringeth not forth good fruit, shall be hewn down and cast into the fire; I the Lord have spoken it. Verily I say unto you, all among them who know their hearts are honest, and are broken, and their spirits contrite, and are willing to observe their covenants by sacrifice; yea, every sacrifice which I the Lord shall command, they are all accepted of me, for I the Lord will cause them to bring forth as a very fruitful tree which is planted in a goodly land, by a pure stream, that yieldeth much precious fruit.

3 Verily I say unto you, that it is my will that an house should be built unto me in the land of Zion, like unto the pattern which I have given you; yea, let it be built speedily by the tithing of my people: behold this is the tithing and the sacrifice which I the Lord require at their hands, that there may be an house built unto me for the salvation of Zion: for a place of thanksgiving, for all saints, and for a place of instruction for all those who are called to the work of the ministry, in all their several callings, and offices: that they may be perfected in the understanding of their ministry: in theory; in principle, and in doctrine, in all things pertaining to the kingdom of God on the earth, the keys of which kingdom have been conferred upon you.

4 And inasmuch as my people build an house unto me, in the name of the Lord, and do not suffer any unclean thing to come into it, that it be not defiled, my glory shall rest upon it; yea, and my presence shall be there, for I will come into it, and all the pure in heart that shall come into it, shall see God: but if it be defiled I will not come into it, and my glory shall not be there, for I will not come into unholy temples.

5 And now behold if Zion do these things, she shall prosper and spread herself and become very glorious, very great, and

very terrible; and the nations of the earth shall honor her, and shall say, surely Zion is the city of our God; and surely Zion cannot fall, neither be moved out of her place, for God is there, and the hand of the Lord is there, and he hath sworn by the power of his might to be her salvation, and her high tower: therefore verily thus saith the Lord let Zion rejoice, for this is Zion, THE PURE IN HEART: therefore let Zion rejoice, while all the wicked shall mourn: for behold and lo, vengeance cometh speedily upon the ungodly, as the whirlwind, and who shall escape it: the Lord's scourge shall pass over by night and by day; and the report thereof shall vex all people; yet, it shall not be stayed until the Lord come: for the indignation of the Lord is kindled against their abominations, and all their wicked works: nevertheless Zion shall escape if she observe to do all things whatsoever I have commanded her, but if she observe not to do whatsoever I have commanded her, I will visit her according to all her works: with sore affliction; with pestilence; with plague; with sword; with vengeance, with devouring fire: nevertheless, let it be read this once in their ears, that I the Lord have accepted of their offering; and if she sin no more, none of these things shall come upon her, and I will bless her with blessings, and multiply a multiplicity of blessings upon her, and upon her generations, forever and ever, saith the Lord your God. Amen.

SECTION LXXXII.

Revelation given May, **1833.**

1 Verily thus saith the Lord, it shall come to pass that every soul who forsaketh their sins and cometh unto me, and calleth on my name, and obeyeth my voice, and keepeth my commandments, shall see my face, and know that I am, and that I am the true light that lighteth every man that cometh into the world: and that I am in the Father and the Father in me, and the Father and I are one: the Father because he gave me of his fulness; and the Son because I was in the world and made flesh my tabernacle, and dwelt among the sons of men: I was in the world and received of my Father, and the works of him were plainly manifest; and John saw and bore record of the fulness of my glory; and the fulness of John's record is hereafter to be revealed: And he bore record, saying, I saw his glory that he was in the beginning before the world was: therefore, in the beginning the Word was; for he was the **Word,** even the messenger of salvation, the light and the **Redeemer** of the world; the Spirit of truth, who came into the world

because the world was made by him; and in him was the life of men and the light of men. The worlds were made by him. Men were made by him. All things were made by him, and through him, and of him: And I John bare record that I beheld his glory, as the glory of the Only Begotten of the Father, full of grace and truth; even the Spirit of truth which came and dwelt in the flesh, and dwelt among us.

2 And I John saw that he received not of the fulness at the first, but received grace for grace: and he received not of the fulness at first, but continued from grace to grace, until he received a fulness: and thus he was called the Son of God, because he received not of the fulness at the first. And I John bare record, and lo, the heavens were opened and the Holy Ghost descended upon him in the form of a dove, and sat upon him, and there came a voice out of heaven saying, this is my beloved Son. And I John bare record that he received a fulness of the glory of the Father; and he received all power, both in heaven and on earth; and the glory of the Father was with him, for he dwelt in him.

3 And it shall come to pass that if you are faithful, you shall receive the fulness of the record of John. I give unto you these sayings that you may understand and know how to worship, and know what you worship, that you may come unto the Father in my name, and in due time receive of his fulness for if you keep my commandments you shall receive of his fulness and be glorified in me as I am in the Father: therefore, I say unto you, you shall receive grace for grace.

4 And now verily I say unto you, I was in the beginning with the Father, and am the first born; and all those who are begotten through me, are partakers of the glory of the same, and are the church of the first born. Ye were also in the beginning with the Father: that which is Spirit, even the Spirit of truth; and truth is knowledge of things as they are, and as they were, and as they are to come; and whatsoever is more or less than this, is the spirit of that wicked one, who was a liar from the beginning. The Spirit of truth is of God: I am the Spirit of truth. And John bore record of me, saying, he received a fulness of truth; yea, even of all truth, and no man receiveth a fulness unless he keepeth his commandments. He that keepeth his commandments, receiveth truth and light, until he is glorified in truth, and knoweth all things.

5 Man was also in the beginning with God. Intelligence, or the light of truth was not created or made, neither indeed can be. All truth is independent in that sphere in which God has placed it, to act for itself, as all intelligence also, other-

14*

wise there is no existence. Behold here is the agency of man, and here is the condemnation of man because that which was from the beginning is plainly manifest unto them, and they receive not the light. And every man whose spirit receiveth not the light, is under condemnation, for man is spirit. The elements are eternal, and spirit and element, inseparably connected, receiveth a fulness of joy; and when separated, man connot receive a fulness of joy. The elements are the tabernacle of God; yea, man is the tabernacle of God, even temples; and whatsoever temple is defiled, God shall destroy that temple.

6 The glory of God is intelligence, or, in other words, light and truth: light and truth forsaketh that evil one. Every spirit of man was innocent in the beginning, and God having redeemed man from the fall, men became again in their infant state, innocent before God. And that wicked one cometh and taketh away light and truth, through disobedience, from the children of men, and because of the tradition of their fathers. But I have commanded you, to bring up your children in light and truth: but verily I say unto you, my servant Frederick G. Williams, you have continued under this condemnation; you have not taught your children light and truth, according to the commandments, and that wicked one hath power, as yet, over you, and this is the cause of your affliction.— And now a commandment I give unto you, if you will be delivered, you shall set in order your own house, for there are many things that are not right in your house.

7 Verily I say unto my servant Sidney Rigdon, that in some things he hath not kept the commandments, concerning his children: therefore, firstly set in order thy house.

8 Verily I say unto my servant Joseph Smith, jr. or, in other words, I will call you friends, for you are my friends, and ye shall have an inheritance with me. I called you servants for the world's sake, and ye are their servants for my sake, and now verily I say unto Joseph Smith jr. you have not kept the commmandments, and must needs stand rebuked before the Lord. Your family must needs repent and forsake some things, and give more earnest heed unto your sayings, or be removed out of their place. What I say unto one I say unto all: pray always lest that wicked one have power in you, and remove you out of your place.

9 My servant Newel K. Whitney, also a bishop of my church, hath need to be chastened and set in order his family, and see that they are more diligent and concerned at home, and pray always or they shall be removed out of their place.

10 Now I say unto you, my friends, let my servant Sidney Rigdon go his journey, and make haste, and also proclaim the

acceptable year of the Lord, and the gospel of salvation, as I shall give him utterance, and by your prayer of faith with one consent, I will uphold him.

11 And let my servants Joseph Smith, jr. and Frederick G. Williams, make haste also, and it shall be given them even according to the prayer of faith, and inasmuch you keep my sayings, you shall not be confounded in this world, nor in the world to come.

12 And verily I say unto you, that it is my will that you should hasten to translate my scriptures, and to obtain a knowledge of history, and of countries, and of kingdoms, of laws of God and man, and all this for the salvation of Zion. Amen.

SECTION LXXXIII.

Revelation given same date.

1 And again, verily I say unto you, my friends, a commandment I give unto you, that ye shall commence a work of laying out and preparing a beginning and foundation of the city of the stake of Zion, here in the land of Kirtland, beginning at my house: and behold it must be done according to the pattern which I have given unto you. And let the first lot on the south, be consecrated unto me for the building of an house for the presidency, for the work of the presidency, in obtaining revelations; and for the work of the ministry of the presidency, in all things pertaining to the church and kingdom.

2 Verily I say unto you, that it shall be built fifty-five by sixty-five feet in the width thereof, and in the length thereof, in the inner court; and there shall be a lower court, and an higher court, according to the pattern which shall be given unto you hereafter: and it shall be dedicated unto the Lord from the foundation thereof, according to the order of the priesthood, according to the pattern which shall be given unto you hereafter: and it shall be wholly dedicated unto the Lord for the work of the presidency. And ye shall not suffer any unclean thing to come in unto it; and my glory shall be there, and my presence shall be there: but if there shall come into it any unclean thing my glory shall not be there; and my presence shall not come into it.

3 And again, verily I say unto you, the second lot on the south shall be dedicated unto me for the building of an house unto me, for the work of the printing of the translation of my scriptures, and all things, whatsoever I shall command you; and it shall be fifty five by sixty five feet in the width thereof, and the length thereof in the inner court; and there shall be

a lower and a higher court; and this house shall be wholly dedicated unto the Lord from the foundation thereof, for the work of the printing, in all things whatsoever I shall command you, to be holy, undefiled, according to the pattern in all things, as it shall be given unto you.

4 And on the third lot shall my servant Hyrum Smith receive his inheritance. And on the first and second lots on the north shall my servants Reynolds Cahoon and Jared Carter receive their inheritance, that they may do the work which I have appointed unto them, to be a committee to build mine houses, according to the commandment, which I the Lord God have given unto you. These two houses are not to be built until I give unto you a commandment concerning them.

5 And now I give unto you no more at this time. Amen.

SECTION LXXXIV.

Revelation to Joseph Smith, jr. given March, 1833.

1 Thus saith the Lord, verily, verily I say unto you, my son, thy sins are forgiven thee, according to thy petition, for thy prayers and the prayers of thy brethren, have come up into my ears: therefore thou art blessed from henceforth that bear the keys of the kingdom given unto you; which kingdom is coming forth for the last time.

2 Verily I say unto you, the keys of this kingdom shall never be taken from you, while thou art in the world, neither in the world to come: nevertheless, through you shall the oracles be given to another; yea, even unto the church. And all they who receive the oracles of God, let them beware how they hold them, lest they are accounted as a light thing, and are brought under condemnation thereby, and stumble and fall, when the storms descend, and the winds blow, and the rains descend, and beat upon their house.

3 And again, verily I say unto thy brethren Sidney Rigdon, and Frederick G. Williams, their sins are forgiven them also, and they are accounted as equal with thee in holding the keys of this last kingdom: as also through your administration the keys of the school of the prophets, which I have commanded to be organized, that thereby they may be perfected in their ministry for the salvation of Zion, and of the nations of Israel, and of the Gentiles, as many as will believe, that through your administration, they may receive the word, and through their administration, the word may go forth unto the ends of the earth, unto the Gentiles first, and then behold, and lo, they shall turn unto the Jews: and then cometh the day when the

arm of the Lord shall be revealed in power in convincing the nations, the heathen nations, the house of Joseph of the gospel of their salvation.

4 For it shall come to pass in that day, that every man shall hear the fulness of the gospel in his own tongue, and in his own language, through those who are ordained unto this power, by the administration of the Comforter, shed forth upon them, for the revelation of Jesus Christ.

5 And now verily I say unto you, I give unto you a commandment, that you continue in the ministry and presidency, and when you have finished the translation of the prophets, you shall from thenceforth preside over the affairs of the church and the school; and from time to time, as shall be manifest by the Comforter, receive revelations to unfold the mysteries of the kingdom, and set in order the churches, and study and learn, and become acquainted with all good books, and with languages, tongues and people. And this shall be your business and mission in all your lives to preside in counsel and set in order all the affairs of this church and kingdom. Be not ashamed neither confounded; but be admonished in all your highmindedness and pride, for it bringeth a snare upon your souls. Set in order your houses; keep slothfulness and uncleanness far from you.

6 Now verily, I say unto you, let there be a place provided as soon as it is possible, for the family of thy counsellor and scribe, even Frederick G. Williams: and let mine aged servant Joseph Smith, sen. continue with his family upon the place where he now lives, and let it not be sold until the mouth of the Lord shall name. And let thy counsellor, even Sidney Rigdon, remain where he now resides, until the mouth of the Lord shall name. And let the bishop search diligently, to obtain an agent; and let it be a man who has got riches in store; a man of God and of strong faith: that thereby he may be enabled to discharge every debt; that the storehouse of the Lord may not be brought into disrepute before the eyes of the people. Search diligently, pray always, and be believing, and all things shall work together for your good, if ye walk uprightly, and remember the covenant wherewith ye have covenanted one with another. Let your families be small, especially mine aged servant Joseph Smith, sen. as pertaining to those who do not belong to your families: that those things that are provided for you, to bring to pass my work, are not taken from you and given to those that are not worthy, and thereby you are hindred in accomplishing those things which I have commanded you.

7 And again, verily I say unto you, it is my will that my

handmaid, Vienna Jaques, should receive money to bear her expenses, and go up unto the land of Zion; and the residue of the money may be consecrated unto me, and she be rewarded in mine own due time. Verily I say unto you, that it is meet in mine eyes, that she should go up unto the land of Zion, and receive an inheritance from the hand of the bishop, that she may settle down in peace inasmuch as she is faithful, and not be idle in her days from thenceforth.

8 And behold, verily I say unto you, that ye shall write this commandment, and say unto your brethren in Zion, in love greeting, that I have called you also to preside over Zion in mine own due time: therefore let them cease wearying me concerning this matter. Behold, I say unto you, that your brethren in Zion begin to repent, and the angels rejoice over them; nevertheless, I am not well pleased with many things: and I am not well pleased with my servant William E. McLelin, neither with my servant Sidney Gilbert; and the bishop also: and others have many things to repent of: but verily I say unto you, that I the Lord will contend with Zion and plead with her strong ones, and chasten her, until she overcomes and is clean before me: for she shall not be removed out of her place: I the Lord have spoken it. Amen.

SECTION LXXXV.

Revelation given August, 1833.

1 Verily I say unto you, my friends, fear not, let your hearts be comforted; yea, rejoice evermore, and in every thing give thanks, waiting patiently on the Lord: for your prayers have entered into the ears of the Lord of Sabaoth, and are recorded with this seal and testament: the Lord hath sworn and decreed that they shall be granted: therefore he giveth this promise unto you, with an immutable covenant, that they shall be fulfilled, and all things wherewith you have been afflicted, shall work together for your good, and to my name's glory saith the Lord.

2 And now verily I say unto you, concerning the laws of the land, it is my will that my people should observe to do all things whatsoever I command them, and that law of the land, which is constitutional, supporting that principle of freedom, in maintaining rights and privileges belongs to all mankind and is justifiable before me: therefore I the Lord justifieth you, and your brethren of my church, in befriending that law which is the constitutional law of the land: and as pertaining to law of man, whatsoever is more or less than these,

cometh of evil. 'I the Lord God maketh you free: therefore ye are free indeed: and the law also maketh you free: nevertheless when the wicked rule the people mourn: wherefore honest men and wise men should be sought for, diligently, and good men and wise men, ye should observe to uphold; otherwise whatsoever is less than these, cometh of evil.

3 And I give unto you a commandment, that ye shall forsake all evil and cleave unto all good, that ye shall live by every word which proceedeth forth out of the mouth of God: for he will give unto the faithful, line upon line; precept upon precept: and I will try you, and prove you herewith: and whoso layeth down his life in my cause, for my name's sake, shall find it again; even life eternal: therefore be not afraid of your enemies, for I have decreed in my heart, saith the Lord, that I will prove you in all things, whether you will abide in my covenant, even unto death, that you may be found worthy: for if ye will not abide in my covenant, ye are not worthy of me: therefore renounce war and proclaim peace, and seek diligently to turn the hearts of their children to their fathers, and the hearts of the fathers to the children. And again the hearts of the Jews unto the prophets; and the prophets unto the Jews, lest I come and smite the whole earth with a curse, and all flesh be consumed before me. Let not your hearts be troubled, for in my Father's house are many mansions, and I have prepared a place for you, and where my Father and I am, there ye shall be also.

4 Behold I the Lord am not well pleased with many who are in the church at Kirtland, for they do not forsake their sins, and their wicked ways, the pride of their hearts, and their covetousness, and all their detestable things, and observe the words of wisdom and eternal life which I have given unto them. Verily I say unto you, that I the Lord will chasten them and will do whatsoever I list, if they do not repent and observe all things whatsoever I have said unto them.— And again I say unto you, if ye observe to do whatsoever I command you, I the Lord will turn away all wrath and indignation from you, and the gates of hell shall not prevail against you.

5 Now I speak unto you, concerning your families: if men will smite you, or your families, once and ye bear it patiently and revile not against them, neither seek revenge, ye shall be rewarded; but if ye bear it not patiently, it shall be accounted unto you as being meeted out a just measure unto you.— And again if your enemy shall smite you the second time, and you revile not against your enemy, and bear it patiently, your reward shall be an hundred fold: And again if he shall smite

you the third time, and ye bear it patiently, your reward shall be doubled unto you four fold: and these three testimonies shall stand against your enemy, if he repent not, and shall not be blotted out. And now verily I say unto you if that enemy shall escape my vengeance that he be not brought into judgment before me, then ye shall see to it, that ye warn him in my name that he come no more upon you, neither upon your family, even your children's children unto the third and fourth generation: and then if he shall come upon you, or your children, or your children's children, unto the third and fourth generation: I have delivered thine enemy into thine hands, and then if thou wilt spare him thou shalt be rewarded for thy righteousness; and also thy children and thy children's children unto the third and fourth generation: nevertheless thine enemy is in thine hands, and if thou reward him according to his works, thou art justified, if he has sought thy life, and thy life is endangered by him; thine enemy is in thine hands, and thou art justified.

6 Behold this is the law I gave unto my servant Nephi; and thy father Joseph, and Jacob, and Isaac, and Abraham, and all mine ancient prophets and apostles. And again this is the law that I gave unto mine ancients, that they should not go out unto battle against any nation, kindred, tongue, or people, save I the Lord commanded them. And if any nation, tongue, or people should proclaim war against them, they should first lift a standard of peace unto that people, nation, or tongue, and if that people did not accept the offering of peace, neither the second nor the third time, they should bring these testimonies before the Lord; then I the Lord would give unto them a commandment, and justify them in going out to battle against that nation, tongue, or people, and I the Lord would fight their battles, and their children's battles and their children's children until they had avenged themselves on all their enemies, to the third and fourth generation, behold this is an ensample unto all people, saith the Lord your God, for justification before me.

7 And again verily I say unto you, if, after thine enemy has come upon thee the first time, he repent and come unto thee praying thy forgiveness thou shalt forgive him and shall hold it no more as a testimony against thine enemy, and so on unto the second and the third time; and as oft as thine enemy repenteth of the trespass wherewith he has trespassed against thee, thou shalt forgive him, until seventy times seven; and if he trespass against thee and repent not the first time, nevertheless thou shalt forgive him; and if he trespass against thee the second time, and repent not, nevertheless thou shalt for-

give him; and if he trespass against thee the third time and repent not thou shalt also forgive him; but if he trespass against thee the fourth time, thou shalt not forgive him but shall bring these testimonies before the Lord, and they shall not be blotted out until he repent and reward the four fold in all things wherewith he has tresspassed against you; and if he do this thou shalt forgive him with all thine heart, and if he do not this, I the Lord will avenge thee of thine enemy and hundred fold; and upon his children, and upon his children's children, of all them that hate me, unto the third and fourth generation: but if the children shall repent, or the children's children and turn unto the Lord their God with all their hearts, and with all their might, mind, and strength, and restore four fold for all their trespasses, wherewith they have trespassed, or wherewith their fathers have trespassed or their father's fathers then thine indignation shall be turned away and vengeance shall no more come upon them, saith the Lord your God, andtheir trespasses shall never be brought any more as a testimony before the Lord against them. Amen.

SECTION LXXXVI.

Revelation given April, 1832, showing the order given to Enoch and the church in his day.

1 Verily, verily I say unto you, my servants, that inasmuch as you have forgiven one another your trespasses, even so I the Lord forgive you; nevertheless there are those among you who have sinned exceedingly; yea, even all of you have sinned, but verily I say unto you, beware from henceforth and refrain from sin lest sore judgments fall upon your heads: for unto whom much is given much is required; and he who sins against the greater light shall receive the greater condemnation. Ye call upon my name for revelations, and I give them unto you; and inasmuch as ye keep not my sayings which I give unto you, ye become transgressors, and justice and judgment is the penalty which is affixed unto my law: therefore, what I say unto one I say unto all, watch, for the adversary spreadeth his dominions and darkness reigneth; and the anger of God kindleth against the inhabitants of the earth; and none doeth good, for all have gone out of the way.

2 And now verily I say unto you, I the Lord will not lay any sin to your charge: go your ways and sin no more: but unto that soul who sinneth shall the former sins return, saith the Lord your God.

3 And again, I say unto you, I give unto you a new com-

mandment, that you may understand my will concerning you; or, in other words, I give unto you directions how you may act before me, that it may turn to you for your salvation. I the Lord am bound when ye do what I say, but when ye do not what I say, ye have no promise.

4 Therefore, verily I say unto you, that it is expedient for my servant Alam and Ahashdah, Mahalaleel and Pelagoram, and my servant Gazelam, and Horah, and Olihah, and Shalemanasseh, and Mehemson, be bound together by a bond and covenant that cannot be broken by transgression except judgment shall immediately follow, in your several stewardships, to manage the affairs of the poor, and all things pertaining to the bishopric both in the land of Zion, and in the land of Shinehah, for I have consecrated the land of Shinehah in mine own due time for the benefit of the saints of the Most High, and for a stake to Zion: for Zion must increase in beauty, and in holiness: her borders must be enlarged; her stakes must be strengthened: yea, verily I say unto you, Zion must arise and put on her beautiful garments: therefore I give unto you this commandment, that ye bind yourselves by this covenant, and it shall be done according to the laws of the Lord. Behold here is wisdom, also, in me, for your good. And you are to be equal, or in other words, you are to have equal claims on the properties, for the benefit of managing the concerns of your stewardships, every man according to his wants and his needs, inasmuch as his wants are just: and all this for the benefit of the church of the living God, that every man may improve upon his talent, that every man may gain other talents; yea, even an hundred fold, to be cast into the Lord's storehouse, to become the common property of the whole church, every man seeking the interest of his neighbor, and doing all things with an eye single to the glory of God.

5 This order I have appointed to be an everlasting order unto you and unto your successors, inasmuch as you sin not: and the soul that sins against this covenant, and hardeneth his heart against it, shall be dealt with according to the laws of my church, and shall be delivered over to the buffitings of satan until the day of redemption.

6 And now verily I say unto you, and this is wisdom, make unto yourselves friends with the mammon of unrighteousness, and they will not destroy you. Leave judgment alone with me, for it is mine and I will repay. Peace be with you; my blessings continue with you, for even yet the kingdom is yours, and shall be forever if you fall not from your steadfastness; even so. Amen.

SECTION LXXXVII.

Revelation given January, 1832.

1 Verily, verily I say unto you, I who speak even by the voice of my Spirit; even Alpha and Omega, your Lord and your God: hearken, O ye who have given your names to go forth to proclaim my gospel, and to prune my vineyard. Behold I say unto you, that it is my will that you should go forth and not tarry, neither be idle, but labor with your mights lifting up your voices as with the sound of a trump proclaiming the truth according to the revelations and commandments which I have given you, and thus if ye are faithful ye shall be laden with many sheaves, and crowned with honor, and glory, and immortality, and eternal life.

2 Therefore verily I say unto my servant William E. McLelin I revoke the commission which I gave unto him, to go unto the eastern countries, and I give unto him a new commission and a new commandment, in the which I the Lord chasteneth him for the murmurings of his heart; and he sinned, nevertheless I forgive him and say unto him again, go ye into the south countries; and let my servant Luke Johnson go with him and proclaim the things which I have commanded them, calling on the name of the Lord for the comforter, which shall teach them all things that are expedient for them, praying always that they faint not; and inasmuch as they do this, I will be with them even unto the end. Behold this is the will of the Lord your God concerning you; even so. Amen.

3 And again, verily thus saith the Lord, let my servant Orson Hyde and my servant Samuel H. Smith take their journey into the eastern countries, and proclaim the things which I have commanded them: and inasmuch as they are faithful, lo I will be with them even unto the end. And again, verily I say unto my servant Lyman Johnson, and unto my servant Orson Pratt, they shall also take their journey into the eastern countries: and behold and lo, I am with them also even unto the end. And again I say unto my servant Asa Dodds and unto my servant Calves Wilson, that they also shall take their journey unto the western countries, and proclaim my gospel even as I have commanded them. And he who is faithful shall overcome all things, and shall be lifted up at the last day. And again, I say unto my servant Major N. Ashley and my servant Burr Riggs, let them take their journey also unto the south country; yea, let all those take their journey as I have commanded them, going from house to house, and from village to village, and from city to city; and in whatsoever

house ye enter, and they receive you, leave your blessings upon that house; and in whatsoever house ye enter, and they receive you not, ye shall depart speedily from that house, and
shake off the dust of your feet as a testimony against them;
and you shall be filled with joy and gladness and know this,
that in the day of judgement you shall be judges of that house,
and condemn them; and it shall be more tolerable for the heathen in the day of judgment, than for that house: therefore
gird up your loins and be faithful and ye shall overcome all
things and be lifted up at the last day; even so.   Amen.

4 And again thus saith the Lord unto you, O ye elders of my
church, who have given your names that you might know his
will concerning you: behold I say unto you that it is the duty
of the church to assist in supporting the families of those, and
also to supprt the families of those who are called and must
needs be sent unto the world to proclaim the gospel unto the
world: wherefore I the Lord give unto you this commandment,
that ye obtain places for your families, inasmuch as your
brethren are willing to open their hearts; and let all such as
can, obtain places for their families, and support of the
church for them, not fail to go into the world; whether to the
east, or to the west, or to the north, or to the south, let them
ask and they shall receive; knock and it shall be opened unto
them, and made known from on high, even by the Comforter,
whither they shall go.

5 And again verily I say unto you that every man who is
obliged to provide for his own family, let him provide and he
shall in no wise lose his crown; and let him labor in the church.
Let every man be diligent in all things.   And the idler shall
not have place in the church, except he repents and mends his
ways.   Wherefore let my servant Simeon Carter and my servant Emer Harris be united in the ministry.   And also my
servant Ezra Thayre and my servant Thomas B. Marsh. Also
my servant Hyrum Smith and my servant Reynolds Cahoon;
and also my servant Daniel Stanton and my servant Seymour
Brunson; and also my servant Silvester Smith and my servant
Gideon Carter; and also my servant Ruggles Eames and my
servant Stephen Burnett; and also my servant Micah B. Wel-
ton and also my servant Eden Smith; even so. Amen.

SECTION LXXXVIII.

Revelation given April, 1832.

1 Verily thus saith the Lord, in addition to the laws of the
church concerning women and children, those who belong to

the church, who have lost their husbands or fathers: women have claim on their husbands for their maintainance until their husbands are taken; and if they are not found transgressors they shall have fellowship in the church, and if they are not faithful, they shall not have fellowship in the church; yet they may remain upon their inheritances according to the laws of the land.

2 All children have claim upon their parents for their maintainance until they are of age; and after that, they have claim upon the church; or, in other words upon the Lord's storehouse, if their parents have not wherewith to give them inheritances. And the storehouse shall be kept by the consecrations of the church, that widows and orphans shall be provided for, as also the poor. Amen.

SECTION LXXXIX.

Revelation given December, 1831.

1 Hearken and listen to the voice of the Lord, O ye who have assembled yourselves together, who are the high priests of my church, to whom the kingdom and power has been given. For verily thus saith the Lord, it is expedient in me, for a bishop to be appointed unto you, or of you unto the church in this part of the Lord's vineyard: and verily in this thing ye have done wisely, for it is required of the Lord, at the hand of every steward, to render an account of his stewardship, both in time and in eternity. For he who is faithful and wise in time, is accounted worthy to inherit the mansions prepared for them of my Father. Verily I say unto you, the elders of the church in this part of my vineyard, shall render an account of their stewardship, unto the bishop which shall be appointed of me, in this part of my vineyard. These things shall be had on record to be handed over unto the bishop in Zion; and the duty of the bishop shall be made known by the commandments which have been given, and the voice of the conference.

2 And now, verily I say unto you, my servant Newel K. Whitney is the man who shall be appointed, and ordained unto this power: this is the will of the Lord your God, your Redeemer; even so. Amen.

3 The word of the Lord, in addition to the law which has been given, making known the duty of the bishop, which has been ordained unto the church in this part of the vineyard; which is verily this: to keep the Lord's storehouse; to receive the funds of the church in this part of the vineyard; to take an account of the elders as before has been commanded, and

to administer to their wants, who shall pay for that which they receive, inasmuch as they have wherewith to pay; that this also may be consecrated to the good of the church, to the poor and needy: and he who hath not wherewith to pay, an account shall be taken and handed over to the bishop of Zion, who shall pay the debt out of that which the Lord shall put into his hands: and the labors of the faithful who labor in spiritual things, in administering the gospel and the things of the kingdom, unto the church, and unto the world, shall answer the debt unto the bishop in Zion: thus it cometh out of the church, for according to the law every man that cometh up to Zion, must lay all things before the bishop in Zion.

4 And now, verily I say unto you, that as every elder in this part of the vineyard, must give an account of his stewardship unto the bishop in this part of the vineyard, a certificate from the judge or bishop in this part of the vineyard, unto the bishop in Zion, rendereth every man acceptable, and answereth all things, for an inheritance, and to be received as a wise steward, and as a faithful laborer; otherwise he shall not be accepted of the bishop in Zion. And now, verily I say unto you, let every elder who shall give an account unto the bishop of the church, in this part of the vineyard, be recommended by the church or churches, in which he labors, that he may render himself and his accounts approved in all things. And again, let my servants who are appointed as stewards over the literary concerns of my church, have claim for assistance upon the bishop or bishops, in all things, that the revelations may be published, and go forth unto the ends of the earth, that they also may obtain funds which shall benefit the church, in all things; that they also may render themselves approved in all things and be accounted as wise stewards. And now, behold this shall be an ensample for all the extensive branches of my church, in whatsoever land they shall be established. And now I make an end of my sayings. Amen.

5 A few words in addition to the laws of the kingdom, respecting the members of the church; they that are appointed by the Holy Spirit to go up unto Zion; and they who are privileged to go up unto Zion. Let them carry up unto the bishop a certificate from three elders of the church, or a certificate from the bishop, otherwise he who shall go up unto the land of Zion, shall not be accounted as a wise steward. This is also an ensample. Amen.

SECTION XC.

Revelation given December, 1831.

1 Behold, thus saith the Lord unto you my servants, Joseph Smith, jr. aad Sidney Rigdon, that the time has verily come, that it is necessary and expedient in me that you should open your mouths in proclaiming my gospel, the things of the kingdom, expounding the mysteries thereof out of the scriptures, according to that portion of spirit and power, which shall be given unto you, even as I will.

2 Verily I say unto you, proclaim unto the world in the regions round about, and in the church also, for the space of a season, even until it shall be made known unto you. Verily this is a mission for a season, which I give unto you, wherefore, labor ye in my vineyard. Call upon the inhabitants of the earth, and bear record, and prepare the way for the commandments and revelations which are to come. Now, behold this is wisdom: whoso readeth let him understand and receive also; for unto him that receiveth it shall be given more abundantly, even power: wherefore, confound your enemies; call upon them to meet you, both in public and in private; and inasmuch as' ye are faithful their shame shall be made manifest. Wherefore, let them bring forth their strong reasons against the Lord. Verily thus saith the Lord unto you, there is no weapon that is formed against you shall prosper; and if any man lift his voice against you, he shall be confounded in mine own due time: wherefore, keep these commandments: they are true and faithful, even so. Amen.

SECTION XCI.

A Vision.

1 Hear, O ye heavens, and give ear, O earth, and rejoice ye inhabitants thereof, for the Lord is God, and beside him there is no Savior; great is his wisdom; marvellous are his ways; and the extent of his doings, none can find out; his purposes fail not, neither are there any who can stay his hand: from eternity to eternity, he is the same and his years never fail.

2 For thus saith the Lord, I the Lord am merciful and gracious unto those who fear me, and delight to honor those who serve me in righteousness, and in truth unto the end; great shall be their reward, and eternal shall be their glory; and to them will I reveal all mysteries; yea, all the hidden mysteries

o

of my kingdom from days of old; and for ages to come will I make known unto them the good pleasure of my will concerning all things pertaining to my kingdom; yea, even the wonders of eternity shall they know, and things to come will I show them, even the things of many generations; their wisdom shall be great, and their understanding reach to heaven: and before them the wisdom of the wise shall perish, and the understanding of the prudent shall come to nought; for by my Spirit will I enlighten them, and by my power will I make known unto them the secrets of my will; yea, even those things which eye has not seen, nor ear heard, nor yet entered into the heart of man.

3 We, Joseph Smith, jr. and Sidney Rigdon, being in the Spirit on the sixteenth of February, in the year of our Lord, one thousand eight hundred and thirty two, by the power of the Spirit our eyes were opened, and our understandings were enlightened, so as to see and understand the things of God; even those things which were from the beginning before the world was, which were ordained of the Father, through his only begotten Son, who was in the bosom of the Father, even from the beginning, of whom we bear record, and the record which we bear is the fulness of the gospel of Jesus Christ, who is the Son, whom we saw and with whom we conversed in the heavenly vision; for while we were doing the work of translation, which the Lord had appointed, unto us, we came to the twenty ninth verse of the fifth chapter of John, which was given unto us as follows:—speaking of the resurrection of the dead, concerning those who shall hear the voice of the Son of man—and shall come forth; they who have done good in the resurrection of the just, and they who have done evil in the resurrection of the unjust. Now this caused us to marvel, for it was given unto us of the Spirit: and while we meditated upon these things, the Lord touched the eyes of our understandings, and they were opened, and the glory of the Lord shone round about; and we beheld the glory of the Son, on the right hand of the Father, and received of his fulness; and saw the holy angels, and they who are sanctified before his throne, worshiping God and the Lamb, who worship him forever and ever. And now, after the many testimonies which have been given of him, this is the testimony, last of all, which we give of him, that he lives; for we saw him, even on the right hand of God; and we heard the voice bearing record that he is the only begotten of the Father; that by him, and through him, and of him, the worlds are and were created; and the inhabitants thereof are begotten sons and daughters unto God. And this we saw also, and bear record, that an angel of God,

who was in authority in the presence of God, who rebelled against the only begotten Son—whom the Father loved, and who was in the bosom of the Father—and was thrust down from the presence of God and the Son, and was called Perdition; for the heavens wept over him; he was Lucifer, a son of the morning; and we beheld and lo, he is fallen! is fallen! even a son of the morning. And while we were yet in the Spirit, the Lord commanded us that we should write the vision: for we beheld satan, that old serpent, even the devil, who rebelled against God, and sought to take the kingdom of our God, and his Christ; wherefore he maketh war with the saints of God, and encompasses them round about. And we saw a vision of the sufferings of those with whom he made war and overcame, for thus came the voice of the Lord unto us.

4 Thus saith the Lord, concerning all those who know my power, and have been made partakers thereof, and suffered themselves, through the power of the devil, to be overcome, and to deny the truth, and defy my power: they are they who are the sons of perdition, of whom I say it had been better for them never to have been born; for they are vessels of wrath doomed to suffer the wrath of God, with the devil and his angels, in eternity: concerning whom I have said there is no forgiveness in this world nor in the world to come: having denied the Holy Spirit, after having received it, and having denied the only begotten Son of the Father, having crucified him unto themselves, and put him to an open shame: these are they who shall go away into the lake of fire and brimstone, with the devil and his angels, and the only ones on whom the second death shall have any power; yea, verily the only ones who shall not be redeemed in the due time of the Lord, after the sufferings of his wrath; for all the rest shall be brought forth by the resurrection of the dead, through the triumph and the glory of the Lamb, who was slain, who was in the bosom of the Father before the worlds were made. And this is the gospel, the glad tidings which the voice out of the heavens bore record unto us, that he came into the world, even Jesus to be crucified for the world, and to bear the sins of the world, and to sanctify the world, and to cleanse it from all unrighteousness; that through him all might be saved, whom the Father had put into his power, and made by him; who glorifies the Father, and saves all the works of his hands, except those sons of perdition. who deny the Son after the Father has revealed him: wherefore he saves all except them; they shall go away into everlasting punishment, which is endless punishment, which is eternal punishment, to reign with the devil and his

'angels in eternity, where their worm dieth not and the fire is
not quenched, which is their torment, and the end thereof, neither the place thereof, nor their torment, no man knows, neither was it revealed, neither is, neither will be revealed unto
man, except to them who are made partakers thereof: nevertheless I the Lord show it by vision unto many, but straightway
shut it up again: wherefore the end, the width, the height,
the depth, and the misery thereof, they understand not, neither any man except them who are ordained unto this condemnation. And we heard the voice saying, Write the vision
for lo! this is the end of the vision of the sufferings of the ungodly!

5 And again, we bear record for we saw and heard, and this,
is the testimony of the gospel of Christ, concerning them who
come forth in the resurrection of the just: they are they who
received the testimony of Jesus, and believed on his name,
and were baptized after the manner of his burial, being buried
in the water in his name, and this according to the commandment which he has given, that, by keeping the commandments,
they might be washed and cleansed from all their sins, and receive the Holy Spirit by the laying on of the hands of him who
is ordained and sealed unto this power; and who overcome by
faith, and are sealed by that Holy Spirit of promise, which the
Father sheds forth upon all those who are just and true: they
are they who are the church of the first-born: they are they
into whose hands the Father has given all things: they are
they who are priests and kings, who have received of his fulness, and of his glory, and are priests of the Most High after
the order of Melchizedek, which was after the order of Enoch,
which was after the order of the only begotten Son: wherefore, as it is written, they are gods, even the sons of God:
wherefore all things are theirs, whether life or death, or things
present, or things to come, all are theirs, and they are Christ's,
and Christ is God's; and they shall overcome all things: wherefore let no man glory in man, but rather let him glory in God,
who shall subdue all enemies under his feet: these shall dwell
in the presence of God and his Christ forever and ever: these
are they whom he shall bring with him, when he shall come
in the clouds of heaven, to reign on the earth over his people:
these are they who shall have part in the first resurrection:
these are they who shall come forth in the resurrection of the
just: these are they who are come unto mount Zion, and unto
the city of the living God, the heavenly place, the holiest of
all: these are they who have come to an innumerable company of angels; to the general assembly and church of Enoch,
and of the first born: these are they whose names are written

in heaven, where God and Christ are the judge of all: these are they who are just men made perfect through Jesus the mediator of the new covenant, who wrought out this perfect atonement through the shedding of his own blood: these are they whose bodies are celestial, whose glory is that of the sun, even the glory of God the highest of all; whose glory the sun of the firmament is written of as being typical.

6 And again, we saw the terrestrial world, and behold and lo! these are they who are of the terrestrial, whose glory differs from that of the church of the first born, who have received the fulness of the Father, even as that of the moon differs from the sun of the firmament. Behold, these are they who died without law; and also they who are the spirits of men kept in prison, whom the Son visited, and preached the gospel unto them, that they might be judged according to men in the flesh, who received not the testimony of Jesus in the flesh, but afterwards received it: these are they who are honorable men of the earth, who were blinded by the craftiness of men: these are they who receive of his glory, but not of his fulness; these are they who receive of the presence of the Son, but not of the fulness of the Father: wherefore they are bodies terrestrial, and not bodies celestial, and differ in glory as the moon differs from the sun: these are they who are not valiant in the testimony of Jesus: wherefore they obtained not the crown over the kingdom of our God. And now this is the end of the vision which we saw of the terrestrial, that the Lord commanded us to write while we were yet in the Spirit.

7 And again, we saw the glory of the telestial, which glory is that of the lesser, even as the glory of the stars differ from that of the glory of the moon in the firmament; these are they who received not the gospel of Christ, neither the testimony of Jesus: these are they who deny not the Holy Spirit: these are they who are thrust down to hell: these are they who shall not be redeemed from the devil, until the last resurrection, until the Lord, even Christ the Lamb, shall have finished his work: these are they who receive not of his fulness in the eternal world, but of the Holy Spirit through the ministration of the terrestrial; and the terrestrial through the ministration of the celestial; and also the telestial receive it of the administering of angels, who are appointed to minister for them, or who are appointed to be ministering spirits for them, for they shall be heirs of salvation. And thus we saw in the heavenly vision, the glory of the telestial which surpasses all understanding; and no man knows it except him to whom God has revealed it. And thus we saw the glory of the terrestrial, which excels in all things the glory of the telestial, even in glory,

and in power, and in might, and in dominion. And thus we saw the glory of the celestial, which excels in all things; where God, even the Father, reigns upon his throne forever and ever: before whose throne all things bow in humble reverence and give him glory forever and ever. They who dwell in his presence are the church of the first born; and they see as they are seen, and know as they are known, having received of his fulness and of his grace; and he makes them equal in power, and in might, and in dominion. And the glory of the celestial is one, even as the glory of the sun is one. And the glory of the terrestrial is one, even as the glory of the moon is one. And the glory of the telestial is one, even as the glory of the stars is one for as one star differs from another star in glory, even so difiers one from another in glory in the telestial world: for these are they who are of Paul, and of Apollos, and of Cephas: these are they who say they are some of one and some of another; some of Christ; and some of John; and some of Moses; and some of Elias; and some of Esaias; and some of Isaiah; and some of Enoch, but received not the gospel; neither the testimony of Jesus; neither the prophets: neither the everlasting covenant; last of all, these all are they who will not be gathered with the saints, to be caught up unto the church of the first born, and received into the cloud: these are they who are liars, and sorcerers, and adulterers, and whoremongers, and whosoever loves and makes a lie: these are they who suffer the wrath of God on the earth: these are they who suffer the vengeance of eternal fire: these are they who are cast down to hell and suffer the wrath of Almighty God until the fulness of times, when Christ shall have subdued all enemies under his feet, and shall have perfected his work, when he shall deliver up the kingdom and present it unto the Father spotless, saying: I have overcome and have trodden the wine-press alone, even the wine-press of the fierceness of the wrath of Almighty God: then shall he be crowned with the crown of his glory, to sit on the throne of his power to reign forever and ever. But behold and lo, we saw the glory and the inhabitants of the telestial world, that they were as innumerable as the stars in the firmament of heaven, or as the sand upon the sea shore, and heard the voice of the Lord saying: These all shall bow the knee, and every tongue shall confess to him who sits upon the throne forever and ever: for they shall be judged according to their works; and every man shall receive according to his own works, and his own dominion, in the mansions which are prepared, and they shall be servants of the Most High, but where God and Christ dwell they cannot come, worlds without end. This is the end of the vision which we saw, which we were commanded to write while we were yet in the Spirit.

8 But great and marvellous are the works of the Lord and the mysteries of his kingdom which he showed unto us, which surpasses all understanding in glory, and in might, and in dominion, which he commanded us we should not write, while we were yet in the Spirit, and are not lawful for man to utter; neither is man capable to make them known, for they are only to be seen and understood by the power of the Holy Spirit, which God bestows on those who love him and purify themselves before him; to whom he grants this privilege of seeing and knowing for themselves; that through the power and manifestation of the Spirit, while in the flesh, they may be able to bear his presence in the world of glory. And to God and the Lamb be glory, and honor, and dominion forever and ever.— Amen.

SECTION. XCII.

Revelation given March, 1833.

1 Verily, thus saith the Lord unto you, concerning the Apocrypha, there are many things contained therein that are true, and it is mostly translated correct: there are many things contained therein that are not true, which are interpolations by the hands of men. Verily I say unto you, that it is not needful that the Apocrypha should be translated. Therefore, whoso readeth it let him understand, for the Spirit manifesteth truth; and whoso is enlightened by the Spirit shall obtain benefit therefrom; and whoso receiveth not by the Spirit, cannot be benefitted: therefore, it is not needful that it should be translated. Amen.

SECTION XCIII.

Revelation to Enoch, on the order of the Church for the benefit of the poor, given to the saints in Kirtland, March, 1833.

1 Verily, thus saith the Lord, I give unto the united order, organized agreeable to the commandment previously given, a revelation and commandment concerning my servant Shederlaomach, that ye shall receive him into the order. What I say unto one I say unto all.

2 And again, I say unto you, my servant Shederlaomach, you shall be a lively member in this order; and inasmuch as you are faithful in keeping all former commandments, you shall be blessed forever. Amen.

SECTION XCIV.

*Revelation given in Perrysburgh, N. Y. to Joseph Smith jr.
and Sidney Rigdon, October, 1833.*

1 Verily, thus saith the Lord unto you my friends, Sidney, and Joseph, your families are well: they are in mine hands, and I will do with them as seemeth me good; for in me there is all power: therefore, follow me, and listen to the council which I shall give unto you: Behold, and lo, I have much people in this place, in the regions round about, and an effectual door shall be opened in the regions round about in this eastern land: Therefore, I the Lord have suffered you to come unto this place; for thus it was expedient in me for the salvation of souls: therefore, verily I say unto you, lift up your voices unto this people; speak the thoughts that I shall put into your hearts, and ye shall not be confounded before men; for it shall be given you in the very hour, yea, in the very moment, what ye shall say.

2 But a commandment I give unto you, that ye shall declare whatsoever things ye declare in my name, in solemnity of heart, in the spirit of meekness, in all things. And I give unto you this promise, that inasmuch as ye do this, the Holy Ghost shall be shed forth in bearing record unto all things whatsoever ye shall say.

3 And it is expedient in me that you, my servant Sidney, should be a spokesman unto this people; yea, verily, I will ordain you unto this calling, even to be a spokesman unto my servant Joseph; and I will give unto him power to be mighty in testimony; and I will give unto thee power to be mighty in expounding all scriptures, that thou mayest be a spokesman unto him, and he shall be a revelator unto thee, that thou mayest know the certainty of all things pertaining to the things of my kingdom on the earth. Therefore, continue your journey and let your hearts rejoice; for, behold, and lo, I am with you even unto the end.

4 And now I give unto you a word concerning Zion: Zion shall be redeemed, although she is chastened for a little season. Thy brethren, my servants, Orson Hyde and John Gould, are in my hands, and inasmuch as they keep my commandments they shall be saved. Therefore, let your hearts be comforted, for all things shall work together for good to them that walk uprightly, and to the sanctification of the church; for I will raise up unto myself a pure people, that will serve me in righteousness; and all that call on the name of the Lord and keep his commandments, shall be saved; even so. Amen.

SECTION XCV.

Revelation given June, 1833.

1 Verily thus saith the Lord unto you, whom I love, and whom I love I also chasten, that their sins may be forgiven, for with the chastisement I prepare a way for their deliverance, in all things out of temptation: and I have loved you: Wherefore ye must needs be chastened, and stand rebuked before my face, for ye have sinned against me a very grevious sin, in that ye have not considered the great commandment in all things, that I have given unto you, concerning the building of mine house, for the preparation wherewith I design to prepare mine apostles to prune my vineyard for the last time, that I may bring to pass my strange act, that I may pour out my Spirit upon all flesh. But behold, verily I say unto you, there are many who have been ordained among you, whom I have called, but few of them are chosen: they who are not chosen have sinned a very grievious sin, in that they are walking in darkness at noon-day; and for this cause, I gave unto you a commandment, that you should call your solemn assembly; that your fastings and your mourning might come up into the ears of the Lord of Sabaoth, which is, by interpretation, the Creator of the first day; the beginning and the end.

2 Yea, verily I say unto you, I gave unto you a commandment, that you should build an house, in the which house I design to endow those whom I have chosen with power from on high: for this is the promise of the Father unto you: therefore I commanded you to tarry, even as mine apostles at Jerusalem: nevertheless my servants sinned a very grevious sin; and contentions arose in the school of the prophets, which was very grievious unto me, saith your Lord: therefore I sent them forth to be chastened.

3 Verily I say unto you, it is my will that you should build an house: if you keep my commandments, you shall have power to build it; if you keep not my commandments the love of the Father, shall not continue with you: therefore you shall walk in darkness. Now here is wisdom and the mind of the Lord: let the house be built, not after the manner of the world, for I give not unto you, that ye shall live after the manner of the world: therefore let it be built after the manner which I shall show unto three of you, whom ye shall appoint and ordain unto this power. And the size thereof shall be fifty and five feet in width, and let it be sixty-five feet in length, in the inner court thereof; and let the lower part of the inner court

be dedicated unto me for your sacrament offering, and for your preaching: and your fasting; and your praying, and the offering up your most holy desires unto me, saith your Lord.—And let the higher part of the inner court, be dedicated unto me for the school of mine apostles, saith Son Ahman; or, in other words, Alphus; or, in other words, Omegus; even Jesus Christ your Lord. Amen.

SECTION XCVI.

A Revelation to Enoch, showing the order of the city or stake of Zion, Shinehah, given for a sample to the saints in Kirtland, June, 1833.

1 Behold, I say unto you, here is wisdom whereby ye may know how to act concerning this matter: for it is expedient in me that this stake that I have set for the strength of Zion, should be made strong: therefore, let {my servant Ahashdah take charge of the place which is named among you, upon which I design to build mine holy house: and again let it be divided into lots according to wisdom, for the benefit of those who seek inheritances, as it shall be determined in council among you. Therefore, take heed that ye see to this matter, and that portion that is necessary to benefit mine order, for the purpose of bringing forth my word to the children of men, for behold verily I say unto you, this is the most expedient in me, that my word should go forth unto the children of men, for the purpose of subduing the hearts of the children of men, for your good; even so. 'Amen.

2 And again, verily I say unto you, it is wisdom and expedient in me, that my servant Zombre, whose offering I have accepted, and whose prayers I have heard; unto whom I give a promise of eternal life inasmuch as he keepeth my commandments from henceforth: for he is a descendant of Seth, and a partaker of the blessings of the promise made unto his fathers Verily I say unto you, it is expedient in me that he should become a member of the order, that he may assist in bringing forth my word unto the children of men: therefore ye shall ordain him unto this blessing: and he shall seek diligently to take away incumbrances, that are upon the house named among you, that he may dwell therein; even so. Amen.

SECTION XCVII.

Revelation given December, 1833.

1 Verily, I say unto you, concerning your brethren who have been afflicted, and persecuted, and cast out from the land of their inheritance, I the Lord have suffered the affliction to come upon them, wherewith they have been afflicted in consequence of their transgressions; yet, I will own them, and they shall be mine in that day when I shall come to make up my jewels.

2 Therefore, they must needs be chastened, and tried, even as Abraham, who was commanded to offer up his only son; for all those who will not endure chastening, but deny me, cannot be sanctified.

3 Behold, I say unto you, there were jarrings, and contentions, and envyings, and strifes, and lustful and covetous desires among them; therefore by these things they polluted their inheritances. They were slow to hearken unto the voice of the Lord their God; therefore, the Lord their God is slow to hearken unto their prayers, to answer them in the day of their trouble. In the day of their peace they esteemed lightly my counsel; but in the day of their trouble, of necessity they feel after me.

4 Verily, I say unto you, notwithstanding their sins my bowels are filled with compassion toward them: I will not utterly cast them off; and in the day of wrath I will remember mercy. I have sworn, and the decree hath gone forth by a former commandment which I have given unto you, that I would let fall the sword of mine indignation in the behalf of my people; and even as I have said, it shall come to pass. Mine indignation is soon to be poured out without measure upon all nations, and this will I do when the cup of their iniquity is full. And in that day, all who are found upon the watch tower, or in other words, all mine Israel shall be saved. And they that have been scattered shall be gathered: and all they who have mourned shall be comforted; and all they who have given their lives for my name shall be crowned. Therefore, let your hearts be comforted concerning Zion; for all flesh is in mine hands: be still, and know that I am God. Zion shall not be moved out of her place, notwithstanding her children are scattered, they that remain and are pure in heart shall return and come to their inheritances; they and their children, with songs of everlasting joy; to build up the waste places of Zion. And all these things, that the prophets might be fulfilled.— And behold, there is none other place appointed than that

which I have appointed; neither shall there be any other place appointed than that which I have appointed for the work of the gathering of my saints, until the day cometh when there is found no more room for them; and then I have other places which I will appoint unto them, and they shall be called stakes, for the curtains, or the strength of Zion.

5 Behold it is my will, that all they who call on my name, and worship me according to mine everlasting gospel, should gather together and stand in holy places, and prepare for the revelation which is to come when the veil of the covering of my temple, in my tabernacle, which hideth the earth, shall be taken off, and all flesh shall see me together. And every corruptible thing, both of man, or of the beasts of the field, or of the fowls of heaven, or of the fish of the sea, that dwell upon all the face of the earth, shall be consumed; and also, that of element shall melt with fervent heat; and all things shall become new, that my knowledge and glory may dwell upon all the earth. And in that day the enmity of man, and the enmity of beasts; yea, the enmity of all flesh shall cease from before my face. And in that day whatsoever any man shall ask it shall be given unto him. And in that day satan shall not have power to tempt any man. And there shall be no sorrow because there is no death. In that day an infant shall not die until he is old, and his life shall be as the age of a tree, and when he dies he shall not sleep, (that is to say in the earth,) but shall be changed in the twinkling of an eye, and shall be caught up, and his rest shall be glorious. Yea, verily I say unto you, in that day when the Lord shall come he shall reveal all things; things which have passed, and hidden things which no man knew; things of the earth by which it was made, and the purpose and the end thereof; things most precious; things that are above, and things that are beneath; things that are in the earth, and upon the earth, and in heaven. And all they who suffer persecution for my name, and endure in faith, though they are called to lay down their lives for my sake, yet shall they partake of all this glory. Wherefore, fear not even unto death; for in this world your joy is not full, but in me your joy is full. Therefore, care not for the body, neither the life of the body; but care for the soul, and for the life of the soul: and seek the face of the Lord always, that in patience ye may possess your souls, and ye shall have eternal life. When men are called unto mine everlasting gospel, and covenant with an everlasting covenant, they are accounted as the salt of the earth, and the savor of men.— They are called to be the savor of men. Therefore, if that salt of the earth lose its savor, behold it is thenceforth good

for nothing, only to be cast out and trodden under the feet of men. Behold, here is wisdom concerning the children of Zion; even many, but not all: they were found transgressors, therefore, they must needs be chastened. He that exalteth himself shall be abased, and he that abaseth himself shall be exalted.

6 And now, I will show unto you a parable that you may know my will concerning the redemption of Zion: a certain nobleman had a spot of land, very choice; and he said unto his servants, go ye into my vineyard, even upon this very choice piece of land, and plant twelve olive trees; and set watchmen round about them and build a tower, that one may overlook the land round about, to be a watchman upon the tower; that mine olive trees may not be broken down, when the enemy shall come to spoil, and take unto themselves the fruit of my vineyard. Now the servants of the nobleman went and did as their lord commanded them; and planted the olive trees, and built a hedge round about, and set watchmen, and began to build the tower. And while they were yet laying the foundation thereof, they began to say among themselves, and what need hath my lord of this tower? and consulted for a long time, saying among themselves, what need hath my lord of this tower, seeing this is a time of peace? Might not this money be given to the exchangers? for there is no need of these things! And while they were at variance one with another, they became very slothful, and they hearkened not unto the commandments of their lord: and the enemy came by night, and broke down the hedge, and the servants of the nobleman arose, and were affrighted, and fled: and the enemy destroyed their works, and broke down the olive trees.

7 Now behold, the nobleman, the lord of the vineyard, called upon his servants, and said unto them, Why! what is the cause of this great evil? ought ye not to have done even as I commanded you? and after ye had planted the vineyard, and built the hedge round about, and set watchmen upon the walls thereof, built the tower also, and set a watchman upon the tower, and watched for my vineyard, and not have fallen asleep, lest the enemy should come upon you? and behold, the watchman upon the tower would have seen the enemy while he was yet afar off: and then ye could have made ready and kept the enemy from breaking down the hedge thereof, and saved my vineyard from the hands of the destroyer. And the lord of the vineyard said unto one of his servants, Go and gather together the residue of my servants; and take all the strength of mine house, which are my warriors, my young men, and they that are of middle age also, among all my ser-

vants, who are the strength of mine house, save those only whom I have appointed to tarry; and go ye straightway unto the land of my vineyard, and redeem my vineyard, for it is mine, I have bought it with money. Therefore get ye straightway ur to my land; break down the walls of mine enemies; throw down their tower, and scatter their watchmen: and inasmuch as they gather together against you, avenge me of mine enemies; that by and by, I may come with the residue of mine house and possess the land.

8 And the servant said unto his lord, when shall these things be? And he said unto his servant, when I will: go ye straightway, and do all things whatsoever I have commanded you; and this shall be my seal and blessing upon you; a faithful and wise steward in the midst of mine house: a ruler in my kingdom. And his servant went straightway, and done all things whatsoever his lord commanded him, and after many days all things were fulfilled.

9 Again, verily I say unto you, I will show unto you wisdom in me concerning all the churches, inasmuch as they are willing to be guided in a right and proper way for their salvation, that the work of the gathering together of my saints may continue, that I may build them up unto my name upon holy places; for the time of harvest is come, and my word must needs be fulfilled. Therefore, I must gather together my people according to the parable of the wheat and the tares, that the wheat may be secured in the garners to possess eternal life, and be crowned with celestial glory when I shall come in the kingdom of my Father, to reward every man according as his work shall be, while the tares shall be bound in bundles, and their bands made strong, that they may be burned with unquenchable fire. Therefore, a commandment I give unto all the churches, that they shall continue to gather together unto the places which I have appointed; nevertheless, as I have said unto you in a former commandment, let not your gathering be in haste, nor by flight; but let all things, be prepared before you, and in order that all things be prepared before you, observe the commandments which I have given concerning these things, which saith, or teacheth, to purchase all the lands by money, which can be purchased for money, in the region round about the land which I have appointed to be the land of Zion, for the beginning of the gathering of my saints; all the land which can be purchased in Jackson county, and the counties round about, and leave the residue in mine hand.

10 Now verily I say unto you, let all the churches gather together all their moneys; let these things be done in their time, be not in haste; and observe to have all things prepared

before you. And let honorable men be appointed, even wise men, and send them to purchase these lands; and every church in the eastern countries when they are built up, if they will hearken unto this counsel, they may buy lands and gather together upon them, and in this way they may establish Zion. There is even now already in store a sufficient; yea, even abundance to redeem Zion, and establish her waste places no more to be thrown down, were the churches, who call themselves after my name willing to hearken to my voice. And, again I say unto you, those who have been scattered by their enemies, it is my will that they should continue to importune for redress, and redemption, by the hands of those who are placed as rulers, and are in authority over you, according to the laws and constitution of the people which I have suffered to be established, and should be maintained for the rights and protection of all flesh, according to just and holy principles, that every man may act in doctrine, and principle pertaining to futurity, according to the moral agency which I have given unto them that every man may be accountable for his own sins in the day of judgment. Therefore it is not right that any man should be in bondage one to another. And for this purpose have I established the Constitution of this land, by the hands of wise men whom I raised up unto this very purpose, and redeemed the land by the shedding of blood.

11 Now, unto what shall I liken the children of Zion? I will liken them unto the parable of the woman and the unjust judge, (for men ought always to pray and not faint,) which saith, There was in a city a judge which feared not God, neither regarded man. And there was a widow in that city, and she came unto him, saying, avenge me of mine adversary.—And he would not for a while, but afterward he said within himself, though I fear not God, nor regard man, yet because this widow troubleth me I will avenge her, lest by her continual coming, she weary me. Thus will I liken the children of Zion.

12 Let them importune at the feet of the Judge; and if he heed them not, let them importune at the feet of the governor; and if the governor heed them not, let them importune at the feet of the President; and if the President heed them not, then will the Lord arise and come forth out of his hiding place, and in his fury vex the nation, and in his hot displeasure, and in his fierce anger, in his time, will cut off these wicked, unfaithful, and unjust stewards, and appoint them their portion among hypocrites and unbelievers; even in outer darkness, where there is weeping, and wailing, and gnashing of teeth.—Pray ye therefore, that their ears may be opened unto your

cries, that I may be merciful unto them, that these things may not come upon them. What I have said unto you, must needs be, that all men may be left without excuse; that wise men and rulers may hear and know that which they have never considered; that I may proceed to bring to pass my act, my strange act, and perform my work, my strange work. That men may discern between the righteous and the wicked, saith your God.

13 And, again I say unto you, it is contrary to my commandment, and my will, that my servant Sidney Gilbert should sell my store house, which I have appointed unto my people, into the hands of mine enemies. Let not that which I have appointed, be polluted by mine enemies, by the consent of those who call themselves after my name: for this is a very sore and grievous sin against me, and against my people, in consequence of those things which I have decreed, and are soon to befall the nations. Therefore, it is my will that my people should claim, and hold claim, upon that which I have appointed unto them, though they should not be permitted to dwell thereon; nevertheless, I do not say they shall not dwell thereon; for inasmuch as they bring forth fruit and works meet for my kingdom, they shall dwell thereon; they shall build, and another shall not inherit it: they shall plant vineyards, and they shall eat the fruit thereof; even so. Amen.

SECTION XCVIII.

Revelation given to Enoch, concerning the order of the church for the benefit of the poor.

1 Verily I say unto you my friends, I give unto you counsel and a commandment, concerning all the properties which belong to the order, which I commanded to be organized and established, to be an united order, and an everlasting order for the benefit of my church, and for the salvation of men until I come, with promise immutable and unchangeable, that inasmuch as those whom I commanded were faithful, they should be blessed with a multiplicity of blessings; but inasmuch as they were not faithful, they were nigh unto cursing. Therefore inasmuch as some of my servants have not kept the commandment, but have broken the covenant, by covetousness and with feigned words, I have cursed them with a very sore and grievous curse: for I the Lord have decreed in my heart, that inasmuch as any man, belonging to the order, shall be found a transgressor; or, in other words, shall break the covenant with which ye are bound, he shall be cursed in his life, and

shall be trodden down by whom I will, for I the Lord am not to be mocked in these things: and all this that the innocent among you, may not be condemned with the unjust; and that the guilty among you may not escape, because I the Lord have promised unto you a crown of glory at my right hand. Therefore inasmuch as you are found transgressors, ye cannot escape my wrath in your lives; inasmuch as ye are cut off by transgression, ye cannot escape the buffetings of satan until the day of redemption.

2 And I now give unto you power from this very hour, that if any man among you, of the order, is found a transgressor, and repenteth not of the evil, that ye shall deliver him over unto the buffetings of satan; and he shall not have power to bring evil upon you. It is wisdom in me: therefore a commandment I give unto you, that ye shall organize yourselves, and appoint every man his stewardship, that every man may give an account unto me of the stewardship which is appointed unto him: for it is expedient that I the Lord should make every man accountable, as stewards over earthly blessings, which I have made and prepared for my creatures. I the Lord stretched out the heavens, and builded the earth as a very handy work; and all things therein are mine; and it is my purpose to provide for my saints, for all things are mine: but it must needs be done in mine own way: and behold this is the way, that I the Lord have decreed to provide for my saints: that the poor shall be exalted, in that the rich are made low; for the earth is full, and there is enough and to spare, yea, I prepared all things, and have given unto the children of men to be agents unto themselves. Therefore if any man shall take of the abundance which I have made, and impart not his portion, according to the law of my gospel, unto the poor, and the needy, he shall, with the wicked, lift up his eyes in hell, being in torment.

3 And now, verily I say unto you, concerning the properties of the order: let my servant Pelagoram have appointed unto him the place where he now resides, and the lot of Tahhanes, for his stewardship, for his support while he is laboring in my vineyard, even as I will when I shall command him; and let all things be done according to counsel of the order, and united consent, or voice of the order which dwell in the land of Shinehah. And this stewardship and blessing, I the Lord confer upon my servant Pelagoram, for a blessing upon him, and his seed after him; and I will multiply blessings upon him, inasmuch as he shall be humble before me.

4 And again, let my servant Mahemson have appointed unto

him, for his stewardship, the lot of land which my servant Zombre obtained in exchange for his former inheritance, for him and his seed after him; and inasmuch as he is faithful I will multiply blessings upon him and his seed after him. And let my servant Mahemson devote his moneys for the proclaiming of my words, according as my servant Gazelam shall direct.

5 And again, let my servant Shederlaomach have the place upon which he now dwells. And let my servant Olihah have the lot which is set off joining the house which is to be for the Lane-shine-house, which is lot number one: and also the lot upon which his father resides. And let my servant Shederlaomach and Olihah have the Lane-shine-house and all things that pertain unto it; and this shall be their stewardship which shall be appointed unto them; and inasmuch as they are faithful, behold I will bless, and multiply blessings upon them: and this is the beginning of the stewardship which I have appointed them, for them and their seed after them; and inasmuch as they are faithful, I will multiply blessings upon them and their seed after them; even a multiplicity of blessings.

6 And again, let my servant Zombre have the house in which he lives, and the inheritance, all save the ground which has been reserved for the building of my houses, which pertains to that inheritance; and those lots which have been named for my servant Olihah. And inasmuch as he is faithful, I will multiply blessings upon him. And it is my will that he should sell the lots that are laid off for the building up of the city of my saints, inasmuch as it shall be made known to him by the voice of the Spirit, and according to the counsel of the order; and by the voice of the order. And this is the beginning of the stewardship which I have appointed unto him, for a blessing unto him, and his seed after him; and inasmuch as he is faithful, I will multiply a multiplicity of blessings upon him.

7 And again, let my servant Ahashdah have appointed unto him, the houses and lot where he now resides, and the lot and building on which the Ozondah stands; and also the lot which is on the corner south of the Ozondah; and also the lot on which the Shule is situated: And all this I have appointed unto my servant Ahashdah, for his stewardship, for a blessing upon him and his seed after him, for the benefit of the Ozondah of my order, which I have established for my stake in the land of Shinehah; yea, verily this is the stewardship which I have appointed unto my servant Ahashdah; even this whole Ozondah establishment, him and his agent, and his seed after him, and inasmuch as he is faithful in keeping my commandments, which I have given unto him, I will multiply blessings upon him, and his seed after him, even a multiplicity of blessings.

8 And again, let my servant Gazelam have appointed unto him, the lot which is laid off for the building of my house, which is forty rods long, and twelve wide, and also the inheritance upon which his father now resides; and this is the beginning of the stewardship which I have appointed unto him, for a blessing upon him, and upon his father, for behold, I have reserved an inheritance for his father, for his support: therefore he shall be reckoned in the house of my servant Gazelam; and I will multiply blessings upon the house of my servant Gazelam, inasmuch as he is faithful, even a multiplicity of blessings.

9 And now a commandment I give unto you concerning Zion, that you shall no longer be bound as an united order to your brethren of Zion, only on this wise: after you are organized you shall be called the united order of the stake of Zion, the city of Shinehah. And your brethren, after they are organized, shall be called the united order of the city of Zion; and they shall be organized in their own names, and in their own name; and they shall do their business in their own name, and in their own names: and you shall do your business in your own name, and in your own names. And this I have commanded to be done for your salvation and also for their salvation in consequence of their being driven out and that which is to come. The covenants being broken through transgression, by covetousness and feigned words: therefore, you are desolved as a united order with your brethren, that you are not bound only up to this hour, unto them, only on this wise, as I said, by loan, as shall be agreed by this order, in council, as your circumstances will admit, and the voice of the council direct.

10 And again, a commandment I give unto you concerning your stewardship which I have appointed unto you: behold all these properties are mine, or else your faith is vain, and ye are found hypocrites, and the covenants which ye have made unto me are broken: and if the properties are mine then ye are stewards, otherwise ye are no stewards. But verily I say unto you, I have appointed unto you to be stewards over mine house, even stewards indeed: and for this purpose I have commanded you to organize yourselves, even to shinelah my words, the fulness of my scriptures, the revelations which I have given unto you, and which I shall hereafter, from time to time, give unto you, for the purpose of building up my church and kingdom on the earth, and to prepare my people for the time, when I shall dwell with them, which is nigh at hand.

11 And ye shall prepare for yourselves a place for a treasury, and consecrate it unto my name; and ye shall appoint one.

among you to keep the treasury, and he shall be ordained unto this blessing; and there shall be a seal upon the treasury, and all the sacred things shall be delivered into the treasury, and no man among you shall call it his own, or any part of it, for it shall belong to you all with one accord; and I give it unto you from this very hour: and now see to it, that ye go to and make use of the stewardship which I have appointed unto you, exclusive of the sacred things, for the purpose of shinelane these sacred things, as I have said: and the avails of the sacred things shall be had in the treasury, and a seal shall be upon it, and it shall not be used or taken out of the treasury by any one, neither shall the seal be loosed which shall be placed upon it, only by the voice of the order, or by commandment. And thus shall ye preserve all the avails of the sacred things in the treasury, for sacred and holy purposes: and this shall be called the sacred treasury of the Lord: and a seal shall be kept upon it that it may be holy and consecrated unto the Lord.

12 And again, there shall be another treasury prepared and a treasurer appointed to keep the treasury, and a seal shall be placed upon it; and all moneys that you receive in your stewardships, by improving upon the properties which I have appointed unto you, in houses or in lands, or in cattle, or in all things save it be the holy and sacred writings, which I have reserved unto myself for holy and sacred purposes, shall be cast into the treasury as fast as you receive moneys by hundreds or by fifties, or by twenties, or by tens, or by fives, or in other words, if any man among you obtain five talents let him cast them into the treasury; or if he obtain ten, or twenty, or fifty, or an hundred, let him do likewise; and let not any man among you say that it is his own, for it shall not be called his, nor any part of it; and there shall not any part of it be used, or taken out of the treasury, only by the voice and common consent of the order. And this shall be the voice and common consent of the order: that any man among you, say unto the treasurer, I have need of this to help me in my stewardship: if it be five talents, or if it be ten talents, or twenty, or fifty, or an hundred, the treasurer shall give unto him the sum which he requires, to help him in his stewardship, until he be found a transgressor, and it is manifest before the council of the order plainly, that he is an unfaithful, and an unwise steward; but so long as he is in full fellowship, and is faithful, and wise in his stewardship, this shall be his token unto the treasurer that the treasurer shall not withhold. But in case of transgression the treasurer shall be subject unto the council and voice of the order. And in case the treasurer is found an

unfaithful, and an unwise steward, he shall be subject to the counsel and voice of the order, and shall be removed out of his place, and another shall he appointed in his stead.

13 And again, verily I say unto you, concerning your debts, behold it is my will that you should pay all your debts; and it is my will that you should humble yourselves before me, and obtain this blessing by your diligence and humility, and the prayer of faith: and inasmuch as you are diligent and humble, and exercise the prayer of faith, behold I will soften the hearts of those to whom you are in debt, until I shall send means unto you for your deliverance. Therefore write speedily unto Cainhannoch, and write according to that which shall be dictated by my Spirit, and I will soften the hearts of those to whom you are in debt, that it shall be taken away out of their minds to bring affliction upon you. And inasmuch as ye are humble and faithful and call on my name, behold I will give you the victory: I give unto you a promise, that you shall be delivered this once, out of your bondage: inasmuch as you obtain a chance to loan money by hundreds, or thousands, even until you shall loan enough to deliver yourselves from bondage, it is your privilege, and pledge the properties which I have put into your hands, this once, by giving your names, by common consent, or otherwise, as it shall seem good unto you: I give unto you this privilege, this once, and behold, if you proceed to do the things which I have laid before you, according to my commandments, all these things are mine, and ye are my stewards, and the master will not suffer his house to be broken up: even so. Amen.

SECTION XCIX.

Revelation given November, 1834.

1 It is my will that my servant Warren A. Cowdery should be appointed and ordained a presiding high priest over my church in the land of Freedom and the regions round about, and should preach my everlasting gospel and lift up his voice and warn the people, not only in his own place, but in the adjoining countries, and devote his whole time in this high and holy calling which I now give unto him, seeking diligently the kingdom of heaven and its righteousness, and all things necessary shall be added thereunto; for the laborer is worthy of his hire.

2 And again, verily I say unto you, the coming of the Lord draweth nigh, and it overtaketh the world as a thief in the night: therefore, gird up your loins that you may be the chil

dren of the light, and that day shall not overtake you as a thief.

3 And again, verily I say unto you, there was joy in heaven when my servant Warren bowed to my scepter, and separated himself from the crafts of men: therefore, blessed is my servant Warren, for I will have mercy on him, and notwithstanding the vanity of his heart I will lift him up inasmuch as he will humble himself before me; and I will give him grace and assurance wherewith he may stand; and if he continues to be a faithful witness and a light unto the church, I have prepared a crown for him in the mansions of my Father: even so.— Amen.

SECTION C.

APPENDIX.

1 Hearken, O ye people of my church, saith the Lord your God, and hear the word of the Lord concerning you; the Lord who shall suddenly come to his temple: the Lord who shall come down upon the world with a curse to judgment; yea, upon all the nations that forget God, and upon all the ungodly among you. For he shall make bare his holy arm in the eyes of all the nations, and all the ends of the earth shall see the salvation of their God. Wherefore, prepare ye, prepare ye, O my people; sanctify yourselves; gather ye together, O ye people of my church, upon the land of Zion, all you that have not been commanded to tarry. Go ye out from Babylon. Be ye clean that bear the vessels of the Lord. Call your solemn assemblies, and speak often one to another. And let every man call upon the name of the Lord; yea, verily I say unto you, again, the time has come when the voice of the Lord is unto you, Go ye out of Babylon; gather ye out from among the nations, from the four winds, from one end of heaven to the other.

2 Send forth the elders of my church unto the nations which are afar off; unto the islands of the sea; send forth unto foreign lands; call upon all nations; firstly, upon the Gentiles, and then upon the Jews. And behold and lo, this shall be their cry, and the voice of the Lord unto all people: Go ye forth unto the land of Zion, that the borders of my people may be enlarged, and that her stakes may be strengthened, and that Zion may go forth unto the regions round about: yea, let the cry go forth among all people; Awake and arise and go forth to meet the Bridegroom: behold and lo the Bridegroom cometh, go ye out to meet him. Prepare yourselves for the great day of the Lord. Watch, therefore, for ye know neither the day nor the hour. Let them, therefore, who are among the Gentiles, flee unto Zion. And let them who be of Judah, flee unto Jerusalem, unto the mountains of the Lord's house. Go ye out from among the nations, even from Babylon, from the midst of wickedness, which is spiritual Babylon. But verily thus saith the Lord, let not your flight be in haste, but let all things be prepared before you: and he that goeth, let him not look back, lest sudden destruction shall come upon him.

3 Hearken and hear O ye inhabitants of the earth. Listen ye elders of my church together, and hear the voice of the Lord, for he calleth upon all men and he commandeth all men every where to repent: for behold the Lord God hath sent

forth the angel, crying through the midst of heaven, saying:
Prepare ye the way of the Lord, and make his paths strait,
for the hour of his coming is nigh, when the Lamb shall stand
upon mount Zion, and with him a hundred and forty four
thousand, having his Father's name written in their foreheads:
wherefore, prepare ye for the coming of the Bridegroom: go
ye, go ye out to meet him, for behold he shall stand upon the
mount of Olivet, and upon the mighty ocean, even the great
deep, and upon the islands of the sea, and upon the land of
Zion; and he shall utter his voice out of Zion, and he shall
speak from Jerusalem, and his voice shall be heard among all
people, and it shall be a voice as the voice of many waters,
and as the voice of a great thunder, which shall break down
the mountains, and the vallies shall not be found: he shall
command the great deep and it shall be driven back into the
north countries, and the islands shall become one land, and
the land of Jerusalem and the land of Zion, shall be turned
back into their own place, and the earth shall be like as it was
in the days before it was divided. And the Lord even the Savior shall stand in the midst of his people, and shall reign over
all flesh. And they who are in the north countries shall come
in remembrance before the Lord, and their prophets shall hear
his voice, and shall no longer stay themselves, and they shall
smite the rocks, and the ice shall flow down at their presence.
And an high way shall be cast up in the midst of the great
deep. Their enemies shall become a prey unto them, and in
the barren deserts there shall come forth pools of living water;
and the parched ground shall no longer be a thirsty land.—
And they shall bring forth their rich treasures unto the children of Ephraim my servants. And the boundaries of the everlasting hills shall tremble at their presence. And then shall
they fall down and be crowned with glory, even in Zion, by
the hands of the servants of the Lord, even the children of
Ephraim; and they shall be filled with songs of everlasting joy.
Behold this is the blessing of the everlasting God upon the
tribes of Israel, and the richer blessing upon the head of
Ephraim and his fellows. And they also of the tribe of Judah,
after their pain, shall be sanctified in holiness before the Lord
to dwell in his presence day and night forever and ever.

4 And now verily saith the Lord, that these things might be
known among you, O inhabitants of the earth, I have sent
forth mine angel, flying through the midst of heaven, having
the everlasting gospel, who hath appeared unto some, and
hath committed it unto man, who shall appear unto many that
dwell on the earth: and this gospel shall be preached unto every nation, and kindred, and tongue, and people, and the sea-

vants of God shall go forth, saying, with a loud voice: Fear
God and give glory to him: for the hour of his judgment is
come: and worship him that made heaven, and earth, and sea,
and the fountain of waters, calling upon the name of the Lord
day and night, saying: O that thou wouldst rend the heavens,
that thou wouldst come down, that the mountains might flow
down at thy presence. And it shall be answered upon their
heads, for the presence of the Lord shall be as the melting fire
that burneth, and as the fire which causeth the waters to boil.
O Lord, thou shalt come down to make thy name known to
thine adversaries, and all nations shall tremble at thy presence.
When thou doeth terrible things, things they look not for;
yea, when thou comest down and the mountains flow down at
thy presence, thou shalt meet him who rejoiceth and worketh
righteousness, who remember thee in thy ways: for since the
beginning of the world have not men heard nor perceived by
the ear, neither hath any eye seen, O God, besides thee, how
great things thou hast prepared for him that waiteth for thee.

5 And it shall be said, Who is this that cometh down from
God in heaven whith died garments: yea, from the regions
which are not known, clothed in his glorious apparel, travelling in the greatness of his strength? And he shall say I am
he who spake in righteousness, mighty to save. And the
Lord shall be red in his apparel, and his garments like him
that treaddeth in the wine vat, and so great shall be the glory
of his presence, that the sun shall hide his face in shame; and
the moon shall withhold its light; and the stars shall be hurled
from their places: and his voice shall be heard, I have trodden
the wine-press alone, and have brought judgment upon all people; and none was with me; and I have trampled them in my
fury, and I did tread upon them in mine anger, and their blood
have I sprinkled upon my garments, and stained all my raiment: for this was the day of vengeance which was in my
heart. And now the year of my redeemed is come, and they
shall mention the loving kindness of their Lord, and all that
he has bestowed upon them, according to his goodness, and
according to his loving kindness, forever and ever. In all their
afflictions he was afflicted. And the angel of his presence
saved them; and in his love, and in his pity, he redeemed
them, and bare them, and carried them all the days of old;
yea, and Enoch also, and they who were with him; the prophets who were before him, and Noah also, and they who were
before him, and Moses also, and they who were before him,
and from Moses to Elijah, and from Elijah to John, who were
with Christ in his resurrection, and the holy apostles, with
Abraham, Isaac and Jacob, shall be in the presence of the

Lamb. And the graves of the saints shall be opened, and they shall come forth and stand on the right hand of the Lamb, when he shall stand upon mount Zion, and upon the holy city, the New Jerusalem, and they shall sing the song of the Lamb day and night forever and ever.

6 And for this cause, that men might be made partakers of the glories which were to be revealed, the Lord sent forth the fulness of his gospel, his everlasting covenant, reasoning in plainness, and simplicity, to prepare the weak for those things which are coming on the earth; and for the Lord's errand in the day when the weak should confound the wise, and the little one become a strong nation, and two should put their tens of thousands to flight; and by the weak things of the earth, the Lord should thresh the nations by the power of his Spirit. And for this cause these commandments were given; they were commanded to be kept from the world in the day that they were given, but now are to go forth unto all flesh. And this according to the mind and will of the Lord, who ruleth over all flesh; and unto him that repenteth and sanctifieth himself before the Lord, shall be given eternal life. And upon them that hearken not to the voice of the Lord, shall be fulfilled that which was written by the prophet Moses, that they should be cut off from among the people.

7 And also that which was written by the prophet Malachi: For behold the day cometh that shall burn as an oven, and all the proud; yea, and all that do wickedly, shall be stubble: and the day that cometh shall burn them up saith the Lord of hosts, that it shall leave them neither root nor branch. Wherefore this shall be the answer of the Lord unto them: In that day when I came unto my own, no man among you received me, and you were driven out. When I called again, there was none of you to answer, yet my arm was not shortened at all, that I could not redeem, neither my power to deliver.— Behold at my rebuke I dry up the sea. I make the rivers a wilderness: their fish stinketh, and dieth for thirst. I clothe the heavens with blackness, and make sackcloth their covering. And this shall ye have of my hand, ye shall lay down in sorrow.

8 Behold and lo there are none to deliver you, for ye obeyed not my voice when I called to you out of the heavens, ye believed not my servants; and when they were sent unto you ye received them not: wherefore they sealed up the testimony and bound up the law, and ye were delivered over unto darkness: these shall go away into outer darkness, where there is weeping, and wailing, and gnashing of teeth. Behold the Lord your God hath spoken it. Amen.

SECTION CI.

MARRIAGE.

1 According to the custom of all civilized nations, marriage is regulated by laws and ceremonies: therefore we believe, that all marriages in this church of Christ of Latter Day Saints, should be solemnized in a public meeting, or feast, prepared for that purpose: and that the solemnization should be performed by a presiding high priest, high priest, bishop, elder, or priest, not even prohibiting those persons who are desirous to get married, of being married by other authority. We believe that it is not right to prohibit members of this church from marrying out of the church, if it be their determination so to do, but such persons will be considered weak in the faith of our Lord and Savior Jesus Christ.

2 Marriage should be celebrated with prayer and thanksgiving; and at the solemnization, the persons to be married, standing together, the man on the right, and the woman on the left, shall be addressed, by the person officiating, as he shall be directed by the holy Spirit; and if there be no legal objections, he shall say, calling each by their names: "You both mutually agree to be each other's companion, husband and wife, observing the legal rights belonging to this condition; that is, keeping yourselves wholly for each other, and from all others, during your lives." And when they have answered "Yes," he shall pronounce them "husband and wife" in the name of the Lord Jesus Christ, and by virtue of the laws of the country and authority vested in him: "may God add his blessings and keep you to fulfill your covenants from henceforth and forever. Amen."

3 The clerk of every church should keep a record of all marriages, solemnized in his branch.

4 All legal contracts of marriage made before a person is baptized into this church, should be held sacred and fulfilled. Inasmuch as this church of Christ has been reproached with the crime of fornication, and polygamy: we declare that we believe, that one man should have one wife; and one woman, but one husband, except in case of death, when either is at liberty to marry again. It is not right to persuade a woman to be baptized contrary to the will of her husband; neither is it lawful to influence her to leave her husband. All children are bound by law to obey their parents; and to influence them to embrace any religious faith, or be baptized, or leave their parents without their consent, is unlawful and unjust. We believe that all persons who exercise control over their fellow

beings, and prevent them from embracing the truth, will have to answer for that sin.

SECTION CII.

Of Governments and Laws in General.

That our belief, with regard to earthly governments and laws in general, may not be misinterpreted nor misunderstood, we have thought proper to present, at the close of this volume, our opinion concerning the same.

1 We believe that Governments were instituted of God for the benefit of man, and that he holds men accountable for their acts in relation to them, either in making laws or administering them, for the good and safety of society.

2 We believe that no Government can exist, in peace, except such laws are framed and held inviolate as will secure to each individual the free exercise of concience, the right and control of property and the protection of life.

3 We believe that all Governments necessarily require civil officers and magistrates to enforce the laws of the same, and that such as will administer the law in equity and justice should be sought for and upheld by the voice of the people, (if a Republic,) or the will of the Sovereign.

4 We believe that religion is instituted of God, and that men are amenable to him and to him only for the exercise of it, unless their religious opinion prompts them to infringe upon the rights and liberties of others; but we do not believe that human law has a right to interfere in prescribing rules of worship to bind the consciences of men, nor dictate forms for public or private devotion; that the civil magistrate should restrain crime, but never control conscience; should punish guilt, but never surpress the freedom of the soul.

5 We believe that all men are bound to sustain and uphold the respective Governments in which they reside, while protected in their inherent and inalienable rights by the laws of such Governments, and that sedition and rebellion are unbecoming every citizen thus protected, and should be punished accordingly; and that all Governments have a right to enact such laws as in their own judgments are best calculated to secure the public interest, at the same time, however, holding sacred the freedom of conscience.

6 We believe that every man should be honored in his station: rulers and magistrates as such—being placed for the protection of the innocent and the punishment of the guilty; and that to the laws all men owe respect and deference, as without

them peace and harmony would be supplanted by anarchy and terror: human laws being instituted for the express purpose of regulating our interests as individuals and nations, between man and man, and divine laws, given of heaven, prescribing rules on spiritual concerns, for faith and worship, both to be answered by man to his Maker.

7 We believe that Rulers, States and Governments have a right, and are bound to enact laws for the protection of all citizens in the free exercise of their religious belief; but we do not believe that they have a right, in justice, to deprive citizens of this privilege, or proscribe them in their opinions, so long as a regard and reverence is shown to the laws, and such religious opinions do not justify sedition nor conspiracy.

8 We believe that the commission of crime should be punished according to the nature of the offence: that murder, treason, robbery, theft and the breach of the general peace, in all respects, should be punished according to their criminality and their tendency to evil among men, by the laws of that Government in which the offence is committed: and for the public peace and tranquility, all men should step forward and use their ability in bringing offenders, against good laws, to punishment.

9 We do not believe it just to mingle religious influence with civil Government, whereby one religious society is fostered and another proscribed in its spiritual privileges, and the individual rights of its members, as citizens, denied.

10 We believe that all religious societies have a right to deal with their members for disorderly conduct according to the rules and regulations of such societies, provided that such dealing be for fellowship and good standing; but we do not believe that any religious society has authority to try men on the right of property or life, to take from them this world's goods, or put them in jeopardy either life or limb, neither to inflict any physical punishment upon them,—they can only excommunicate them from their society and withdraw from their fellowship.

11 We believe that men should appeal to the civil law for redress of all wrongs and grievances, where personal abuse is inflicted, or the right of property or character infringed, where such laws exist as will protect the same; but we believe that all men are justified in defending themselves, their friends and property, and the Government, from the unlawful assaults and encroachments of all persons, in times of exigencies, where immediate appeal cannot be made to the laws, and relief afforded.

12 We believe it just to preach the gospel to the nations of

the earth, and warn the righteous to save themselves from the corruption of the world; but we do not believe it right to interfere with bond-servants, neither preach the gospel to, nor baptize them, contrary to the will and wish of their masters, nor to meddle with, or influence them in the least to cause them to be dissatisfied with their situations in this life, thereby jeopardizing the lives of men: such interference we believe to be unlawful and unjust, and dangerous to the peace of every Government allowing human beings to be held in servitude.

GENERAL ASSEMBLY.

At a General Assembly of the Church of the LATTER DAY SAINTS, *according to previous notice, held on the 17th of August, 1835, to take into consideration the labors of a certain committee which had been appointed by a General Assembly of September 24, 1834, as follows:*

"The Assembly being duly organized, and after transacting certain business of the church, proceeded to appoint a committee to arrange the items of doctrine of Jesus Christ, for the government of his church of the Latter Day Saints, which church was organized and commenced its rise on the 6th day of April, 1830. These items are to be taken from the bible, book of Mormon, and the revelations which have been given to said church up to this date, or shall be until such arrangement is made.

"Elder Samuel H. Smith, for the assembly, moved that presiding elders, Joseph Smith, jr. Oliver Cowdery, Sidney Rigdon and Frederick G. Williams compose said committee. The nomination was seconded by elder Hyrum Smith, whereupon it received the unanimous vote of the assembly.

(SIGNED.) OLIVER COWDERY, } *Clerks.*"
ORSON HYDE. }

Wherefore Presidents O. Cowdery and S. Rigdon, proceeded and organized the high council of the church at Kirtland, and Presidents W. W. Phelps and J. Whitmer proceeded and organized the high council of the church in Missouri. Bishop Newel K. Whitney proceeded and organized his counsellors of the church in Kirtland, and acting Bishop John Corrill, organized the counsellors of the church in Missouri: and also Presidents Leonard Rich, Levi W. Hancock, Sylvester Smith and Lyman Sherman, organized the council of the seventy; and also, Elder John Gould, acting President, organized the travelling Elders; and also Ira Ames, acting President, organized the Priests; and also Erastus Babbit, acting President, organized the Teachers; and also William Burgess, acting President, organized the Deacons; and also Thomas Gates, assisted by John Young, William Cowdery, Andrew H. Aldrich, Job S. Lewis and Oliver Higley, as Presidents of the day, organized the whole assembly. Elder Levi W. Hancock appointed chorister: a hymn was then sung and the services of the day opened by the prayer of President O. Cowdery, and the solemnities of eternity rested upon the audience. Another hymn was sung: after transacting some business for the church the audience adjourned for one hour.

AFTERNOON.—After a hymn was sung, President Cowdery arose and introduced the "Book of doctrine and covenants of the church of the Latter Day Saints," in behalf of the committee: he was followed by President Rigdon, who explained the manner by which they intended to obtain the voice of the assembly for or against said book: the other two committee, named above, were absent. According to said arrangement W. W. Phelps bore record that the book presented to the assembly, was true. President John Whitmer, also arose, and testified that it was true. Elder John Smith, taking the lead of the high council in Kirtland, bore record that the revelations in said book were true, and that the lectures were judiciously arranged and compiled, and were profitable for doctrine; whereupon the high council of Kirtland accepted and acknowledged them as the doctrine and covenants of their faith, by a unanimous vote. Elder Levi Jackman, taking the lead of the high council of the church in Missouri, bore testimony that the revelations in said book were true, and the said high council of Missouri accepted and acknowledged them as the doctrine and covenants of their faith, by a unanimous vote.

President W. W. Phelps then read the written testimony of the Twelve, as follows. "The testimony of the witnesses to the book of the Lord's commandments, which he gave to his church through Joseph Smith, jr. who was appointed by the voice of the church for this purpose: we therefore feel willing to bear testimony to all the world of mankind, to every creature upon the face of all the earth, and upon the islands of the sea, that the Lord has borne record to our souls, through the Holy Ghost shed forth upon us, that these commandments were given by inspiration of God, and are profitable for all men, and are verily true. We give this testimony unto the world, the Lord being our helper: and it is through the grace of God, the Father, and his Son Jesus Christ, that we are permitted to have this privilege of bearing this testimony unto the world, in the which we rejoice exceedingly, praying the Lord always, that the children of men may be profited thereby." Elder Leonard Rich bore record of the truth of the book and the council of the Seventy accepted and acknowledged it as the doctrine and covenants of their faith, by a unanimous vote.

Bishop N. K. Whitney bore record of the truth of the book, and with his counsellors, accepted and acknowledged it as the doctrine and covenants of their faith, by a unanimous vote.

Acting Bishop, John Corrill, bore record of the truth of the book, and with his counsellors, accepted and acknowledged it as the doctrine and covenants of their faith, by a unanimous vote. Acting President, John Gould, gave his testimony in favor of the book, and with the travelling Elders, accepted and acknowledged it as the doctrine and covenants of their faith, by a unanimous vote.

Ira Ames, acting President of the Priests, gave his testimony in favor of the book, and with the Priests, accepted and acknowledged it as the doctrine and covenants of their faith, by a unanimous vote.

Erastus Babbit, acting President of the Teachers, gave his testimony in favor of the book, and they accepted and acknowledged it as the doctrine and covenants of their faith, by a unanimous vote.

Wm. Burges acting President of the Deacons, bore record of the truth of the book, and they accepted and acknowledged it as the doctrine and covenants of their faith, by a unanimous vote.

The venerable President, Thomas Gates, then bore record of the truth of the book, and with his five silver-headed assistants, and the whole congregation, accepted and acknowledged it as the doctrine and covenants of their faith, by a unanimous vote. The several authorities, and the general assembly, by a unanimous vote, accepted of the labors of the committee.

President W. W. Phelps then read an article on Marriage, which was accepted and adopted, and ordered to be printed in said book, by a unanimous vote.

President O. Cowdery then read an article on "governments and laws in general," which was accepted and adopted, and ordered to be printed in said book, by a unanimous vote.

A hymn was then sung. President S. Rigdon returned thanks, after which the assembly was blessed by the Presidency, with uplifted hands, and dismissed.

THOMAS BURDICK,
WARREN PARRISH, } CLERKS.
SYLVESTER SMITH,

Q

INDEX.

17*

CONTENTS.

[*The arrangement of the Lectures supercedes the necessity of any other reference than the Index.*]

PART SECOND.

A

B

C

viii

D

E

F

G

K

L

M

N

O

P

S

T

U

NOTES TO THE READER.

Several errors have escaped the eye of the proof reader: They will be carefully sought, and, in the next edition, *correc ted*:lest, however, that any should be mislead, the last paragraph of the article on Marriage, page 251, should read: "We believe that husbands, parents and masters who exercise control over their wives, children, and servants and prevent them from embracing the truth, will have to answer for that sin."

In the proceedings of the General Assembly, page 255, it should read: "Wherefore O. Cowdery and S. Rigdon, Presidents of the first presidency, appointed Thomas Burdick, Warren Parrish and Silvester Smith, Clerks, and proceeded to organize the whole assembly, as follows: "They organized," &c. And it should read at the 9th line from the bottom, "And they also, as the assembly was large, appointed Thomas Gates, John Young, William Cowdery, Andrew H. Aldrich, Job S. Lewis, and Oliver Higley, as assistant presidents of the day, to assist in preserving order, &c. in the whole assembly." And on the 257th page, 5th paragraph, it should read: "The venerable assistant President," &c. And the whole proceedings should be signed,

OLIVER COWDERY, ⎱ *Pres'ts.*
SIDNEY RIGDON,   ⎰

Thomas Burdick,   ⎱
Warren Parrish,   ⎰ *Clerks.*
Silvester Smith,

SOUTH DAVIS STAKE
ELDERS' ANNUAL SOCIAL

President David O. McKay will discuss

"A VISION OF THE PRIESTHOOD 100 YEARS HENCE"

The South Davis Stake Annual Elders' Social will be held

Thursday, Nov. 8 at 8 p. m. in
the Bountiful Tabernacle
1934

GOOD PROGRAM   -:-   LIGHT REFRESHMENTS   -:-   GOOD TIME

Admission Free

Pictures showing the First Edition of the Book of Mormon, a Priesthood Convention with Apostle Charles A. Callis, President David O. McKay and Samuel O. Bennion of the First Council of Seventy, also President George Albert Smith going over the old Mormon Trail. The lower picture shows Wilford Wood sitting on the fence that the Prophet came to after leaving his father working in the field. Here he fell exhausted and the Angel appeared to him telling him to return and tell his father of his vision, which he did.

President David O. McKay watches Wilford C. Wood deliver the deed to President Heber J. Grant for the first purchase of property on the Temple Block in Nauvoo, Illinois in 1937.

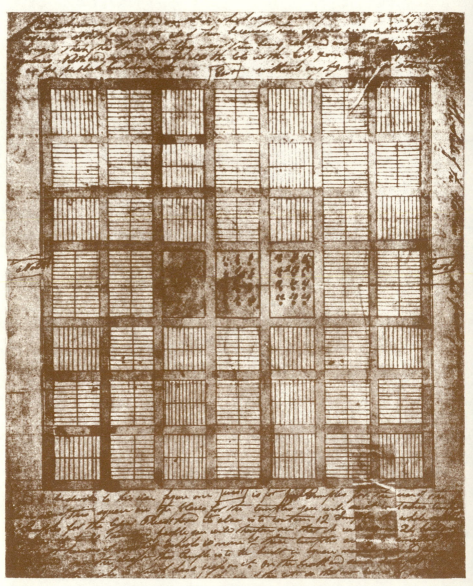

Reproduction of the plat of the City of Zion drawn by the Prophet Joseph Smith

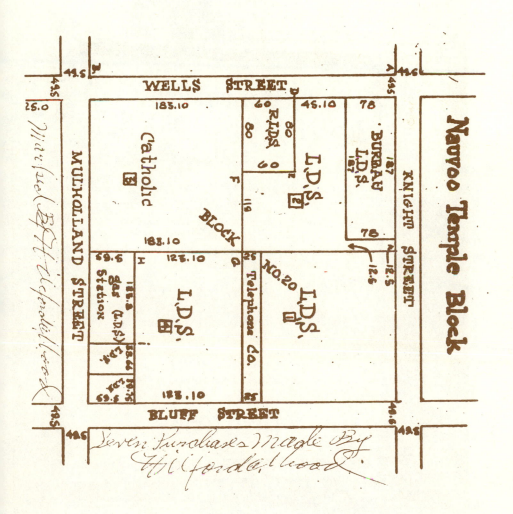

Nauvoo Temple Block

WELLS STREET

MULHOLLAND STREET

KNIGHT STREET

BLUFF STREET

Catholic

Block G

L.D.S.

L.D.S.

L.D.S.

BUREAU L.D.S.

R.L.D.S.

gas (L.D.S.) Station

Telephone Co.

NO.20

41.5

495

25.0

183.10

45.10

78

80

60

127

183.10

123.10

119

F

12.6

12.5

78

25

25

495

49.6

425

Seven purchases made By Wilford Wood.

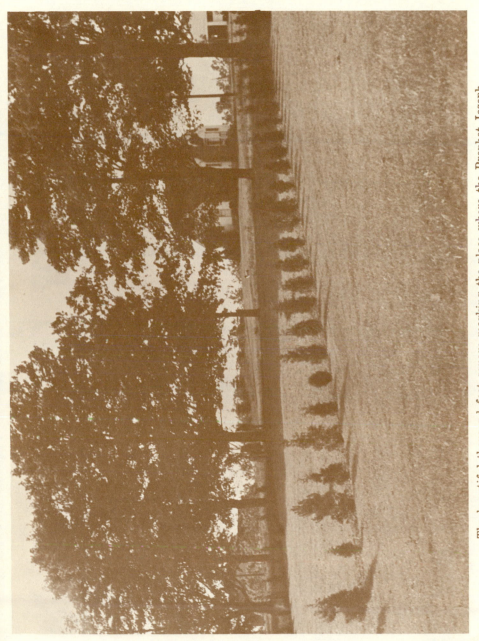

The beautiful thousand foot square marking the place where the Prophet Joseph Smith was tarred and feathered at Hiram, Ohio. Over one hundred trees have been planted as a monument to the Prophet Joseph Smith, a monument made by God as only God can make a tree.

Wilford Wood's two grandchildren, Wilford Cannon and Richard Glade, learning about old historical records of the Church while they are young.

Wilford Wood's two sons-in-law, Larkin Glade and Ralph Cannon, fathers of the two grandchildren, are studying old historical records of the Church.

George D. Pyper, former General Superintendent of the Sunday School, examines stone floor where the Prophet Joseph Smith was in prison in Liberty Jail, Missouri. When he was a small boy his mother taught him about the Prophet Joseph Smith.

THE DESERET NEWS SALT LAKE CITY WEDNESDAY DECEMBER 23 1936

Utahn Has Death Mask Casts Of Prophet, Brother

With the advent of the 131st birthday anniversary of the Prophet Joseph Smith, Wilford C. Wood, prominent Church man and member of the South Davis Stake High Council, has come into the possession of the original casts of the death masks of the Prophet and his brother, Hyrum. Above is a facsimile of the agreement for the purchase of the casts made between Philo Dibble, the Prophet's bodyguard, who made casts, and J. H. (Harrie) Brown.

Pres. David O. McKay and Mr. Wood are shown below examining the original casts at a recent meeting of bishops and the stake presidency of South Davis Stake.

Original casts of the death masks of the Prophet Joseph Smith and his brother, Hyrum Smith, martyred at Carthage Jail nearly a hundred years ago, have come into the possession of Wilford C. Wood, of Woods Cross, prominent Church member and official photographer for the Utah Pioneer Trails and Landmarks Association.

Copies of the originals are kept in the historian's department in the Church Office Building.

The casts were taken two days after the murder of the Prophet. The one of Hyrum Smith clearly shows the bullet hole the left nostril. Made by Philo Dibble, who was the Prophet's bodyguard during the last weeks of his life, the casts remained for four decades in the possession of this pioneer who made his home in Springville. They were purchased Nov. 21, 1885, by Harrie Brown of Logan, Utah, for the sum of $50. Dibble had been traveling through the Territory of Utah at the time ex-

hibiting the casts and other Church relics, charging a small admission fee to finance the showing. Brown had taken a course in sculpture and was preparing to make busts of the martyrs when the opportunity to buy the originals came to him.

While Mr. Wood was attending dedication ceremonies at Florence, Neb., this fall and taking pictures of historical sites and collecting antiques along the Mormon Trail, he learned that the original casts were in the possession of Mrs. C. Alzina Brown, the widow of Harrie Brown. He immediately wrote to Mrs. Brown. Arrangements for the purchase were consummated Dec. 14.

Mr. Wood considered the casts the most remarkable relics in his collection. He also recently obtained the belt buckle from the sword belt of the Prophet Joseph Smith, worn when he was commanding the Nauvoo Legion.

Court Records of the Martyrdom. The Torah

DEATH MASKS

Masks of the faces of Joseph and Hyrum Smith were made three days after they were martyred. Plaster casts were made from the death masks. The two bronze faces on this plaque were made from the original casts of the death masks.